The Monster of Newark:

The Life and Adventures of an Historian

Brian Regal

Typeset by Richard Heath and Jonathan Downes,
Cover and Layout by SPiderKaT for CFZ Communications
Using Microsoft Word 2000, Microsoft Publisher 2000, Adobe Photoshop CS.

First published in Great Britain by CFZ Press

CFZ Press
Myrtle Cottage
Woolsery
Bideford
North Devon
EX39 5QR

ISBN: 978-1-905723-40-9

Acknowledgements/dedication

This entire book, and indeed my entire life is dedicated to my longtime partner of 36 years Dr. Lisa Nocks, who passed away shortly before I finished the manuscript. She was the best person I ever knew. I will love her and miss her for all eternity. When I met her I knew my heart had found a home.

In addition to all the people mentioned in this book, whether by name or not, I'd like to thank Alice Wyman, Sheila Tartaglia, Benjamin Radford, and Jack Pollack for reading all or parts of the manuscript. Thanks to Jonathan Downes and everyone at the Fortean Zoology Press.

Made in New Jersey.

FOREWORD

I don't like social media, and think that it is probably responsible for far more of the ills of the modern world than we actually accept. However, it was Facebook that first introduced me to Dr Brian Regal. I read about something that he had written, and was so enthused, that I wrote to him. We soon became friendly and upon his next visit to England I invited him and his girl-friend Lisa to come and visit us for lunch. My wife cooked a delicious meal and we had a very pleasant time. Sadly, my wife and Lisa have now gone onto the next stage of the journey, and both Brian and I are lost without them.

Reading this book has given me a very valuable insight into the events that made this eminent historian what he is today, and it is both amusing, informative, and indeed inspiring. Brian has that rare gift, so rare amongst much of academia, of being able to write prose in an entertaining manner, and so I have absolutely no compunction in recommending this book to anybody who is interested in the modern history of cryptozoology and indeed all sorts of other things. And I'm not just saying that because I'm the publisher.

Jon Downes
Bideford,
September 2024

Introduction

Travel through the world's archives
We will find things no one else will ever see
Fear not if you linger to read what you find
I will wait
I would wait forever for you
To find me

-- Quintus Severus, *Historia Mundi*, 231 CE

I'm in my office at home at my desk writing. Across from me, against the wall, a side table. There are a couple of lamps with monkeys holding them up, and some books, including an original 1672 edition of Gaspar Schott's *Physica Curiosa* (with its disturbing period drawings of fantastic monsters once thought to be real). There is a wooden-handled magnifying glass Lisa bought me when she really didn't have the money to, and a plaster copy of the famous bust of Ben Franklin I found on sale at the Morgan Library in New York. There is also a small multicolored cardboard box about one inch by three inches by one inch. It's decades old and a little frayed. Just poking out of one end of the box is the nose of a vintage toy Matchbox Car: the *Alvis Stalwart* cargo carrier. Writers often point to something in their lives as an important metaphor, like the sled in *Citizen Kane*. I guess the *Alvis* is my Rosebud.[1] It represents everything I have dreamed of since I was a kid. It represents freedom, a global perspective, and exploration as adventure: a vehicle to chase monsters.

The bust of Ben Franklin looks at me skeptically.

I woke up not knowing where I was. Something was pounding on the door. I thought it was a ghost, but it was only a monster. I study the history of monsters.[2] To be more precise, I study the history of the people who study monsters. I've had a whole career writing books about them, and have appeared on television, radio, and podcasts talking about them. I'm less interested in monsters on their own, however, than I am in how we chase them. It's what I do for a living. To study the history of monsters and monstrosity is more than just biology or folklore. It is the study of the history of human hatred and fear, as well as obsession and isolation.

Whether it's Frankenstein's creation, werewolves, Bigfoot, Loch Ness, the Jersey Devil, immigrants, the socially unacceptable and marginalized, or outcasts of any kind, I tell stories of isolation.[3]

I chose monsters and the history of science as a field of study because I wanted to do something that was fun. I never considered "making an impact" and it is questionable as to whether I have. Monsters are fascinating. They are those terrible things we create for ourselves. The concept of Monster Theory says monsters have always served psychological

---

[1] The original left my possession years ago, but I was able to get another recently thanks to the wonders of eBay. I wrote an homage to the *Alvis* and its impact on my development as an adult in an Op Ep. "Why I Became a Globalist," *Star-Ledger*, February 24, 2019.
[2] Monsters can be defined in many ways. I will leave it up to the reader to assign whatever meaning they like. My interest here, however, is in creatures sometimes referred to as Cryptids.
[3] I have consciously chosen to not include criminals, murderers, dictators, people who drive Hummers, etc. That is for other scholars to do.

purposes. They are symbolic of cultural and individual unease, and even help give us identity.[4] They grow from the hate and fear filled reactions we have to the world. Sometimes they look like scaly fiends or large menacing felines, but more often, they look like us. They hide in the dark corners of our minds, as well as streets and forests and lakes. They occupy our souls and our back pockets. They can jump out with ease no matter how much we push them down or run away from them. They have the power we give them, which is why, I think, we chase them: to take back that power or eliminate that fear. It is a lonely path. We are alone when surrounded by our monsters, and we are even alone surrounded by our friends and loved ones.

Aloneness and loss are central themes here.

I think I can say I've lived a varied and interesting life which I'm now going to tell you about. I've had a number of jobs and careers though there was always one underlying focus and dream that helped keep me going in even the worst of times. Since I was a kid I wanted to be an historian, and an adventurer: an adventuring historian, who is also a writer, and maybe an artist, one who chased monsters. At first I wasn't even really sure what that meant. I held on to this idea until my fingers bled, and rarely ever told anyone about it. I knew if I ever let it go I'd be dead. I enlisted in the United States Army when I was seventeen years old and left home because I wanted to pursue that dream.

It is just one example of how I spent my life trying to make it what I wanted, because I was so disappointed in what it actually was. I wanted to run away and shed my old skin, and become someone new. The Earth, however, is spherical. When you keep going in any direction long enough you wind up back where you started.

Throughout this running I had adventures, weathered tempests and hairbreadth escapes, romanced femme fatales, carried secrets, and stole artifacts. I found treasure and lost it. I supped with Sciopodii. I have searched for werewolves in the Black Forest of Europe and the oldest libraries in the world. I've swam in the Blue Danube. I've held a document in my hand, written by the Jersey Devil. I hobnobbed with spies in a bar in China. I discovered dinosaur tracks and ancient fossils. I communed with the stones at Avebury on a misty morning. I saw terrible things and wonderful things, encountered good people and bad.

I stood alongside heroes and cowards (and was never sure which one I was). I learned from geniuses and fools. I studied for years, yet still felt uneducated. I saw men launched into space, heard the bells chime at midnight, and the echo of the countdown to the end of the world. I had my heart broken, but never any bones. Eventually, I looked up and I was back where I started. At least I was now an adventuring historian, a writer about monsters. What follows is the story of how that happened.[5]

While sitting in the Shakespeare pub in Bristol, England in July of 2010, with my partner Lisa, and our friend, the well-known British cryptozoologist Richard Freeman talking about all manner of things monstrous, an idea that had been bouncing around in my head bounced back. What was my role in all this? When the barman brought our food over, he

---

[4] J. J. Cohen, ed. *Monster Theory: Reading Culture* (University of Minnesota Press, 1996). Also see Cohen's *Medieval Identity Machines* (University of Minnesota Press, 2003).
[5] While I always had this goal, I really had no clue how to achieve it until I was in my thirties. As with everything else, I just went off alone and did the best I could trying to figure it out along the way.

overheard part of or conversation and eyed us suspiciously. Those who chase monsters, to either prove them real or to prove them hoaxes have been around almost as long as the monsters themselves. I, like Richard, have been part of that chase. Whereas Richard chased the actual monsters, I chased the chasers. I have spent my adult professional life writing about the lives of sad, lonely people on deeply personal, but isolated quests to find monsters, explain monsters, or rid themselves of monsters. I try to tell their stories and to understand them. Writing about myself then will be no different.

It was a few years after my conversation with Richard and Lisa that I began to write this book. It had to wait as I dealt with Sasquatch and the Jersey Devil, and even Christopher Columbus. The final nudge came on a British Airway's overnight (BA0188) to London on Sunday, April 3, 2016 (my beloved partner of thirty years Dr. Lisa Nocks had just been diagnosed with cancer, yet she insisted I make this trip anyway). I was eating cheese ravioli and drinking a lot of Spanish red wine, and trying to figure out what my life meant, if anything. A further catalyst was a discussion with the skeptical author, researcher, and editor, Benjamin Radford. After he heard me tell some crazy anecdote about my life, he jokingly said he looked forward to reading my autobiography someday. So this is all his fault. Sitting on this plane, having enough wine in me, I decided to begin, but all I had to write on—I was too lazy to get my backpack out of the overhead—was the menu card. I started scribbling various thoughts as they randomly entered my head.[6]

As an historian, I have examined a number of different intellectual communities, in the realm of what could be vaguely—though not always accurately—referred to as the paranormal or the Fringe, although where the fringe is depends upon where you are standing on the map. I've been called many things and been accused of even more for doing so. I have always sought to learn something about these communities that was of value. I am not a debunker or a skeptic, though I have been called these too. While I am skeptical of paranormal activity and the existence of ghosts or flying craft from other worlds, or most cryptids, and all conspiracy theories, I have, I hope, helped to show the underlining origins of some of these things. I am first and foremost an historian. I tell the history of monsters and their pursuers. I follow the historical and archival trail to reach some sort of position. I try to follow that trail wherever it leads me with no preconceived notion of what the answer should be.

I am primarily a biographer, though now I will attempt to be an autobiographer. What must be accepted here, or nothing wonderful will come from this story, is that autobiography writing is parts self-indulgent, self-aggrandizing, and self-pitying. I plan to have a healthy dose of them all. Another thing to keep in mind is that we do not search for and study monsters to find out about them alone, we search for them as a way of finding out about ourselves. As a result, there will be a good bit of 'dark night of the soul' here. It could get a little uncomfortable. Just a warning.

Autobiographies are by their very nature, products of propaganda. They are designed by the author to make the author look the way the author wants to look. They can also be tools for the author to address wider issues of culture and religion and politics. Augustine of Hippo

---

[6] This sort of thing has been a habit of mine. I've written parts of my work on napkins, the backs of restaurant place matts, boxes, and candy wrappers. I have used anything that could be written on in a pinch. I've written while riding trains, in parks, on airplanes, in bathrooms, sitting on walls, and on the grass. I once was so desperate to get something down that I wrote a sentence on the back gate of a Plainfield city, DPW truck. When I came back with a piece of paper to copy it down the truck had driven off. I've written some of my best work in bars.

(354-430), when he wrote his *Confessions,* for example, wanted to show what a superior Christian he was, having converted from philandering sex maniac, pagan. Benvenuto Cellini (1500–1571), the art historian, said you shouldn't begin an autobiography until you're over forty. In *Between the World and Me*, Ta-Nehisi Coates talks to his son as a way of explaining the place of African people in America. Maya Angelou wrote about her experiences growing up poor, and how *I know Why the Caged Bird Sings*. Charles Darwin wanted to explain to his children why he had done the things he did. In *Life and Death in Shanghai* Nien Cheng used her harrowing story to discuss the ravages of the Cultural Revolution in China. Ben Franklin, well, he was just having a good time.

With these, and other autobiography writers whispering in my ear I will embark down the road myself. One of my goals here is to not just do a chronological telling of my life. There will be places where I jumble the narrative structure and chronology quite a bit in order to address certain issues at certain points in hopefully a more effective way. I will treat my life the way I have treated other lives I have written about: to try and learn something about the time and place of the person's life in wider context and where it fits in.

I will try to make this story as un-cringe worthy as possible, but I make no promises. I have tried to be accurate, but with exceptions. I have used some people's real names and hidden a few. There are moments I will write about in painfully excruciating detail and moments that I will never discuss with anyone. A couple of important people appear only vaguely or not at all. I could not mention everyone who had a role in my life and I apologize if they feel left out. I made those decisions for my own reasons, which need no explanation. I have probably confused people and unintentionally conflated them, especially in the early chapters. As a kid I had issues grasping and understanding what was going on around me. People, shapes, and light often seemed indistinct, misshapen, unreal, sometime appearing as terrifying monsters I didn't understand. I had no way to articulate any of this so I turned inward looking for explanations. This led most people to think of me as the dumb kid who never seemed to pay attention. A nun once told me in front of class that I must be brain damaged. Years later, I found out some of my learning issues came from dyslexia. I also distinctly remember eating paint chips in the hallway of the tenement I grew up in. In 1960s Newark, New Jersey that meant lead paint. No teacher ever thought to investigate or ask questions as to why I had learning issues. Their way of dealing with me, like they did with so many others, was to just relegate me to dumb kid status, and get on with their lives.

Despite all this, I did have several advantages. My father was a construction worker, and my mother was a waitress, neither of whom ever made more than a subsistence living. Their lack of pedigree and position, and the circumstances of my life growing up allowed me to choose who I wanted to become. That is a freedom not everyone had. In my fractured provenance, I come from a long line of Celtic and Silesian people who were never more than serfs and peasants and dirt farmers. They discovered no new lands, inventions or secrets of the universe. None of them were kings or queens or bishops or generals. None of them were philosophers or scientists. The only world travelling they ever did was packed on an immigrant boat (by the standards of today's anti-immigrant pundits, they would be called illegals). In their ordinariness, they were extraordinary for having fought and toiled to simply make the lives of their children a little bit better than their own. Appearing in this book may be the only time they are ever mentioned. I am the product and the beneficiary of this anonymous tribe. I would not be who I am without them, and I didn't even know most of them directly. I am a mongrel birthed by mongrels.[7]

---

[7] Rest easy, this book is not a genealogy.

I was also lucky in that, despite being a product of lower working-class, inner-city America, I was a white male, and so did not have the obstacles in front of me that bedeviled and held back others. I had the luxury of being able to focus on myself and while I had obstacles to overcome, they were as nothing compared to others. I had fairly decent parents who, their considerable flaws and lack of economic power aside, did genuinely love me, and sacrificed for me. I did not have to deal with the racial discrimination and gender bias so prevalent in American society and which held so many back. As a child I could stand by and watch the Newark Riots, for example, and be hurt and confused as to why these innocent people were being treated so badly, without ever really understanding the forces that brought them on. I could then be excited by watching a National Guard armored personnel carrier clatter slowly down the middle of Broad Street and how it was meant to scare the people of the neighborhood into knowing who had the real power.

I'm not a victim. Others have made much greater sacrifices and have been hurt far more profoundly than I have ever been. My trials and tribulations were not particularly unique or unusual. As a kid I had the naive luxury of not seeing the walls in front of me despite their existence. This wasn't an arrogant "nothing will stop me" sort of thing. There were things I wanted to do and so I tried to do them. My circumstances taught me that I wasn't destined for anything or deserved anything. The idea of 'winning' has never meant much to me. To my view, the world was mostly horrible and filled with horrible people and so I tried to move around them and make it a little less horrible. I was lucky enough to see a few slivers of a life I thought I might want to have. That is what saved me. I headed in the direction I thought would get me there as best I could. It was not always easy. It was a circuitous, retrograde course, never a straight line, and never assured of success. Many people with greater intellect and ability than I went much further while some never reached as far as I did. I've always tried to make the best of what I had. In all this motion, I fell many times. I changed strategies and directions, but always was able to keep one goal in my eyesight: well, at least mostly. My successes were more to doggedness, luck, and fear rather than any innate ability. Some obstacles were easy, others not so much. Some left scars where they broke things or left cuts or bruises. I just kept trying to move forward. My White Privilege allowed me to do this. I could worry about scholarship and rare books and manuscripts, art, and adventuring. I could travel to archives and libraries without being looked at suspiciously, or as if I were a child playing at adult research, or as a sex object. I could walk around the museums of the world without being followed, as if I were about to steal something. I've never been pulled over by the police because of the color of my skin. I've never been paid less because of my gender. I was never kept from a job because of my religion. I was never assaulted because of my sexual orientation. In addition, about halfway through I managed to find a partner that felt the same way I did and who loved and supported me unconditionally as I loved and supported her unconditionally in return. There were people who I hoped respected me, but 'liked' was not part of the equation. I never thought about appeal. But for most people, I didn't care one way or another. I never fought for promotion, not in the army, not in any academic job I ever held. If I received a promotion, I didn't turn it down, but I never went looking for it. I had an ability to not care. If I felt fulfilled in some way, it was alright. This gave me an advantage not every one of my peers had, and which I was not always aware of, and should have been more appreciative of.[8]

I am not a 'self-made man.' There is no such thing as being self-made. I had huge amounts of help as everyone has. Some people helped me intentionally, some unintentionally. Some were positive role models many were negative role models. I was able to follow some

---

[8] When I expressed this attitude in an Op Ed piece in May of 2020 at the beginning of the Covid pandemic I was roundly ridiculed and cursed in hate mail exclusively from white people who argued that there was no such thing as White Privilege. "Karen wants to go to the Salon," *Star-Ledger*, May 10, 2020.

who never knew I was following them. I followed some I never knew I was following. Either way I had help which had I not had it, my life would have been very different. I benefitted from the hard work of others, and I had a good deal of plain old, stupid luck. Lots of luck. Never trust anyone who claims they were self-made or that they weren't lucky. They are lying.

I'm going to write this story the way I lived my life: selfishly, from my point of view. I'm not proud of being a selfish ass, but for better or worse (probably worse) that's what I am. I will tell stories as I remember them, which may not always be the way they actually happened.

I blame no one for any negative part of my life, ultimately all the responsibility is mine. We all walk amongst the monsters on our own and in our own way. As a kid I tried to make my life an escapist fantasy, so as an adult I'm going to write it that way. I did consider briefly, writing this as a novel rather than an autobiography. In darker moments I considered naming this *All You People can Go Straight to Hell*. Slightly less angry title possibilities were, *Major Matt Mason was Right*, and *My Apologies to Sasquatch*. Finally, I wish I had been able to make this funnier, but I'm not a funny guy. I also wish I could have been more poetic, but I don't have the heart of a poet. So, whether you like it or not, this is my life: it's the only one I have. With this as a background, I present the story of how I became a historian of monsters.

Chapter 1

The Monster of Newark

"Deformity is visible to every eye; but the effects of it are known to very few;
intimately known to none but those who have them…"

– William Hay, *On Deformity* (1754)

The English born, religious firebrand, Robert Treat (1624-1710), founded Newark in the year 1666.[1] He left Boston, and then New Haven, because he felt the Puritans there not strict enough. He served as governor of Connecticut before coming to what colonists had only recently started calling East Jersey (along the banks of the river called Passaic from the local Hackensack people who had already lived there for a thousand years). Briefly called Pesayak Towne, Treat wanted to officially call the settlement Milford, but his partner, Abraham Pierson, because it was to be a form of protection from the evils and the monsters of the world, insisted they call it the New Ark of the Covenant.

Sometimes, dreams do come true. Once upon a time, I'm not sure which one, I don't remember being born. They tell me it was June 25, 1960.[2] You'd think I would remember as it was an important moment. The problem was that, like so many other things in my life, I didn't notice. I was thinking about something else. As such, I started this journey already a few years behind. It was a quiet moment before a storm of revolutionary upheaval in the world. The Berlin Wall was about to go up. Four young Englishmen were about to become a phenomena. John F Kennedy was about to be elected the 35th President. For me it all began when a monster tried to get into my room. It may account for a good bit of my adult life. It was the 1960s after all, and monsters were everywhere.

I grew up in a lead-painted, three-floor, walk-up tenement on Fleming Avenue in Newark, New Jersey, USA. The neighbourhood was sometimes called 'Down Neck' (because of the way it was bordered by the Passaic River), and sometimes as 'The Ironbound' (because it had been an industrial hub). It was made up of working class people of many ethnic groups, Norkies, each struggling to get by in its own little concrete enclave. Newark had been a manufacturing powerhouse through the First and Second World Wars, but now was starting a slide into decline.

My grandparents, then my Uncle Billy Costigan owned the building. He was one of my mother's many brothers. The Costigan clan were an Irish-American family constantly angry at God knows what. Just angry for the sake of being angry. Billy was my Godfather, though not a very good one. He was the kind of guy who would occasionally get you a nice birthday present, but who mostly forgot the day of your birthday and so stopped off at the drug store at the last minute and bought you one of those sad pharmacy toys that said more about the giver than the receiver. He laughed at everything, even stuff that wasn't supposed to be funny. Whatever you said to him, he'd let out a laugh that was less an indication of him

---

[1] This area was known to the Leni Lenape people as Scheyichbi. The Dutch called it New Netherlands. When the English took over in 1664 they began calling it Jersey after the island in the English Channel.
[2] On other June 25th the war in Korea began, Charles Starkweather was executed, Custer's Last Stand, and George Orwell was born.

finding all of life amusing than it was of him viewing the world with contempt. When he talked, it was in a big, blustery voice you could hear a mile away. He was a career fireman who called Black people *Shines*, Jewish people *Kikes*, Puerto Ricans *Spiks*, and Portuguese *Chadnees*. He failed to see the irony of this as he and other Irish-Americans were derogatorily known as *Micks*, *Hillbillies*, and *Paddy's*. The complaints he made about other ethnic groups—that they were lazy, shiftless, smelly, drunks and criminals—were the exact things that were said about the Costigans; many of which were accurate appraisals. He drove the back of the hook & ladder fire truck. During the Newark riots, he built a plywood and Plexiglas box for his position in case anyone threw a bottle or rock at him, which they did.[3] The Irish half of my family was filled with alcoholics, drug addicts, jailbirds, and adulterers. There was chronic depression, and even a touch of suicide.[4] While I liked the Reigele side of the family, I disliked the Costigan's intensely. I hated them in fact with a hatred that a four or five year old should never have. Once, the Costigan boys and their father were having a disagreement that had escalated quickly into a screaming, shouting and punching fest. Instead of having it in one of their homes, they came to our apartment. They were in the kitchen and had knocked chairs over and spilled our dinner. My father came home from work in the middle of it all and had to throw them out physically. I remember spending the rest of the night shaking. As a result, I've never liked loud noises and I have an aversion to loud, annoying people.[5]

Billy and his family were on the first floor. We were on the second floor, and my ageing Irish grandparents were on the top floor. There were porches with steps at the back and one of my earliest memories was standing on our porch watching as my grandfather, drunk and angry about something, threw furniture off the upper porch down into the yard.

The one side of our yard was the wall of the next door dry cleaners and was just this massive, featureless, concrete surface. The back of our yard butted up against the yard of the house behind us that fronted on Mott Street. Our yard was separated in two by a little wooden fence that ran from the wall to the fence of the tenement next to ours. There was a little gate that allowed you to pass between the front and rear sections. The back half was a garden where my father grew flowers. There was a little tree that produced sour, pea-sized fruits. This back garden seemed miles away from the urban chaos of the Ironbound, just a few steps outside. Happily, I could dig in the ground—I was convinced there were tunnels of some kind hidden just below the surface—have adventures by myself, and feel like I had escaped a little.

The other great thing about the back garden was that that it butted up against another yard that belonged to the two men who lived there. I always assumed they were brothers. I think I remember some aunt referring to them as, 'confirmed bachelors', and one of them was called Dzudzy. I'm not sure if that was his name or a nickname. In the summer they would sit outside their back door, in their yard, under a beach umbrella, attached to a table by ropes.

---

[3] This was a common field modification done to a number of Newark's fire trucks during the riots. You could see some of those veteran engines with the plywood bunkers built onto them still operating with various fire companies into the 1980s when the city began to retire them.

[4] To this day, I am amazed that I somehow did not go down that path. There were plenty of times, though, where I came perilously close.

[5] When I was eleven years old we had an especially hot summer. My grandmother had a little window air conditioner that she offered to my mother. My mother hated air conditioning so she let me have it. I placed it in the window of my room. Then Uncle Billy decided he wanted it for his house (which already had several large air conditioners). He just showed up one morning and took it out of my window without saying a word, and walked off with it. My mother's reaction was to say, "Just let him have it."

14

They sat in collapsible lawn chairs with frayed, vinyl straps, and would sit all day listening to the little AM radio they kept in the kitchen widow facing out. My image of summer, burned into my brain like the ghostly image on a computer screen that can never be erased, is the sight of these two men sitting there listening to the ball game or the music station that only ever seemed to play, "The Lazy, Hazy, Crazy Days of Summer."

What drew my attention to Dzudzy and his brother was that they had a bowling alley in their yard. A full-sized, single lane, outdoor, wooden bowling alley. I don't know if they built it or had it built or if the previous owners of the house had built it. It had some sort of set -up where the ball would knock over the pins then somehow be traversed onto the track which rolled the ball back to the player.

They would sometimes let us kids play with the bowling alley, while they had their lunch. Their favourite was Rueben sandwiches with extra sauce, and some beer. The beers were in cardboard containers with lids that pressed on. They were like the soup bowls you get at *Panera*, a cardboard tube the size of a large beer can today, with no markings or logos, just blank white cardboard. You went to the bar, ordered a beer to go, and the bartender took one of these cardboard cups and filled it from the beer tap. Dzudzy and his brother's favorite beer was Rheingold. It had a strong stench of hops; very bitter. I think the smell, which I did not like, kept me away from alcohol for years after. That, and the fact that my parents were borderline alcoholics. My parents had a number of monsters in their lives they wanted to forget, but never could.

I shared a bedroom with my older sister. It was a front room off the living room with a window that fronted on Fleming Avenue, one building in from Mott Street. As it was an old building, it had those iron fire escapes that *film noir* directors were so enamoured with in the 1950s because of the way moonlight shone through them. An entire row of similar buildings were attached to ours along the street, with no spaces between them. The neighbourhood teemed with people, many of whom of unusual characterisation. A guy my dad always called, 'The Mayor', lived a couple of doors down. He'd squeeze his considerable bulk into a lawn chair on the sidewalk in the summer time and sit there all day no matter the temperature. People would wave to him and yell, "Yo, Toe-Nay!" as they drove by. He would smile back, knowingly, while chomping on a cigar.

In the mornings, I would walk up Fleming Avenue to go to school. Towards the other corner, there were small storefronts on the ground floor. The sidewalk was made of those large, grey, slate sheets. We kids loved these as they made great surfaces to draw on with coloured chalks. Continuing on, I'd pass a large apartment and business office complex that filled the entire block; a huge concrete cube like the Kaaba in Mecca. Everyone called it 'The Prudential Building'. Just past 'The Pru' was Saint Aloysius Catholic Church. It was named for Aloysius de Gonzaga (1568-1591) an Italian Jesuit who died young treating plague victims. Everyone in the neighborhood, of course, called it Sain' Al's.

Across the street from the church was Saint Aloysius grammar school which I attended. Once, the nuns decided it would be a fun exercise to have all the kids in my first grade class stand up individually, and say aloud where we lived. I knew I was in trouble since, although I knew exactly where I lived, I did not know the official street address (27 Fleming Avenue). Details like that often eluded me. As they crept closer and closer, each student dutifully standing up and reciting their address perfectly to the approving smiles of the nuns, I grew more and more agitated. Finally, it was my turn to stand. I was nervous. I tried to

15

remember as best I could, but couldn't. The more I tried the more my brain seized up. The nun smiled and said, "Okay, Brian tell us all where you live." I stood and began stuttering. She snapped, "come along young man." By now a fully blown panic had seized me and I began shaking. The other kids in class all turned to stare at me accusingly. I was holding up the entire project (there had been a promise of cookies for when we had finished). The Mother Superior assumed my stuttering was me acting up. Completely untrained as psychologists or sociologists or child behavior specialists, or even as teachers, the nuns reacted to everything as if you were intentionally making trouble for them personally. Her smile disappeared and the nun scowl appeared.[6] She smacked her stick on the teacher's desk and barked, "Tell us your street address!" On the verge of wetting myself from anxiety, I blurted out the only thing that came into my head. "I live on 42nd Street, New York!" The class burst out laughing, and the Mother Superior began screaming at me. Thinking I was being a smart ass, she suddenly rushed down the aisle raising her stick as she came at me in a lunge of fluttering black robes, well in advance of J.K. Rowling's invention of Harry Potter's Dementors. In a smooth, practised movement, she smacked me across the head with her stick. It would not be the last time a nun had beaten me on the head hard enough to give me a headache for the rest of the day.

I had to find a way out of this. Even then, I knew I had to get out. Luckily, I found a possible escape route. It wasn't long after, that I was at home leaving the kitchen to go to my room. My parents kept the television in the living room against the outside wall of the apartment facing Fleming Avenue, between the two living room windows. The set was on. As I was about to enter my room I heard this sound coming from the TV. It was music; it was syncopated bongos, backed up with a horn section. It sounded exciting, so I went back to look. It was a cartoon of a kid. He was riding a hovercraft. Bad guys dressed in frog suits were shooting at him as he swung on a rope. What was this? It was incredible. It was *The Adventures of Jonny Quest*.

I sat down to watch. Jonny Quest was simply the coolest kid I'd ever seen; his dad was a scientist, he had a cool Secret Service agent as a bodyguard, a fun, barky dog, and his brother was a Hindu child mystic. They travelled the world having adventures and battling evil-doers. The show had already been on the air for a year, and was, in fact, about to get cancelled when I encountered it. The first episode I saw was, "The Robot Spy". When the legs come out of the big black bowling ball, all I could think was, "Wuuut?" Then as it tried to escape, the troops guarding the compound are shooting at it. The machine gun team is firing. I loved the way they animated the spent casings flying out of the Browning .30 caliber as they shot. Then the tank, an actual Walker Bulldog not a childish, 'cartoony' tank, fires at the mechanical spider. It was all a little too much to process. All I knew was I had discovered my path. I had no idea why, or how I was going to make this work, but I was going to become Jonny Quest.

Sometime later my desire to see the world received a boost. My favorite aunt, Wanda (my father's sister), lived a few blocks from us on Filmore Street. During the Newark riots she bought a police scanner which she kept on an end table against the couch in her living room. This way she could hear what was going on as the city burned. It was on twenty-four hours a day. Once the riots ended she kept it and kept it on well into the 1980s. When we were over for a visit, we'd sit in the living room talking or watching a ball game (Wanda's house was the designated Thanksgiving dinner house—it was always the Houston Oilers

---

[6] Anyone who has ever attended a Catholic grammar school knows the 'nun scowl'.

versus the Detroit Lions). Every once in a while the scanner would suddenly burst into life as it picked up communications between officers in the field and the dispatcher. It could be a little jarring. About halfway between her house and ours was the neighborhood Boys' Club. Also known as the 'Red Shield' because of the large metal logo bolted to the outside wall over the entrance, the Boys' Club was a popular community centre that everyone went to.[7] Along with the sports activities, they had a ceramics class that was popular (Aunt Wanda made everyone one of those foot tall ceramic Christmas trees with the lights in them for the holidays).[8] They also ran day trips to various sites around the region. Once we went to Cheesequake Park, once to Crystal Caves. It was a way to get city kids out in the world. Then we went to the United Nations in Manhattan. It was a big deal and the bus was packed. I had to wear my special events suit. Decked out in my dress slacks, dress shoes, shirt, tie, and brown sweater vest, I assumed no one would see I was a kid; I felt I looked so adult. We did the entire UN tour. The best part was that our tour guide was a young Chinese woman who was more likely a 20 or 21-year-old college intern, exchange student. I was dumbstruck by her beauty, her jet black hair cut in straight bangs, and her accent—I was five by the way. I followed her around like a starry-eyed puppy dog. Aunt Wanda, who I normally adored, embarrassed me by chanting, "Brian's got a girlfriend!" The young woman saw my embarrassment, smiled at me and said it would be okay. Internationalism has seemed like a good idea to me ever since.

Despite the two-legged monsters in medieval outfits at Sain Al's, and the monsters on *Jonny Quest*, the Ironbound was not the sort of neighborhood where cryptids showed up.[9] One night as I fell asleep, the fire escape outside our room began to rattle and shake violently. It was late June and the heat was such that we slept with the window open. I looked up and there was this hairy monstrous face peering in the window. It had a deranged look in its gaunt eyes. It seemed very big, but emaciated as it pulled on the metal stairs of the fire escape mechanism. A primordial beast seemed to be trying to get in to eat us. The figure darted away just as my father came in the room. We pointed at the window and he looked out. He muttered under his breath some ancient Chinese expletive he had learned as a tank driver in the Korean War then turned to us. His angry face instantly turned to one of sympathy and fatherly concern. He smiled and said everything was okay, and not to worry.

A night or two later, it happened again. This time there was shouting outside and some great rattling commotion. In my Flintstones PJs I bravely looked out just as the monster darted between two parked cars yelping in pain. It was being pursued by another monster that chased him with what looked suspiciously like a baseball bat.

That was the last time we saw the creature, and all seemed to return to normal on Fleming Avenue. There were still monsters running around, but none of them tried to get into my room. It got me thinking. How did such a creature know how to operate a fire escape? How did no one notice it walking down the street in the middle of the Ironbound? There were plenty of strange things on those streets, of course, but even this thing must have aroused comment. I filed those questions away and continued to dream of being an historian or a

---

[7] One day I found the firefighting hose attached to the wall just outside the gymnasium. It was one of those wheels with the hose wrapped around it and a solid brass nozzle hanging down. It looked like it could be used as a swing, but all I did was bring the nozzle down on my head and cracked it open. There was blood everywhere and my mother, who could not drive, walked me to a local doctor's office who proceeded to put several surgical steel clamps in my head without anesthetic.

[8] As I write this my nostrils were suddenly filled with the distinctive smells of ceramics class.

[9] A much shorter version of this story appears in Karen Stollznow ed, *Would You Believe it? Mysterious Tales From People You'd Least Expect* (2017).

writer, or at least a tank driver like Pop.

A few years later I was in the candy store with my mother. She was buying some household things while I perused the magazine rack on my knees. Then I saw it. There on the cover of a magazine was a picture of the thing that attacked us. The magazine had a title I found difficult to say, AR-GO-SEE. "Mom! Mom! That's the thing I saw…" Just as I blurted that out, she grabbed my hand and dragged me towards the door. "Don't play with the books! Come on, we still have to go to the deli and then to the…" I didn't hear the rest, I kept looking at the magazine cover.

"But…but!" I waved and pointed feverishly, but ineffectively, back at the magazine rack and tried to get her to understand. It was no use. The pot-roast and pirogues awaited and there was no way she was going to detour for some foolish magazine that her weird little kid was yammering on about. However, I was determined. I managed to save my pennies and a few weeks later went back to the candy store to get a copy of the magazine with my creature on the cover. Of course, they were all sold out. Like the monster in my window, it was gone.

The modern English word monster comes from the Latin monstrum. In Greco/ Roman theater the Monster was a character that when they appeared on stage the audience knew something significant was about to happen. They were portents of things to come. In the European Middle Ages, the term monster was applied to children, or animals, born deformed. People believed these monstrous births to be portents of catastrophes to come. God was warning people of an impending doom by having the child be born against the normal. This is where the term began to change. Monster took on the modern meaning of not only a portent of evil, but of physical ugliness.

It wasn't until years later at a typically drunken family baby christening that I finally learned what had happened that night, what strange creature had intruded upon our lives. It seems a youngish newlywed who lived in the tenement next-door had rapidly grown weary of her husband and began an affair with a wiry, bakery truck driver. Beau Brummell was not the smartest loaf in the basket, and would wait until the husband was going in the front door and coming up the stairs before he climbed out on the fire escape to leave unnoticed. That night he had climbed over to go down our fire escape. That's when we saw him.

My father knew what happened and that we were never in danger. My Irish grandfather, however, felt action was required. He took to hiding in the darkened, street-level glass entry doors with a Louisville Slugger, waiting. His patience was rewarded when the hapless lover came scrambling down the fire escape ladder a few nights later. As he was about to swing down to the sidewalk and safety, gramps stepped out and swung for the fences with an expertise that would have made the Great Bambino proud. The poor guy fell from the rusty ladder and began to run and hop wounded down the street, his legs aching from where my grandfather had hit him in the shins several times. As gramps swung he growled, "Ya bastid, scare my grankids will ya!" As the poor creature ran away into the hot Ironbound night he yelled back, "I'm not a burglar, I'm not a burglar!" The story passed into the lore of Fleming Avenue to be told at every family gathering from then on.

Incidents such as this give useful insight into the formation of myths and legends. Some tales of monsters undoubtedly have their origins in some event that was poorly remembered by those involved. From Grimm's fairy tales, to Jack and the Beanstalk, to the Blemmyae of the Middle Ages, to El Chupacabras, to Spring Heeled Jack, more than a few fantastical stories began with mundane events expanded out of proportion. This can also teach us about the differences between rural and urban legends. They are a wealth of primary source material.

It is difficult to prove the existence of monsters: they are annoyingly elusive and require a good bit of work to find. Often, when we do find them they turn out to be just as annoyingly prosaic. That, however, is the nature of the monster hunting game: lot's of work to find out it was just a guy climbing out a fire escape in the middle of the night, scaring some kids. It makes the entire enterprise so much more interesting and fun, at least if you begin with the idea that there is probably no flying devil horse or scaly aquatic beast to be found.

Years later, while I was working on my biography of Grover Krantz, the University of Washington anthropologist who believed Bigfoot was real, I was finally able to acquire a copy of the *Argosy* magazine with Ivan Sanderson's article with the Paterson Film stills.[10] It seemed different to me as an adult than I remembered it as a kid. That's the faulty nature of memory, especially the memory of monsters. We always seem to embellish them beyond the facts of what happened. As an historian, I have been trained to see past the memories, to analyze the texts, to see the correspondences, and to compare against the actual data. This is something the large majority of monster hunters and cryptozoologists need to do more of. Maybe they were not lucky enough to be born in the Ironbound or have a grandfather who was handy with a baseball bat?

Kearny

A fire in the building next door convinced my father we should leave the Ironbound. It happened late at night and we had to frantically get out onto the sidewalk. Fire engines were everywhere with their lights flashing, reflecting off the buildings and walls like the psychedelic dreams that a few adventurous people were just beginning to have. The noise and the people and the screaming sirens freaked me out, and so I had plastered myself against the building and shook unable to run away. Pops saw me so he picked me up and held me. It wasn't a big fire and it was put out quickly; no one was injured. The fire was the excuse he always used for why we moved. My father Henry hated the Costigans as much as I did. Uncle Billy was considering raising the rent—on his sister. Also, racial tensions were growing and violence was spreading around the city. Just after we moved out, the Newark Riots began. As a kid I didn't understand the deep and legitimate causes of the riots and why the city's Black population had reached a point where they could no longer stand the poor treatment meted out to them by the White political establishment that ran the city and controlled the police and fire department that Uncle Billy was a part of.

A pair of Newark police officers arrested and beat African American cab driver John Smith, because he was foolish enough to pass a double parked police car. Smith's arrest and beating enflamed an already tense situation. Newark had been a Victorian jewel noted for stately homes and breweries and then a WWII industrial boom town. With the war over, white flight set in as families began moving out of the city for perceived better opportunities in the outlying suburbs. With the outrage over Smith's beating, the 'Long Hot Summer' of 1967, which had been visiting other American cities, came to Newark. Civil unrest had already struck at Chicago, Boston, Atlanta, Cincinnati, and other places. It then came to Newark, and my future home town of Plainfield. For more than a week, violence ebbed and flowed, dozens

---

[10] Brian Regal. *Searching for Sasquatch: Crackpots, Eggheads, and Cryptozoology* (Palgrave-Macmillian, 2013).

were killed and hundreds injured across town. The New Jersey National Guard and State Police were called in and a city that had been a thriving multi-ethnic place descended into economic and cultural oblivion from which it would not begin to recover until the 21st Century.

My parents started looking around for a new place to live and Kearny, just across the Passaic River, seemed as good as any. Originally called New Barbados, the town was renamed in 1867 in honour of Union, Civil War General, and one-armed globetrotting adventurer, Phil Kearny, who once fought with Napoleon III, and who died at the battle of Chantilly in 1862. The town was just urban and ethnic enough to feel like Newark, but not too much.[11] Back then, it had a large Scotts-Irish population that made my mother feel at home. Hispanic families had begun to move in as well as a sprinkling of Black families just well-off enough to escape Newark, though not well-off enough to make the lower working class white population nervous.

The town sat on a high ridge that sloped down to the Passaic River and Newark on the West side then down to the vast expanse of Meadowlands and New York City on the eastern side like the long sinuous back of a triceratops. Kearny Avenue—'The Ave'—ran along the crest of the ridge. Kearny Avenue actually started in the Ironbound with Jackson Street. Only a few blocks from Fleming Avenue, it was just over from Somme Street, named in remembrance of the First World War battle. Despite this pedigree, Norkies never called it Somme Street they always called it *Sohm-eee* Street. It then crossed the Passaic River at the PSE&G gasworks, at the Jackson Street Bridge, a short distance from where Robert Treat first made landfall. There was a huge gas storage tank here. Originally constructed in 1926, on the side of it in big letters was painted 'Go Navy.' Why it had this exhortation, I never knew.

It was at the gas company that the street began the slow rise through Harrison— named for President William Henry Harrison—into Kearny. It then went on through Lyndhurst—named for Lord Lyndhurst of Boston—and then North Arlington. It then continued on to cross Route 3—named for Congressman Rhutt Tree. It ended in Rutherford—named for Senator John Rutherford who owned some land in the area—and the Meadowlands where so many secrets were buried. The total distance was about ten miles of old, dead, forgotten white politicians.

My parents looked at several places including a single family house on Schuyler Avenue. My father liked it, but passed because Schuyler Avenue, which ran along the edge of the Meadowlands, was a heavily used truck route and he was worried for our safety. Also, the property was a house and my mother was dead set against buying or even living in a genuine house. My mother, Elizabeth, who everyone called Betty, had grown up on a small farm in upstate New York before they moved to Newark. Her family had emigrated from Ireland in the 19th century, pushed out by the leftover effects of the potato famine, and claimed mixed Irish/English/Scots descent that had married into some German. She often

---

[11] Settled during the early Colonial period, New Barbados was located along the edge of the Meadowlands, the swamp that separated New York from New Jersey. Pirates from the Caribbean could sail their boats a good way in off the ocean and offload their booty unmolested by the authorities. They set up a small settlement that grew even after the pirates no longer came by. Phil Kearny served many years in France with the cavalry there including fighting alongside Napoleon III at Solferino. In 1855 Kearny built an elaborate home he called *Belle Grove*, but who everyone else called Kearny Castle. See, William Styple, *Letters from the Peninsula: Civil War Letters of General Philip Kearny* (Bellgrove Pub., 1988).

went on about how much she hated living on that farm so, my father, who grew up in the inner city, had to give up his dream of suburban home ownership to make her happy. They finally settled on a three-storey tenement building on the corner of Tappan and Devon Street not unlike the one we were moving out of. The building's number was 1 and we moved into the second floor apartment. It was at the highest point in Kearny. I always hated it. It was owned by a local shyster furniture store owner, slumlord. With three bedrooms off a central hall it always felt cramped and restrictive to me. It did have access to the roof and when I grew older I would carefully sneak up there and sit in the hatch. I'd stare out at the New York skyline and the Meadowlands, and dream. There was a back porch area (where I built my first laboratory), and a small concrete covered yard where all the kids played. It was immediately across the street from Saint Cecilia's grammar school and later an eight block walk to Kearny High School. Its best feature—as far as I was concerned—was that it was just a couple of blocks away from a set of Hudson County parks. My mother would live in this awful place for the next fifty years.

One of the first things I tried to do after we moved to Kearny was to dig my way to China. I saw *Journey to the Centre of the Earth* on television and wanted to have an adventure like Professor Lindenbrook. I started to dig down in a secret spot amongst some trees I found. I thought that if I just dug far enough I'd find a tunnel system I could follow and disappear like in the movie. It was great fun, but as I went I realized two things: I wasn't going to be able to go all the way to China, and I began finding interesting rocks. This led me to my weekly Saturday morning rock hunting expeditions, and the journey to my interest in science and then history that *Jonny Quest* had started me on.

The park was actually three parks separated by Devon Street and Davis Avenue. The one that butted up against Kearny Avenue was the smallest, known to all and sundry as 'Park N°1' or the 'Little Park'. It was just a flat, tree-filled zone about half the size of a football field with winding black top covered walking paths and a central raised dais with a shrub hedge around it and a water fountain. The two long sides of the park were hemmed in by the backs of houses.[12] Out each side were stone step entryways of four or five steps and smooth, river rock stone retaining walls. Someone had put some design thought into them to generate a rustic aesthetic in the center of an urban landscape. The main entrance on Kearny Avenue had grand, sweeping staircases leading up and into the park that was above the level of the street. There was a big, Adirondack style sign that said "Welcome to Hudson County Park." Residents saw it as something worthy of public pride in its day. By the late 1960s, it had all the air of a forgotten ruin. This appealed to my budding interest in archaeology. To me it seemed like the entrance to Atlantis or some pre-Columbian capital city. If I explored enough, I thought, I might encounter an Aztec princess or a beautiful, Black Forest witch, and we could live in our very own tree house there, and be happy forever.

All this rudimentary exploration contributed to my growing interest in something I learned was called 'scholarship.' Along with everything else the *Ben Franklin's* store on the Ave sold books. They had those tiny paperback Golden Nature Guides. The edition titled *Rocks and Minerals* had a section on how to be a rock hound. I read it over and over standing in front of the shelves until I could afford the $1.95 cover price. The book said you should have a backpack with geology equipment when you went rock hunting. I didn't have one so I made a backpack out of sheets of thin plywood I found in the garbage, some duct tape and

---

[12] Once when I was riding my bike as fast as I could through the Little Park I lost control and crashed. I landed on my knee and skidded along the ground on it. When I came to a stop I discovered I had sliced all the flesh off my knee cap.

with string for shoulder straps.[13] Every Friday night I would carefully pack my adventuring gear while I watched *Chiller Theater* on channel 11, the WPIX local station.[14] Cheese and crackers in the little plastic pack with the red plastic spoon, for a snack, a magnifying glass, a bottle of *Yoohoo* and a notebook to keep careful track of my work, was my kit.[15] Herbert Zim told me I needed a special hammer to be a real geologist, but they were expensive, and I had never seen one in any of the stores I had ever been in.[16] I saved up my allowance and went to Mr. Finger's on the Ave and bought a tack hammer for seventy-five cents, because it sort of looked like the hammers real scientists used that I had seen in Zim's book. Seeing me with the tack hammer my father asked what I was doing so I explained. Without ever saying he was going to do it, for my next birthday, the old man made a professional grade Estwing geologist's hammer magically appear "off the back of a truck" in the way some dads could in Newark in those days.[17]

The neighbourhood was full of kids, many of whom went to St. Cecelia's, but not all. Some of them were nice, most were awful. Like their parents they all seemed mean, stupid, and always ready to make others feel bad. None of them seemed interested in learning about the world. There were the neighbourhood tough guys who I tried to avoid, but still got beaten up by once or twice. They were the kind of kids who grew up to drive those huge pickup trucks with Trump flags flying from them. In the first floor apartment was a kid who was taking saxophone lessons. He had sort of, kind of, learned to play the Batman theme.

There was a mix of apartments and single family homes and bad parking all packed together. In one house was Mrs. Carchitti. She was one of those tiny Italian women whose husband died when they were in their twenties and now in her eighties she still wore black mourning outfits all the time. She was generally sweet, but when we acted up she gave us the horns and the 'Malocchio.' For all her years in America she never really learned to speak English well, and she would often break into Italian. Around the corner from there lived a couple whose grown son was severely mentally and physically handicapped. He could walk around outside with shuffling difficulty, his hands bent in perpetual and painful claws, and who sometimes went to the park by himself. He couldn't speak coherently and often drooled copiously. He always frightened me because of his monstrosity. Some of the crueller kids would taunt him, causing him to yell and splutter. All anyone ever called him was 'Junior.' After I went off to the service I lost touch with these people. I have no idea what happened to any of them, and I never really cared.

---

[13] Eventually my mother discovered my homemade backpack and so took me on the bus into Newark and brought me to an Army/Navy store and bought me a genuine army surplus map case complete with a shoulder strap and places to put pencils.

[14] This was a popular show. They ran science fiction and horror movies from the 1950s. Its distinctive feature was the opening of the show which had a stop motion animation of a giant hand (which took viewers a while before they realized it had six fingers) sinking into a fog covered swamp. As it did, an unearthly voice would groan "Chilllli-errrrrr."

[15] Published by Western Publishing and mostly written by Dr. Herbert Zim (1909-1994), and wonderfully illustrated by James Gordon Irving (1913-2012), Raymond Perlman (1923-2015) as well as other artists, the Golden Guides were a series of tiny paperbacks designed for children to learn science. In addition to the one on *Rocks and Minerals,* I also eventually had the one on *Zoology, Fossils,* and *The Stars.* They didn't just discuss the content, but had sections on how a kid could pursue these areas themselves. It would be interesting to see how many scientists, astronomers, archaeologists, and historians first became interested in their fields by reading Golden Guides.

[16] This information was on pages 10 and 11.

[17] He also got me a little portable typewriter with a plastic carry cover. He saw it on a shelf in a construction site office trailer not being used, and took it. He thought it would help me do better in school. To me it was the greatest computer in the world. I wrote on it so much it eventually broke. Despite his best efforts, I still graduated at the bottom of my class, twice. I still have that hammer. It's rusted and pitted with the marks of a thousand adventures.

Saint Cecelia

My parents were never quite sure what to make of me and my hobbies. They were glad I was reading books and wanted to do something 'sciencey' (after showing interest in astronomy Henry took me to a local camera store and bought me an inexpensive telescope. He and I would set it up at night and look at the stars together through the kitchen window). I think they sensed on some primordial level that my interests could lead to better things for me. I also think it frustrated them that I was doing this work at home on my own, but in class I was failing. My parents feared I would follow a bad path, as so many in my family and in the neighbourhood had, so did everything in their power to keep that from happening. 'M&D' also thought keeping me in a Catholic school would prepare me for the future. It did, but not for the reasons they expected.

Despite my reading, history and science interests, at Saint Cecelia's I was far from the smartest kid in the class. In fact, I was considered one of the dumbest. In grammar school I knew I was in the classes for dummies. I knew this because Sister Louise told me to my face, "You're in this section because you're stupid!" She also once told me in front of the entire class that not only did she think I was brain damaged, but that I was the Antichrist as well. The eighth grade teacher yelled at me because I was in the back of the class reading the *Encyclopedia Americana*.

It wasn't all the nun's fault. I did seem to have learning issues. It was difficult for me to understand complicated ideas, and I had trouble memorizing and remembering things. My parents had me fitted for glasses, but that didn't help (I eventually lost the glasses in the park). Because of all this, I always felt alone even in a crowded classroom. We all sat in those desks with the lift-up tops. I would lift the desktop and stick my head down inside. The teachers thought I was mentally disturbed. They didn't realize I was in my imaginary library having an adventure. I was developing a sense of isolation that would follow me all my life, interpreted by others as distance, disinterest, and even mean-spiritedness. I just wanted to be left alone, I had world exploring to do. I assumed that out in the world I'd meet people who were not as awful as those I actually knew. To my teachers I had little ability or intelligence. My final report card for the eighth grade (my last year at St. Cecelia's) bears witness to the nuns assessment of my potential. I received a C in history, a D in science, C for study habits, and a D in conduct. The final slight to God himself, a D in Christian Doctrine.

The world I saw always seemed to be different from the one everyone else experienced. As a student, I tried hard. I wanted to be smart. I liked reading and history of course though the letters would seem to spin around. I was especially bad at math. Our 7th grade math teacher was a young guy with dark hair, a big moustache, and a penchant for white, proto-disco suits. He was not particularly good at explaining things. His way of dealing with you if you didn't understand was to say the same thing again only louder, and then smack you. He would get frustrated easily with kids like me who did not pick it up quickly or not at all. He enjoyed physically hitting kids. It was standard procedure at St. Cecelia's for the faculty, both the religious and lay people, to physically assault the children under their supposed 'pastoral care'. These monstrous adults hit me with open hands, closed fists, rulers (both wooden and steel), and once with a Crucifix: the nun beat me with Jesus! You never told your parents because doing so would usually get you a beating from them as well, so you suffered in silence and ultimately became a priest, a nun, an atheist, or a serial killer.

23

The nuns were always reminding us that if we didn't behave God would know and he and Jesus would send us to hell where we would burn in fire forever. As if to remind us of that, Saint Cecelia's grammar school was a designated nuclear war fallout shelter. Over the main entry way was one of those black and yellow 'Fallout Shelter' signs, designed by William Blakeley in 1961, with the triangles. If Jesus didn't vaporize us the Russians would. Throughout the 1960s and '70s the government told us to expect the Communists (probably the Soviets, but also the Chinese) would launch a nuclear strike on us without warning. They also told us that we could survive if we made it to a special shelter like the basement of Saint Cecelia's. Homework was more of an immediate worry, though.

My parents tried to help me with my homework, but it usually ended with them angry. Mom would make me sit at the kitchen table as she tried to teach me to spell, but the letters moved around. I told her this, but she didn't get it. Dad would do the same and try to teach me math with mixed results. I felt that all I ever did was disappoint my father. I always seemed to screw everything up and that frustrated him, which in turn frustrated me, and so on. Eventually, he stopped asking me to help him with various things because he knew I'd just fumble it somehow and it was just easier for him to do it himself. None of us had ever heard the word dyslexia.[18] I had trouble understanding what was going on around me. I had trouble processing information. Everything went by too fast. I had trouble seeing things sometimes. Under any type of pressure my mind would seize up and my vision go out of focus. I had no idea how to articulate this to anyone. To my parents and teachers I was just being a wise ass or not paying attention. "Doesn't pay attention" was the most common critique my teachers made of me. When I tried to explain they would just get angry at me. All this taught me that when disappointments or failures came along the best thing to do was smile a little, say, "It's okay, it's not really that important," and walk away. That would end it. I'd go to the safety of my room, lock the door, and calculate the distance from the Earth to Jupiter so I could fly there. I was never able to explain to my parents what was going on inside my head. After a while, I just gave up trying, and went off on my own, alone. If I could do something on my own, I did it. If I couldn't do something on my own, I didn't do it. While I wanted someone to help me, I never asked for help because that would just complicate things.[19] It was a habit I could never quite break.

The Secret Alley

One of the reasons we moved to Tappan Street was because St. Cecelia's church and Catholic school were right across the street. I enjoyed the physical church: I loved the statues, the stained glass, and the carved wood. The God stuff not so much. I liked the nuns and priests even less. Don't get me wrong, I was not some pioneering eight-year-old atheist. I didn't not believe. I just wasn't interested in God or Jesus. Religion did not interest me. Only the architecture. I liked the trappings, but not the theology. I would blandly do the rituals and sing along if that kept them from hitting me, but it never took.

Saint Cecelia's Church sat on Kearny Avenue. First established in 1893, it catered to

---

[18] Heading down Jackson Street in Newark, just past the bridge there was a large advertisement painted on the wall of a building there. It was for a place that sold baby clothes and furniture. One day driving past looking at the sign—we were stuck in traffic—I asked my parents what 'Jun-eh-vill' meant. They had no idea what I was talking about. Then I pointed to the billboard for the baby furniture store. Part of the advertisement read, "We have everything for Babies and Juveniles too!" I was reading Juveniles as Jun-eh-vill. My mother busted out laughing. She found it very funny. She would repeat this story many times to friends and relatives over the years. They had no idea it was a sign that I suffered from a cognitive learning issue.

[19] It puzzles me today to think I was able to create a career as a writer and teacher with these learning issues. Please don't tell anyone.

the Scots and Irish immigrants of the neighborhood. An imposing façade, it was elevated about a dozen feet over the street level. To the right, as you looked at it, was the Rectory where the priests lived. Behind the church was the convent where the nuns lived. To me the nuns and priests were like these weird, savage creatures that took delight in tormenting the children. Any sign of resistance brought retribution from them. Even as a child I wondered what had happened to these women so that they took on the job of tormentors of innocent children. They certainly seemed to enjoy it. Their attempts to stifle us only led to some of us finding ways to squeeze out the sides. This was the time of the Second Vatican Council, Vatican II. This move to a more liberal church ended the mass in Latin. During the school week we studied religion one day then science the next. It was in Catholic school that I first learned about dinosaurs and evolution. [20]

The shift in doctrinal attitudes didn't change everything. We still did confession. This is where you kneel inside a little cabinet box inside the Church—I of course liked the carving and the wood work—and told the priest, who was in another box with his face hidden, about your sins. It was like a hockey penalty box for your soul. When you were done, the priest would give you a 'penance.' This usually amounted to saying a number of prayers, 'Hail Mary's' or 'Our Fathers', as punishment. As an eight or nine year old, I never knew what to confess. I hadn't broken any of the commandants as far as I could tell. I hadn't killed anyone or robbed a bank (though I had kissed a girl for the first time in the school basement). I never "coveted my neighbor's ass." I wasn't even sure what that meant, though it did make us giggle when the priest or especially a nun said it. I started to make stuff up just to get through it, just so no questions were asked. I'd say I used bad language or acted up in class or ran in the hallway. That was easy. All vague, no details. It got you in and out without too much trouble. Then I heard Pauli Ditillo tell a priest that he had 'bad thoughts.' He seemed to get out of the box even faster. I was unsure what 'bad thoughts' meant, but it sounded good. Anything to shorten the time in the confessional. I started telling the priests in confession I was having bad thoughts. A few weeks later Monsignor Corrigan came to class and made all the girls leave then started yelling at us about having bad thoughts, and that he expected us to give details in the confessional. Apparently, everyone was saying they had bad thoughts. After that, I went back to saying I'd been running in the halls.

On the grounds of the actual church there was a set of garages that fronted onto Chestnut Street. Across this street sat the grammar school and high school. Behind the rectory was my favorite spot in those days. There was a semi-hidden walkway that started at Chestnut Street and ran along the inside edge of the property down to where the little library was. The church owned a small house that faced Kearny Avenue in the corner of the property. They used this house as a library. I really enjoyed going there. [21] The librarian seemed nice, and this place was one of the only ones in my life at the time that didn't give me anxiety attacks. The nuns always behaved as if these few moments of respite set aside for books and reading were somehow suspect. When they came to gather us up to go back to class, they would scowl and growl at us as if to say, "fun time is over, back to breaking rocks." In that library, I began to

---

[20] Thanks to Vatican II, St. C-ecelia's also experimented with 'Guitar Mass.' One Sunday, instead of the usual organ music they had a twenty-something hippy girl come in, sing, and play acoustic guitar. She was really cute with big permed hair, round granny glasses, and a flowing skirt. She sat in a chair near the altar. At the appropriate moment the priest smiled, and gave her the nod and she began to sing. There were smiles all around. She did a few numbers over the course of the mass, then she did her big finale: a spirited rendition of *White Rabbit*. The priest stopped smiling. I was in love, but the priests, nuns, and parents were aghast. That ended the great guitar mass experiment in Kearny. We never saw her again.

[21] We were visited a few times by the Book Mobile. That was a very special treat. To be able to climb up into a truck and find a library inside it. This simple act, sponsored by the city government, opened me to vistas I never thought existed.

enjoy the idea of being surrounded by books. It made me feel safe, and helped with the shaking. I read a lot (though I actually mostly just looked as the words spun around), but my favorites were Virginia Lee Burton's *The Little House* (1943) and Jean Merrill's *The Pushcart War* (1964). I decided I was going to save my pennies and start buying my own books. That way the nuns wouldn't be involved at all, no one would be, and they'd never be able to tell me to stop.[22] I realized that if I didn't involve anyone in my adventures I could do what I wanted, go where I wanted, and think what I wanted. Also, if I didn't tell people what I was doing or let them get too close, they couldn't make fun of me or steal it away from me.

To access the walkway that led to the library along the outer edge of the church property, you entered through a thick oaken door set into the wall that connected the edge of the property to the garages along Chestnut Street. The door seemed ancient and heavy, and you had to really push to get it to open. Not many people ever used it. There was a rusty iron ring for a door handle. Along that boundary line was a wall that seemed ancient to me. As we were in the middle of the city, the other side of the wall was fronted by houses just like the park. The wall seemed made of medieval bricks. I had only recently read about this thing called The Middle Ages. It had cool stuff like castles and monasteries and really old books. Inset into the wall at regular intervals were bas-relief Stations of the Cross. In my mind I saw the depictions of the execution of Jesus, done in what had originally been colourful, glazed ceramics, as carvings of knights battling monsters.[23] There was ivy growing on it. There were a few concrete and marble benches along the walkway. There was one under a large shady tree that was my favorite place to sit. The whole thing was shielded by the back of the Convent and the Rectory as well as a large half-shell altar to Saint Cecelia. The whole thing formed a kind of secluded cloister. The few instances I ever heard anyone refer to this place, they called it 'The Grotto.' This little precinct had been used for outdoor ceremonies and rituals in the past, but by the time I came along it was all but abandoned. When we were walked to the library as a class we went around the other side of the newly built Rectory. In all my time at St. Cecelia's—from second to eighth grade—I never saw a nun or priest come to this place. You couldn't see it from Kearny Avenue. You had to know where it was. In that shielded area I could see the whole of the Middle Ages in a crumbled wall, see into the cosmos, and travel through time and space.

When I discovered this lost world, I immediately wanted to make it mine. I never told anyone else about it. I knew from experience that if I did, they would ruin it with their stupid angry faces and cruel ways as they had done with other things I discovered, thought fun and wanted to share. With the silently staring statues and the overgrown ivy, the secret alley appealed to me. I would go there whenever I felt afraid or lonely which was pretty much all the time. Despite its close proximity to Kearny Avenue and the honking horns and groaning buses it was quiet. I could sit there and think. While I was there no one was screaming at me, or hitting me, or correcting me, or yelling at me, or bullying me, or telling me I was worthless, or stupid, that I had done this or that thing the wrong way, or that I had no future. It was in this place that I caught a fleeting glimpse of what might be. My suspicions grew that I might find a life out in the world away from here. I certainly wasn't going to have one in Kearny. If

---

[22] *The Little House* taught me how to reify a physical place into the idea of 'home.' Home would be a concept I'd wrestle with all my life, but never really get comfortable with. *The Pushcart War*, as it told the story of working people who fight an evil corporate owner, helped turn me into a socialist.

[23] The 'Stations of the Cross' was this weird ritual where you recreated the trial and execution of Jesus. There were fourteen 'stations' each depicting, in a diorama, a moment where Jesus drags his cross to Calvary to be torture murdered by the Romans. At each station you stopped and said prayers. The whole thing was designed to inspire deep contemplation over the suffering of Jesus.

the janitor came along, I would leave.[24] For protection, whenever I went there, I always carried my favorite Matchbox car in my pocket.

A British company, Lesney Products, unveiled 'Matchbox Cars' in the 1950s. In our area, they sold them out of a display in the hobby/toy section of the *Two Guys* department store on River Road in Harrison.[25] The *Two Guys* was an adventure land for me. There were all sorts of wondrous things there. Unfortunately, it was a bit too far for me to walk. Luckily, our family had a Friday night ritual. My father was paid on Fridays and after he came home and cleaned up, we'd pile into the car and go down to River Road to go shopping at the *Two Guys* which also had a grocery store attached to it. While my parents were shopping I'd wander off and entertain myself in the toy and hobby department. One Friday when I was nine, I was walking past a rack of glass-bowled candy machines something caught my eye. One of the glass bowls had 'Genuine Moon Rocks' on the label. The Apollo missions were big at the time and I was totally following it. I could see the objects in the bowl looked just like what I thought moon rocks should look like. You had to put a dime in and turn the crank to get these valuable objects. I went to ask Pops for a dime, but my parents were done with the shopping and heading home so I had to leave. I thought about it all week. I managed to save a couple of dimes and waited for the next Friday. As soon as M&D were in the grocery store I went to find the candy machines. I went stealthily because I didn't want anyone to know I had found this incredible treasure and I didn't want to look too eager. Hiding behind a clothes rack I carefully peered out. There was no one near the candy machine. I thought, this can't be. Why is there not a line of people waiting to get genuine moon rocks for ten cents? Was I the first to discover this repository of interstellar artifacts? I sidled up to the machines, again trying not to look too eager. I looked around to make sure the coast was clear. I put a dime in, turned the crank and heard that sound of objects tumbling down the chute to rest just behind the little door. I scooped five or six grey mineral-like rocks out. Then I put in my other dime and repeated the procedure. I now had a handful of actual, genuine, real-life, honest, moon rocks. I shoved them into my pocket. I didn't want anyone to see I had them. In the car on the way home I took them out to examine them. I remembered a news report on television where they said the moon rocks brought back by Apollo 11 had to be quarantined in case they had a space virus in them. I had an old peanut butter jar with a screw top lid and I figured that it would make a perfect moon rock quarantine. On closer inspection as we drove home, however, my moon rocks looked like a sample in my collection of rocks and minerals the old man had

---

[24] The school only had one janitor who had to take care of all the buildings in the complex. Everyone, including the nuns and priests called him 'Mr. Fix.' I have no idea if that was his actual name or that they called him that because it was his job to fix everything. Once while I was sneaking around the basement of the grammar school building exploring, I found the boiler room. I was fascinated by the machinery. Then I saw Mr. Fix had set up a cot with a little night stand with a lamp on it with a little rug and two wall lockers. He lived there. One of the wall lockers was open and I looked inside. To my surprise, there was a World War I vintage army pistol belt and shoulder harness with a canteen attached to it. There was one of those old dishpan style helmets, and a fully functioning M1903 Springfield battle rifle just like Sargent York carried. The school was designated a fallout shelter in case of nuclear attack, but I never learned why Mr. Fix had a combat outfit in the locker next to the place where he lived in the basement of a grammar school next to the boilers.

[25] *Two Guys* was a chain of department stores. The one we went to every Friday night after my father came home with his paycheck was on River Road at the Passaic River in Harrison. It was the original location founded in 1946 by brothers Sidney and Herbert Hubschman. I loved going there for a number of reasons. Harrison and Kearny were still industrial. There was still barge traffic on the Passaic River, and a series of railroad tracks serviced the foundry next the department store. This meant, if you were lucky, you could see those little bulldog switcher engines pushing freight cars through the big parking lot up to where the sidings connected with the main shunt line that came out of the meadowlands. Seeing a working engine was always a treat for me. The other thing that I loved about the *Two Guys* was they had a hobby department. As long as I can remember the same man worked behind the counter. To me he seemed very old though he was probably in his early 40s. He always wore a blue lab coat and he seemed to know everything about model trains, laboratory glassware, and any other aspect of hobbying.

bought me: the ones glued to the cardboard box. Once at home I examined them more closely with my magnifying glass. To my great disappointment, I realized that the 'genuine' moon rocks were, in fact, a handful of industrial gravel with a bit of glitter sprinkled on them. I felt a little cheated. Next week at the *Two Guys* I went back to dreaming in the hobby department.

I had a much better experience with Matchbox Cars than with moon rocks. They were a revelation to me. Not only were Matchbox Cars inexpensive—as opposed to Corgi Toys which were out of my league, in terms of price—but they were exacting in their scale realism despite their diminutive size. They were brightly colored and exotic and from a far off place. The collection included vehicles I had never seen before. They spelled words like color as colour. Inside the box were instructions in French and German. It was all so enticing.

I preferred the working truck models to the cars. I loved the yellow 'stake truck' and the blue 'refuse truck.' My favorite, however, was the six-wheeled *Alvis Stalwart* cargo carrier (Number 61B in the original series). This pushed me further along the road to being interested in the world and wanting to travel the globe. I wanted to go visit England and maybe France and Germany, maybe Egypt or China. I wanted to have adventures, to explore. I mean, the *Alvis* even had the word EXPLORATION written on the side of it. There was a bit of a problem, though. Everyone around me—except for mom and pop—told me that I had no future because I wasn't bright and that I would never amount to anything. The nuns at Saint Cecilia's told me so on a regular basis.[26]

These toys told me different. These toys, along with TV shows like *The Thunderbirds,* and *Jonny Quest,* and *Herge's Adventures of Tin Tin*, told me different. Matchbox Cars cost fifty cents. That's all it took to show a kid from a crappy neighborhood with no prospects that you weren't stuck in the life you were in. You could have a future.

When I went to the secret garden, I thought about these things. I thought about what I wanted to be. It was there that I dreamed my dreams of escape. I would carry the *Alvis* in my pocket and hold it in times of need like a talisman that could ward off evil, in the way Abraham Pierson envisioned Newark doing for its citizens. It would leave grooves in my hand I held it so tightly while I shook. What helped was to see myself through the windshield of the *Alvis* sitting in the driver's seat in that way only a little kid can. I would use it to escape. No matter what. No matter what it took I was going to get out. I wouldn't let anyone or anything stop me. Someday, I'd jump in the *Alvis*, drive away, become an historian, and never, ever come back.

Virgil

In the seventh grade, I became fixated on the planet Jupiter. I began reading everything I could on it and decided to go have a visit. I had a metal *John Glenn Globe* that

---

[26] The television was my best friend during this period. Along with American shows, I was fascinated by the material coming out of England. There was *UFO* and the short-lived *Strange Report* about a London detective who was also a scientist. I fell in love with Diana Rigg as Mrs. Peel in *The Avengers*, and Carol Cleveland of *Monty Python's Flying Circus*. Of course, there was *The Prisoner*. The 1960s and 70s were a Golden Age of weird, stylish British television. In addition, the PBS channel in the New York area, Channel 13, showed incredible children's content. Not just *Sesame Street* and the *Electric Company*, but *Zoom!* and a strange Canadian show, *The Friendly Giant*. I also loved watching *Mr. Roger's Neighborhood*. While watching Mr. Rogers I had a brief respite from uncontrollable shaking and anxiety attacks I had as a kid. Mr. Rogers was one of the only people in my life in those days who told me I was worthwhile as a person: the complete opposite of what the nuns told me. The last thing I will remember on my deathbed is the closing credits from *Zoom!* "Send it to Zoom, Zee-double oh-em, Box 3-5-oh, Boston, Mass, 0-2-1-3-4!"

had all the planets on the base, and all the tracks of Glenn's triple orbit mission around the Earth marked over the top of the continents. I used it to plan my mission because it also gave the distances to each planet from the sun. The Apollo moon missions were now everywhere in the news and in pop culture. It seemed like we as a society were on the verge of making space an abode for us all. That Christmas, Pop had gotten me one of the best presents of all time, a Major Matt Mason action figure. Major Matt Mason was an astronaut who wore an authentic NASA space suit. I was never really interested in fantasy stuff (the one exception was Hot Wheels Cars, because, well, come on). Even the *Thunderbirds*, which were a fantasy show set in the future, went through a lot of trouble to look realistic and to seem like it was everyday technology. Major Matt Mason was a rubber figure about six or seven inches tall with a wire armature which allowed you to pose him in different positions. He had cool accessories like a moon crawler and a moon base. GI Joe and all of his equipment were hyper realistic, but a bit pricey for our household. The major was more affordable. He had a helmet with an orange visor that flipped up. When I excitedly took him out of the plastic package blister on Christmas morning he looked at me, flipped up his visor and said, "Let's go kid!" and I went. I was so desperate to get out I built a spaceship. I made it out of an old metal file cabinet with wheels that Pops had found on one of his job sites . As I flew, the cosmos passed by and opened a universe of possibilities to me. My ship was modelled on the *Jupiter II* from 'Lost in Space'. It took me away from everything in my life in New Jersey. The life that I hated. I was as alone as I wanted to be. It made me feel as though I might be able. To accomplish something. To be something.

My first flight was just a shakedown to make sure everything worked: a couple of orbits around the earth just like NASA did with Apollo 8. The big trip was going to be to Jupiter. Like my rock hunting expeditions, I planned ahead of time. I had cheese & crackers and a bottle of *Yoo-Hoo*. I had my exploration gear and my Monkey Division helmet. My dog, Sherman came along too. We set down on the moon of Io so we could have a good view of the planet. I popped the hatch and just peered over the edge (I had seen the movie *Angry Red Planet* on Chiller Theater and saw that there were giant rat-bat creatures on Mars. I knew Jupiter was a gas planet so it was unlikely such creatures lurked there, but I wasn't taking any chances. I wondered why the colours didn't look like those I saw in books. Then I realized I had the yellow blast visor of the Monkey Division Helmet down and that was effecting the colours. I flipped it up and that fixed everything. I thought very seriously about staying a while, but then Sherman barked. We took off and headed back to earth. I'm not sure how long I was away. Nobody noticed I was gone. That was just fine by me. Anyway, there was something I had to do in church.

Catholics have a ceremony called 'Confirmation' that is sort of their version of a Bar Mitzvah. Depending which diocese you were in, the ceremony could be done anywhere between the ages of 10 and 18. I had mine at 13, the most common age. It's done for the reason of welcoming the child into the larger religious community as an adult. One of the things you had to do, along with memorizing various prayers and special ways to walk up to the altar, was to choose a Confirmation name. For girls it was Mary or Maria or some variation on that. For boys it was often Michael or John. The name had to be that of a saint. I chose Virgil. The nuns, who usually thought me defective in some way and who took delight in beating me, suddenly acted differently to me. They were impressed I had chosen the name of the highly regarded Roman poet. Even though there was no Saint Virgil, they let me do it. I put on my special Confirmation suit, was wrapped in the Rosary Beads and other accoutrements and kneeled along with Ray and Mikey and Frankie and Richie and Jimmie, and the others at the altar, our hands clasped in fervent prayer as our parents watched from the pews and snapped pictures. As the priest finally stood before me I was welcomed into the bosom of the Catholic Church as Brian Virgil Regal. With swirling organ music, we processed down the main aisle then out the front doors and into the sunshine of Kearny Avenue. The parties then ensued and after that we all went back to our regular routine. I think Sister Louise and the others would have reacted differently had they known that the Virgil I chose as my namesake was not the Roman Poet, but Virgil Tracey, the pilot of Thunderbird 2.

It was around this time that I discovered the public library on Kearny Avenue. Built with a Carnegie grant in 1913 the Kearny Public Library became as much an oasis to me as the secret garden had. I was very proud of myself when I applied for and received my first library card. At night, with the books I borrowed from the library, I analyzed Farragut's strategy at Mobile Bay, and began to learn to read French. Every chance I had, I found a retreat at the library. It had all that polished wood, tall windows, shelves and shelves of books, and that great smell of leather bindings. It was even better than the library at St. Cecilia's. I would collect a pile of texts in a quiet corner and sit on the floor and read and dream for hours. I read literature, art, science, engineering, religion, everything, even a book on how to become a Private Eye. Along with those other things the library increased in me the belief that I, too, could succeed and have a life worth living. I learned an important lesson sitting on the floor of the Kearny Public Library; though I walk through the valley of the shadow of death, I will fear no evil for I have books with me.

I didn't want to be totally isolated. I did make an effort to fit in and be like everyone else. Down the bottom of the hill, practically in the swamps of the Meadowlands was the Boys Club. It had been a bowling alley in the past, but was turned into a refuge for kids. They had bumper pool tables, ping-pong, and arts & crafts. In the summer if you were one of the first twenty kids in line in the morning, you were given a ticket for a free lunch. There were all sorts of kids there: black, white, Hispanic, and Asian. They also had 'Day Camp.' This program ran all summer long, but my parents could only afford one week. Day Camp was where you went to places during the day, but didn't sleep over. Each night you went home then returned to the club house the next morning. We piled into a rickety yellow school bus the Boys Club owned and headed off for some destination, usually a park or other sightseeing location. We went to Cheesequake State Park and ran through the woods. Then we went to *Jungle Habitat*. A popular destination before it was shut down because of the unsanitary and unhealthy conditions for the animals. It still holds a strange place in the lore of New Jersey; along with the safari park it had a sea-world style exhibition area. We went and watched the dolphin show. When it was over they said we could stand next to the glass wall of the big pool and watch the dolphins up close. They also said not to bang on the glass or put our hands in the water. In our group was Johnny Cartucci. He was one of those kids who immediately did whatever you told him not to. As soon as the Boys Club counsellor turned his back, Johnny stuck his hand in the water and started splashing it around laughing. A dolphin swam over, and thinking he was being fed, grabbed Johnny Cartucci's thumb and tried to bite it off. He started screaming and pulled his hand out of the water which was now turning red from his blood. Forever to be known as Oohchy Cartucci, he then proceeded to run around screaming at the top of his lungs as blood flew everywhere. We kids just stood there watching saying, "whoa, cooooolllll!" With the end of that summer, I had one last year to go at Saint Cecelia's.

Miraculously, I managed to make it through that year without too much turmoil and graduate from Saint Cecelia's Grammar School in 1974. It was never a sure thing that I would. Henry gave me a graduation congratulations card. Inside, only partly as a joke, he wrote

"Weeoohh, we never thought you'd make it!" I was in trouble a lot, and my grades of course were awful, and I acted up. I was often angry for reasons I never understood and couldn't articulate. My homework was spotty. They thought I was lazy and didn't want to do the work. The reality was I had trouble reading the textbooks. When I told the nuns they just screamed at me saying I was lying to get out of doing the work.

Kearny High

After escaping from the Catholic confinement of St. Cecilia's I went to the public, Kearny High School. It was just two blocks from the library. Built in 1920, Kearny High catered to the working class children of the area. My father, who had graduated from high school told me over and over again "be sure to sign up for college prep!" Though he had not gone to college he knew going meant a ticket to future success. I applied to college prep and began. Filled with positive anticipation of finally getting to become the scholar I dreamed of, my academic work turned out about the same in high school as it was in grammar school. I took my social position as one of the weird stupid kids no one knew or was really interested in knowing. Invisible.

I initially tried to ingratiate myself into the circle of some smart kids. Georgie and Howie and the others at first allowed me in. Then I realized it had just been so they could make fun of me. I had foolishly told them I wanted to be a writer and an historian. The snickering became louder and I stopped hanging out with them. I did find a small coterie of friends: Mike Uhlick, whom I had gone to St. Cecelia's with, and Al Malet and Kenny Williams (who eventually became an FBI agent). Jim Poncek was another. Al had brothers who were all motor heads. They eventually opened their own body shop. Al had a magnificent 1969 Chevy Chevelle convertible that he rebuilt with a juiced up 385 v-8 big block. I painted a Frank Frazetta-like scene on the trunk. This was my little circle. It would be with these guys that I went cruising on the avenue, haunting the Jersey shore and the Meadowlands, and listening to music.

I didn't take much part in the usual high school hijinks. That was because, other than the few friends, listed above, I was never part of the scene; any scene. My high school years would not be a model for *Sixteen Candles* or *Pretty in Pink*, *The Breakfast Club* or *Fast Times at Ridgemont High*. I was never ousted for not being cool enough because I was never allowed in to begin with. I was involved in no romantic dramas or power plays. I didn't like any of those people or cliques so why would I try to be part of them? I learned my lesson the first time. As far as I knew, none of them dreamed of escaping to the outside world the way I did. None of them would appreciate Harlan Ellison. None of them had the kinds of plans I did. I did enjoy being in the student science club, but even there I was closed mouth about my plans. I was just marking time until I could do the big "see you suckers later!" Even then I didn't actually do that. I just quietly walked away. It wasn't like I didn't want anyone to know, it was just that none of these people mattered to me or figured in my designs.[27]

You had to take a language in your freshman year. All the other kids I knew from St. Cecilia's took Spanish because it was the easiest. I wanted to do something more challenging so I took Russian. I quickly found myself way in over my head and flunked out by the end of the first semester. I desperately begged the administration to take me out of college prep and put me in general education (what was sometimes called 'gas pump jockey track'). Again, the

[27] I received an invitation to take part in my graduating class's tenth anniversary in 1988. I thought about it for a minute, then didn't bother to reply. I never received another.

greatest pain was that I had let Henry down. He didn't yell at me over it, but the disappointment in his eyes was obvious. Not even the *Thunderbirds* or *Jonny Quest* could get me out of my depression. It only got worse.

I muddled along as best I could. I took 'small engines' which was a class where you learned to strip down and rebuild gasoline engines. It was one of the few classes I genuinely enjoyed. My sophomore year I took my first dedicated history class, which I enjoyed quite a bit. This was what I wanted. You had to do a classroom presentation. I launched myself into it planning to do a presentation so great everyone would be impressed. I recreated the battle of Hampton Rhodes with models of the Monitor and Merrimack I built. I even practised my presentation. On the day I gave it in class, I could see some of the cool girls in the back of the room giggling and making fun of me because I was a nerd playing with toys.

In my third junior year at Kearny High, it was time for us to go see the guidance counsellor for advice on what to do after graduation. For the kids who had good grades, and were headed somewhere this was when you began to apply to university and line up your letters of reference from faculty members and local politicians. I never realized you had to start lining up schools and reference letters from faculty and local politicians. This had all gone right past me while I was flying to Jupiter. I still, however, harboured dreams of academia. I went into the guidance councillor's office at the prescribed time and sat down. I had met with her a few times since school began.

In an obviously disinterested rote fashion, she asked me what my plans for the future were. I took a deep breath and explained, as seriously as I could, what I wanted to do with my life. She sat quietly smiling as I talked. I later realized, this was the dream I should have kept to myself, but I got excited and told it. I told her how I wanted to go to college to be an historian and that I wanted to chase monsters. I told her, though it was difficult and made my head hurt, how I had read so many books on my own. I told her how I wanted to be a writer, how I collected books and had started to write little stories of my own, and how much time I spent in the library reading Roger Zelazny and Harlan Ellison and H. P. Lovecraft, and tons of history.[28] I told her how I wanted to explore the world and make something of my life. I had never said any of this so eloquently or completely before, not even to my parents. When I had gotten it all out I sat back, a little winded, smiling like Ralphie when he turns in his Christmas theme. This was the most personal and protected aspect of my life and now it was out. She studied my transcripts for a moment and then looked up at me. Still smiling she said, "Kids like you don't go to college." I didn't know how to react to that. She smiled and said nothing else. It was like encountering a door with no handle on it. I stood up, turned and walked out into the hall and back to my class a little dazed. As always, because the nuns had beaten it into me that once a person in authority told you something you said, "okay" and left. You didn't question, you didn't ask why, you just took it and left. I never felt safe telling anyone my aspirations again until I met Lisa.

Later that night I told Henry about my encounter with the guidance counsellor. This time he became upset. He had been drinking because of having a bad day, now he had come home to find out his strange, stupid son would not be going to college as he had hoped: one more of his dreams dashed. One more way I had disappointed him.[29] He started to pepper me

---

[28] When I was 16yo I read Harlan Ellison's "Adrift Just off the Islets of Langerhans." After I read the main character's need to find "The coordinates for the location of my soul" I was never the same.
[29] As a kid my father never told me he was disappointed in me. He never ridiculed me. I just got a sense from him. Years later as an adult he told me he was proud of me. I realized he had as much trouble articulating to me as I had articulating to him.

with questions: his voice getting louder. Why didn't I say anything to the guidance counselor? Why hadn't I questioned her? What was going to happen now? Will I ever get into college?" I had no answers for any of this. Just a shattering realization of my titanic failure. I kept saying, "I don't know, I don't know!" Finally, I went to my room. I climbed under my bed and rolled up into a ball. I hated that guidance counselor, I especially hated myself. The pressure inside my head was overwhelming. If I had had a gun, I would have shot myself right there and then without the slightest hesitation.

In the lunch hall the next day I was still depressed. Not even the meatloaf and mashed potatoes helped. Then it came to me. A way out of all this. To hell with college, I'd join the army. Jim Ponczek was going down to see a recruiter about enlisting in the Rangers. I went with him. The recruiter showed us a Ranger promotional film then he asked me what I was interested in? I said my dad was a tank driver, and that I built model tanks. "Ah!" he said, "then check this out!" He had an early portable video tape player that sat on his desk. He put another tape in the machine and pushed play. The film was about the 11th Armoured Cavalry Regiment's antics in Vietnam. I was hooked. I could have a paying job, not have to worry about my grades or college, and since Pops had been a tank driver I could be like him and he'd be happy. Ponczek never did join up--he later became an actor--but I did. I enlisted in the United States Army.

It wasn't long after that when another depressing event occurred. It's weird the way sometimes things happen to us where everyone knows, and then there are incidents only we know of, only we have to live with. I was pathologically shy in high school. The thought of actually getting physically close to someone made me shake. I wasn't a germaphobe or anything like that. I didn't dislike girls, quite the opposite. I just feared intimacy would lead to pain. I could simply not talk to girls, at least talk to them with an eye towards asking them out. I wanted to ask them out. When I tried, it always came out terribly. I would shake and stutter. This pegged me as a weirdo. I wanted to be a smooth operator, I wanted to be James Bond. I wanted to exude confidence the way they taught me boys were supposed to. There were a number of girls I had crushes on, but I could never approach them and tell them (a couple of teachers as well!).

Then one day I saw this girl in the cafeteria. She stopped me in my tracks. She had jet black hair cut in a page boy style. She wore black clothes and cat glasses. As a kind of proto-goth, she appealed to me greatly. She also read books. I thought, do such magical creatures exist? Girls who read books? All the girls I had encountered up to this point were giggle girls or frosty cheerleaders. She looked like Natalie Merchant or Janeane Garofalo later would. I thought, well, this girl would understand. She wasn't a cool kid; she didn't hang out with the cheerleaders. In fact, she was shunned by the cool kids. She read books, she would understand, she would see me as a kindred spirit.

So, seeing this girl I had to force myself to overcome my blinding hesitation. After thinking about it for a few days I finally mustered up the courage to go and talk to her. It was fish stick day at the cafeteria. I went over. She was sitting there reading something. I haltingly said, "hi, mmmmy nnnname is Brian Rrreeegal, would you like to go to a movie sssome time?" I said that because I didn't know what else to say and that sounded like it might be okay. I gave her the best smile I could muster. I thought to myself, "well, you did it. It didn't come out too bad. I only stuttered a little." She looked up at me. I thought this was it; this was where it would all come together. She would see how we were similar, and how we felt the same way about so many things. Her face suddenly changed. The bright smile changed to a frown and she said, "What? No, leave me alone."

I stood and stared for a moment; a skinny, stick insect with longish, unkempt hair and a dumb, pimple-covered face, wearing my Apollo/Soyuz t-shirt with the hole under the one arm from when it got caught on a barb as I climbed over a barbed wire fence.

"Uh, Okay," I said weakly and I turned and walked away. I went out into the hallway and walked down to the corner then around. The sounds of the cafeteria--clinking china and glasses with that metallic sound of cutlery in plastic trays--fading behind me. A hallway lined with metal lockers. I walked a few paces then satisfied that no one was around, turned and rammed my head into a locker door as hard as I could. The sound reverberated, but no one heard. I hit the door with such force I left a dent in it. Then I did it again. After the second hit I paused, rubbed my now aching forehead, and waited for the lights to stop flashing. Then I went off to gym class. I know that sounds a bit extreme, but you have to do this sometimes in order to get the goblins out.

I never took my frustrations out on others, I always took them out on myself. If doctors did a brain scan today they'd probably find all sorts of scar tissue up there. I've bashed my head into doors, and walls, and other inanimate objects most of my life (I once hit myself in the head with a hammer) in frustration and self-loathing. I always did it privately. If anyone had noticed while I was in school, they would have had my parents make me wear one of those helmets. All I could do was resign myself to what I was and try to make myself feel better by thinking that at least at the end of the school year, I'd head off to the army and would leave all these people behind.

Another year and then you'll be happy. Just one more year and you'll be happy...[30]

The KSA

One of the few bright points of my high school career was membership of a student club called the Kearny Space Administration (KSA). The 1970s was the height of the Space Age. The club was started by one of the school's science teachers, John O'Hara. Mr. O'Hara was one of the very few faculty members that did not make me feel like an idiot. He had connections at NASA and knew astronauts. He had been at the launch of Apollo 11 and Skylab. The KSA was great for me because all the kids who were members were nerds and geeks. We all loved science and history and *Star Trek* and board games. In 1975 the KSA sponsored a trip to the Kennedy Space Center in Florida to witness the launch of the Apollo-Soyuz Mission. Apollo-Soyuz was a joint mission with Soviet Russia. It was an attempt at interstellar détente. The Russian Cosmonauts learned to speak English while the Americans learned to speak Russian. With NATO and Warsaw Pact armies nose to nose around the world ready to start World War III, everyone thought this space mission was a positive step in East/West relations. It was amazing to be standing there on that day in the Everglades watching this huge Saturn 1B rocket take off. The launch pad was over a mile away yet you could still feel the heat of the engines and feel the vibration in the ground. After the launch we toured the cape and went to the control center and inside the VAB (Vehicle Assembly Building). Then we went to Disney World. The new Space Mountain ride had just opened up. We all hotly anticipated what we thought would be a brand new approach to amusement rides. We were all disappointed that the reality was that Space Mountain was just a roller coaster inside a building in the dark. One ride was enough. The Pirates of the Caribbean boat ride, however,

---

[30] Jerry Rafferty, "Baker Street," *City to City*, 1978.

was a different story. I rode that twelve times that day.

John O'Hara had somehow sweet-talked the town of Kearny into giving him a narrow strip of land on the town's large sports complex down in the meadowlands known as Gunnell Oval. There he would build a public science building. He was able to line up donations from several sources and we students did the construction work. It was a grand, beautiful, crazy idea. I had enormous fun carrying cinder blocks and mixing concrete. Pops gave me one of his old construction helmets to wear. The center would have a space simulator, classrooms, lecture hall, and an astronomical observatory on the roof. By the time I went off to the army the wide public interest in space had waned, unfortunately, and donors became harder to find. By the time I returned I went down to see what had become of the KSA. O'Hara had run out of money with only the shell of the building complete. The city then confiscated it. Instead of a public science center it became a garage for city trucks and snow plows. John O'Hara folded the KSA and became Kearny High's athletic sports medicine consultant eventually retiring from teaching in the early twenty-first century. A number of the KSA students did go on to science and other academic careers. We all owe a debt of gratitude to Mr. O'Hara.[31]

Conclusion

I'm not sure exactly when I decided I wanted to be an historian, but it was likely while I sat on the rug in the living room watching *Jonny Quest* in 1966 or so. *Jonny Quest* originally broadcast on Friday nights. He got to travel the world and have cool adventures. All of these inspirational shows—even Mr. Rogers—were about travel, about seeing the world, going places. That's what I wanted. Along with *Jonny Quest* there was *The Thunderbirds*, a British series about a family of astronauts and engineers who flew cool airplanes and spaceships, and who rescued people from disasters around the world. The characters were realistic looking puppets, and the machinery, while futuristic all had a feeling of realism to them. The whole thing had a wonderfully odd charm to it. Made by Gerry Anderson, who also made the precursor to the *Thunderbirds*, *Fireball XL5*, and others, wanted the series to inspire kids to want to be involved in science, technology, and history. The final show of the trio which inspired me was *Herge's Adventures of Tin Tin*. This was a straight forward animated series based upon the wildly popular comic book series by Belgian artist Georges Remi. Tin Tin was a young journalist who along with his friends Captain Haddock, the detectives the Thompson Twins, Professor Calculus, and his trusty dog Snowy travelled the world fighting evil and having adventures. All three of these shows had an enormous influence on me. I lived in a world of horrible people, of monsters, and no possibilities. These shows told me there were possibilities.

In 1971, a new British series debuted on American TV, *UFO*. This was made by the same people who made *The Thunderbirds*. It concerned a secret organization called SHADO (Supreme Headquarters Alien Defense Force) that was based out of a movie studio in the English countryside. SHADO fought the invasion of aliens. The show as incredibly stylish in a very 70s British sort of way. It was based in the far off 1980s. While I loved the space ships

---

[31] The next year after Apollo/Soyuz Mr. O'Hara was contacted by one of the people he knew at the Redstone Arsenal in Huntsville, Alabama. They were throwing away some old space hardware and did he want it for the Kearny Space Center? He piled me and another kid into his station wagon and we drove to Alabama. We wound up at a garage that when we walked in the large floor was covered with space gear. We picked up everything we could cram into the station wagon, including an almost complete Gemini era space suit. I worked on refurbishing that suit for months and was able to wear it to presentations. It looked exactly like Major Matt Mason. So, yes, I've worn a space suit. An actual space suit.

and the stories—which were rather cutting edge and dark for the time involving questions of race and gender and discrimination and ethnic hatred—the thing which most caught my eye was Lieutenant Gabrielle Ellis.

SHADO operated a base on the moon as a forward defense. They had a squadron of 'Interceptors' which tangle with the flying saucers of the alien invaders. The Interceptors would scramble after they were alerted by an orbiting sentient computer early warning satellite called SID (Space Intruder Detector). SID would then warn the moon base. I thought it was very cool that SID spoke with what to me was a posh British accent. The Interceptors would then be vectored to their target by the command center on the moon base. The Moon Base commander was Lt. Ellis. All the moon base controllers were women and they all wore the same silvery jump suits and all wore purple page-boy wigs. Not once in the entire two year run of the series, however, was it ever explained why the moon base controllers wore the purple wigs. As a kid I didn't care, they just looked incredibly hot. That has always been my type: smart girls, glasses, bangs. That's why I fell in love with Velma Dinkely from *Scooby-Doo*, and why I fell in love with Lisa when we met. Though, that was still a way off.

Chapter 2

Sturmpanzer 43

"I've always been a selfish being…"

– Mr. Darcy

Machinery and military history fascinated me as a little kid. I was too young to understand war and its consequences, of course, but the hardware was interesting. By the mid -1960s, World War II had only ended some twenty years before, a ceasefire had been signed over Korea, and the Cold War had begun in earnest. The Russians launched Sputnik and put up the Iron Curtain. Many people still had direct memories of war or had personally taken part in it. I had uncles who fought in the war, and friends who had dads and uncles who had been in WWII or Korea. American involvement in Vietnam was also growing. Reference to military subjects and the glorification of war was considered appropriate. After all, now that the Nazis and the Fascists and Japanese Militarists were gone we still had to deal with the Commies. It was unremarkable that kids of my generation were exposed to all sorts of reminders of war and the military. We ran in the streets 'playing army' all the time. We watched television shows like *Combat!* and *Rat Patrol*. We didn't see it as unusual. My father, despite his harrowing service in the Korean War regularly bought me war toys, including the *Monkey Division Army Helmet* as well as a large motorized version of the M26 Pershing tank he served on. In this landscape, the notion of adventuring not only attracted me, but encouraged me. I embraced the notion completely. Simultaneously, there was the notion that with World War II over the world might unite into a greater whole to fight evil. This was reflected in such television programs as *The Man from UNCLE*, and *Star Trek*, and the James Bond movies. The world I saw on television and in pop culture was one looking outward and forward to wide vistas. People respected the notion of a United Nations. Despite all the death and destruction there was a sense that the future would bring better days. To this stew I added my own ingredients of science and history. I would not just go off adventuring with a helmet and boots chasing monsters, I'd be carrying books and a microscope, and I'd draw pictures of it.

On Kearny Avenue there was the *Ben Franklin's*. One of the earliest franchise systems in America, *Ben Franklin Stores* first opened in the late 1920s though the original parent company went back to the 1870s. Each store was owned and operated by individual proprietors. They eventually gave rise to both *Walmart* and *Michaels*. *Ben Franklin's* was a store where you could buy just about anything one would need for the home short of food and furniture. It smelled of clean and dry and possibilities. I could stand in the office supply isle staring at the pens, pencils, notebooks and filing card systems imagining how I was going to build and organize my private library and keep track of monsters. My mother always bought window shades there. They had that machine that cut the shades to the length you needed as you waited. If I was in the store and heard an employee turn the window shade machine on I would go and watch. We purchased all our school supplies there. A few doors up there was a smaller place called *John's Bargain Store* where everything was really cheap, because, well, it was really cheap. For cash-strapped working-class families it was necessary to shop there.

In addition to the park, my first field of adventuring was Kearny Avenue. The Ave was where everything went on. It was the central shopping zone—wall to wall stores from Newark all the way to Rutherford. It's where you ran with your pack, your troops. I would have run with a pack if any pack had wanted me to run with them. As with most things in my life my forays up the Ave tended to be solitary excursions which I was perfectly happy with. Along with *Ben Franklin's* there were shoe stores, banks, bars, bakeries, pizzerias (.25 cents a slice), and an ethnic deli that had that great deli smell of meat.

In the middle of the *Ben Franklin's* was a wide set of stairs leading down. It had those shiny, aluminum handrails that were thought to be very modern and stylish, at the time. As you reached the bottom of the stairs off to the right was the toy department. One summer day in 1971 I was there to get some army men. Everyone had those same army men. I don't know who did the original carvings, but I hope they received residuals (probably not though). That same platoon of guys was everywhere. There was the kneeling rifleman, the standing rifleman, the bazooka man, mortar man, and the crawling guy. It always struck me as odd that these figures were modeled on Vietnam era American troops with all the equipment and weapons of that period. Except for the machine gunner. The machine gunner was firing a British made Bren gun (it should have been an M60 machine gun). They came in plastic bags that held about thirty figures, and were neatly piled up on the lower shelf of the toy isle. Next to them loose were several matching vehicles: a wheeled cargo truck, a jeep with a machine gun mounted at the back seat, and an M48 tank.

It was my 11th birthday I wanted a new M48—the gun barrels often became bent so I wanted to pick out one with the straight barrel. I happened to look to the left and there was the isle for plastic model kits. With a few exceptions, I had not really been that interested in plastic, scale models as they were really only cars, airplanes, and ships.[1] This was different. There on the shelf was the plastic kit version of the M48 Patton tank I was holding in my hand as a toy. It was the Monogram 1/35 scale model. I also saw they had several more US military vehicle kits. Monogram's 'Armor Series' had originally come out a decade before, but had just been reissued in new boxes and graphics. What put this all over the top was that each kit came with a special additional set of instructions for building dioramas. I pulled my pockets inside out to get every penny I had to buy this. I didn't have enough. I put the toy tank back on the lower shelf then bounded up the stairs, through the aisles, past the window curtain cutter, to the back door of the *Ben Franklin's*. I hopped on my bike and was racing home through the heat.

I had two single dollar bills hidden in my room for emergencies. This was an emergency. I retrieved the singles, with my dog Sherman barking at what I was doing, and in a flash was racing back to the *Ben Franklin's*. Upon returning, I realized I still didn't have enough for the M48, but I did have enough for the jeep with the 37mm anti-tank gun. I could also get a tube of the *Testor's* plastic glue needed to assemble it.

The 1960s and 70s were the Golden Age of military model building. The way kids talk about and obsess over video games in the 21st century, plastic model building held kids, especially boy's, imaginations. I first started building military vehicles because there was a small general store on the Ave near St. Cecelia's owned by a man named Mr. Finger. He sold

---

[1] Part of this was because I had trouble reading the instructions. With the words swirling around I would try to follow the drawings on how the parts went together. As a result it took me a while before I came to appreciate plastic model building. This also ruined me for following printed instructions from then on. All my life I have encountered the lament, "why don't you just follow the instructions?" It's not that I didn't want to, I was just too embarrassed to answer that with, "Because I have trouble reading them."

everything, and he had a small section with toys and plastic models. The Aurora company released a line of 1/48 scale tank models that were of acceptable details and complexity for a kid. They also had a strange, but enticing, line of models taken from the pages of the magazine *Famous Monsters of Filmland*. The line included such staples as *Frankenstein*, *The Wolfman*, *Dr. Jekyll and Mister Hyde*, and the unique *Forgotten Prisoner of Castle Mare* (that no one seemed to know anything about as it was not from a movie). Once when I was sick my mother bought a tank model there for me to build as I lay in bed recuperating. Along with Aurora (who also made HO scale slot cars) there was Lindberg, and Revell. The quality of the kits varied though of these American manufacturers Monogram was probably the best. One of the things I always loved about the plastic kits was the artwork on the covers. While later kits had photographs of the completed model, the ones from this period had lavishly created artwork showing the vehicle in some kind of action. I could stare at them, imagining myself in the picture, for hours.

It wasn't very long after discovering the Monogram models at *Ben Franklin's* that me and my friends discovered Tamiya. This Japanese company produced the very best plastic models (Airfix, a British company, also made quality kits, but they were harder to find in New Jersey). The Tamiya kits were more expensive than the Monogram or Aurora kits—and you couldn't buy them at the *Ben Franklin's* or Mr. Finger's—but they were a league ahead in detail. The Monogram models were good, but the Tamiya models were the best. They had the best cover art as well. I noticed that many were in the same style. I later learned that they were done by an amazing Japanese artist named Yoshiyuki Takani. With the flair of a genius, Takani could suggest hyper realistic machinery with just a few sinuous brush strokes.

The advantage the Monogram kits had was the guide sheets for building dioramas. I had discovered Sheperd Paine. Starting off as a sculptor of scale military figures Sheperd Paine (1946-2015) had already established a reputation in that world. When Monogram Models decided to re-release its small range of military vehicle kits in 1970, they came up with a novel idea. Military vehicles had not yet gained popularity amongst builders. To add an extra attraction to the military vehicles—the M48 was then the only tank in the line—the company decided to include 'Tip Sheets' with instructions on how to create realistic dioramas for the vehicles. They asked Sheperd Paine to do them. He took to the assignment with gusto and created a series of dioramas that still inspire model builders. [2]

Going back to Ben Franklin's a few weeks later, I saw more Monogram kits. They were different because they were in 1/32 scale whereas the original kits were in the slightly smaller 1/35 scale. These kits were all exclusively tanks and armoured fighting vehicles. The one that caught my eye was the German, Sturmpanzer 43. This vehicle was not really a tank in its purest form. It was an assault gun. It was the basic Panzer 4 chassis with the turret replaced by a large thick, boxy superstructure mounting a short-barreled demolition gun. It was designed to trundle up to pillboxes and fortresses and blast them to rubble. The box art called it a 'Brumbar' that they translated as Grizzly Bear. The reality was that the Germans did not call it a Brumbar: that was an Allied forces designation. It also did not exactly mean Grizzly Bear, but grouch, as in grouchy old man.

Summer Afternoons in 1974

Not long after this my friend Mark told me about a hobby shop up the Ave all the

---

[2] Jim DeRogatis. *Sheperd Paine: the Life and Work of a Master Modeler and Military Historian* (Schiffer, 2008).

way in North Arlington right across from the cemetery. They were more HO and N Gauge model trains, but they carried the Monogram Armor Series. They also started to have model building contests every year. I entered the first one with a diorama of a Sherman tank—the Monogram Sherman with the hedgerow cutter—splashing through the mud to attack a German pillbox. Incredibly, I won first prize. The next year I entered with the Monogram halftrack (not in a diorama) covered in equipment and men in the back. I won again. Mark's uncle came to watch and began yelling "Fix!" because I won twice in a row. While that particular hobby shop was not great for plastic models, I enjoyed going there.[3] Sometimes Henry would drive me, but mostly I went alone.[4]

It became an excuse for me to travel. In the summer I would save my allowance and take back some bottles to the candy store for the deposits (Henry might slip me a couple of bucks). Getting up early on the Fourth of July, I strapped on my backpack, and got on my vehicle that to me was of course, the *Alvis Stalwart*, but to everyone else's eyes looked suspiciously like a heavily repaired bicycle. When ready, I rode down along the Saint Cecelia's schoolyard fence. As I did I remembered the awful things that went on in there (I always felt like I had been sent to that place as punishment for something I had done, but couldn't remember what it was). I continued on down to the intersection where the hulking structure of Saint Cecelia's church stood guard on Kearny Avenue. There was the occasional Cicada rattling in the distance. It was very hot, but I liked it.

I paused on the corner. Deep breath. Facing right I pushed down on the gas pedal and headed north up Kearny Avenue. I sped along, dodging the people and cars in the summer heat. In my mind's eye I saw a map of the world. I passed pyramids, ancient fortresses, and futuristic skyscrapers. I passed the *Ben Franklin's, John's Bargain Store*, then the Kearny Public Library. Just before the Town Hall I passed Liberty Street that was originally Berlin Street. In a fit of patriotic fervor in 1917 the city fathers decided to give it a more pro-American name. Upon reaching the Town Hall I'd stop and wheel into the little park next to it. They had a shell carried by the *USS Olympia* at the Battle of Manila Bay in 1898 during the Spanish-American War. They had it displayed on a marble plinth made to look like a ship's capstan with flowers around it.[5] Painted with a thousand layers of silver paint I could still make out the grooving on the back of the round where it would fit into the gun breach. For a moment I'd imagine myself on the bridge of the *Olympia* standing next to Commodore Dewey as he famously shouted, "You may fire when ready Gridley!" After paying my respects, I'd head off again.

Another couple of blocks was a smaller public park that was little more than a triangle shaped green lawn with a pair of German artillery pieces captured and brought back by local Doughboys from the First World War. I'd pass the Lincoln Theater where I took my few accordion lessons. Past the Bellville Turnpike that climbed the hill from the Passaic River, crossed Kearny Avenue, then descended the other side of the hill out into the Meadowlands like a giant X marks the spot. From this point on Kearny Avenue was Ridge Road. Years later I discovered just a block down on the Meadowlands side was *Pizza Land*.

---

[3] It went out of business a few years after this, replaced by a beauty salon.
[4] The really best local hobby shop was in East Rutherford. *Paul's Hobby and Marine* was a mecca for model railroad enthusiasts as it carried a wide range of the top of the line materials: engines, cars, track accessories.
[5] I have no idea how this particular artifact wound up here.

The place that made what I still consider the most delicious pizza I've ever eaten.[6] From the house to the hobby shop in North Arlington was about four miles. About half a mile or so beyond the North Arlington Public Library—where I found they had a rather good collection of books on model building—there was a *Dairy Queen Brazier Burger*. As I passed I could smell the char broil. I knew I would be back here in a while. I'd continue up to the cemetery then cross the street, dodging cars, to the store entrance. I never just dropped my bike on the ground the way everyone else did. I'd carefully 'park' it. I'd reverse the *Alvis* up so the back wheel just touched the building, and use the kick stand. That way if I had to make a quick escape I could just jump on it and speed off.

I'd then go in and peruse the shelves. Once I was finished staring at what was on the shelves--looking, scheming, and planning--I would begin the journey back. I'd stop at the *Brazier Burger* for lunch. I felt so much like an adult. I didn't like being a kid, and unlike Holden Caulfield did not want to remain one. Innocence is about not knowing anything. I wanted to know things. Well, I wanted to know most things. As long as it wasn't too close to me or painful.

At the *Brazier Burger*, I'd order a burger and fries with a soda. The taste of the greasy charbroiled meat and the crinkle cut fries was like heaven. I had learned the enjoyable taste of certain foods could help push away my bad grades, hateful neighborhood kids, and my parent's fighting when they were drunk. The interior of the restaurant looked like a mountain cabin. There were lots of exposed wooden beams and stone work. You could see the brazier from the sitting area. Flames would occasional leap from the grill, the air sizzling. It was all very close and cozy. Sitting there by myself, not feeling lonely at all, I'd inspect my purchases: Once a *Panzer IV*, maybe a *Wirblewind*, or a *Sherman Calliope*. Most of the time I hadn't purchased anything. I felt like a great explorer. I could sit there and think; think about big things like what I wanted to do with my life, and if Carol Cleveland from *Monty Python's Flying Circus* was married. These trips were less about buying things than as a journey into personal freedom. I was on my own and in charge of my own life. I felt like I was moving forward. It felt good. The more I pedaled the more room I put between myself and all that stuff I wanted to leave behind. I never went back by the Ave. I always turned off and headed home by the side streets. To travel back along the avenue, the way I came, felt too much like going backwards. I hated that feeling. In many ways, my life as an adult has been one long effort to regain that sense of freedom I experienced riding my bike alone to the hobby shop.[7]

Betty

Eventually, I had collected all the Monogram Models' tip sheets. All the black and white ones and all the full color ones. I saved the instruction sheets from every plastic model I ever built. I could spend hours going over them, memorizing every detail. As she did with much of my things when I went off to the army, my mother threw them all out. When I asked her why, she said, "Oh, you didn't want those anymore." She had no idea what I went through to collect them, what they meant to me, what they represented.

---

[6] It was run by a gruff guy named Fred, who looked like an Italian Mr. Clean. Even though it was officially *Pizza Land*, we always called it Fred's. It was later immortalized by appearing briefly in the opening credits of the series, *The Sopranos*. I've had pizza all over the world and no one ever made it as deliciously as Fred. Once, Lisa and I went in and I ordered an Italian hotdog "with just potatoes." An 'Italian hotdog,' sometime called a Newark Style, is a hot dog with peppers, onions, and potatoes. All I wanted on my dogs were potatoes. When we got home I discovered he had taken my order a bit too literally. It was just a bun with potatoes on it.

[7] To this day, I will say I need to get something from this store or that, or ask Lisa if she wants to go to an antiquing village. It's really just an excuse for me to take a ride. To spend some time thinking. To be away from everything.

O Superman
Oh mom and dad
Hello? This is your mother
Are you there?
Are you coming home? [8]

My mother Elizabeth was born into a large family of boys on a farm in Upstate New York. She was made to be the workhorse. She was expected to take care of her horrid parents as well as her equally horrid brothers. She had aspirations of being a fashion designer and going to art school, but her family said a girl's place was taking care of the family. As a result, not only did she not get to go to art school, she didn't graduate from high school either.

With few exceptions, I never liked any of my Mother's family, the Costigans. Her brother Danny loved to tell off color jokes, especially in front of kids. His wife Marion became mentally disturbed, but deep down was a decent soul (the most decent of all of them in fact). As my Godmother Marion always went out of her way to be nice to me. She was the only adult to ever sit with me and watch an entire episode of the Thunderbirds. Even after Danny dumped her for a trophy wife, she still would send me birthday cards into my late twenties. Then dementia took her, and she forgot who I was. My uncle, Eddie Costigan, had five sons each a year apart with his wife Stella. When they came over for a holiday or some other family event they made a terrible row, running and screaming. My dog Sherman would hide under my bed to avoid the torture. My father called them all 'The Wallbangers.' Eddie loved to torment his own kids and us as well. He liked to eat raw hamburgers in front of us in order to creep us out. Once he called the house to speak with my mother and I picked up the phone. Seeing a chance, he told me he was calling from a contest agency and that I had won a brand new bike. I wanted a fancy new ten-speed bike, but Henry couldn't afford one. I became very excited that I had won a bike. Then I heard hilarious, cackling laughter from the other side of the phone. Eddie said "surprise!" it was all a joke and I was a little idiot for believing him. I was so angry and humiliated. I never liked Eddie to begin with, now I genuinely hated him. He thought it was all terribly funny.

When Elizabeth married Henry they moved into the tenement her family owned. I think my parents genuinely loved each other. Henry rearranged his entire life and changed his plans to make her happy. When he injured his foot in his late sixties and the doctors said they should amputate it, she carefully, laboriously, and faithfully treated his wounds herself and saved his foot. They came from that generation were even married couples rarely showed affection for each other in public. She alternately worked outside—once in the Entenmanns factory around the corner in Newark which I loved because we would go down to meet her to walk her home and the place smelled so good—and was a stay-at-home mom. Despite her Irish ancestry she often thought of herself as Italian, and while a devout Catholic could behave like a stereotypical Jewish mother. She was the one who introduced me to Manhattan. The two of us would get dressed up and take the bus in. We went to several of the Flower Shows, to Broadway plays, and to the American Museum of Natural History where I met the fourth floor Tyrannosaur. Once we went to FAO Schwartz, the famous toy store, just before Christmas, but we couldn't buy anything because it was too expensive.

My mother was an incredible cook. She would invent food for us. My dad liked tuna

---

[8] Laurie Anderson. "O Superman," *Big Science*, 1982.

fish so she engineered her own style of *hors d'oeuvre*. She put fresh tuna on sliced cucumber sections with herbs and spices and a little onion that she lovingly assembled by hand. She called them 'Tuna Guys' and made them special for him. For me she invented 'Hot Dog Casserole' that was *au gratin* potatoes with hot dog pieces mixed in. I would get that on Friday or Saturday nights if I had been a good boy all week. It was all made from inexpensive, poor people ingredients. I loved it like it was the ambrosia of the gods.

For all her positive qualities, Betty had her foibles and idiosyncrasies. There are few photos of her looking into the camera. She had this fear of looking at the person taking her picture, or even looking into anyone's eyes. She would choose odd moments to tell you little bits of strange information, like that she had a twin brother named Michael who died in childbirth, or that we had Native American blood in us (the second I found out was that her uncle had once had an affair with a Native woman in upstate New York. Betty didn't really understand genetics and heredity). In order to get me to not eat chocolate as a child she told me I was allergic to it and if I did eat any I'd die. She could be distant and cold one minute then incredibly helpful the next. She never learned to drive a car, and she constantly would give our things away. Whenever she did give our stuff away she would say, "You didn't want that!" She never asked she just did it. When I returned from the army I discovered she had given or thrown away all my most precious possessions, including the *Alvis Stalwart*.

When she was in her final years her behavior became stranger. The way I dealt with it was to say, "but she's always been this way." When she was in the last month or so of her life we had to hospitalize her, the attending physician took me and Lisa aside and said, "your mother is demented." It really wasn't any different from when I was a kid. Only then did it dawn on me that she likely was disturbed all her life. As kids you simply accept your parent's whacky behavior as normal. She could be quick to cut you down or dismiss you, yet at the same time to her dying day encouraged my attempts to better myself.

In the end, despite her support of me, my mother and I were never close. I always envied those people who had close relations with their parents. We were never a touchy-feely kind of family. I never ran to my mom when I was upset the way other kids could. Whenever I was scared or lonely and needed a hug or someone to tell me everything was going to be alright there was no one. I hid in my room or in the secret alley or the park, and shivered by myself until it went away. I might try to play with a favorite toy to distract myself from what was going on round me: my parents fighting, my awful relatives and neighborhood people, my terrible grades at school, my inability to understand what was going on around me. I'd take a trip in my mind to Jupiter or China or London, or lose myself in books or in building a model kit. That way I'd have a few moments where the torment stopped. I'd squeeze my eyes as tight as I could hoping that when I opened them the monsters would be gone and everything would be better. It usually wasn't. I learned that life was one long torment, with a few enjoyable moments here and there. I never doubted that my parents loved me, they just had a hard time showing it: we all did. They tried to make up for it by supporting our various endeavors and giving us what little money they had whenever we needed it. None of us ever forced the issue. As far as I can remember, my mother never once asked me "is everything alright?"

By the year 2000 Henry's health had begun to deteriorate. His back had been oddly itchy for over a year. No creams or salves helped. Doctors told him it was nothing. Eventually it was discovered that he had kidney disease (that's what was causing the itching). He had smoked and drank heavily all his life. Spending most of his life out in all kinds of weather as a crane operator didn't help either. It had all caught up with him. He began a series of hospital stays and then dialysis. He became weaker and weaker. I knew it was all over one day when Lisa and I went to see him at St. Michael's in Newark. He looked so incredibly frail. He had been the coolest guy I had ever known. With his work jeans tucked into the tops of his construction boots army style, facing down the Commies on the 38th Parallel, running the big cranes, sneering in the faces of mobsters, he was one tough monkey. Now he was like a sickly baby bird in a nest.

Henry was always very fastidious about his appearance. When we were kids and he had been able to save enough money he would take the family out for a Sunday dinner to a fancy restaurant: or at least as fancy as he could manage. He always put on a suit and tie. He always went clean-shaven and showered.[9] Now he lay here unable to wash himself. He asked me to shave his face. His stubble was hard and I tried to wet his face then do it. I couldn't handle it; I couldn't handle seeing him reduced to this. On the pretense I was afraid I'd hurt him I went and found a helpful orderly who did it. I stayed out in the hall trying desperately to not get emotional.

Standing out there in the hospital hallway I found myself thinking about our first dog, Fuzzy. There is a picture of dad holding Fuzzy in our kitchen in Newark while I, dressed in a little army uniform, was preparing to throw a football pass. In the back you can just see my bike. When I was five years old I wanted a bike, but he couldn't afford to buy a new one. So, he found a guy at one of his job sites who sold him a broken down bike with training wheels for a couple of bucks. He cleaned it up, fixed it, and painted it black then carefully painted 'Bat Mobile' on the side of it in red. He would always try to find a way to get something of what you wanted.

Our only other dog, I picked out when we lived in Kearny. Pops and me jumped into the car and drove to New York to the Bideawee Home on East Thirty Eighth Street. It was a charity kennel where you gave a donation then picked out a pet. We walked around looking at the various dogs. Then I saw a tiny puppy in the back of one of the big room sized cages. He was sort of orangey red and was shivering uncontrollably just the way I always did. He looked at me and I knew he was the one. Henry gave them a donation and the three of us got in the car to come home. After a bit of silent driving Pops asked what I was going to name him. I thought about it for a while then said, Sherman. "Like the tank?" he said. "No," I replied, "Like Sherman and Mr. Peabody." Henry seemed to like that. The dog licked my face. Sherman would accompany me on many adventures.[10] He was Arrow to my Oblio. I was Vic and he was Blood.[11] He was the only one who always stood by me in those days. In later years he had a group of other dogs that he would run around the neighborhood with like a little doggy gang. One night in 1985 while I was away in Providence attending the Rhode Island School of Design Sherman came in, laid down on his favorite blanket and went to sleep. He never woke up.

Henry succumbed to his kidney disease in June of 2004. In the hospital we went to see him to assure him everything was going to be okay. He had already filled out all the paperwork so that Betty would inherit his union pension and their meager bank account. Like Sherman, he went to sleep and never woke up.

---

[9] Thanks to my dad, I always get dressed up when Lisa and I go to a nice restaurant, and I get oddly annoyed at men who go to nice restaurants dressed like slobs.

[10] 'Sherman and Mr. Peabody' was a popular kids cartoon. Mr. Peabody was a college educated talking dog, who took his boy sidekick, Sherman, on various adventures to learn about history. My dog Sherman was a Wire Haired Terrier.

[11] The *Boy and His Dog* from the Harlan Ellison short story.

Darby O'Gill and the Little People

I was lucky in that my parents never put too much pressure on me to be one thing or another. They simply wanted me to succeed at something I wanted to do, and to be happy. When I was born my mother wanted to name me after her father, Daniel. My father said absolutely not. Then she suggested Henry name me after his father Antoni. He said no to that as well. He didn't want me to be held down by some ancestor's name. He wanted me to have a clean start. Antoni never taught Henry to speak Polish for the same reason, he said the family was American and they would speak English. In the end my father agreed to have my mother pick a non-relative's name for me. They had just seen a movie called *Darby O'Gill and the Little People* (1959).[12] A comedy where an Irish drunkard has an encounter with leprechauns. The King of the leprechauns is named, Brian. So, I was named after a fictional leprechaun ruler. Right from the start I had a paranormal beginning. Also, my mom had a thing for the actor Brian Keith.[13]

Born in Newark in 1929 (the year of the stock market crash) my father dreamt of being a big league baseball player when he was young. There is a picture of him in the Newark newspaper with Mel Ott (1909-1958). A well-known player Mel 'Master Melvin' Ott was on a promotional visit to East Side High and their team. In the picture Ott is holding a bat with my dad and they're smiling into the camera. He looks exactly like what he was, a tough Norkie from the streets. He had that smile of someone who knew all the angles. He'd kick your ass and not break a sweat. The caption says that young Henry Regal has a lot of professional potential. For a brief moment a career as a professional athlete beckoned to my dad, but it didn't work out.

I spell my last name REGAL as Henry did. That's not how the family spelt it originally, however. The proper spelling of my Paternal family's name is Rygiel (It's also sometimes spelled Reigele in the western, more German parts of Poland).[14] This is the way my father's father spelled it. A number of family members spell it differently. The version I use was not changed at Ellis Island as many think. Indeed, the whole, "our name was changed at Ellis Island" thing is a myth. The customs officers had to account for every person coming off the boat. They would receive a manifest from the steamship line and had to make the list match. If it didn't match, there was a major problem. So, almost no one's name was ever changed in this mythical fashion. My father's name was changed when he went to grammar school. The administrators in Newark at the Hawkin's Street School thought the right way was too much for them so they anglicized it. My cousins Jason and Joseph, for example, use Reigal because their grandfather, my father's brother Michael, ran into a different set of lazy, administrators. Not as romantic as the mythology, but there you arc.

My mother's parents were the only grandparents I knew; they were the horrible grandparents. Grams never liked my father. I'm not quite sure why, but it was obvious. She would always call him 'Regal' instead of Henry. She would do it with a sneer. [15] My father's

---

[12] This Disney movie's cast included a young, pre-James Bond, Sean Connery
[13] In 1997 Brian Keith committed suicide in despair over the suicide of his daughter. He did it on my birthday.
[14] There is a brewery in Augsburg, Germany called Reigele (the oldest private brewery in Augsburg!). I was able to obtain a Reigele coaster and beer glass while I was over there. The glass eventually was broken, but I still have the coaster.
[15] My maternal grandmother's cousin was the actor, Paul Fix (1901-1983). He gained fame as a character actor in films and television and in a number of John Wayne movies. When his first big TV part came along, as the sheriff in the popular series *The Rifleman*, my grandmother called him to tell him how everyone in the family and in upstate New York, where he grew up, was proud of him. His response was to yell at her and accuse her of only wanting his money.

parents, Antoni and Anna were the good grandparents, but both of them died while I was an infant. Antoni met Anna Pisarczyk in Newark. They had both come over to America in 1907 as children. Anna spent time in the St. Joseph's Immigrant Home. Though they arrived around the same time Antoni travelled on the SS *Abraham Lincoln* (3rd Class) Hamberg-American Line out of Bremen, Germany while Anna came on the SS *Barbarossa* also out of Bremen (also 3rd Class), North German Lloyd Line.[16] Their parents scrapped together what little money they had to put their children on a boat out of the hellscape that was then central Europe. This was not uncommon. Parents sacrificed everything to send their children to this far off place called America, where, they were told, their kids might have a chance to survive. They both wound up in the Ironbound because there was already a European, Catholic, immigrant community there that included some relatives. Antoni was born in Koslaw and Anna in Bizescie (Brzeszcze) in the Carpathian Mountains, both in Silesia close to the modern Czechoslovakian border along the Oder River. The coal-mining region of Silesia has a turbulent history. It has passed from various kingdoms and duchies over the centuries: at one time part of Germany, then Russian then Bohemia then Austria then the Prussians took over. It was largely dominated by Germanic culture and by the 1870s became part of the German Empire, hence the way some of the family spell it Reigele like the Augsburg brewery.[17] It was not until after WWI, well after Antoni and Anna came to Newark, that Silesia became part of modern Poland.

Antoni and Anna were kindred spirits. Both children of national imbalance and uncertainty: refugees fleeing political turmoil. Antoni's parents, Maciey Rygiel and Maria Mankiewicz, sent him to America to avoid him being conscripted by the Cossack armies then running around Eastern Europe. Sent alone as children with no official documentation by their desperate parents they travelled to the other side of the world to wind up in a new country in a large, urban, heavily populated city none of them knew anything about, speaking a language they didn't know. From the same region, they found in each other a sense of calm and tradition. Anna took up the role of loving homemaker while Antoni became a rabbit skin tanner at a local factory.

They found a place to live above a bar at 9 Fleming Avenue in the Ironbound and proceeded to raise a family.[18] They had five kids, Michael (1913), Frank (1916), Edward (1918), Wanda (1926), and Henry (1929). I never really knew Frank. My father's brothers and sister were my favorite relatives though. Wanda was my favorite aunt. She was a tiny woman, and an incredible cook. I still miss her Thanksgiving and Christmas meals. I would look forward all year to stuffing myself with her handmade Swedish meatballs, potato and onion filled pierogis, and potato platzskis. She always treated me nicely and always got me the best

---

[16] The *President Lincoln* was confiscated in New York at the outbreak of WWI and used by the Americans as a troop transport. In 1918 it was sunk by the U-90. The *Barbarossa* was also confiscated and renamed the *USS Mercury*. It too served as an Allied troop transport and was eventually scraped in 1924.

[17] This information is taken from Antoni's naturalization papers. In the 21st century right wing bigots love to go on about 'illegal immigration.' A common refrain is that new immigrants don't come here "like our ancestors did." Antoni arrived in the US in 1907. He did not even file for citizenship until 1941 and then only at the insistent prodding of his children. During the interim he would have been considered an "illegal" by the standards of Right Wing anti-immigrant types.

[18] As a kid I was always hearing about a bar called 'Number 9.' "Let's meet at Number 9s," "Oh, you can find him over at Number 9s." Only in 2019 did I discover, while doing the research for this story, that 9 Fleming Avenue was the tenement where Antoni and Anna made their home and where Wanda and Henry grew up. On the ground floor of that building was a bar. Whatever the actual name of the bar was, everyone called it 'Number 9' because of its street address. The bar is still there and is called, as of this writing, The Ironbound Bar & Grill.

Christmas presents.[19] I never really knew Eddie that well either. I'm not sure if he served in WWII, but I assume he did. He seemed a frail man. His son, also named Eddie, became a cop in Kearny and eventually rose to the rank of Captain before he retired. When he was young Eddie learned to play the trumpet. At family gatherings he would be made to come out and in front of the assembled family and play 'Taps.' His father would sit quietly with tears running down his cheeks.

Uncle Mike was the one of all my uncles on either side of the family I was drawn to. I always wanted to get to know him, but I never really could. Even as a little kid I sensed a deep sadness in him. Several years older than my dad, he fought in World War II. Trained as a combat engineer he saw action at both the Battle of the Bulge, and Remagen Bridge. During the Bulge his unit helped stop the German advance by running back and forth across the country side in their halftracks and Greyhound armoured cars blowing up bridges. The heavy Nazi tanks needed the bridges to advance, but as Mike and his fellow engineers blew them up it stymied them.

Mike came back from the war with issues he tried, like so many did, to drown in alcohol. He moved into a small house in the Ironbound, not many blocks from where he grew up, to raise his sons Dennis and Michael. It was just a few blocks from where I would grow up in our apartment on Fleming Avenue. It was in front of the Ballantine Brewery at 451 Ferry Street. Next to it on the right was the Ferry Street Diner: one of those chrome diners out of the 1950s nostalgia buffs love (The apartment at Number 9 where Mike grew up also had a small diner right next to it). There was nothing else there except a big gravel lot where the delivery men would park the beer trucks. At the opposite corner was *Lancers Tavern*. Wanda, after she married Tommy Higgins, moved into a house just a few blocks from there on Filmore Street.[20] Everyone lived within a mile or so of each other. It was like some weird little village, but wrapped inside a great city.

Mike also brought back a captured Nazi pistol, a mint condition 9mm, Walther P-38. One night he became upset at a guy in *Lancers* who was pushing his girlfriend around. Mike had nothing to do with it, but he broke it up and the guy got mouthy with him. Mike calmly went home and came back with the loaded P-38 like Stagger Lee to settle the score with Billy Lyons. Without saying a word Mike grabbed the girlfriend beater by the collar, shoved the P-38 into his face and cocked the hammer. Having killed Nazis in the war, Mike was not averse to knocking off one more schmuck who liked to beat on women. Somehow, after a few tense moments, everyone calmed down and went home without further incident. When Wanda found out she took Mike's pistol down the nearby Passaic River and threw it in.[21]

Once when I was five or six years old, Mike was babysitting me. We were watching the TV and there was a war movie on. He suddenly looked at me and said, "Brian, you know what you do with Nazis?"

"No, Uncle Mike…" I replied.

"You give them a chance to surrender, and if they don't, you just kill them all." I didn't quite know what to say. "Okay, Uncle Mike," was the best I could muster. He then flashed a smile and said, "Let's have hotdogs!" to which I replied, "Yay!"

Mike's health began to deteriorate and he went into the hospital. My father would go to see him and bring me along. I wanted to go up and see Mike, but Henry said I had to wait downstairs. I would be left in the hospital snack bar by myself with a little hamburger and a small milkshake. On one visit Henry bought me my first Matchbox car—the road roller—to keep me occupied while he went upstairs. There were many times in my life as a kid when I was told to sit alone and wait, and be quiet, while adults did their adult things. I didn't need to know what was happening, I just needed to sit quietly and wait.[22] I was overseas in 1980 when Mike died so I missed the funeral. Except for when Wanda died, Mike was the only one of my relatives I mourned when they passed.

The Bar Room Life

I spent a lot of time in bars when I was a kid. That was because my parents spent a lot of time in bars when I was a kid. The bar was a central element in my parent's lives. In the lives of all the adults I knew. You had the place where you lived, you had your work, and then you had the bar. It was more than just a community center where family gatherings and celebrations were held. It was where you went to get away from it all, to avoid the Madding Crowd: you could be left alone there or you could talk the night away. You might not even know the person next to you on the stool, but there was type of odd, unspoken fellowship of the lost and lonely and the downhearted. Mostly, the only food was a large glass jar on the bar with weird green water in it in which floated hard boiled eggs, or occasionally hotdogs that cooked on one of those fryers with the slowly rotating steel cylinders. I think my fascination with contraptions began with me looking at, and trying to figure out the mechanism, of hotdog cookers in bars. These establishments were not trendy or fashionable. These were neighborhood drinking bars, gin mills.

Lancers was a popular watering hole for my family. There were countless christenings and birthday parties held in its large back room, event hall. In front was the bar. Family gatherings at places like *Lancers* inevitably ended with a fight or screaming match and the arrival of the police. My father would sit there for hours, sometimes with Mike, sometimes alone, while I would sit at a table with a soda by myself. The bartender would give me one of those tall thin fancy glasses with ice cubes in it. Sometimes the bartender would put a red plastic straw in it to make it festive. Henry would give me a handful of nickels to get pistachios out of the machine (I loathed hard boiled eggs and still do). Even at a young age,

---

[22]My parents never told me anything about what was going on. If I asked they wouldn't hide things, but they never offered any information voluntarily. They would occasionally tell me if anyone died, but they never told me if someone was getting ready to die. They never involved me in any decision making. This unconsciously taught me that my input was not of value. It taught me such things were not necessary for me to know. It taught me to think only of myself and of my concerns. It taught me to reflexively always look inwardly and not care about anyone else. I would make decisions about what to do in any given situation on my own, and not ask for any help or advice. I never rejected good advice, but my initial instinct has always been to not ask, or expect anyone to want to help me. This has occasionally benefitted me in adult life, but has mostly caused problems. Lisa was the only person I really ever opened up to and whose advice I sought.

however, I could sense that my father's hard, quiet, exterior masked a deep melancholy that he worked to keep under control.

In the bar the juke box was always playing just loud enough, but not overpowering like in a dance club. The dark was illuminated by the mood lights behind the liquor bottles, the small hanging ceiling lights, and the colored lights from the jukebox. Those lights seemed like stars in the sky. They showed me the way to the universe. During this period English Tudor architecture became a popular motif for bars and restaurants, especially the interiors. Shadows abounded. I would stare at my father's back as he sat at the bar and slowly drank in the gloom. I could see the other patrons as well, most looked like my dad: working men wearing working clothes, a work helmet or two on the bar. Occasionally a woman or two. Sometimes there would be one that was different. Occasionally, I would see someone way down the end of the bar in the shadows, or in a darkened both by themselves. They didn't seem the same as the others, you could never really see their faces. They seemed disjointed or misshapen, they seemed to be weird creatures. Such instances made me think maybe there were special rules that allowed lost and lonely monsters to come into the bar and drink. As long as they didn't attack or eat anyone, I surmised, they would be allowed in and left alone.

Bringing me along was an easy way to make sure I didn't get into trouble. As a child who had already learned not to cry and scream in public, but to find a private spot by myself and do it there, I didn't intrude on Henry's solitude.[23] I learned a number of life lessons there. Sitting in those bars I subconsciously saw what adulthood was supposed to be. I sat there, my feet not touching the floor, with my soda and pistachios that turned your fingers red, near the shuffle board table, and watched these men try to cope with their lives and pains by numbing themselves with alcohol. I learned to like polished wood surfaces and tall chairs with backs. The sound of the cash register ringing and the rattle of coins dropped into the coin boxes inside the register. I could stare at the novelty advertising gismos all the bars had: mechanical horses pulling the *Budweiser* beer barrel wagon, or the *Schlitz* emblems. I learned to feel at home around neon. I learned lessons about violence, and race, and gender, and how blood looked streaming out of someone's nose, and what a real black eye looked like. I heard what a broken heart sounded like when someone groaned, "no, please don't leave!" I didn't realize at the time that it didn't matter if I didn't understand any of this, it was being lodged in the filing cabinet of my mind for later reference.

While he taught me to catch and throw a ball, and how to fix things with tools (you can fix almost anything with a screwdriver, pair of vice grips, a hammer, and a roll of electrical tape) my father never taught me things in that TV or movies way of sitting me down and explaining. I learned by watching him. I learned you had responsibilities that you had to uphold no matter what. I learned it was easier and faster to do things by yourself rather than ask anyone for help (he always seemed disappointed by my efforts to help him do things). People depended upon you and you put all your needs second to theirs. Girls could get away with stuff, but boys were always responsible. You were supposed to know what to do at all times (and reinforced by my later military service and career as an academic) and have all the answers to all the questions. This was not showing off, it was simply your responsibility. I learned that life was one long compromise and sacrifice. My mother taught me to cook, and

---

[23] Well into my adulthood, Henry always had bars he could go to. Whether it was a local gin mill, the Elk's Hall, or the Union Hall, he needed a place to be by himself. He brought me along as a child, but not as an adult. Even after I came home from the service he wouldn't bring me with him. I would have liked to sit and have a drink with my dad in the bar, but for him this was something not even I could partake in. He had wounds no salve could ever heal. There were aspects of his self even I couldn't ever be allowed to learn. It hurt, but I think I understood.

she also taught me a lot about sacrifice. My parents had been forced by the laws of the universe to give up on almost all their dreams. They were denied those things they wanted for themselves. They made up for that by working so their kids could have a better life than they did: that they might realize some of their dreams. You just had to learn to accept it, to smile grimly and go on.

Walk it off. Just walk it off.

It was difficult for me to understand this at the time. My lifelong obliviousness was my coping mechanism developed during this period. This might account for why it took me so long before I began drinking. I had all these unintentional negative role models. Even in high school where illicit drinking was a rite of passage I only joined in a few times. It wasn't until I went overseas that I drank more, yet I still never approached the level of consumption of many of my colleagues or my family members.[24] Not until I was in my late forties did I start consuming alcohol on a regular basis: in part because I had discovered English beer which was far and away better than any American brew I had ever had, and in part because the anxiety attacks returned with a vengeance.[25] Only then did I really come to appreciate those men like my dad in the *Star-Z*, *Lancers*, and *Number 9*, and what they were doing and why, and that monsters chased everyone. To this day I prefer old style bars and pubs that subconsciously remind me of those places I spent so many hours in as a kid. When I go into a saloon now and I look down the long bar, I see my dad sitting there. I see him every time. I can never not see him there.

My Sporting Career

The 1970s is often described as the "me era." It certainly was for me. All I cared about was myself. I didn't, however, like any of the 70s clothing styles: I didn't like flowing silk shirts, and I hated bell bottom jeans. My mother always bought them, but I would never wear them. This was also the period in which I toyed briefly with the idea of being an athlete as most boys do. It was mostly my father's idea though. At his urging, I played Little League baseball in Kearny for three years (I also played one year of Little League football and one of basketball with less than stellar results). All the teams had ethnic civics groups as sponsors. There was the Polish American team sponsored by the Polish American Club, and Irish American team sponsored by the Irish American Club, the team I was on, the Scotts American team was sponsored by, well, the Scottish American Club. There was also the Fireman's Benevolent Association team. They had the letters FMBA emblazoned across the chest of the cotton uniform. We, of course, called it Fat Man's Belly Ache and thought ourselves wildly creative and funny for doing so.

Boys are supposed to love sports. We are told this from very early on. Our dads buy us balls and gloves and helmets so we will love sports. We always think in terms of little girls being under undue pressure about how they look and how they act and what sort of lives they should lead as adults. That pressure certainly is there and it's unfair to girls, and it causes great harm. Little boys have a similar problem to deal with. Boys are pressured into being good at sports, athletic, strong, 'manly' and tough. If you're not, then the ridicule begins, the bullying, the ostracism, and violence. Sissies aren't manly and you better not be a sissy.

---

[24] I also managed to not turn to drugs while I was in the service, despite the fact that I was surrounded by them. I suppose growing up around alcoholics and drug addicts inured me to the 'romance' of drug addiction. I also never learned to smoke, drink coffee, or play poker while I was in the service. Go figure.

[25] My personal favorites—at least as of this writing—are Smithwicks, Samuel Smith, and Old Speckled Hen.

My first year on the Scot's American was a good year. Most of the team was made up of really good third years. We worked hard and won the Kearny Southern Little League championship. The prize was a trophy and a blue windbreaker with 'Scotts American' across the back. Then they took us to the Scotts American Club for lunch. The 'club' was just a bar and lunch was hotdogs. Henry was happy as now he had a new place he could go drink to get away from his wife and kids. There is a photo that Henry took with me in my uniform with my championship windbreaker holding the trophy, with my usual bewildered look on my face. The next two years all those actual athletes on the team went off to their respective High School teams or moved up to the Pony League, then off to college. We didn't do as well with me as senior guy.

Then I went to High School.

The country came out of the '60s unsure of itself. After World War II the nation could look proudly on the idea they had fought a horrific war, but had fought it for a good reason: the Nazis, the Italian Fascists, and the Japanese Militarists had to be stopped. With the country's involvement in Korea then Vietnam that certainty seemed less so. Gender roles had begun to morph as well. The image of manliness was changing. Women and ethnic minorities were vocal about achieving their rightful due. Fathers told their sons to cut their hair. I started wearing my hair longer. I was lucky in that Henry never gave me a hard time about the length of my hair. In fact, he bought me my first hair dryer for Christmas. Only Aunt Wanda would ask me every time she saw me, "When are you going to get a haircut?" The previous generation saw the world in a certain way and my generation ignored all that and went their own way. I never hated my parents the way some kids did, though. I understood that despite their shortcomings, they were trying their best to do right by us and help us achieve the lives we wanted.

My sports career ended the summer before I began high school. While enrolling for Kearny High I somehow ticked a box somewhere indicating my interest in playing on the school baseball team. I then received notice to report for the summer, pre-school training camp. Henry was thrilled and even drove me over for the first day (he never drove me to school). Kearny High had only recently built a brand new complex on campus. A large sports center attached to the original 1920 brick building by futuristic sky tubes and underground tunnels: all very 1970s. The lower portion was a state of the art sports facility with three side-by-side indoor basketball courts with those giant movable bleacher sections. Downstairs were offices for the teams and the locker rooms. On the ground floor were the large, main entry doors to the gym. This is where girls who were interested in athletes would congregate to flirt with them. My wall locker was just to the right of these doors. This forced me to watch the cheerleaders, none of whom were interested in me, throw themselves at the sports heroes. On the upper floors were a large music room and a suite of nicely furnished art studios. The city had spent quite a bit of money on the whole thing and was rightly proud of it. I spent some of the few happy times at Kearny High in the art department learning to paint, do graphic design, and photography. There I met fellow student Bill Styple, another artist with an interest in history. He went on to become a well-known Civil War historian and author, and Kearny's town historian.

Showing up for baseball camp we had to fill out more forms one of which asked for your sports experience and what position you were interested in playing. I put down that I had played second base, and was a catcher in Little League. "A catcher!" yelled the coach who I later learned everyone called No-Neck Pauli. With that I was whisked off to the pitcher's practice area. I enjoyed being a catcher because you didn't have to run around too much, and you got to wear all that body armour.

In the practice area they had a pitcher's mound made out of plywood and 2x4s set to the correct height of an outdoor pitcher's mound. They had a batter's box laid out with tape on the floor and I and the coach walked over to it. No-Neck Pauli handed me a facemask and catcher's glove. "Warm him up." He said. There was an older kid there. I remembered him vaguely from one of the other Little League teams though as usual, I didn't remember his name. I said to Pauli, "Uh, where is the chest protector and shin guards?" He looked at me incredulously. "We're indoors, you don't need that stuff." I thought about asking what being indoors had to do with it, but he walked off to talk to the pitcher and they went out to the mound. The coach said some words of instruction to the pitcher and they both looked at me. I crouched down into position and prepared to help the pitcher practice.

After a few more words of instruction from the coach the kid went into his wind up.

Set, focus, windup, throw.

With practiced effortlessness he went through the serpentine undulations of throwing a baseball, and the bright white sphere was hurtling at me. The instant the ball left his hand I knew I was in trouble. He had thrown a curve ball. I watched in fascinated terror at the ball curved in the distinctive looping arc getting larger and larger as it came at me. Curve balls are notoriously difficult to throw correctly, but this young man had mastered it. I tried to follow the ball as it described its spinning trajectory with my glove. As I watched I thought of the opening sequence of *Dr. Who* with the spinning vortex of infinity and that weird electronic music. Somehow, I managed to keep the glove between my face and the ball and I caught it, though I did it incorrectly. A sharp sting raced through my hand and up my arm, but I couldn't show fear or pain. Catcher's gloves look the way they do for a reason. They have a webbed upper area that is where you are supposed to actually catch the ball. You must avoid catching the ball with the palm of the glove where your hand is. If the ball hits the part where your hand it it's like catching the ball barehanded. It stings like lightning.

I managed to throw the ball back without showing, at least as far as I could tell, how much my hand now hurt. The next couple of pitches went by without incident. I was able to catch everything with the glove's webbing the way you are supposed to. Then the coach said some more instructional things to the pitcher. All I could hear was "fastball."

Set, focus, windup, throw.

As a little league catcher I never had much of a problem as most of our pitchers couldn't throw that fast or powerfully. This kid was way beyond that level. At seventeen he was already throwing fast balls like a pro. As it came towards me it began to dip. I followed with my glove. It went up and I followed with my glove. Then it dipped again and couldn't follow it with my glove.

The ball hit me square on the right kneecap at 80 miles per hour. Everything went white for a second or two. The ball ricocheted off my knee like an anti-tank round. I jumped up and yelled, "Owwww!" and began hopping around hissing through my teeth in abject, electric pain. I threw the glove down and tore off the mask and threw it. The coach looked annoyed that I was now interrupting his pitching practice session. Without saying another word I hobbled past everyone who was practicing and stretching and trying to be real men, and headed down to the locker room. I changed back into my jeans and t-shirt. As I sat there, the waves of pain finally subsiding, I saw that the ball had left an imprint of the laces in my knee quite distinctly.

I took my things and left. I limped all the way home down Devon Street. Tellingly, no coach ever came after me or called the house to see if I was okay. Dad had just come home and he excitedly wanted to know all about my first day at baseball spring training. I told him what happened. He seemed like he was about to say, "oh, well, just walk it off, you'll be fine."

'Walking it off' was the tried and true answer to every injury, physical or emotional. Sprain your ankle? Walk it off. Pull a muscle? Walk it off. Spear through the head? Walk it off. Stray bullet through the chest? Walk it off. Broken heart? Walk it off. Nobody likes you? Walk it off. You've got no future? Walk it off.

I sat down at the kitchen table. We had that table with the cheap Formica top and the aluminum tube legs. The kitchen ceiling light was that one with a small, cylindrical, pickle jar shaped glass covering that barely stopped the harsh, unrelenting glow of the bulb. It was the same one you'd find in every tenement, put there by cheapskate landlords trying to save a few pennies. They still sell the exact one in all the home stores.

I looked at my dad and told him I didn't want to go back. He was disappointed and began to try to talk me into changing my mind. As he did, I pulled down my jeans and showed him the imprint of the laces in my knee which was rapidly turning an ugly black and blue. He stopped. He looked at it. "Does it hurt?" he asked quietly. "Yes," I said. My mother, who had come into the room, filled the cloth-covered, screw-top 'headache' bag with ice and put it on my knee. "Okay, go into your room, keep the ice on it and rest a bit. We'll order a pizza."

We never talked about me playing sports again.

I wanted to learn to play a musical instrument. When I applied to Kearny High they asked if I wanted to join the marching band or the orchestra. I asked if I could take piano lessons. The councillor said that you couldn't take classes in a musical instrument unless you already knew how to play it. That seemed odd to me. When I was in seventh grade, my mother asked if I wanted to learn to play the guitar? If I did, she would spring for private lessons. The next week a music teacher showed up at the apartment. I was rather excited. I was going to learn to play the guitar. When he came in he was carrying two large black boxes that didn't look like guitars. He proceeded to open them and out came two accordions. I was a bit confused. I asked Ma what was going on. I thought I was going to have guitar lessons. "Oh, you'll like this better," was her answer. So, I get my music lesson and then it is announced that I would have to travel to the guy's studio for the rest of the lessons. His studio was way up the Ave over the Lincoln Movie Theater near the Bellville Turnpike. The whole top floor of the movie theater was taken up with music and dance rehearsal spaces. As you went in you could hear people playing and tuning. Through another door I could see dancers' plieing. I went to a few lessons and became bored. I would not pick up an accordion again until I was in my late '40s. Only in my dotage would I get to play at being a part time rock star.

Korea

Dreams of a sports career all ended for my father when he was drafted. He had been too young to go to World War II like Mike, but he was old enough to go to Korea. Originally, he was sent to Fort Hood, Texas to learn to be a tank driver.

Shrewd young whipper snapper loved to run and play
but the Draft Board got him they inducted him today.
It wasn't me sarg no, no, it wasn't me
It must have been some other body, uh huh, but it wasn't me...[26]

He trained on both the older M4A1E8 Sherman (the 'Easy Eight') and the more modern M26 Pershing heavy tank. While in Texas, Henry engaged in the usual army trainee behavior; he got drunk with his friends and went into Mexico and danced with Mexican girls. They were training to go and fight in Korea. Beginning on June 25, 1950 the Korean War began when the communist north decided to unify the entire country by invading the democratic south. It became a major engagement that threatened to escalate into a nuclear war. It was the first conflict being dealt with by the new United Nations.

By 1953 the fighting had degenerated into a series of smaller scale encounters rather than large foraging armies bashing away at each other. Being such a hilly land, many of the battles of the Korean war were fought over the control of hill tops where tanks were much less effective. The Chinese began using mass infantry wave attacks. Hundreds, sometimes thousands, of North Korean and Chinese troops would storm up the side of a particular hill intending to throw off the United Nations units on top of it by sheer weight of numbers. This was often done at night to the accompaniment of blaring bugles projected from loudspeakers.

Though trained as a tanker, Henry and his fellows were reassigned to anti-aircraft duty. During the Second World War, all sides experimented with anti-aircraft weapons. One of the more effective American-made anti-aircraft weapons was the M16. This was a standard M3 half-track with a rotating turret mounted in the open back bed of the vehicle. The one-man turret had four .50 caliber, heavy, machine guns mounted on it and arranged to fire in unison. The fifty caliber was, and still is, a formidable weapon.[27] Firing a copper slug the size of a grown man's thumb, the .50 cal—also known as a 'Ma Deuce' because its official designation was M2—could devastate a low-flying aircraft. By the time of Korea the M16 was essentially useless in the anti-aircraft role as the skies were now full of jets. In the rocky, hilly terrain of Korea with the Chinese employing the mass wave attack strategy, the M16 found a new job. Its heavy rate of fire and devastating impact worked well in breaking-up infantry assaults. Dug in to a pit an M16 could sweep the lines of advancing enemy and obliterate them. The M16 was so effective in this role the crews who manned them and the United Nations troops who came to depend on them for their survival called them 'Meat Choppers.' No longer needed as a tank driver, this is where they sent Henry. He traded in his Pershing for a 'Meat Chopper' and was sent into the front lines. He was there in the last half of the war, 1953.

My father saw a good bit of action in Korea, but didn't talk about it much.[28] He once told me of an incident after a battle where the ground in front of their position was covered in dead Chinese soldiers. The decision was made to dig a large hole and bury them all together and so an armoured bulldozer was brought in. Gasoline was dumped over the corpses and set

---

[26] Chuck Berry, It Wasn't Me (1965).

[27] The 50 Cal is the oldest still serving weapon in the American military arsenal. It first entered service in the early 1920s.

[28] He served with Battery B, 82nd AAA (Anti-Aircraft Artillery), AW Battalion (Automatic Weapons), (SP) Self Propelled.

on fire. As Henry and his fellows sat on their halftrack watching, one of the Chinese bodies on the edge of the pile sat up as if it were alive. The intense heat of the fire caused the muscles in the dead man to contract suddenly. Henry did not want his family to know any of this, and only told me once when he was drunk. In those days they had not yet developed the idea of PTSD. They called it Battle Fatigue or Shell Shock. The only pictures I have of pops after the war where he is smiling are all where he is with us. I wish he had been able to talk to me about it. I wish I had known the right questions to ask. There had been a time or two as a kid when I tried to ask him things about the war, but it obviously made him uncomfortable so I stopped. That caused me to hardly ever ask him questions about anything. I would have liked to ask him about his parents or growing up in Newark, but I never did for fear of upsetting him needlessly and making him suffer. The rest of the family did enough of that. He didn't need me pestering him. We would just stand there next to one another not talking, but wanting to, but being unable to. We both thought that maybe just a close proximity would be enough. I went through life knowing very little about his inner most thoughts and beliefs. If maybe he knew he could talk to me he wouldn't have drank so much.[29]

As a construction worker, my dad never had much money, but he always tried to get us things. He wanted to pay for me to go to college or buy a house, but he simply did not have that kind of money. So, in place of that he would get us little things he thought we'd like. In 2004 while out grocery shopping with Betty he bought me a frozen 99 cent pot pie that came in a little cardboard box. He knew I liked pot pies and figured 99 cents was a bargain. I had had one these before and I knew they were awful, but I smiled and said thanks. I knew he did it because he loved me and wanted me to be happy.[30] A few weeks later he went into the hospital for the last time then passed away. I carried that potpie around with me for years after. As the last thing he ever gave me I couldn't bring myself to throw it away. Every time we moved I'd pack it up and bring it to the next place and put it in the freezer. Finally, it deteriorated to the point where I had to get rid of it. Throwing away that little frozen mess of a potpie left me unable to speak for the rest of the day. Though I didn't want to think it, I felt like he was finally gone.

The .50 Caliber Bullet

When my mother became too ill and demented to live on her own, Lisa and I moved her in with us. I went back to that horrid apartment again to pick up any valuables or keep sakes that she might want. I couldn't take everything because she had somehow contracted scabies and we didn't want to contaminate our place too. As I packed up some of her things; some framed pictures, an old painting I had done as a kid, and a few other sentimental odds and ends from the bottom drawer of her ancient broken down clothes dresser, I saw a small, old, cardboard box. It was maybe two inches long by about half-an-inch deep, wrapped in some equally old men's dress socks. When I picked it up I could feel something rattling around inside it. I had never seen it before. I opened it up and found a single, fifty-caliber machine gun round. Not the brass casing, just the copper slug. It had been kept carefully in

---

[29] My father eventually did stop drinking. A few years before he died, doctors told him he had to stop smoking and quit drinking. With a will power I still envy, he just stopped. One day he was a two pack a day smoker, the next nothing. His health greatly improved, but the years of abuse had taken its toll and no amount of abstinence would save his kidneys and lungs at that point. He was offered a kidney transplant, but he turned it down. "Give it to someone young," he told the doctor.

[30] Another way I knew Lisa was a keeper was because of the girlfriends I brought home for my parents to meet, she was the only one Henry took a liking to. Though, when I did bring Lisa over for the first time my mother called her Gina: which was the name of the girl I had been seeing previously. That all got straightened out.

this box over the course of half a century.

It had been fired.

I went and sat down at the old kitchen table where I had so many meals as a kid; where I had watched my mother cook, and where countless Christmas, birthday, and Thanksgivings had been celebrated; where relatives laughed, fought, and screamed at each other. This was where Betty had taught me to spell and where Henry tried to teach me maths. Inside the door of the battered old kitchen sink cabinet still lurked the little drawings of mice I made in the wood every time Sherman caught a mouse. You could just make them out. That refrigerator, that god damned broken down old refrigerator they refused to replace, and which I wanted to replace for them, but they wouldn't let me. The one that held the Oxford University wall magnet we got her the first time Lisa and I went there. Next to it was a magnet of the Pope and some long-forgotten saint with clasped hands staring wistfully up at heaven.

I stared at the 50-caliber bullet. I never knew Henry had brought it back from Korea. Like so many things, he kept it hidden. Was it a reminder of his experiences? Was it to remember all the bullets he had fired into men's bodies taking their lives? Did he keep it to help scare the ghosts and goblins and monsters away? Did it keep him from bashing his head into the wall? I don't know. I'll never know. The only person who might have known was my mother. I wanted to ask my mother about that bullet, but she could barely remember what time of day it was, so I didn't bother.

I loaded the wreckage of her life into my car. After leaving that wretched place for the last time to go back to Plainfield and to Lisa, I drove to Rutherford first. There in the swamps of Jersey Henry and I once flew model rockets together. Flying model rockets became a thing in the 1970s inspired by the NASA space program. Anything that I was interested in that seemed sciencey or something intelligent people did, my father supported. I would spend all week carefully building them. Cardboard tubes, with balsa wood wings you had to cut out and glue together. Then I'd paint them. On Friday nights we would go down to the hobby shop together and he would buy the rocket engines. Saturday morning, we would come down here to the swamp to fly them. I think he was happy when he and I were together alone. He never cursed me, or insulted or humiliated me in public, or hit me (the way Eddie and Billy often did to their sons). We did fight as father's and son's do, though it was mostly me disappointing him or not knowing how to articulate how I felt about things. There were times when I was much younger he would bring me to one of his construction sites and let me play on the crane. With him carrying me on his shoulders, I watched the big machinery work, greased cables lifting steel girders to the 'Iron Men' who climbed the girders effortlessly, so cocky and sure of themselves they did it without harnesses, and never fell. Sometimes when I was nine or ten years old he and I would walk down to a small greasy spoon snack bar on the avenue. They made the most incredible 'Newark Style' hotdogs there.

A large, fresh, Greek pita bread sliced in half with two fat, grilled hotdogs. The kind that were crunchy on the outside, soft on the inside. That topped off with potatoes, peppers and onions (I always picked the peppers out, I still do). All of it fried in oil on the grill. We would sit at the counter. I'd spin slowly back and forth on the stool and he never told me to stop. The hotdogs would be brought over—the smell, that smell, grease and oil and meat fat— and we'd eat. The glass door would open making the little bell attached to the top jingle as a customer came in. There were only a few other times in my life I can remember seeing my father look this happy. He was not at a job site; he was not around his crazy wife or her insane relations. It was just him and me and I would never judge him. We all have moments in our lives that we would go back to if we could. They are usually times we think we were happy. Sitting in that tiny restaurant with my dad and a couple of hotdogs, with the traffic of Kearny Avenue outside, is one of those moments for me. He had been happy there, and for me that's all that mattered.[31]

I used to get up early and secretly watch my father get ready to go to work. He rose at 5am, took a shower, got dressed putting on his jeans and his work boots, and had a cup of coffee. He'd rub his knee and wince. It was an old wound from Korea. Then he would rise, take his coat, and head quietly out the back door to work making as little noise as possible so as not to wake us. I watched, hiding at the end of the long hallway of that horrible apartment. He didn't do this because he liked it. He didn't think it ennobling. He did it because that was the way he knew to take care of his family. To him, no one could call themselves a real man unless you took care of your family. He put away all his own hopes and dreams in order to take care of us.

> A union man, a union man, a union man am I
> I joined up when I came home from the war
> And I'll stay in it
> Until I die.

Watching my dad like that filled me with rage. Not at him of course, but at a world that crushed good and honest men like him. Watching Henry I learned to hate liars, and frauds, bullies, those who shield the evil, and those who start wars, but never fight in them. In the service I learned the term REMF (Rear Echelon Mother F***r). These are people who talk tough about what patriots they are and how they love guns and fighting. They say all this however, from the safety of the background, they say it while carrying assault rifles into a grocery store to intimidate housewives, and from the comfort of places where they never have to actually sacrifice anything. I met a lot of REMFs over the years. I still hate them. I always will.[32]

After leaving the Kearny apartment I drove down to our rocket launching place in Rutherford just off Route 3. By now the swamp that once had been a quiet place with reeds in the wind was different. When we came here no one else did. It was our special place. No one intruded. It was now the cloverleaf for the highway system that connected Routes 3 and 17, and led out to the New Jersey Turnpike entrance. They built the now infamous *Legendary Times* restaurant there where you can play at being a medieval knight. They filmed *The Cable Guy* there, which was the first time I saw Janeane Garofalo. A mile or so across the swamp they built what was originally called the Brenden Byrne Arena, and next to it the horse race track, and next to that Giant's Stadium. In the early 21st century they built the huge and

---

[31] Once, years after he had died I had this odd dream about my dad where he was wearing a three-piece suit. He smiled at me and asked, "How do I look?" I said, "You look good!" That was it.

[32] My father was in the construction union during what some call the Golden Age of organized crime. He knew such heavy hitters as Anthony 'Tony Pro' Provenzano, Frankie Fitzsimmons, and Jimmy Hoffa. I would listen to him as he sat at the kitchen table talking with disgust about these men. Despite their mob ties, many union members considered them heroes because Hoffa had genuinely benefitted union members on occasion. Henry did not think they were heroes. He saw the workings of mob guys, but was never impressed by them. He never engaged in the flag waving, backslapping, hysteria men like Hoffa—with their pro-labour rhetoric—engendered from members. He knew the big corporate bosses took advantage of workers, but he also saw the mob guys steal and abuse workers just as much. He supported the idea that unions helped protect worker's rights, but was wary of how mob figures had infiltrated the unions. His Korea experiences gave him the ability to see through people.

intensely ugly American Dream Mall, with its indoor ski jump which as of this writing had still not opened after more than a decade. Standing in the dirt with fake knights behind me and the white noise of the highway traffic out ahead of me I threw the 50 caliber bullet as far as I could into the reeds. It would never be found now. Henry's secrets were safe forever.

Chapter 3

Garrison at the Edge of the Empire

"I met your children, what did you tell them?"

– Video Killed the Radio Star

I did not join the United States Army for patriotic reasons. In fact, such thinking never entered my mind. Despite the on-going Cold War there was no grand cultural impetus to sign up in 1977. The nation's love affair with the military had waned with the end of its involvement in Vietnam. I did have my reasons for volunteering, however. I wanted to leave everything behind. With a few exceptions, I disliked everything about my life. Joining the army would give me a chance to create a new one. I had developed the crazy notion that I could, with my books, art, and words, create a life of my own. I was going to pursue the dream of becoming an adventuring historian, and a slayer of monsters. My enlistment was a means to that end.

My earliest musical memories came from sitting in the corner of the *Star Z* and *Lancers*, and other down neck bars waiting patiently for my parents. The music on the juke box was always Tony Bennet, Frank Sinatra, and Nat King Cole. When we moved to Kearny, my parents changed over to Irish bars so the music was more Tom Jones, Engelbert Humperdinck, and an annoyingly insistent song about unicorns not making it onto Noah's Ark. Also, the intensely depressing *Honey*, by Bobby Goldsboro, where the singer laments the loss of his love at a young age. She had planted a tree and now he watches alone as it grows always reminding him of her. All this music was well suited for sitting in a darkened bar slowly drinking your life away.

The Music of the Spheres

In 1973 my father, as a crane operator, was sent by the union over to JFK Stadium in Jersey City to help set up the stage for a big weekend concert. Henry wasn't that much into pop music—though in the early '80s he developed an odd liking for *Southside Johnny and the Asbury Jukes*—so it was just another job for him. Ever since the phenomenon of Woodstock, weekend long, multi-performer shows were popular. The big headliner for this show was the *Allman Brothers Band*. They had had a number of hits including 'Sweet Mellissa,' 'Whipping Post,' and 'Ramblin'Man.' They were part of a growing genre called 'Southern Rock' that would include the likes of *The Marshall Tucker Band*, *ZZ Top* and *Lynyrd Skynyrd*. At noon on that day Henry and the other construction guys stopped work to have lunch. Pops did his usual by climbing out of the control cab of the big crane to sit on the caterpillar track. He took out his lunch pail with the built in thermos and began to eat the meal Betty had prepared for him. As he sat there, a young man with long blonde hair came up to him and started asking questions about the crane. He asked about how much weight it could handle and other technical issues. After a moment the young man asked if he could sit down and Pop said "sure." The two of them sat there on the track of the crane chatting in the late summer sun. After half an hour or so my father said he had to get back to work. The young man smiled, shook his hand, and said thanks for all the effort putting up the stage. Henry smiled, took the compliment and climbed back into the rig as the young man walked off. He never saw him again.

As he was telling us this story that night we asked my father if he knew who it was. Pops said the young man had introduced himself as 'Gregg.' It was Gregg Allman. "He seemed like a very nice guy," the Old Man said. We would forever tell the story of how my dad had lunch with Gregg Allman while sitting on his crane.

In 1975 Bruce Springsteen, who was then still little more than an obscure, struggling, local Jersey shore rocker, released his third album, *Born to Run*. A rock-n-roll record as black and white *Film Noir* soundtrack. The characters and situations he sang about were familiar to me *and* my friends. We knew these people; we knew these characters. We knew these emotions. They were us. I've loved the work of lots of bands and singers, but I never felt such a connection between them and myself the way I felt with Springsteen. He spoke directly to me. He told me things. He said everything might be awful now, but there's a chance it might work out okay. [1]

Shortly after that, English singer/songwriter Al Stewart released *Year of the Cat*. He wrote about characters too. Unlike Springsteen's garage mechanics and Jersey girls in black leather jackets running wild in the street, Al Stewart wrote about sophisticated world travelers who had wild affairs with beautiful and mysterious women who spoke with exotic accents. They travelled to other countries and stood before huge antique wall maps. They flew in Tiger Moth airplanes, and knew secret places out of H. Rider Haggard and *Arabian Nights*. Al Stewart also wrote about historical events and people. Both *Born to Run* and *Year of the Cat* were concept albums: They told complete stories with a beginning, middle and an end. You were meant to listen to them in their entirety in the order they appeared on the record. An album was not just a collection of songs, it was meant to be an experience. The order of the songs, even the album cover artwork, meant something to the whole.

Then, I heard it.

It was March of 1976. I heard the voice of an angel, a voice from another realm. A voice that allowed me to see other vistas, other spheres. Bruce Springsteen and Al Stewart pointed me towards things; this voice took my hand and led me there. It was a transformative voice.

I heard Ann Wilson sing 'Magic Man.'

The first 'Heart' album, *Dreamboat Annie*, highlighted her incredible voice as well as the red-hot guitar playing of her sister Nancy. Part of the appeal of this record for me went beyond the simple appreciation of the music or what the sight of Ms. Wilson did to my sixteen -year-old soul. *Dreamboat Annie* is about escape. It's about riding the euphonious ship away from all those things that hurt us and make us feel bad about ourselves, that deaden our souls. That "little ship of dreams" was a vessel of escape. I would sit in my room staring out the window with my giant 1970s headphones on listening to these records over and over,

[1] I have listened to or played the Bruce Springsteen song 'Fourth of July, Asbury Park' every Fourth of July since 1977.

dreaming.

This was the most influential music in my life: *Born to Run, Year of the Cat,* and *Dreamboat Annie*. They were all released around the same time. While they are wildly different stylistically, they all sent me the same message. The same message that Jonny Quest, the Thunderbirds, Tin Tin, libraries, and the *Alvis Stalwart* sent me: you could get out. You didn't need to stay in that life you hated. A life you feared you might be stuck in forever. The closing line from *Dreamboat Annie*, is "heading out to somewhere, won't be back for a while." That line resonated with me. I have always been afflicted with this almost pathological need to get out, to run away, to leave all those fools behind. I've never really been sure what it was I was running away from. I only knew I had to run. This music told me it was okay. It said you could run from what you were to something you wanted to be.

That's why I joined the army.[2]

D-3-1

When I joined the US Army no one from my graduating high school class that I'm aware of enlisted at the same time.[3] With World War II and Korea now distant memories, and Vietnam over at last, few people were interested in military service in the 1970s. The few people who said anything to me about it said I was a chump for doing so because only losers joined the army. I find it humorous today, in the third decade of the twenty-first century, how many politicos and pundits who love to go on about what great patriots they are, and how we should go to war with this country or that were the people laughing at me when I enlisted. And whom themselves never served.

I was not the only kid who wanted to get out of New Jersey, of course. I just had fewer options. Higher Education would not be my out, the way it was for others. It was made clear I wasn't going to go to college. My parents couldn't afford it and everyone at Kearny High, except John O'Hara, told me I was too stupid to go. So, without the slightest regret or hesitation, I headed off to begin a life of adventure on Uncle Sam's dime.[4]

It took some convincing, but eventually M&D saw I was determined. Henry was not thrilled. Pops and I would often sit together in the living room and watch the news in 1968 and 1969. At 6pm the local news came on then at 6:30 the national/international news. In the late 1960s and early 1970s the first thing Howard K. Smith would start the broadcast with was announcing how many American troops had been killed in Vietnam that day.

"Five Americans were killed in Vietnam today."
"Eighteen Americans were killed in Vietnam today."
"Fifteen Americans were killed in Vietnam today."

---

[2] Years later Lisa and I went to see Al Stewart perform at *Club Bene* on Rt. 35. An old style Dinner Theater of a type that doesn't really exist anymore, *Club Bene* was famous for having some of the best pop acts of the day perform there. It was small and intimate. You had dinner then the act would come out. When we saw Al Stewart we sat right up against the stage with the band just a step or two away. After a great show, Al stayed after to sign things and talk to fans. I was going to go over and tell him how his music inspired me to join the army and go adventuring and to thank him. I got in line, but then thought it would sound weird so I stepped out of line and we left. It was enough to just be there.
[3] My model-building friend Mark enlisted the year after I did and became a paratrooper. My cousin Tommy joined the Navy Reserve, while my Costigan cousins (Billy's sons) Patrick and Billy Jr. enlisted a few years after that. Patrick became a radio specialist while Little Billy, who was five years older than me, also became a paratrooper. On one of his earliest jumps he was injured and was mustered out. He spent the rest of his life on a disability.
[4] Warning, your experience may differ.

Social unrest was growing. Television shows like *All in the Family*, *Good Times*, *Mary Tyler Moore*, and even *Rowan and Martin's Laugh In*, mixed social commentary not only on the war, but on race relations and women's equality. College students were protesting the war by marching on their campuses. Violence was breaking out as the anti-communist older generation clashed with the younger anti-war generation who saw American involvement in places like Vietnam and Korea as insane and counterproductive. Mostly poor kids were drafted while rich White kids could easily get deferments or bribe a local doctor to say you had a condition that disqualified you. Clashes between anti-war protesters and the authorities were becoming common. At Kent State University in Ohio, students were shot down by National Guard troops who were mostly the same age. Sitting in front of the television, my father would sometimes make remarks about the 'hippies.'

He saw the younger generation as a disappointment. He had served why didn't they? They were just layabout drug addicts who didn't want to grow up. When that lifestyle invaded his family it made him even angrier. The actions of such groups as the Black Panthers, the Weathermen, and others were committing violence across the country—in ways that these members saw as acts of righteous outrage against the war in Vietnam, gender and racial inequality, and an immoral government. These were people and movements my dad never really understood.

My father's attitude to the Vietnam War and the hippies began to change when he saw how many veterans were leading the anti-war cause. Despite being a Nixon Republican, he was troubled by the Watergate scandal. The nation saw that the top leaders, including the president himself, could be lying, petty, vindictive criminals as much as any street thug. He also saw how close the war was coming to him. Fortunately, by the end of the 1960s and into the 1970s American involvement in Vietnam—thanks in large part to the anti-war movement and the hippies—began to end.

One morning in 1973, Henry came into my room and woke me up. Without saying a word, he hugged me and then left. He never did that sort of thing. It wasn't until some years later that I learned that morning they had announced on the radio that the last American troops had left Vietnam. It was one thing for him to support the American effort to stem the tide of Communism. As time crept by, however, as more and more young Americans were being killed for no apparent reason he changed his mind. It was becoming clear that his son might have to go to Vietnam, fight, and likely die. His politics changed. As a result, me announcing that I was going to solve all our problems by enlisting did not really go over well. He eventually saw I was determined so he supported me in my decision. Still, I know now that he couldn't bear to stand there as I walked off on that summer day. He left for work earlier than usual.[5]

Welcome to the 'G' kid…

Though I had officially enlisted at seventeen, I couldn't go on active duty until I had turned eighteen: which I did on June 25th, 1978. I decided to leave right after graduation from Kearny High. I was so happy about being done with high school that I even skipped the graduation.[6] Mom asked if I wanted a graduation party? I said no, I did not. I didn't want

---

[5] On the day I returned from basic training, wearing my dress uniform, he picked me up at Newark Airport. When he pulled into a parking space in front of the apartment, he blasted the horn to let everyone in the neighborhood know his son was home.

[6] I skipped my grammar school graduation as well. In fact, the only graduation I ever went to was my doctoral degree ceremony at Drew University.

anything more to do with that place or those people. I couldn't wait to get away.[7] I wanted to shed my high school experience like shedding a skin. I didn't want anything of it left. It was now June 28 and it was my reporting day. By 6 a.m. I sat on the edge of my bed dressed and ready to go. They told me to only bring a shaving kit—though I hadn't actually started shaving yet—so I only had to have a small bag: everything else would be provided once I had arrived at basic training.[8] Sherman sat at my feet looking up at me, his head on my thigh. I gave his ear a rub. At the appointed time I stood up, went out into the kitchen and said goodbye to my mother. We didn't have much to say to one another. We didn't hug. She stood on one side of the kitchen and I on the other. What she might have been thinking I hadn't a clue. We never really expressed our feelings in words in my family, certainly not my mother. She smiled and said, "good luck." I smiled back and said, "thanks, I'll write as soon as I can." As I was walking out the back door she said, "do good!" Other than M&D I didn't say goodbye to anyone. One day I was there, and the next I wasn't. No one noticed I was gone. No one ever noticed me anyway, even when I was there. I went down the quiet back steps of the apartment building with my little bag and walked past the reeking garbage cans all piled up in the alley for collection. I went around to the corner of Tappan and Devon Streets and stood there by myself. The sun had just come up. It was already hot. No one was around. I could hear Sherman up in the window sniffing for me. He knew I was going off on this adventure without him. I had been waiting for this day for a long time. It was my independence day. All strings were now cut. I had met all my obligations. I had made my bed and tidied my room. There was nothing to go back for. I was on my own and I liked it. It was a bit scary, but exhilarating. At this point, it would have been more difficult to go back then go forward. I wanted to change everything about myself, my clothes, my hair, my face. I didn't care for most of the people in my life. Now I was going to fill it with some new ones. I might not like any of them either, but at least they'd be different. Like Toby Tyler I was running away to join the circus and live a life of adventure.[9] Standing there on the corner I was filled with the overwhelming feeling that I was now…free.

Right on schedule, the sergeant recruiter picked me up and dropped me at the indoctrination center downtown. I spent the next few hours in the Newark Federal Building, being examined, poked, prodded, and injected. I filled out the first of what eventually seemed like a million pieces of paperwork I'd fill out over the course of my military career. At noon they put us, a little group of about six or so, in a van to Penn Station, and then onto a train to Kentucky. I was the last one to board the bus. As I did the army doctor who saw us off slapped me on the shoulder good naturedly and said, "Welcome to the 'G' kid!" Somehow, we wound up on a bus that in the late afternoon the next day finally pulled into the bus stop at the gate of tank school, of armoured cavalry school: Fort Knox. This was the place they filmed *Goldfinger* in 1965 and *Stripes* in 1980. There was a little open bus stop shed with a sign on the wall over a phone with no dial that said, "If you are a newly arrived recruit pick up this phone." We did and a voice said someone would be right over. They put us in an old style barracks you'd see in the movies. They verified who we were, fed us, and told us to get some

---

[7] In December of 1978 I had been in Germany for three months. I then received through the mail my high school yearbook. I looked through it. I saw all those people who had never really liked me or treated me well, who made fun of me or shunned me or made me feel bad about myself. I saw my picture, which I hated, and decided I never wanted to be reminded of this again. The first day off I had, after we returned from a three week bridging exercise, I took the yearbook for a walk into downtown Bamberg. Snow flurries were falling. It was two days before Christmas. The first bridge I came to that crossed the Regnitz River (which ran through the center of the city) I walked halfway across. Looking down into the dark water, I dropped in my yearbook. I walked back to the barracks smiling.
[8] Henry helped me pick out the shaving things. He introduced me to Barbasol shaving cream.
[9] *Toby Tyler, or Ten Weeks with a Circus*, 1960.

rest. There was about forty of us by now as other buses arrived.[10] Early the next morning, names were called, orders were barked, and other vans took us to brigade barracks. They separated us into the platoons we would be part of for the remainder of our training. Our drill sergeants introduced themselves by screaming and cursing at us. That's when the fun really began.

Delta Company, third battalion, first training brigade, D-3-1. That was my very first US army unit. The battalion had four companies of six platoons each; Alpha, Bravo, Charlie, and Delta. I went into the sixth platoon. My MOS, (Military Occupational Specialty), was 19F10 (nineteen, foxtrot, ten), tank driver, private. In my mind I was now a soldier-historian. We did the entire clichéd indoctrination: stand in line to have your head shaved, stand in line and fill out forms, stand in line to eat. Stand in line to stand in line, so you could then go stand in line.

Then the clothing line. At the end of a long concrete, cider-black building you stepped through a door and up to the first counter. You yelled out your last name. They checked off your name on the list then gave you a large duffel bag. You then side-stepped along from one counter to the next. Hats here, step down, pants here, step down, shirts here, two belts, and two pair of black leather combat boots. Green socks, underpants, and shirt, step down. Step down, step down, step down. Some guy measuring you. Lots of yelling. Then they sewed your name and 'US ARMY' on every shirt and your field jacket. As it was summer we stuffed the cold weather gear, leather gloves, field jacket, bunny ears wool cap, and rain coat down into the bottom of the duffel bag which they then painted your name on. At the end of the clothing line they had benches. We were told to sit here and get dressed into our work uniform for the first time. The uniforms were a solid, dull-olive drab—like everything else—with a baseball cap as head gear. When I foolishly asked the drill sergeant when would we get our black tanker berets his eyes almost bugged out of his head. "You ain't no tanker yet, boy!" he screamed. Another drill sergeant stood on a bench yelling orders at somebody, "put the underwear on first, idiot. Then the pants!"

As we dressed, the other drill sergeant came around to each of us and painted yellow dots on the back of the pair of boots we were not wearing. From then on we were to alternately wear the yellow dot boots and the non-yellow dot boots each day. Woe betide the 'crute' who fell out for roll call with the wrong pair of boots on. As I sat there buttoning my shirt, I noticed the guy next to me. Bobby Lee Newsom was from a little, destitute, stereotyped, rural Southern town outside Decatur, Georgia. He looked upset, even a little watery-eyed. I whispered to him, "you okay?" He sniffled, sat up straight, scowled and growled that he was fine. Later that day he came over to me and apologized for being gruff. "It's just," he said pointing down at his boots, "This is the first pair of brand new shoes I've ever had."

Over the next fifteen weeks along with military etiquette (including who to salute and who not to), we learned how to operate and repair tanks and armoured personnel carriers. It was great fun driving a tank. It was easier than I expected. We got to crash over walls and through mud puddles. They taught us how to negotiate ditches and trenches (always straight on, never at an angle). We learned how to neutral steer, which was when you made one track

---

[10] The end of June and early July were peak periods for the arrival of new recruits as it was right after high school graduation.

turn forward while the other turns backward. This allowed the tank to spin in a circle. If you know what you're doing you can make a tank behave like a ballerina. We learned to shoot pistols, shotguns, and machine and sub-machine guns of all types. It took me a while to acquire any proficiency with the 45 auto (the standard side arm for a tank crewmember). My hand shook so much when I tried to aim at a target and shoot I couldn't hit anything. I eventually did master it and even attained a rating of 'expert'. We learned how to throw a hand grenade, how to read a map, how to work a radio, and how to bandage a "sucking chest wound." They showed us how to stick a bayonet in someone's back, and to not punch with a closed fist, but to hit the opponent at the base of the nose with the heel of your hand, or in the neck with the side of the hand. We learned to survive in a nuclear and biologically contaminated environment.[11]

The technology stuff I found interesting, but the PE was rough. I was never a good runner and we did a lot of running. I never really had much upper body strength and so of course, we did about a million push-ups. You get into shape very quickly. As it was summer in Kentucky the heat and sunshine were intense. It made every object outside red hot including the apparatus we had to climb and swing from. Our drill sergeant loved to march us into a parking lot to do pushups on the boiling hot blacktop. I tore the flesh off the palms of my hands doing the overhead monkey bars, which we did several times a day every day. I didn't go on sick call. I surreptitiously took napkins from the mess hall and duck taped them around my hand to absorb the blood. When the drill instructor saw my improvised bandages he screamed—he was always screaming—"what the hell is wrong with your hands boy?" He tore the tape off and instead of sending me to the medic told me to go do more chin-ups. As I did, only then did I realize the upper part of the chin-up bars and monkey bars were covered in dried blood. I wasn't the only one losing skin. I didn't mention it to anyone. To show pain could be fatal. A real soldier, a real man we were told, works through it and doesn't complain. Very few went on sick call even when legitimately injured. Cuts, bruises, sprains, and worse all went unreported. One kid broke his thumb and didn't report it. One might have cracked his elbow, but didn't report it either. This was not empty bravado, it was survival. If you were injured you didn't complain. If you were sick you didn't complain. We saw the ridicule heaped upon the weak.

Walk it off, boy! Walk it off.

So, that's what I did too. Monkey see, monkey do.

We marched a lot: "left right, left right, left right." I still hear that in my head when I walk. We sang cadence songs as you marched:

"Standing tall and looking good ought to be in Hollywood…"

"I knew a girl in old Nairobi, If she was married she never told me…"

"Mama mama can't you see, what the army's done to me. They put me in a barber's chair, spun me around then I had no hair…"

---

[11] You were not really learning to fight, you were learning to kill.

"I met a girl in Madagascar, first I kissed her, then I asked her…" There were also lots of songs about a guy named Jodie, who seemed to be a real schmuck.

We did a good bit of our training at the Holder Armoured Reconnaissance Facility. It was a learning complex with classrooms and lecture halls, and what today would be called smart rooms. One of the things I liked about Holder was that in the auditorium sized lecture halls they had these huge, floor to ceiling, photo murals of black & white pictures of old tanks and armoured cars from the history of armoured warfare, on the walls. Those ancient, grinning, dust and dirt covered faces looked down on us like ghosts. One day, a week or so before we graduated, a general walked in and spoke to our company. He wore the slightly older green work uniform. These were made of cotton, rather than the polyester/cotton blend of our uniforms, and so could be starched. The edges of his sleeves and pants were so sharp they looked like you might cut your finger on them. He had seen action in Korea and Vietnam. His steely eyes looked out from under his black tanker's beret that held a single silver star.[12] He was thin and wiry and spoke with sharp, clipped sentences. "Men," he said, "Look at the faces in these pictures." He gestured to one ten foot tall photo, taken in the late 1930s, of an M1 combat car, which looked more like a rattle trap vehicle from old cartoons than a fighting machine. The crew were leaning out of the hatches looking at the camera. They wore those early tank helmets with the thick leather top shell so you wouldn't hurt your head on the sharp edges inside the tank. "Those men," the General went on, "they're our ancestors. They did their duty, now they expect you to do yours. We all know you will. I know you will. We tankers are all brothers now. Look at the man next to you. He's your brother and you're his." Then he thumped his fist against his chest. "You're my brother now too, and I'm yours!" I've always been cynical about stuff like this, but I have to admit, he seemed so serious and genuine I got caught up in it. We all screamed in unison, "Yes Sir! Armor, Sir!"

We learned all sorts of weird little behaviours, some I could never quite lose. I still instinctively never carry anything in my right hand because they taught us that, as tankers, you keep your pistol hand free at all times. In chemical warfare class I learned about 'frothy sputum' and how to tell the presence of nerve agents by their smell (the smell of almonds always brings me back to that). I can never just end something I'm doing, I have to make sure broken parts are fixed or replaced, and that everything is clean and put away in its proper place. I can't go to sleep if there are dirty dishes in the sink. Only then can I try to relax. I also learned what Grits were. They looked appetizing at first, sort of like mashed potatoes with sugar in them. They were not. There was a lot of southern food on the US army menu. I never cared for most of it.

They taught us that every button on your clothes must always be buttoned. If not it was 'push up time.' They taught us to pay attention to the state of our 'gig line.' This is the imaginary line from the pit of your nose down your chest along where your shirt buttons were through to the position of your belt buckle, then down along the zipper on your pants. If they all didn't line up it was 'push up time.' It was all about getting the details right. I still reflexively check my gig line to this day every time I get dressed.[13]

---

[12] One of the sources of our *Esprit de corps* was that armor and cavalry troops were allowed to wear black beret as a sign of our elite status. In the 1990s the black beret became the head gear for all US Army members. It took the specialness of it out for us. As reaction to that, cavalry units began to wear black cowboy hats.

[13] I still get annoyed when I see a guy wearing a hat indoors. They taught us that a real man always wears his hat outside, and takes his hat off indoors.

Each platoon had two drill instructors: one senior one junior. The senior, older drill sergeant didn't scream, but would frown scream. The junior drill sergeant screamed all the time. His eyes were always bloodshot. If he liked you he'd call you by your last name or some offensive nickname. If he didn't he called you 'Slick.' He always called me Slick. He was a real redneck. His treatment of me was the same as the way Sister Louise treated me, so it was nothing new. The main problem I had in basic training was keeping a straight face while he was screaming in my face. His eyes would bug out and he'd get all red. He wore a weedy little mustache that reminded me of Mr. Finger. He'd say all that stereotypical drill sergeant stuff:

"You're nothing but a piece of shit boy!"

"The best part of you ran down your momma's leg!"

"Are you some kind of queer faggot?"[14]

The insults were always sexual in some way, and weirdly obsessed with mothers. I had to exert a lot of energy to not smile at this. It was so absurd and over the top. I couldn't believe he was really saying it with a straight face. It was supposed to be intimidating, but to me it was just comical. Fortunately, I somehow retained my composure and simply stared straight ahead, which is the reaction you were supposed to have. In my platoon there were these three African American guys who were friends. Because one of them was very dark skinned the junior sergeant called him Dark Chocolate. One was lighter skinned and he called him Milk Chocolate, while the third was more light skinned and so called him White Chocolate. It went on like this all summer and into the fall.

At the conclusion of tank school the survivors were given their dress greens and orders to report to their first duty station.[15] I was headed to West Germany. Along with volunteering for combat arms I took an extra year of service so I could choose my first duty station along the Iron Curtain. I didn't join for a job, I joined for the adventure. I didn't want to be a clerk or a supply specialist. I was so naive I told the recruiter that I wanted to be in a front line unit, "where the action is." For this I received a signing bonus of a whopping $2,500.00 (as of 2019 the signing bonus for the same situation is $45,000.00).

Balance Beam Walking the Iron Curtain

After graduation from tank school, we received a week of vacation time before we had to report to our first duty stations. At the end of the week Henry had to drive me to John F Kennedy airport in New York in the middle of the night to get the *Flying Tiger's* flight to Europe that the army arranged. After the long, mostly silent drive to the airport in the dark, he came into the terminal with me. Just inside the big glass entry doors we stopped. I put down my duffle bag. I was in my dress uniform with my pants tucked inside my polished boots, black beret on my head with a single gold, Private stripe on it that I was so proud of. On the wall there was a giant poster of an airplane taking off that said, "Your adventure begins... NOW!"

We could see a little gaggle of guys in uniform near the ticket counter. At this hour the cavernous terminal was largely deserted except for a single maintenance man running a floor buffer. One of the airline people looked up and saw me. She smiled and waved me over. After a minute I took a breath and said to my father, "I guess I should go." We stood facing

---

[14] It's hard to believe, but all the screaming and physical assaults had a purpose: it was to teach you to remain calm under pressure. In a real situation your very survival, and that of your fellows, depends upon remaining calm.

[15] We started with six platoons of 40 individuals each. By the end that was down to about 30 each.

one another. I listened to the spinning pad on the floor buffer. He hugged me spontaneously for only the second time I could remember. We had never been able to look each other in the eyes, and I never knew why. I guess we were both afraid of what we'd see. He said quietly, "good luck, write your mother when you can." Then he turned and walked back towards the doors we had come through. I didn't want him to go. I wanted to tell him things. I wanted to say thanks for everything, but I didn't know how.

Neither of us could handle long goodbyes or intimacy like this. We would often come to an edge where we were about to say something meaningful to each other, then we couldn't quite make it. When we met again after today I would be a different person than the one leaving now. I wouldn't be a little kid anymore. He would never get to show me how to throw a ball again. He'd never drive me to the hobby shop again. This moment seemed like an ending. I hated the distance between us. I wanted to grab him and hold on forever, but I knew I couldn't. I had to go. We both knew I had to go. So we did what we always did, we just smiled awkwardly, swallowed the pain, and looked away. No more words were spoken.

The army rep was waiting and Pops knew I would be taken care of. He could leave and be stoically emotional in the car by himself on the long drive back home, and I could do the same on the plane on the long flight to Germany. We just could never figure out how do it together. After showing them my paperwork the airline rep led me and the others through the counter and into a hall that led to the plane. As I picked up my bag and went to follow I looked back one last time at the big glass doors. I could just see my father standing outside on the sidewalk of the terminal in the dark watching as I walked away. The red tail lights of my plane grew smaller as I flew away, while the red tail lights of his car faded as he drove off in the opposite direction.

Near the end of tank school in Kentucky I wrote my parents a letter trying to explain to them how much they meant to me. After I sent it I was wracked with the feeling I hadn't said it well enough or that they might not understand. They never mentioned receiving it, and I never asked. It wasn't until several years later that I learned Henry had taken my letter, put it in a little frame, and placed on their dresser. With at best mixed results, I've spent the rest of my life trying to be as good a man as him.

After the nine hour flight we arrived in Frankfurt, West Germany. Europe was very old, and I was very young. All newly arriving US troops were dropped into the replacement centre. I was assigned to Alpha Company of the 3rd Battalion of the 35th Armoured Regiment: the 3/35. It was part of the Bamberg Garrison (The Warner Barracks), 3rd (Bulldog) Brigade, 1st Armoured Division (Old Ironsides), VII Corps, USAREUR (United States Army Europe). As a result, I wore the 1st Armoured Division shoulder patch. There, I was put into the second platoon, tank number five.

Several of the guys I was with in basic training wound up there with me. I was glad to have familiar faces I liked. Our company commander was Captain J.D. Dunn. We were only a short drive from the East/West border separating NATO from the Warsaw Pact: the infamous Iron Curtain, the reason we were all here. It didn't dawn on me at the time, but 'The Wall' was just about the same age as I was. A few days after I arrived, Captain Dunn called me and the other newbies into his office to officially welcome us. On the wall was a large board with silhouettes of every vehicle in the company: seventeen tanks and about a dozen support vehicles. Each little cut out tank or truck had a spot to put the names of the men who served on that particular vehicle. Looking at the A25 I saw my name as driver already there in those plastic strip labels you made with the hand-held letter punch. Captain Dunn telling us what our unit's job was, snapped me out of my reverie. We trained to fight the end of the world, he said solemnly. Tank driving was our world and the end of the world was our trade.

They meant it.

Being in the 'front lines' we were expected to be at the battle ready 24 hours a day. Everything guarded with loaded weapons. All equipment ready to go at a moment's notice. Our tanks carried live ammunition on them at all times. It all had a serious air and sense of urgency to it. The higher ups were constantly telling us we could be at war at any moment.

My platoon mates included 'O.D.', 'The Walls,' 'Red Neck Shields,' and 'Gary P' (from Brooklyn, who was my best friend there). There was a Chicano kid who bragged about being a gang banger, another kid who clearly had emotional problems who turned out to be a self-cutter and was discharged on a Section 8, and Mustafa who was a Moslem from Iran who immigrated with his family to America just a few years before he enlisted. In the rest of the company there was one of those enormous guys from Samoa who insisted everyone call him 'Pineapple,' and Ronald Mitchel who was also from Newark who everyone called 'Chow Hound.' They came from every part of the country in all colors and religions. They were cocky, and full of enthusiasm and bravado, and utterly fearless in a way I envied because I wasn't. They were young, tough monkeys ready and willing to take on the world. They'd bare hand a Russian BMP for the fun of it then look at you and make a goofy face while they were doing it.[16] They reminded me of the guys I saw at the construction sites my father took me to when I was five years old.

Our tanks were the M60A1 Improved Rise/Passive MBTs (Main Battle Tank). The M60 series, for all its night sights, contamination protection, and high kill ability was still really Second World War technology taken as far as it could be taken.[17] It was in essence the last of the Super Sherman's. Our company had three platoons of five tanks each along with a headquarters platoon that had an additional two tanks: one for the company commander, and the blade tank. In addition, there were several jeeps for the company leadership, a trio of trucks made up as an all-purpose carrier, a tool truck, and an armory truck. There was an M113 armoured car (we called them cracker or cookie boxes because of their squarish shape) fitted up as a command and communication vehicle, and a Gama Goat, six wheeled all terrain cargo carrier. Assorted trailers, and finally an M88 heavy recovery vehicle (a sort of tracked, armoured tow truck) rounded out the stable. There were four tank companies (A, B, C, and D) in the battalion, along with a Headquarters Company—which had a mortar platoon, scout platoon, anti-aircraft defense platoon, maintenance and supply vehicles, the mess platoon, and a pair of AVLBs (Armoured vehicle launched bridge). The battalion was integrated and organized as a self-sufficient unit able to go anywhere at a moment's notice, and survive independently or as part of the larger brigade and division and Corps. It was not something you would have wanted to be on the receiving end of.[18]

---

[16] A BMP was a Russian built, full tracked, armoured personnel carrier widely used by Warsaw Pact forces.

[17] The first in the series was simply M60. Then there was the M60A1, then the strange M60A2 that had an unusually shaped turret to hold the short barreled 152mm gun/rocket launcher. The M60A2 was not a particularly successful vehicle and was eventually removed from service. Finally, there was the M60A3 that was an improved version of my M60A1. The new M1 Abrams was just entering the design phase as I enlisted.

[18] We always had an M163 Vulcan anti-aircraft vehicle assigned to our company in the field for close support. The M163 was a cracker box with a specially designed turret containing a 30mm Gatling gun. To keep things simple, their radio call sign was always just, 'Duckhunter.' The armoured ambulance (another modified cracker box) assigned to us was always, 'Bandaid.'

The uniforms, personal weapons, and other gear we wore and carried, while modern, were little different from what my father had worn in Korea and what Uncle Mike wore in World War II. I carried the same 45 caliber pistol, the venerable M1911A1 Colt 45 automatic, as Henry did. The sub-machine guns we were issued, the M3 known commonly as a 'Grease Gun' from its resemblance to the mechanic's tool, were used in WWII. Our CVC helmets— the helmet with a microphone and earphones for talking on the radio—were upgraded versions of the ones Henry and Mike wore.[19]

Every job in the US Army has a nickname. Infantry, for example, are Ground Pounders, artillery were Cannon Cockers, and maintenance people were Monkey Wrenches. Tankers were either Tread Heads or Doggies. Most of our tanks had nicknames. There was *Sure Shot*, *Spirits in the Night*, *Opps Upside Ya Head*, *Yo Mamma*, and others. Every conceivable girl's name: *Angeline*, *Tanya*, and *Bridget*. A fan of the band The Cars called his tank *Candy-O*. The command tank was, *Armoured Cow*. The blade tank was simply, *Dog*.[20] The A25 didn't have a name so I decided to give it one.[21] I went to the company motor sergeant for some stencils and black paint. My TC, Sergeant Moore, didn't care what name I chose. Arranging the three-inch tall, metal letters in the right order and taping then to the side of the turret, I slathered black paint on them. I carefully peeled off the stencils and admired my handiwork: *Dreamboat Annie*.[22]

Not everything was so serious. You could also go into town when you weren't on duty. The closest civilian club to the entrance to the garrison was called *Les Marquis*. It had a restaurant in the front and a dance club in the back. German girls looking to land an American husband would go there as would other young Germans who just wanted to work on their English or meet Americans. I went once in a while and danced very badly with a girl or two and got drunk like my dad going into Mexico when he was in Texas. Up the road from the tank park was a bar restaurant run by the army called the *Rod & Gun Club*. It was much more 'American' and felt like a VFW Hall or Adirondack cabin. They had decent food and it wasn't too expensive. Because the senior sergeants would hang out there to sit at the bar and get drunk all night the younger guys called it the *Rod & Bottle*. It reminded me of *Lancers*.

Vincere Vel Mori!

As we were the first line of defense against Commie aggression, we were often roused from our sleep by 'alerts.' These only ever seemed to happen between 3 and 5 in the morning. All the lights would suddenly come on and we knew what was happening. We'd have to roll out of our bunks, quickly get dressed and head down to the basement to the 'sensitive items' room to get our chemical warfare gear, then to the armory to pick up our pistols, shotguns, submachine guns, and assault rifles. As we were considered front line troops, we kept all the heavy machine guns in the tanks along with the main gun ammunition and our personal

---

[19] CVC – Combat Vehicle Communications.

[20] This is a tank with a bulldozer blade on the front of it. Every tank company had one.

[21] Rules about naming vehicles varied by the unit. It was common that some commanders insisted that the name had to start with the first letter of the company designation: All tank names begin with a 'B' if in Bravo Company, for example. There was no such rule in the 3/35.

[22] Captain Dunn was an unusually free spirit for a West Point graduate. So that his tanks stood apart from all the others in Western Europe, he made custom recognition plaques for each one. He had plywood cut to 1x2 foot pieces. They painted them black with a bright yellow vertical stripe separating the board into half. In each half section there would be a series of yellow dots. For example, my tank had two dots in the left half (second platoon) and five dots in the right half (tank five). The whole effect was to look like dominoes. They hung off the bustle rack of each tank so you could see them from behind.

equipment. Half asleep, and some half in the bag from a night out, we would then trudge to the track park and get the vehicles ready to go. You didn't want to be late to the end of the world.

We would get the engines fired up, mount the machine guns, put our personal gear in the turret bustle rack, get the radio antennas mounted, spin the turrets around into combat position and wait for the signal to move.

What most people don't realize is that tanks and other armoured fighting vehicles cannot go into action on their own. They need a literal army of support vehicles. They need fuel trucks and ammunition trucks and maintenance vehicles. The brigade had a fleet of tactical transports called GOERs. They were large, odd looking, four wheeled beasts. Some were cargo carriers others were fuel tankers. They looked like a moon buggy that Major Matt Mason might drive. They were incredibly ungainly and difficult to operate, and had a tendency to crash if the driver wasn't paying attention. The advantage was they could go almost anywhere. Without them, and the men and women who manned them, there was no army. Truck drivers and maintenance personnel often get overlooked or dismissed as of lesser importance: there are few movies about the glories of being a fuel truck driver or supply clerk. You can have the best tank in the world, but if you can't keep it fueled and armed, all you have is sixty tons of scrap metal.

We also had the occasional 'Health and Welfare' checks. Like an Alert, we'd be rousted from out beds at 4 or 5am and made to go downstairs to the basement corridor to sit around and wait. The officers, and sometimes MPs, would search our rooms for contraband. They were looking for drugs. Pot smoking was fairly common. Occasionally cocaine or a German over the counter diet drug called X112 that affected you like speed. Only the dimmest potheads kept their stash in the barracks. One guy I knew kept his in the rusty tailpipe of the old Sherman tank on display in front of the barracks.

We were often reminded that our job in the 3/35 (and all the other units with us in West Germany) was to die. We were told this in those words. As each new soldier arrived, we were made to write goodbye letters to our families. These would then be kept in Washington (they told us) and sent out once we were all dead from fighting the Russians. They expected WWIII to involve vast hordes of Russian and Warsaw Pact forces bursting across the border on their way to the French or Spanish coast. It was our job to throw ourselves under this juggernaut and rather than stop them, which they considered all but impossible, we were meant to slow them down just long enough for reinforcements to arrive from France, the UK, Canada, Australia, and mainland US. We thought of ourselves grimly as "twenty minute men." That meant from the moment the "balloon went up" (war began) we had about twenty minutes to live. We were told we would die in large numbers and that the wounded would drown in a sea of radioactive blood. Bamberg sat on highway 70 that headed east towards Czechoslovakia thirty miles off. We were to barrel down that highway at the enemy. Once we got going—if the rockets and nukes we knew already targeted our barracks hadn't vaporized us—we were expected hold preselected positions and let the Soviet T-72 tanks come at us in waves. We would likely use up most of our ammunition before the last of us were shot to pieces.

I don't know why all this didn't affect us more. I guess it was because we were all so young. We thought we were invincible. While the senior leadership did, we never took any of it seriously. We knew the reality, but did not dwell on it. Our training instilled that idea in us. Those Commies would never get me and *Dreamboat Annie*. I never lost sleep thinking about it. In fact, all the fear and constant shaking I experienced as a kid had vanished. I no longer had the anxiety attacks. I could talk to girls. I no longer bashed my head into walls in frustration. I felt confident. Even some of the other guys in my company who liked to act tough only made me laugh at their absurd behavior or their occasional attempts to intimidate me. The shaking and head banging only returned when I was in my forties.

When the alert was invariably called off we would have to put all that stuff back so we could be released to go about our everyday duties. This also allowed us to dash to the mess hall. On my first alert in 1978 I was carrying equipment out of the barracks to go up to the track park. I had already retrieved my weapon. I had a belt holster with my pistol in it (I had yet to learn that a shoulder holster was much less cumbersome). I left plenty of slack in the belt so the holster was down by my thigh gun fighter style. I thought it looked cool that way. As I went down the stairs to pass through the double doors to head outside I heard from behind me. "Hey! Hoot Gibson!" I turned around to see the company First Sergeant standing at the top of the stairs looking grim. He pointed at my pistol belt. "Cinch that thing up right. Who the hell do you think you are?" I took a big gulp. "Okay, Top, sorry."[23] I put my stuff down then fixed the belt cinching it up so it hung like a regular belt at the proper height. He stood there the whole time watching. "We're soldiers, not clowns," he said then turned and went about his way. A great deal of energy went into teaching us that there were ways a professional handled firearms. They were not toys. Anyone who showed off, or waved their weapons around, or God forbid, pointed them at someone would receive a severe reprimand, and even the loss of rank.[24]

I had that problem my entire time in the service. I was always looking for little ways to be different in a sea of conformity. I was always getting yelled at for letting my hair grow too long. On our field caps we were supposed to wear our rank and our unit crest. I often went without the unit crest just to be different. Our crest was a little shield with an armadillo on it. The motto in French read 'Vincere Vel Mori' (Victory over Death). Originally constituted in 1941, the 35th had fought in WWII in the Rhineland, Ardennes-Alsace, and others with distinction. The battalion's tattered guidon flag was festooned with battle ribbons. It was treated with reverence as if it were a religious relic. When an honour guard ceremonially brought the guidon to the stage where the battalion or brigade commander was for some formal unit meeting, it would be carried with the same solemnity as they carried the statue of Mary in St. Cecelia's. We called the figure of the armadillo, the Armoured Dildo.

In the field we lived on our tanks. We never pitched tents even though we carried them. The four-man crew included the TC (tank commander), gunner, loader, and driver. The first three lived in the turret, while the driver had the forward hull compartment to themselves. Tanks are not exactly built for comfort, but an experienced crew could make it liveable. There were places you could stretch out on the turret floor, on top of the turret or the back deck, if

---

[23] First Sergeants are the highest ranking enlisted man in a company. They are often called by nicknames such as 'Top Sargent' or often just 'Top.' Sometimes they were called 'Top Kick' because they kicked you in the ass. Less often they might be called the 'First Shirt.' Their rank emblem was three pointed stripes on top, three curved stripes, or rockers, on the bottom, and a diamond in the center.

[24] On an exercise after I had been in Germany about a year, a newbie loader left his submachine gun on the fender of his tank while we were parked along a secondary road. It disappeared and everyone went ballistic. The loss of a weapon was serious business. The entire company ground to a halt to look for it and a swarm of MPs showed up. After an hour or so they found it in the possession of a German kid and his friends who were playing in the woods with it. The newbie who lost it was shaking so bad in fear he could barely control himself. He spent the next few months on perpetual guard duty and was late getting promoted.

the weather was good. The tanks had internal heaters for when the Hawk was about.[25] You quickly learned how to live on one of these things. During long road marching the TC would sit on the swing out seat inside the cupola. As the seat wasn't very comfortable you'd alternate by standing on the platform just under the seat. When I was filling the loader job I'd adjust the seat so I could stand in the loader's hatch with my head just poking out with my arms folded resting on the top of the turret. I could then rest my chin on my arms. A good driver could control the direction of the tank with almost imperceptible touches of the steering bar (called a 'T Bar' because of its shape). When maneuvering cross country, you stood and learned the rhythm of the undulating tank like when a bird sits on a branch swaying in the wind. In the field the turrets would be covered in bags and boxes of personal gear. The brigade commander was always yelling about how the tank crews carried so much stuff festooned on the vehicles. He tried, without success, to establish protocols for exactly where on a tank the crew could keep their personal gear (there was already a protocol for where all tools and other equipment were kept). He often grumbled about how when the 3/35 went into the field, which meant driving around in German towns and villages and highways amongst the civilian population, we went "looking like gypsies."

Each tank carried four or five boxes of C-Rations usually kept in the turret bustle next to the radio. Each of these boxes had twelve meals. Each box was a different meal of metal cans all painted green. There was tuna fish, spaghetti and 'beef chunks' (which for me was the worst of the set because while the spaghetti was fine, the beef chunks looked like road kill, and tasted awful), turkey that looked like mostly skin and necks, and the perennial favourite, hot dog chunks and baked beans that we called 'Beenee Weenies.' Each meal came with salt and pepper packs, awful instant coffee, a sugar pack, a tiny cake in a can (everyone wanted the pound cake, few wanted the chocolate cake, and no one wanted the fruit cake), and peanut butter and jelly with crackers. Finally, some meals contained chocolate and toffy disks that were so hard that we called them John Wayne Bars, because you had to be a real hero to eat them.

We only ever ate the C-Rations unless we had nothing else. When we loaded up to go into the field we always brought grocery bags full of commercially available food. Loaves of bread, cold cuts (if it was winter), and cans of Campbell's soup, *SpaghettiOs*, and other canned goods, and a case of sodas. In the field we would trade our C-Rations for beer when we were stopped for a while, and the requisite groups of German kids would show up to gawk at the vehicles.

You learned to live close with others in a tank. It didn't matter what color skin or religion the other guys in your crew were, whether they were straight or gay, it didn't matter (in the 3/35 we had several guys who were recent immigrants from Iran, and Moslems). You learned what an unwashed body smelled like after three weeks without showers. You didn't flinch as you road marched down a highway while one of your crewmates stood on the fender of the tank, going 25 mph, holding onto the grunt rail with one hand, holding himself with the other, urinating over the side because you couldn't stop for such things when you had to get somewhere: and it was snowing. You learned to not say "eww" as someone squatted behind a tree to defecate, and sometimes not behind a tree. You had no problem with drinking from the same cup or eating from the same plate using the same utensils. You had to learn to depend on

---

[25] The heaters on an M60 were mounted in the driver's compartment. They burned diesel fuel from a line off the fuel pumps. They were notoriously temperamental, and always a pain to get running. They were incredible loud when running and had two settings: high and low. There was little difference in actual temperature between the two. They were lava hot or nothing.

each other.

In the field it was the First Sargent's job to make sure everyone was fed. He had a jeep with a little two wheeled trailer with a custom built box over the top that always looked to me like Snoopy's doghouse, but in camouflage green. Each company also had a mess truck that was a regulation Deuce and a Half with another custom built box filling the carry bed. It then pulled a large two wheeled mess wagon which folded out to become an even larger kitchen like something Willey Coyote might build. They would cook food, scoop it into 'Mermite Cans' (sort of large thermos bottles), and Top would then drive around to find us so we could have a hot meal. They often made Sloppy Joe's, macaroni and beef or something similar. It was easy to make and transport and we mostly liked it.

It was a week before Christmas of 1978, and I was on my very first field mission: a bridging exercise where we captured a spot on the Regnitz and forced our way across by using a temporary bridge the engineers put up. Europe is crisscrossed with rivers and, if the balloon went up we would have to capture and cross many of them or keep the Warsaw Pact from capturing and crossing them. Once the infantry secured the area the combat engineers came in and assembled the bridge with as much haste as possible. Then, our tank battalion raced down to cross. I had never driven across one of these bridges before so my TC Sargent Moore had me drive for the experience. Our platoon swung down to cross. As I drove up and the tracks of *Dreamboat Annie* began to mount the metal bridge ramp I saw off to the side a deuce and a half with a broken back. It seemed a surreal scene. It had just given out from overuse.[26]

Two men were standing there staring at it as if they stared long enough the truck would miraculously become unbroken. Snow was just starting to pile up in little crevices on the vehicle. We couldn't stop to help, others would do that. We had to get across. The bridge groaned and rattled and made loud, metallic creaking sounds. You could feel it undulating up and down in the water. We were trained to do this as fast as we could. Our battalion commander was always telling us, "Hesitation kills! Hesitation kills!" After twenty seconds or so we bounced down the other side onto dry land then up the hill to join the fray.

Later that day we pulled onto wedge-shaped position in a large farmer's field and waited for the opposing forces to attack. We had been in the field for two weeks, and there had been a problem with the mess truck. They kept giving us ham and cheese sandwiches to eat. By the third day of the ham and cheese, I couldn't take it anymore (I had eaten all my store bought food because I had yet to learn how much to bring). The First Sergeant drove up next to us to deliver lunch. He had a trailer full of sandwiches. I climbed down to pick them up.
"Oh, come on Top," I said in despair as he opened the back of his trailer.
"What?"
"I hate ham and cheese; I can't take any more ham and cheese!"
"Well, that's all we have."

"Okay," I said disappointedly and just stared at the sandwich which was in one of those little wax bags, turning it over and over slowly. He was about to get in his jeep to drive over to the next position when he stopped. Our tank, and his jeep, and all of us, were standing in mud. It was cold, and everything was wet. I was wearing about a hundred layers of cold

---

[26] We put huge amounts of were and tear on our vehicles. We repaired ours endlessly, but sometimes a truck or a jeep, like an exhausted old person, would break down to the point where you couldn't fix them anymore. It always seemed to me like they consciously laid down to die, and had decided the world could just go to hell.

weather gear including the wool cap with the long fuzzy bunny ears under my CVC helmet. Snow flurries were falling. He pulled a wrapped sandwich out of his own pack, handed it to me, and roughly grabbed the ham and cheese from my hand and put it back into his trailer with the others. Without saying another word, he got in his jeep and they drove off. I unwrapped the sandwich and saw it was peanut butter and jelly. I never forgot that little act. It taught me how a real leader is supposed to look out for their people. After that, I would never let anyone bad mouth him when he wasn't around. Luckily, the next day we headed back to the barracks for the holidays.

Knowing How to Talk to People

Our secondary duty was to patrol the Iron Curtain. The 2/2 Cav across the street had that as their main function, but when they went off on maneuvers or fire exercises we filled in for them. When you did this you lived in little forward camps just a short drive from the actual border. They looked like something out of an old movie: log cabins in the pines surrounded by barbed wire. We would go off in jeeps and do walking patrols. You carried all of your firearms, ammunition, and protective masks.

As we were in the place we were, the Russians spied on us quite a bit—just as we spied on them. The Russians had these special cars that were allowed to drive around in West Germany and watch NATO troop movements. They were known as Soviet Military Liaison Mission cars. SMLM (we pronounced it smell'um) were groups of four or five guys who would follow field operations and take pictures, though they had supposedly strict orders not to get too close to us. We were all issued these little pocket guides with instructions on what to do if we encountered a SMLM vehicle. We were never to talk to them or get into altercations with them. If we saw one we were to call up to higher headquarters and they'd send out intelligence officers to deal with it. One time we were doing a joint border patrol operation with the British. We occasionally did joint operations with West German, Dutch, and British troops. We were on the border and doing a joint patrol. This gave the different national units a chance to see the areas of operation of the other NATO countries. On this day I found myself in the back of a mutt following along with a British jeep. The British troops were great guys. We spent the day laughing and exchanging stories. The man leading this little group was an English Sargent named O'Rourke. It seemed like he stepped out of one of those old movies. His uniform was impeccable. His entire demeanor was of a hyper professional soldier, but also one enjoyed himself immensely, thank you very much.

We drove into a little town and dismounted to stretch our legs. It was a sunny day. There was an ice cream vendor across the street and I was looking forward to a cone. Just then a SMLM car came around the corner and stopped directly across the street from us. I could see the guy in the back had a camera and was snapping away at us. The sergeant, hands clasped behind his back, calmly walked over. He leaned down and said, as the driver rolled down the window a few inches, "Sorry gent-el-min, you can't be here, you need to turn around and go back. There's a good fellow." The four agents in the car just chuckled and said something, I'm sure was derogatory, in German. Little did they know that sergeant O'Rourke spoke fluent German. The five of us now walked over to back him up. Without missing a beat, still leaning down and smiling, he repeated his command in German. The driver then said something, maybe in Russian or Czech and laughed sinisterly. He then rolled the window down a little more and spit on the sergeant's uniform. In perfect calm and under perfect control, Sergeant O'Rourke took a half a step backward, looked at the front of his uniform. He yanked the door of the car open, then grabbed the driver by his collar and dragged him out of the car.

I had no idea what to do.

You weren't supposed to assault these guys no matter what they said to you. My officers hadn't told me what to do in a situation like this. The other agents in the car started to get out, but we glowered at them so they stayed put. O'Rourke picked the man up, "Be careful, Suh, you'll get urt that way." He brushed off the man's suit jacket and put him back in the driver's seat. He closed the door, and still smiling cheerfully, said, "Now, off you go. There's a good follow." Cursing, they drove away.

By now I was standing next to the Sergeant Major. He never went for his sidearm, he never raised his voice. I must have looked a little bewildered at what just happened. He smiled and said, "Not to worry Lad, sometimes you just have to know how to talk to people."

The border wall—sometimes called the Iron Curtain—ran from the North Sea down to the Alps. In places, it was heavily fortified with a physical wall, loops of barbed wire, ravenous dogs and land mines all on the Eastern side. Despite this, there were places where there was no wall at all. In the area I patrolled it was a bit misleading. The Wall was not built right on the literal border, it was set back a distance from there. The actual border line in these places was marked by little more than plastic traffic cones and concrete bollards. In the wooded areas you couldn't see the wall with the razor wire, the dogs and landmines. It seemed almost peaceful as if there was no Wall.

We were not allowed to cross the border under any circumstances though sometimes we did. We could only approach the border line on foot or in wheeled vehicles. We were not allowed to bring tracked vehicles within a certain distance of the border. At that distance there were large metal signs reminding you that it was '50 Meters to the Border.' On one occasion I was in a walking patrol. These were intelligence gathering activities though we hardly ever saw or did anything unusual.

On another patrol we did heard voices and mechanical sounds in the woods very close to where we were walking. We stealthily moved towards it weapons drawn. When we came to a clearing we saw four East German border guards with a jeep. This was a wooded area with the traffic cones rather than a proper wall. They had the hood up and were poking around the engine. Then we heard that tell-tale sound of trying to get an engine running without any success. Grrr, grrr, grrr…nothing…grrr, grrr, nothing. They looked up at us and there was a moment of tension. We were all armed to the teeth and nervous about each other. My sergeant, who spoke some German, broke the spell by jokingly asking if they were having car trouble. That relieved the tension. We holstered our pistols then walked over—crossing the border in contravention of all of our rules—and helped them finally get the jeep started. It was a clogged carburetor. We then all decided to have lunch. We broke out all our food on the hood of their jeep and enjoyed a warm sunny, spring day. We were not antagonists, we were not enemies, we were a bunch of teenagers and twenty-somethings working on an old car on a Sunday afternoon in a park. The talk was about cars.

As we stood there eating I noticed something about the East German soldiers. Their uniforms seemed old and shabby. Their equipment was not of good quality. Our uniforms were brand new. Our equipment was all new and well taken care of. We had lots of food, they didn't. We had just been paid so I had a large wad of cash in my pocket. When we finally left I felt so badly for one guy I gave him ten dollars. He was very grateful. That money was a monthly salary for him. It was how much I spent on a couple of beers at *Les Marquis*. These guys and their cohorts were not planning on invading the west, they did not want to kill me or my family. They were barely able to feed their own families. All the stuff about the Communist threat I had been taught as a kid, all the air raid drills, Duck & Cover, all the political speeches, the propaganda, the thinly veiled movies, it was all bull. I realized we had been lied to.

My time in West Germany is what made me a political animal. Up to that point I really didn't care much for politics. Seeing what went on there and how I was lied to so much about why we were there made me genuinely angry. I was told that hordes of Commie-Ruskie, bogeymen were waiting to cross the border and kill us all and steal our moms and rape our dogs. There may have been members of the ruling elite who wanted to invade and destroy the West, but the troops on the ground couldn't even get their jeep to run. I never thought about politics the same way again.

When we weren't playing footsy with the bad guys on the border we were on field exercises where we practiced battling the bad guys. War games took up most of our field time. Ten months out of every year we were out in the field on exercises. Bridging exercises 'Bridgex's, blocking exercises, Reforger and, several times a year, live fire missions to Grafenwöhr.[27] It was fun. We'd drive around the countryside, through little German villages. People would come out and wave and we'd wave back. If it was German girls we'd wave with extra enthusiasm. Once during the winter our company was road marching through a little town when our tank began to slide on the black ice (I was not driving). Once 55 tons gets sliding on its own there's nothing you can do but hold on and ride out whatever happens. We slid then the tank hit the sidewalk and stopped us. Unfortunately, it did not stop us in time to keep the tank's gun tube going through the wall of a Gasthaus. In another incident our platoon sergeant's tank slid down the side of a grassy knoll. The incline wasn't even that great, but when it hit a little gully at the base the entire tank rolled over. Luckily SFC Rodriguez and his crew were able to duck inside and ride it out. No one was injured, but they needed the company's M88 heavy recovery vehicle to come pull the tank right side up then take it back to the shop for repairs.

Maneuver exercises lasted anywhere from one to three weeks. We road marched relentlessly back and forth across Germany in all weather, from sunshine to rain to heat to snow, and at all hours of the night and day. The sound of the tanks rolling down the Autobahn at speed was quite distinctive: a combination of metallic clacking and squeaking. This was produced by the tracks being a collection of metal and rubber parts held together by steel pins and collars. I still hear it in my sleep. Anyone who ever did this will always recognize the sound instantly. The hypnotic hum of the highway followed us like background music as we travelled from one place to another. We were getting used to the terrain and where things were. That way when Ivan came we might be able to hold them off for a little while. That sound will follow me into the afterlife.

> I am a passenger
> I ride and I ride
> And I ride and I ride...[28]

---

[27] Pronounced Grafen-veer.
[28] Iggy Pop. 'The Passenger,' *Lust for Life*, 1977.

Werewolves in the Black Forest

While on an exercise the spring after I arrived we had stopped along the edge of a forest. After letting the engines run for a minute to cool we all shut down and adopted a battle quiet posture. To the right of our line was a large open field bordering on woods. To our left, right up against our track, was another wood, much thicker than the one to our right. You could only see in about twenty yards before it became too wooded to see any further in. When you stopped like this the first thing you did was dismount and check the vehicle. You would check the road wheels to see if they needed grease, and do a quick inspection of the tracks. One person always had to stay on the radio and it was my turn. As the TC and the others went about it I sat in the loader's hatch. I could hear the occasional crackle of radio messages, but otherwise all was still. The woods began to hypnotize me and I wanted to see more. I climbed out of the loader's hatch and all the way up to the top of the commander's cupola.[29] My feet straddled the armoured housing for the TC's periscope. I was now about fifteen feet above the ground. I faced into the thick woods. I had never encountered trees like this before in New Jersey. As a city kid the closest thing to this landscape, I had ever seen were the trees in the park I played in. I had never seen a forest so dark and skies so clear. I stared into it caught up in the romance of the Black Forest. The entire place was deathly quiet and there was no air moving. The sun was shining brightly and the sky was painfully blue, but none of that penetrated the woods. I began to get an inkling of how monster stories could begin when people had to deal with places like this. I could imagine all sorts of wild things watching me from just a few feet away. At that moment the platoon sergeant came walking down the line of tanks making sure everything was in order. He looked up and saw me and stopped. In heavily Spanish accented English he asked me what I thought I was doing? I looked down and said, "I'm checking for werewolves." His face never changed its serious expression. He replied, "okay" then resumed walking. I then thought I heard a low cry of sadness coming from deep in the forest. It may have been a warthog, or likely my imagination, but I wanted to think it was sad werewolf mourning the loss of its mate.

We practiced the maneuvers we would need to perform in order to engage with the Russians. One day our platoon was assigned to guarding an intersection in a small German village. As we often did, to stay out of the street we backed our tank into the driveway of a house there. It was a good position. We could back in and turn our turret to face the intersection and shoot any bad guys that tried to come through. As we did, an elderly German man came out of the house. We thought he was going to chase us away, but he smiled and waved. As we were going to be there all day. We climbed down to do the usual road maintenance on the tank. The old grandpa began telling us in broken, but understandable English how he had been the commander of a Panzer IV during the war. As I had built Panzer 4's as models I was interested and we chatted amiably. After a few minutes his wife came out with what must have been the prized family silverware. A large highly polished tray with the handles at either end, a large silver coffee pot and a smaller tray of cookies. Sergeant Moore eagerly took some coffee. As I had never learned to drink coffee I had cookies. The next day we were ordered on to a new position. As we were about to leave the old gentleman, former Nazi tank commander, came out and handed us a case of beer in bottles. We made a half-hearted attempt to say "no thanks," but then we gladly accepted his hospitality. We put the case under a tarp on top of the turret and drove off with some anticipation for later that night.

---

[29] On an M60A1 the commander had a cupola, which was like a smaller version of the main turret. It could turn independently of the main turret and had a short barreled M85 fifty caliber machine gun mounted in it.

After several blocks as we passed out of the town there was a sharp turn. The battalion Sergeant Major was parked there in his jeep watching as the tanks went by. Making the tight sudden turn the plastic case of beer bottles fell on its side. Sargent Moore and I managed to grab them, but two bottles got past us. One fell onto the back deck while the other fell on the side fender. Both bottles exploded and beer and bright white foam went everywhere. This all happened just as we drove past the Sergeant Major, who scowled at us in such a way that could have burned through the side of the tank. I don't know how or why, but we never did get called on it. These sorts of things were fairly regular occurrences.

One night we scrambled to our forward positions. It was December of 1979 (these thing always seemed to happen in December), and there were a few inches of snow on the ground. We pulled into positions in the woods while a cavalry group slipped quietly in behind us. As it started to snow again we waited. Nothing much happened, but we sat there waiting for the end of the world. By three in the morning we were taking shifts to get some sleep and it was my turn to do radio watch. The rest of the crew of my tank were asleep. I stood with my head up and out of the loader's hatch just enough for my eyes to look over the edge. The falling snow made everything quiet and it was pitch black. Then I thought I heard the sound of many engines off on the distance. My mind began playing tricks on me. I thought they were getting closer. If the Russians did attack, their approach would sound just like this. I looked through the binoculars to see if anything was out there in the dark. For an instant I thought I did see some movement, but then it was gone. The Russians were not coming tonight. I had a small cassette player on just loud enough for me to hear. Al Stewart's *Time Passages*. Buy me a ticket on the last train home tonight…[30] By 4 am someone, somewhere had remedied whatever crisis had provoked this alert and we were instructed to 'Index to Base Station.' In other words, go back to the barracks.

Another night without a nuclear holocaust. At least I would know how to describe it when it came. I went to NBC school in Germany. Nuclear, Biological, and Chemical warfare school. I then went through it again in Kansas. I saw the infamous 'Goat Film' that, as far as I know, has never been seen by the public. As a result, I can say that I know what it looks like to watch a living thing vaporize in a nuclear blast. The results of those tests helped doctors devise strategies for treating people with radiation poisoning. One of the things you're taught in NBC school is how to estimate the explosive yield of a nuclear bomb. If you saw an atom bomb go off in front of your position, you were to take off one of your dog tags and hold it up to the mushroom cloud. By comparing the relative size of the cloud to your dog tag you could estimate mega tonnage. You would then call in this information to your higher headquarters. Unfortunately, if you were that close to a nuclear bomb going off you would not be able to call your higher headquarters because as you tried you and your radio would be melting.

Why We Were There

Ostensibly, the reason I and everyone in the 3/35 and every other American, British, Canadian, French, Dutch, and German soldier were there was to prevent the Russians and the Warsaw Pact from invading and capturing Western Europe. That was the big fear (we knew the wall was not to keep us out, but to keep eastern citizens in). At the end of WWII the allies had chopped-up Germany into spheres of influence and each one of the victorious allies took a piece. The eastern half went to the Russians who immediately set about taking control of all

---

[30] Al Stewart. *"Time Passages,"* Time Passages, (1979).

the Eastern European and Balkan countries they had liberated. It was supposed to be a temporary situation until Germany recovered. The Russians, however, had no intention of giving anything back. As a result, the year after I was born they began building the barrier that came to be known as the Iron Curtain. The term came into popular use as a symbol of the Russian wall after a speech by former British Prime Minister Winston Churchill given in Missouri in March of 1946. The wall itself went up in 1961 making it just a year younger than myself.

At home they told us that the Communists were getting ready to invade the West. Since I was a kid we were told this. We rehearsed air raid drills in school. Every Saturday at noon we heard the long whine of the air raid siren. Many of the science fiction films I watched on *Chiller Theater* as I prepared for my Saturday adventures were thinly veiled allegories of attacking Communists. The James Bond films, even Jonny Quest had the Cold War as the underlining narrative foundation. We heard the Emergency Broadcast System test on our radios and televisions: that annoying high-pitched scream after which a voice that told us, "This has been a test." Today that test is heard less. The voice says, "This has been a test. Had this been an actual emergency you would be informed where to tune in order to get further information." As kids we heard the voice say, "Had this been an actual emergency *probably an attack*, you would be informed where to tune…"

I was told us we lived in the best country in the world. When I turned away from the movies and television and looked out the window, however, I saw racial discrimination, gender inequality, religious hatred, oppression of gay people, and disrespect of the poor. I saw towering hypocrisy. I saw monsters running out of control. They told us this stuff, and we believed it. Now, face to face with the supposed enemy, I began to have my doubts.

When I arrived in Bamberg the wall had about a decade to live. We were this odd mass of men and women doing this odd job that no one back home seemed to know was being done. Even fewer cared. Few people ever knew how close we came to nuclear oblivion or how many times. The reality was we only knew in theory what we were doing.

One of the things rarely discussed in talking about the men and women who served in NATO in Western Europe, and indeed all the American military during this period, is their legacy. Members of the Army, Navy, Air force, Marines and the various guards trained to a razor's edge to fight an apocalyptic war that never happened. They were separate from those who served in Vietnam, and did not come into their own until after that conflict ended (though more than few had seen duty in Southeast Asia before coming to Europe). There are no monuments to the troops who 'fought' this part of the Cold War.

These troops, if they are remembered at all, stand as little more than historical placeholders caught in-between Vietnam and the various Gulf conflicts. They engaged in no pitched tank battles as they were told they would. They were not 'nuked' or gassed. They did not shed their blood in the huge quantities they were told to expect. They stood face to face with the Warsaw Pact, with the Russians, the ravenous monster everyone told them to be afraid of (the same enemy that some Western politicians cozied up to in the late twenty-teens). They were the bouncers who kept the belligerent drunks out of the club called Western Europe. They served when few others were willing to, and with little fanfare. They went, though there was no call. They stood at the ready watching for the balloon to go up. They waited for years and no luft balloons ever flew by. They are ghosts now with nowhere to haunt.[31] We were a ship of fools going nowhere and never realized it.

It's easy all these years later to look back on this and say, "well, since the Third World War never happened, there was never really any danger." I've had people say to me several times to my face that my service and the service of all those others really did not count (having served when I did, I was not allowed to join my local VFW Hall). That may be so, but in that moment, it was very real. A war was going to happen. It was not a maybe. We were the garrison at the edge of the empire. We were the sharp end of the sword. Like Roman Legionnaires we were there to preserve some muddled ideas of national relations. Some of those ideas were worthy while most had more to do with economics than liberty and freedom. For us the difference was so negligible we put it out of our minds and concentrated on dating Germans and buying high-end electronics at knock down prices. We knew that when the end came it would all be over quickly. We figured we'd get in a couple of good punches and then we'd be gone. I was never good at long goodbyes anyway. We may not have accomplished much in some people's eyes, but we did keep World War III from happening.

On a couple of occasions when we were on patrol and no one was looking I would balance beam walk along the Iron Curtain just for the fun of it.

---

[31] After the fall of the Soviet Union and German unification, some units in what had been West Germany went off to other duties, some stayed. Some shipped back to the US while others fought in the various Gulf Wars. With no units left to occupy it, they eventually closed the Warner Barracks and the Bamberg Garrison in 2014. As of this writing the track park where we kept our tanks, where *Dreamboat Annie, Sure Shot, Yo Mamma, Angeline, Candy-O*, and the *Armored Cow* waited at the battle ready is now an empty, overgrown lot with the concrete cracking and decaying. The vehicles we trained on to fight the end of the world were scrapped and sold off, their ghosts as forgotten as the crews who manned them. By the twenty-first century several technology companies bought up many of the remaining M60s and rebuilt them with new engines, upgraded gunnery equipment and a host of high-tech bells and whistles. They then sold them to countries who did not have the resources to build their own tanks. I'll always wonder if *Dreamboat Annie* wound up being one of these rebuilds or did she wind up in the ocean just off the coast as an artificial reef.

Chapter 4

Return to the Pointless Forest

In all creation, nothing endures, all is in endless flux, each wandering shape a pilgrim passing by. Time itself glides on endlessly flowing.

– Ovid

With my overseas service at an end, I was reassigned as standard procedure. I had taken a little longer than usual, but by now I had been promoted to 'Specialist Fourth Class', or 'Spec 4', basically a corporal. I have never been much of a climber, and so promotion was not something I thought much about. I had been able to choose myself going to Germany. This time my duty station would be chosen by the army. As my reassignment approached, everyone said they hoped I didn't get sent to Kansas because it was awful. California, Colorado or Washington State, that was good tank duty. Then one morning, a month or so before my scheduled ship out, the First Sergeant stopped me in the company hallway and handed me an official looking letter. We had just finished the morning ritual of waxing and polishing the floors of the company area and dusting before beginning the workday.[1] When I opened my reassignment papers standing outside the Day Room, everyone burst out laughing: it was Kansas. Top smiled, punched my shoulder good-naturedly and said, "Well, hopefully they won't make you eat ham and cheese sandwiches!"

Kansas

After a short visit home, I flew to Kansas City then took a bus from there to Fort Riley. At the moment my name became available for reassignment that old algorithm kicked in. In that cosmic moment of decision, not thought of an instant before and not cared about an instant after, the army decided they needed a body of a tanker in Kansas, so that's where I was sent. Fort Riley was then home to the First Infantry Division. The First Armoured was nicknamed 'Old Ironsides' while the first infantry was 'The Big Red One.'[2] I was assigned to Alpha company of the 1/34 Armour (its unit crest was a disembodied arm holding a shield). I had to spend a week in the reception station before joining the unit. The reason for the delay was that the 1/34 was out on a gunnery exercise when I arrived so I had to wait until they returned to the barracks.

I had to spend a week in the post reception station twiddling my thumbs and doing nothing, but trying to avoid being put on a mindless work detail. One day, I was in the snack bar across the street from reception having lunch (they made a pretty good chilli burger). I was there with another 'Spec 4' who had arrived on the same day as me. He was an anti-aircraft rocket mechanic. As a way of avoiding a work detail, he wore his dress uniform every day. As we sat at the snack bar counter we discussed how to get out of work. I said I was just going to go hide somewhere or maybe walk over to the PX for a while. Just then, an older man in civilian clothes who was just within earshot said to us, "you should be careful talking like that. Someone who gives a damn might overhear you." He smiled paid his bill then left. The next day I received my orders to head over to the 1/34. When I walked into the company

---

[1] To this day, I hate the smell of floor wax.
[2] Insert penis joke here.

office to present myself and my orders I almost choked out loud. The First Sargeant looked at me and smiled. It was the guy from the snack bar. I instantly knew I was totally screwed. "This is your worst and luckiest day, son." The glee in his face was obvious. "This is my last day with the company. I hope you're not as much of an asshole as I think you are." He took my orders and told me to get out. I walked over to the barracks knowing that I had just missed walking off of a cliff.

Overseas service was highly rated in stateside units. In short order, I was promoted to sergeant and was expected to take a leadership role (something I was never comfortable with). Now a tank commander, my call sign became 'Romeo Two-Five'. That was because R in the military phonetic alphabet is Romeo and I was in the second platoon, tank number five, and my last name began with an R. In addition, because I had been to chemical warfare school I was made company NBCNCO. That meant, among other things, I handed out the gas masks, though we were not supposed to call them 'gas masks.'[3] They were 'protective masks'. It also meant I had a 'sniffer' device mounted on the top of my tank. It drew in air from the surrounding atmosphere and checked it for contaminates. If it found any it would suddenly start screaming, and we were to put on our masks and other protective gear including green pants and blouse called a 'MOPP' suit. They were baggy like medical scrubs and were meant to keep contaminates off you. MOPP stood for Military Oriented Protective Posture. On our gas mask bags were attached decontamination kits. It was a plastic box with vials of chemicals and wipe down swabs. If you had a chemical agent on you, you would break the vials and pour it all over the contaminates. We also carried—in Germany but not in Kansas—atropine injectors. These were for if you breathed in any nerve agent. If you did you would immediately start to shake violently as you lost control of your nervous system (nerve agent was, in essence, human-grade insecticide). If that happened, you were supposed to remain calm (which was unlikely) take out the atropine injector from your gas mask bag and jam it into your thigh. Inside the injector, which was about the size of one of those novelty, oversized pencils you'd buy on a class trip to Washington DC or Hersey Park, was a large spring loaded needle that upon activation would automatically stab you and inject nerve agent antidote. You would collapse and continue to shake violently, but the theory said, at least you wouldn't die from nerve agent poisoning.

It all reminded me of going to Saint Cecelia's because, over the front entrance to the school was one of those black and yellow fallout shelter signs called 'Blakeley Shields' after Robert Blakeley, the man who designed it. We were never more than a bingo card away from nuclear oblivion. In a special room in the basement the nuns kept the nuclear war survival gear the government had sent them. The idea was that if the Russkies nuked New York, people would flock to the fallout shelters and safety. Presumably, if that happened all the people within a few blocks of St. Cecelia's would come to the church and school and pile into the basement. We would live off the supplies that were kept there. I remember as a kid reading the instructions on the side of a large reinforced cardboard barrel that held fresh water. The instructions said that once the water was used up, the barrel, which was painted olive drab with yellow lettering on it, would then be used as a toilet. Once that was full, it was to be dumped outside somewhere. As the Civil Defense security man on the spot, the janitor Mr. Fix, was expected to ward off looters, and keep the kids in line while wearing his white WWI era helmet with the triangular Civil Defense logo on it, web gear, and Sargeant York rifle. Once the danger was past we'd come out of the bunker and start to rebuild Kearny by feeding

---

[3] NBC stood for Nuclear Biological & Chemical. It had been called ABC for Atomic Biological & Chemical, and also CBR, Chemical Biological & Radiological.

off the irradiated and decayed flesh of the dead. Down the street was a local fire station. It was also a designated fallout shelter and Civil Defense headquarters. In the yard of the station, they had a white command vehicle.[4] I was fascinated by this and wanted to get inside to see what sort of rescue equipment was in there. I imagined it was like Thunderbird 2. The government told us if we followed the protocols of civil defense we could survive a nuclear war. As a kid I had seen enough monster and science fiction movies to realize this assessment seemed wildly optimistic.

> The first time I kissed a girl
> was in the furnace room of Saint Cecelia's grammar school
> where they kept the flag furled
> it was under a metal sign warning of the end of the world

The Land of Ahs

Fort Riley was an enormous property. Unlike in Germany, where the moment you passed through the tank park gate you were in town, we never left the reservation and did all our maneuvering on base. I missed interacting with civilians on manoeuvres. I had to find ways to entertain myself in the field here as well without the presence of people. As it turned out Kansas was not as bad as everyone said it would be. It was actually quite nice. The weather was pleasant, and I never saw a tornado. It was, however, extremely flat just like the stereotypical image. There were a few places where it wasn't so great.[5]

Just outside the main gate of Fort Riley was Junction City, Kansas. A hell hole at the time, which seemed little more than a main street of dive bars, tattoo parlours, whore houses, laundromats, billiard rooms, greasy spoons, and despair. It was the type of place you'd see on the back cover of a country rock band album. One of these towns exists immediately outside the gate of every stateside American military base. They survive like those sucker fish that attach themselves to the backs of sharks. I never went there voluntarily; I preferred Manhattan, Kansas at the other end of the post. Manhattan was home to Kansas State University so it had a lively student scene.

As a sergeant, I was allocated my own single room in the barracks. This suited me fine as it allowed me privacy and a refuge when I found my companions too much. I told Henry about it and he went out and bought me a little portable TV. Before I could tell him not to, he sent it to me through the mail. Unfortunately, by the time it reached me it was broken. I didn't have the heart to tell him so I said it was great and how much I appreciated it (which I did).[6] I was able to get the same one at the post PX. Cable television was just becoming available and they had wired the barracks for it. I figured out how to splice into the cable and hook it to my set. It allowed me to pull in the local stations without having to pay. There was a pay phone booth just outside the barracks and when I was really bored I'd camp out there with a pocket full of quarters and call my friend Al or my parents for a chat. The adventurous life I had experienced and loved in Germany was all but gone in Kansas.

---

[4] The way the government had of distinguishing the Civil Defense forces from, say the police or military, they painted everything associated with this organization white. From the helmets they were supposed the wear to the vehicles they drove.

[5] The Kansas state motto is *The Land of Ahs*: a pun on Oz the mythical land Dorothy gets sent to because of a tornado.

[6] My father did this sort of thing all my life. Never having much money, and unsure of any other way to do it, he would show me he loved me by buying me little things he thought I'd like. The first Christmas I was in Germany he sent me, completely unsolicited, an HO electric racecar set. It became a popular past time in the barracks. One of the great regrets of my life was that I was never really able to find the words to tell him how much all this meant to me.

Once I was able to afford it, I took a small apartment at 1207, Poyntz Avenue across from the park in Manhattan. We had our own phone and cable TV there. The cable package we signed up for included a new channel called MTV that had only just debuted. It was on MTV that I saw *U2*, and *The English Beat, The Clash, The Motels*, and a host of bands that were now being referred to as New Wave. Bands such as *The Cars* and *Heart*, which I already liked, had videos as well. Memorable songs like 'Don't You Want Me Baby?,' '99 Luft Balloons,' and *Aha's* 'Take on Me' entered our ears to remain forever.

The apartment next to mine was occupied by a pair of Iranian students who were always nervous about living next to soldiers, particularly as it was during the Iranian hostage crisis and there was a prevailing anti-Iranian sentiment in the country. We never gave them a hard time and they never did anything to make us suspect they were anything other than hard working students from a far-off land. Ronald Reagan was president at the time. I disliked him from the start. He seemed superficial and too worried about rich people and against working people. It also upset me that he had clearly colluded with the Iranians to not release the hostages until he could use that news in the election. The reality was that Jimmy Carter had gotten the hostages released, not Reagan. As someone who had recently been on the Iron Curtain, I also knew Reagan had done nothing to end the Cold War either. His pointless sabre-rattling only pushed us closer to nuclear annihilation. Despite his famous "tear down this wall" speech in 1987, the Soviet Union was already beginning to crumble through no effort of his. It wasn't him or his speech that ended Russian communism, it was the efforts of millions of people in Russia and the Warsaw Pact countries who were fed up with waiting in line for three hours just to get a roll of toilet paper you could use to sand a table.

When I wasn't seething about politics there was a movie theatre a few blocks walk from the apartment.[7] One day we went to see a new animated film *Heavy Metal*. I had been reading the magazine *Heavy Metal* since I was in Germany, and I was beginning to harbour notions I might be able to have a career as an illustrator after I left the service. I was filling sketchbook after sketchbook with drawings since I arrived at the 3/35.[8] *Heavy Metal* featured such amazing artists as Enki Bilal, Richard Corben, and Jean Girard, better known as Moebius, whose work influenced mine.[9] The magazine appealed to science fiction and speculative fiction fans; its European sensibility seemed exotic and fascinating; the artwork was as far from the classic American super hero style as you could get. That was something I found inspiring, as I never liked the super hero style. The magazine showed me there were people out there who felt the same way I did about the nature of illustration. As a result, I was anxious to see the film. Also, it was on a double bill with another new movie which I knew nothing about called *Raiders of the Lost Ark*. I thought the 'ark' of the title was Noah's Ark. I didn't realize they were talking about the Ark of the Covenant until the scene with the Feds.

Walking out of the theatre after seeing these two movies, I felt transformed. I had become painfully resigned to the fact that my 'scholarly' endeavors would never be more than a secret hobby. Seeing *Raiders of the Lost Ark*, however, unexpectedly rekindled in me the

---

[7] I saw the film *The Funhouse* in a Drive-In outside Manhattan.

[8] One day JD Dunn asked me, out of nowhere to paint a wall mural in the hallway of the barracks. He said I could do anything I wanted. I did a scene of the 3/35 fighting WWIII. I put in a skeleton handing ammunition to soldiers battling against onrushing Soviet tanks. I also put odd little monsters in the trenches. When I was finished, Captain Dunn took one look at it and said, "cool." I always wanted to know what happened to my mural after I left.

[9] A product of the Franco-Belgian *bandes dessinées* tradition *Heavy Metal* magazine, known in its original French incarnation as *Métal hurlant*, could claim Herge's *Tin Tin* as an ancestor, as well as the Smurfs.

need to be an historian and the desire to go to college.[10] It brought back all the enthusiasm I had built up as a kid imagining myself as a globetrotting academic. I had attained the globetrotting part, now I needed to do the academic part. I determined I was going to someday recreate that early classroom scene in the movie, but for real. I have since done that, and while I never had a student write "Love You!" on her eye lids, I've come close once or twice.

> Individuality?
> You are what you want to be…
> Until tomorrow.[11]

I shared the apartment with a platoon mate named Dwayne. As a 'Spec 4' he had the money to pay half the rent and he wasn't too annoying. He also had a car. As it was close to the bar scene, our apartment became a kind of stop over place for guys in the platoon, either going off to or coming back from a night out. Marcus Beaver, the driver of A23, regularly stopped by at 3am, like Cosmo Kramer, and slept on the floor. In the morning we'd all pile into his pick-up truck and drive onto the post to go to work.

In the 1/34 there were a few of my company mates who were hopeless drunks. A few stoners. There were a couple of religious fanatics, racists, and one or two who were just barely literate who joined rather than live in squalor in some rustic deep South locale. Some had enlisted rather than go to jail. There were several guys from Mexico who had enlisted in order to begin working on their American Dream. They were the hardest workers in the group. It reminded me of the platoon in *The Dirty Dozen*, though not always in a good way. The entire time I was in Germany I was never depressed by my fellow soldiers, it was always exciting. I was amused by a few, and I didn't like a couple of them, but they never depressed me. Every time I stepped outside the barracks it felt like an adventure. Here in Kansas it was, well, dull. There were times my fellows just depressed me for their thinly-veiled racism, their misogyny, and their lack of interest in anything other than drinking and being dopes.

It was not totally laid-back though. Our role in Germany was to hold off the Russians just long enough for reinforcements to arrive from stateside. The 1/34 was one of those units that, if World War III began, would be the first ones on the planes to be sent over in an operation code named REFORGER (Return of Forces to Germany). As a result, we had to stay in ready condition.

Still, the duty at Fort Riley was more like a regular nine to five job. We went out on field exercises every few weeks, but we had no border duty, no alerts, nor did we carry live ammunition on the tanks. Established in 1853 as a cavalry outpost guarding settlers heading west along the Santa Fe trail, Fort Riley was a sprawling property which boasted its own herd of buffalo. George Armstrong Custer famously spent time there prior to going out to have his encounter with Sitting Bull. As I had been relocated from Germany I was seen as an old and experienced hand (at 20 years of age). Except for the platoon sergeant, none of my new platoon mates had ever been overseas, not even the LT. I liked the stripes mostly for the pay increase, and because it meant I would never have to do guard duty or KP again. I was put

---

[10] Yes, of course the character of Indiana Jones is problematic: he mistreats locals, doesn't do his work in a scholarly manner, and is essentially a tomb robber and pot hunter. Still, at the time I saw it, I saw the thrill and it wasn't until later that I realized he was not a good role model for me.
[11] *Psychedelic Furs*. "Pretty in Pink," 1980.

back in the second platoon, and because the platoon sergeant, Joe Matron, and I hit it off, I was made TC of A25. As the five tank in the platoon, I was wingman to the four tank that is always the platoon sergeant's tank (the six tank is always the lieutenant/platoon leader's vehicle). My job was to cover the platoon sergeant and the rear of the platoon as we manoeuvered. Hence, the five tank was sometimes known as 'Ass End Charlie'. Sargent Rusty in the three tank was the best map reader in the platoon, so was always on point.

My stoner gunner on the A25 had hooked up a car cassette stereo player to our tank radio and a set of small speakers nailed to a board, a la *Kelly's Heroes*, so we could listen to music out in the field on exercises. One day, while on a major force maneuver in May of 1981, the platoon was roaring down a road through one of the more wooded areas of the reservation. It was a beautiful sunny day and I had the speakers out on top of the tank turned up to 11. I was sitting on my commander's cupola behind the .50 cal while my loader Dennis Croaker (a white kid from California who grew up in a Chicano community), was sitting out of the loader's hatch, as per procedure, facing rearward so as to spot anyone coming up on us from behind. Dennis had this odd ability to predict the weather. We would be out in the field on a sunny day and he would tilt his head up, sniff a few times and turn to me and say, "Iz goin' to rain Esé!" Within fifteen minutes it would cloud up and start to rain.

As we bounced our way along the path at 55 tons and 25 miles per hour the company, in single file battle line, we passed through a clearing. There were several jeeps and armoured cars sitting there on the side of the road. The battalion commander, Lt. Col. Praxitelis 'Nick' Vamvakias, the battalion Sergeant Major, and a clutch of reporters, were standing there watching us go by. It was not unusual, even here in Kansas, for the media to cover these big scale operations. As it happened quickly, I didn't notice them until the last second so I couldn't duck down inside the turret and turn the music down in time. Just as we went by the VIPs, the local rock station out of Manhattan, K-Rock 101.5fm WMKF that we were listening to, played *The Vapors*. So, as we passed the unit CO, 'Turning Japanese' blared out of our tank, both Dennis and I on top of 'Dreamboat Annie II' doing our best New Wave head shaking and screaming out the lyrics as loudly and enthusiastically as we could:

> I'm turning Japanese
> I think I'm turning Japanese
> I really think so…

One of the news guys had a hand-held motion picture camera and filmed as we went by. The Sergeant Major gave me one of the best stink eyes I have ever received. Incredibly, no one ever chased us down or reprimanded us. It was the second time I had done something odd in front of people who mattered, but somehow had escaped.

Bad Tranny

Shortly after the *Vapor's* incident, the 1/34 was chosen to go on special desert training. They only wanted some troops to go. I immediately volunteered and talked my crew into going with me: I needed that excitement back in my life. They packed up about half the battalion, along with men from our sister unit the 1/63 Armour up the street, onto planes and flew us out to the Fort Irwin National Training Center in Southern California. It was an even larger base than Fort Riley and allowed for both manoeuver and live-fire exercises. Army units rotated through to become familiar with desert conditions. What made the training unique was that there was a permanent unit stationed there which called the OPFOR

(Opposing Forces). They operated US vehicles modified to look like Soviet equipment. They wore soviet style uniforms and manoeuvered according to Warsaw Pact tactics. We spent several weeks there running around the desert chasing and being chased by the OPFOR units.[12]

One day in the desert, we did a mass assault at an OPFOR strategic position. With the call of "Tally Ho!" we charged; an entire battalion of tanks intermingled with an infantry battalion. Overhead roared helicopter gunships and A10 *Warthog* tank busters. As we raced across the sands we fired blank ammunition. The vehicles were festooned with MILES sensors to record hits and misses, and a tank gun simulator called a Hoffman Device. As we raced forward, I noticed that the tank's engine was revving, but we were slowing down. I called down to Dennis, who was driving, and asked what was going on. He said he was pushing on the gas pedal, but the tank continued to slow down eventually rolling to a complete stop. Everyone else went roaring past us. It became clear that we had blown the transmission. I radioed the LT and told him what happened. The battalion had to keep going and we were on our own (they listed us as destroyed in the battle). I radioed the company motor sergeant and he said to sit tight and they'd be by to take a look. I thought about telling him that with a blown transmission there wasn't much else I could do, but sit tight. After a minute or two all the vehicles that had been attacking in the same direction disappeared into the dust which then settled. The sky emptied of aircraft and the area turned quiet. We were left sitting there totally alone in a vast expanse of desert.

After letting the engine cool down, we shut it off and went about opening the back of the tank. We hadn't actually taken our own vehicles to the desert. Fort Irwin had this massive depot full of every conceivable US army vehicle in storage. When units came in they would draw vehicles from this storage and use those then return them at the end of the exercise. The M60 I was handed apparently had a bad transmission that the previous users had managed to conceal. The engine cover on the M60A1 is armored. It's not like popping the hood on your car. It has several large pieces with access panels and vents to allow heat to escape; the entire assembly weighs several tons. It's all held down with large steel bolts the size of railroad spikes. We would need help getting it out.

While we waited under the bright sun, I climbed up on top of the commander's cupola and took a look around with the binoculars. From this vantage point, I could see for miles. The desert in this area was flat as a plate. There were mountains in the distance. I thought of those Golden Books I read as a kid. Herbert Zim had said deserts like these in the Western US were flat because they had been the floors of ancient oceans. When they were full of seawater, massive Mosasaurs (bigger than the tank I was standing on), and huge Nautilus squids roamed these primordial seas. I listened for the sound of waves breaking on shores, but heard the deep growling hiss of a fossil sea scorpion instead. I then realized it was a deuce and a half screaming across the desert floor towards us. It was the motor sergeant driving up in his truck.

I climbed down, grabbed the gun barrel and did the tanker's spin down to the ground, landing on my feet, as he came over. I said, "bad tranny!" He stuck his head in the open engine cover, looked about a bit and said, "yeah, bad tranny." His assistant, looked in as well

---

[12] They also had a museum area with actual Russian vehicles you could climb on to get familiar with. They had several T-55s, and T-72s, along with BMP armored personnel carriers and various other assorted vehicles. These had all been captured by the Israelis from Syrian and Egyptian forces during the various Arab-Israeli wars.

and echoed, "yeah, bad tranny!" Dennis Croaker, was lying flat on top of the engine deck resting his head on one hand, his other arm dangling over the open engine compartment. He smiled at me, and said, "Whoa! bad tranny!" Then the company XO pulled up, looked around and radioed, "bad tranny." It was very difficult to keep from laughing.[13]

Rather than tow the vehicle back to the shop the XO decided it would be good training for all involved to swap out the transmission *in situ*. We would need the company '88' for that. Every tank company has a heavy recovery vehicle that is also a rolling machine shop. It has a bulldozer blade on it and an 'A' frame crane for removing tank engines and other heavy lifts. After an hour, the 88 arrived and positioned itself directly behind the tank as if the two were about to have intimate relations. They raised up the 'A' frame crane and we laboriously removed first the back deck, then the transmission. We then had to wait for a truck to bring out a new transmission: the truck of course became lost in the desert and didn't arrive for some time. Once it did, we put the new transmission in and hooked it all back up and made sure it worked. In the middle of all this, the Battalion Sargeant-Major of the 1/63 drove up in his mutt to see how we were coming along. Not caring that we had spent the better part of the day doing this dirty, exhausting mechanical work, he made a remark about how we needed to put our shirts back on to look like proper soldiers. I gave him a half-hearted, "Yes, Sargeant-Major." He then drove off. We didn't put our shirts back on. By the time the '88' and the mechanics drove off it was two in the morning. I made the decision to wait until daylight to move. We were alone in the desert again.

We made a campfire and cooked our C-rations. We were exhausted, sweat-soaked, and dirty. We used the last of our water to wash up a little. Despite the exhaustion, dirt, and heat it was fun to sit under the cloudless Southern California night sky and relax. We rolled out our sleeping bags, and ate beanie weenies out of a can. They tasted better than almost anything I'd ever had before. It's amazing how you learn to appreciate little things like beans out of a can for dinner in the desert. I've had few meals in fancy restaurants I enjoyed that much, sitting around with the guys making jokes, singing *DEVO* songs, the only humans for miles. I looked at the sky a lot that night.

I'd never seen so many stars. I thought about how Pops and I would look up at the darkness with our cheap, little telescope. In 1973 he and I saw the comet Kohoutek. Here in the California desert there was none of the pollution that restricted our view in New York metropolitan area and so the sky reverberated with astronomical wonder. Flat on my back, arms out like Jesus, watching the belt of Orion as the others nodded off into much deserved sleep, made me think about the expanse of the universe and traveling amongst the stars. It brought back to me those thoughts and dreams I had about what I wanted to do with my life. I had recently begun to have vague thoughts about possibly re-enlisting and making the army a career. I was pretty good at this stuff. It paid well, had full medical coverage, and it was so very easy. Maybe I should stay and finally give up on all the nonsense about being an historian or a writer. Luckily, Orion said I had a destiny outside of the uniform. As I lay there, I kept listening for that high-pitched shriek the giant desert ants from *Them* made. Fortunately, I never did hear it.

As the sun was coming up the next morning, and the guys were rolling up their sleeping bags and getting ready to go, I finally radioed the LT and told him we were repaired

---

[13] XO is the abbreviation for Executive Officer, the second in command.

and were going to rejoin the platoon. I asked for the map coordinates and we'd be on our way. He told me that rather than come straight to where the platoon was I had a special task first. There was a field medical unit nearby where we had broken down. We were to drive over there, hook up with them and lead them to where they were going which wasn't far from our company. We would then rejoin the platoon. We packed up and headed off. The MASH unit was about a thirty minute drive from where we were.

The field medical unit was right where they were supposed to be in a little copse of trees. As we drove up all the med staff came out to gawk at us. They had never seen a tank this close up before. It was hot so we were all in our green t-shirts: the look the Sargent-Major didn't care for. I had cut the sleeves off mine Newark style of course, our shoulder holsters visible. We stopped, and still wearing my CVC helmet with the goggles on it, I climbed down. I told the guys to do the usual field check of the tank to be sure everything was working properly. I found the company commander who turned out to be a blonde captain/doctor I was immediately taken with. She seemed in her mid-thirties or so and reminded me of Florence Henderson from the *Brady Bunch*. We exchanged pleasantries and she said we were a bit early and could I wait around? I said of course. I figured I'd go for it and began a little flirting with her. To my delight, she reciprocated. They had just finished breakfast and she offered us whatever we wanted to eat. The boys wolfed down pancakes and sausages from the line of marmite cans. We also wrapped some up to take with us. People from the med unit crowded around the tank and a few asked if they could look inside to which we said, sure. I asked Captain Florence if she wanted a look. She smiled and said yes, then asked who 'Dreamboat Annie' was.[14] I helped her climb up and gave her the tour.

We sat for a few minutes inside the turret and talked. I knew it was hopeless of course. Even if I came out and said, "I'd like to date you," and she said, "yes, I would like to date you as well," we couldn't. First off, my unit was in Kansas and hers was in Oregon. Also, there are strict rules about sergeants and captains dating. We both knew that, so we enjoyed our flirt: just two people who suddenly found themselves spending a few moments together in the cosmic vortex. I then asked Captain Florence if she had any extra water. We were out, and we were filthy, and it would be nice to wash up a bit. I explained what we had been doing all night. She brushed some dirt off my shoulder smiling and said, "yes, you could use a bath." Just then the med XO came over to the tank, climbed up and stuck his head in the loader's hatch. The medical unit was all ready to go. We both sighed. She said all they had was a water buffalo: a two wheeled tanker trailer especially used for water. The XO then said that they didn't have a vehicle to tow the water buffalo and would have to leave it behind. The captain looked at me and said we could take as much water as we wanted. I thought about it and after all the med people had cleared the tank told Dennis to drive over to where the water trailer was. The M60A1 has a large tow pintle on its backside that is almost never used for anything. So we hooked up the water buffalo to the tank then drove to the head of the med unit which had formed up their vehicles in a line to convoy to their next position. The captain drove up in her mutt just in front of us. She looked up at me and smiled, then waved forward and the whole line began to move. After a while we reached the rendezvous point. We pulled over to let the medical convoy go by. They peeled off and disappeared down the road. We waved goodbye.

Then my LT radioed and said he could see us, and we were just about a quarter mile from the platoon, and why were we towing a water buffalo?[15]

---

[14] Even though this tank was not mine, I had to make it feel that way. I found a big black magic marker in the depot when we requisitioned our vehicles, and I used it to write the name on the side just under my commander's cupola.

[15] It quickly dawned on the LT and everyone in our platoon that having our own 500 gallons of water in the desert wasn't such a bad idea after all.

Only a week or so after that the 1/34 was chosen to partake in that year's REFORGER exercise. They packed us all on planes again, but instead of going to California, we went to Germany. We essentially repeated what we had just done in California—picking up tanks at a depot and using them to maneuver—but in Germany. Once again, I found myself steamrolling around Europe practicing to fight the Warsaw Pact. I was hoping we would go near Bamberg or run into the 3/35 and I could say hello to my old friends, but unfortunately, we didn't. After a month of fun and games the exercise ended and we flew back to Kansas.

Shortly after returning we had our bi-annual live gunnery exercise. Every year, every soldier had to officially qualify with their standard weapon, which in our case was the .45 caliber pistol. We also had to qualify with our tanks. There was a live fire range out in the middle of Fort Reilly and we headed out there for a week of shooting. You had to qualify as an individual vehicle and as a platoon. First, the entire company lined up on a special range to 'bore sight' the guns. This was a technique for ensuring that whatever you saw through the gunsights on the tank, the guns were pointing at the same spot. You did this by firing a series of rounds at targets then adjusting the sights until when you fired the main gun it hit in the exact spot the cross hairs were on. We set the guns to be able to hit a target at one thousand meters distant. This was the mid-range. For targets closer or farther, away there were techniques for adjusting fire on the move.

After bore sighting we moved to the combat course. This was laid out like a drive in the country. You pulled up to the start line and radioed that you were all set. An observer jeep would follow along behind you and give orders and record your shots. Along the route you had certain problems to negotiate. Several were straight forward 'shoot the bad guy's tank' station. Suddenly, a wooden target of a Russian tank would pop up in the distance. The TC (me) would call out, "driver stop!" As the vehicle came to a halt I'd use the override, a pistol grip style handle in the TC's position which let you spin the turret and elevate (and even fire) the guns independently of the gunner. The TC used the override to get the gun on the target quickly (the idea is that whoever shoots first usually wins). As I did this I'd call out, "Tank, left front." Then I would call out what ammunition I wanted the gunner to fire at the enemy and what type of target he was to fire at. "Gunner, HEAT (High Explosive Anti-Tank), Tank." As that was happening the loader would take out one of the heavy rounds from the ready wrack and throw it in the breech of the gun. As it seated it tripped a lever that allowed the breech to snap shut. When the loader finished loading the gun he'd take the safety off, then yell, "Up!" meaning the gun was ready to go. Once the gunner saw the target, he would say "Identified." I would then say "Fire!" The last thing was for the gunner to announce he was going to pull the trigger, by saying "On the way!' Then, boom. At a thousand meters, it took the round barely a second or two to reach the target. You could follow it with your eyes because each round had a tracer on the back of it so you could watch the light of the tracer fly through the air and hit the target.

Other stations were more complicated: fire the main gun on the move (the M60A1's turret was power stabilized). Shoot at infantry in the open with the machine guns, and my favorite, shoot down a helicopter with the fifty-caliber machine gun. They simulated this with a series of telephone poles with a steel cable running along the top like a ski resort cable car. They suspended a wooden helicopter shaped target from it that has pulled along by another cable.

By the end of the week long exercise my tank came in first in the company of seventeen tanks, and third in the battalion of fifty-four. It was pretty damn good shooting. The

CO gave us each a three-day pass—which in Kansas meant a long weekend without having to come to work. It was late Spring of 1982, my original enlistment was up.

Despite this gunnery success, I was feeling done with it all. My position during this period bounced back and forth. Should I stay or should I go? I decided to take my end of tour. They tried to get me to reenlist, of course. They offered me promotion to Staff Sergeant. They offered me a chance to go back to Ft. Knox to train on the new M1 Abrams tank that was just going into service. Though I did seriously consider reenlisting, I eventually turned them down. Finally, after more prodding I said I would reenlist if they sent me to helicopter pilot school. I figured that was so outlandish they'd never go for it. Then they called my bluff and said okay, they'd send me to Ft. Rucker, Alabama to become an Apache gunship pilot. That made me pause, but then I said no thanks. It was time to move on. I signed a mountain of paperwork on a sweltering day in mid-June, and said my goodbyes. I shook Dennis Croaker's hand, gave away all my stuff, took my severance money, and hoped a plane out of Kansas. And just like that, it was over.

Home Again

Upon my arrival back home everyone was happy. I was too, sort of. After the return home party at my Cousin Michael's house in Boonton, and the backslapping and congrats and welcome homes, and the we're so proud of you's, I took a few days to let the dust settle and clear my head. After the years of receiving a paycheck from Uncle Sugar, however, I needed to find a real job. I also needed to think. I went for a walk in Park #2 through some of my old rock hunting grounds. I found a spot on a bench next to the Bowling Green and overlooking the Hollow. I sat on this bench many times before as a budding adventurer kid and now I sat and contemplated my future as an adult. I had just turned twenty-two years old.

There were birds around and kids playing. Sherman came running along, hoped up on the bench, and sat next to me as if the time we hadn't seen each other had never happened. I gave his head a rub as his tail waged excitely. It seemed odd to have been doing the job I had been doing just a few days before. I had spent the last few years training to fight the end of the world, to literally fight Armageddon, now I was sitting in the park where I tried to dig to China. I felt strangely out of place in this environment I once knew so well. This is where Sherman and I, like Oblio and Arrow, explored the Pointless Forest. For a time I had been someone others looked up to, a man in charge of things. A man required to make decisions. I stood down the Commies. Now, I was just an anonymous guy sitting on a bench wondering what to do.

Nobody's seen where I've been
Nobody feels what I've done
Not a one…[16]

My childhood was over. I didn't want to go back to it anyway. I didn't want to move back in with my parents regardless of how happy they were to have me do so. I didn't have much choice right now. Sitting there on that bench as kids ran by and young mothers pushed baby carriages past me, I knew the skills I had learned in the Cav would not really translate

---

[16] Heart. "Nada One," *Dog and Butterfly*, 1978.

well into a civilian life.[17]

    At night I'd drive down the public sports field called the Gunnel Oval and sit on the trunk of my car in the heat trying to figure out what to do now that I was no longer working for the 'G.' I could call in an arty strike on an enemy position. I could put a 105mm Sabot or HEAT round through a one-foot square target a mile away. I could swap out a tank's engine and reattach a thrown track in the mud. I could decontaminate a nerve agent victim or puncture a person's throat with my thumb. I couldn't exactly put any of that on a resume.[18] I wanted to be a writer, but all I was really good at was shooting and blowing up stuff. I needed to figure out who I was now.

    I needed to get something, anything to start earning money. Also maybe some things a little more sociable.

    I began to date Mike's little sister, Carol, briefly. We had known each other for years. She had started writing to me while I was in Kansas and we seemed to like each other though she was four years younger than me (the first movie I brought her to see was *Bladerunner* which in hindsight might not have been the best choice). She was cute and sweet and we went out a couple of times then it all cooled. Part of the reason was that I had changed a bit while I was away. I thought I was the same, but apparently, no one else did. I think Carol might have been a bit nervous about who I had become. I think she saw me as even more weird and odd than before. Also, Mike's girlfriend Lynne, didn't like me so I suspect she told Carol to stay away from me. But, I really don't know. In hindsight it was for the best.

    I wanted a car too. I had saved a lot of my army pay. Every month—we were paid the last day of every month—I'd keep some money for myself then the rest I sent to Henry who put it in a savings account for me. Pontiac had just released the new model of the Firebird: the one they used in the television series *Knight Rider*. I went down to the Pontiac dealer on River Road, put down five grand, and drove away with a jet black car. While it looked great, it was a lemon. In fact, it was probably the single worst financial investment I ever made. It had a terrible transmission and a computer they had to replace twice in the first year. I was constantly repairing it. I was happy when I eventually sold it to one of those cars for cash joints in Manhattan. Then there was the wedding.

    I had known Mike since the second grade at Saint Cecelia's and I assumed we were good friends. Mike—along with Al and Kenny—were the only people, other than my parents,

---

[17] Shortly after I returned, I saw the Kmart down on River Road in Kearny was hiring and one of the positions was in security. I thought, well at least I can have a job and get paid while I looked for something better. I went down and applied. I was ushered into the office of Human Resources across from a young women about my age who was the HR person. She looked at my application the way a dog looks at a bowl of plastic fruit.
"So, you were in the army?"
"Yes."
"You were a tank commander?"
"Yes.'
"Uh, what's a tank?"
I saw she was serious. Without saying a word, I stood up, and walked out.
I also thought about applying for a job as an armored car driver with Wells Fargo. Then I briefly contemplated applying to the New Jersey State Police Academy. Then I thought, what do I want to be a cop for?
[18] Years later, I actually did put my military skills at the end of my CV. It always generated interesting looks from academic committee members.

who wrote to me while I was in. We went down to the Jersey shore to go to clubs and listened to live bands, got drunk, and flirted with girls when I came home on leave. We went to one of the first concerts by *Little Steven and the Disciples of Soul* at the Peppermint Lounge in New York. We often opened up to each other in the way guys do when they are friends and they are drunk and all philosophical. Once, Al and I were on a double date in New York and we went walking in Battery Park. As you do, the two couples wandered off on their own. After a bit, Al and his girl came running over, "Hey, they have a statue here to the guy who invented the skateboard!" I had no idea what he was talking about so we all walked over to look at this statue. Sure enough, it was a statue of a man in 19th century garb holding what looked for all the world like a skateboard. Then it hit me the skateboard looked familiar and I was back in my sophomore history class giving my first lecture in front of the room. The skateboard was a scale model of the *USS Monitor*, the civil war ironclad. The plaque said, John Ericsson: Designer of the *USS Monitor*. And, I thought, the skateboard.

The morning of the Fourth of July after I returned, Al called me and said he heard a good show was about to go on at the *Stone Pony* in Asbury Park. He picked me up and we headed south. To say it was a good show is an understatement. A band with 15 horns—including the Asbury Jukes Horns, and the guys who appeared on the J. Geils Band's recent live album—crowded the stage. Around midnight to everyone's delight Bruce Springsteen showed up.

Sometime later Mike announced he and his long-time girlfriend, Lynne were getting married. We all went to Kearny High together and I had even been in a couple of classes with Lynne. I was happy for them even though Lynne was often not that subtle about her disdain for me (she only tolerated me because I was Mike's friend). The next time we talked on the phone, I said to Carol that we would be in the wedding party together and it would be fun. She sort of laughed nervously and said, "sure."

A few days after they announced their wedding date, Al had bought tickets to a New York Ranger's game at Madison Square Garden. Al drove and when they came to pick me up, Mike came to the door. As we headed down the back stairs and out to the street I asked him, "Hey, this is going to sound odd, but am I in your wedding party?"
All he said was, "no."

I couldn't believe it. I knew his older brother was going to be best man, but I thought I'd be in the wedding party. Al was in the wedding party. It was like a knife in my heart. I barely talked the entire night. I just sat in the stands blankly watching the game. Al even asked me at one point if I was okay. I couldn't move or speak or think clearly. I couldn't believe how bad this made me feel. My entire life has been one long series of events where I've been excluded from the club and avoided because I was the weirdo, and so I was used to it. This was different. I felt like Falstaff when Prince Hal tells him he is going to abandon him, "But, we have heard the bells chime at midnight together," Falstaff says, "oh, the things we have seen."

A few days after that, the wedding invitation arrived. I was just going to be another guest sitting at the loser's table. I was so angry I threw the invitation out the window like a Frisbee. I didn't go to the wedding. With that, a friendship that had lasted over fifteen years was over. Mike and I never spoke again.

Attack of the Lawn Jockeys

  While trying to figure out what to do with myself, Pops showed me a job advertisement in the *Star-Ledger*. It had only been a week since I came home. An aluminum foundry in Bellville was looking for someone with 'artistic skills.' I went down and was hired, but not apparently for my artistic skills. I started out pouring molten aluminum into molds. A week later the owner finally decided to employ my artistic skills and I was 'promoted' to the paint shed. There I was to paint the various aluminium *tchotchke's* they made. They made all sorts of sports related objects: hockey skates that were bottle openers, baseballs that were bottle openers, golf balls that were bottle openers, batting helmets that were…well you get the idea. They also made lawn jockeys. Yes, I couldn't believe it either. They made lawn jockeys. They made three kinds of lawn jockeys. They looked exactly the way you'd expect them to look with the one hand on the hip and the other outstretched holding a large ring. The full sized regulation ones were for the lawn then a smaller half-sized version and an even smaller table top version. The paint foreman was quite clear, "Always paint the lawn jockeys with beige flesh tone, never paint the skin brown!" I only lasted a couple of weeks. I got laid off. I then found a job driving a delivery van for a florist. Then the family came to the rescue.

  Helping me get out of my post-service funk, my cousin Dennis lined me up with a job. He worked at a place called Welco in Newark on the Passaic River. The owner of the florist shop was a very creative and flamboyant, and often snippy, gay man. Dennis asked me why I wanted to drive for a word I can't say here, for so little money. I lowered my head, rubbed my eyes and let out a long, pained,"Ughhhh" when he said it. Welco was a company that supplied natural gas cylinders to businesses and hospitals in the area. It was a union job and paid pretty well, $7.50 an hour. So, I put on my old tank driver's coveralls, ignored my cousin's word faux pas and went to work filling bulk gas cylinders eight hours a day on the picturesque Passaic River. In the days of the Lene Lenape People the Passaic had been crystal clear and full of fish you could eat and water you could drink. Once European settlers and colonizers were through with it the water was the colour and consistency of chocolate milk. If there were any fish left in it you'd never eat them. On occasion a small, Coast Guard ice breaker (complete with an M60 machine gun mounted on a pedestal on the bow), the *USCGC Wire*, would cruise lazily up the river. The *Wire* was one of over a dozen similar vessels operating on the nearby Hudson River. I guess when they got bored they'd cruise the Passaic.

  I was living with my parents, but was desperate to get a place of my own. M&D were happy to have me home and happy to have me live with them. They made every accommodation to make me happy and never imposed rules or anything, but I was 22 years old and a vet and I needed to get out. The job at Welco was easy: roll in empty steel cylinders—that looked like torpedoes—hook them up to the filling rack fifty at a time then stand around for half an hour waiting for them to fill. Once full, you disconnected them from the filling rig, rolled them onto the loading dock, then rolled in fifty more empties. I learned how to roll two cylinders at once by holding the valves and pushing the bottom of the cylinders together with your foot. There was an entire cast of characters working at Welco. There was a Portuguese guy who had a little man complex; a morbidly obese mechanic; a tall skinny, chain-smoking dude whose face and hands were permanently yellow from the nicotine; There was another older guy, Walt, who gave off a weird vibe. He was one of those people who is always bragging about how smart he was, and how much money he had. He hardly had any, but he always talked about making "big scores" down at "AC." [19] He would

---

[19] Atlantic City.

stand on the loading dock as we waited for the tanks to fill, and count the money in his wallet so everyone could watch, which everyone made a point of not watching. Years later, when I was working on my doctoral dissertation, I was at the Newark Public Library doing research. When I was finished, I was walking back to my car and thought I'd stop in at the bar on the corner for a refreshing pint before I headed home. As I approached, I saw a filthy half-naked street guy sitting on the sidewalk with his back up against the wall of a bar. Even from a distance you could tell he smelled. As I walked past I saw it was Walt. He didn't notice me and I kept walking and didn't bother going in.

Welco was located on the bank of the Passaic River right next to the Jackson Street Bridge. To get there I drove straight down Kearny Avenue which at the gas works turned into Frank Rodgers Boulevard to cross the bridge. There was a heavily used PATH train station there, with hordes of people coming home from New York City, and so at 5pm the traffic became very congested with all the people heading back into Harrison and Kearny. It was kind of depressing inching along to get back to my parent's place. Sometimes we do jobs for the love of the work. Sometimes we do a job to help others. Sometimes we do a job because if we don't we starve.

> And my radio says tonight it's gonna freeze
> People driving home from the factories
> There's six lanes of traffic
> Three lanes moving slow…[20]

While rolling bulk gas cylinders around Newark, I decided to try to make a career as an artist. I wanted to be an historian, but I had no idea how to go about doing that. I could draw a bit and so pursued that as a way of having a career other than rolling bulk gas cylinders around Newark. I got laid off from Welco a year after I started anyway. They lost a big account and since I was the new guy, I got canned. The foreman, who was about fifty and really skinny except for his huge beer belly which made him look perpetually pregnant, handed me my paycheck that Friday as always. He said, "You don't need to come in Monday." Because I am the naivest person in the world I said, "Oh, are we off Monday?" He looked at me like I was an idiot and said, "No, you're fired." I didn't care. I hated that job, and I was about to head off to art school. Before I left the army I had heard about a school in Dover where they taught comic book illustration and cartooning. It sounded cool, so in the Fall of 1983 I left Welco and entered as a First Year at the 'Joe Kubert School of Cartoon and Graphic Arts.'

Maybe I would never become an historian of monsters, but maybe I could have a career drawing them.

---

[20] Dire Straits, "Telegraph Road," *Love Over Gold* (1982).

Chapter 5
What is Good?

> Whether you succeed or not is irrelevant, there is no such thing. Making your unknown known is the important thing.
>
> *– Georgia O'Keeffe*

I had been slowly coming to the realisation that what really attracted me to history was the storytelling. I wanted to tell stories, though this idea had yet to take a clear form in my head. I assumed I needed a college degree, but that seemed as unlikely now as ever despite getting all hopped up over *Raiders of the Lost Ark*. Commercial artist seemed a more realistic goal. While in my last winter in Kansas, I applied to the Cooper-Union School of Art in New York. They had a great reputation. I saw one of those college poster ads with the little card you pulled off, and sent in for information, in the Fort Riley post library. They sent me an application pack with a brochure that made it seem the coolest school in the world in what I already knew was the coolest city in the world. The entrance application required you to do a self-portrait. As that was the mood I was in, I did a gouache rendering, on an illustration board, of me in my black leather biker jacket sitting with my back against a tombstone in a cemetery as snow flurries fell. On the stone it read, 'Jonny Quest – 1955 – 1981.' I put a lot of emotion into it and thought it was not half bad.

My drawing and painting always came from inside. Each picture I created always had some kind of narrative; always trying to tell a story. I had created several sets of illustrations since arriving in Kansas, each of which told part of stories I had made up.[1] My ability to tell these stories in words alone was still greatly lacking. Artwork, however, proved a bit more successful. These always had to do with adventures of one kind or another, often with people running away from monsters of one type or another. They were less like comic book pages and more like elaborate film storyboards. In this manner, I was able to articulate, in a small way, some of the things going on inside my head. The Jonny Quest cemetery scene was part of that. I filled out all the paperwork and sent it off with the painting and my high hopes to New York. A few weeks later, I received a letter that began, "Unfortunately, we were unable…" I didn't even bother with the rest.[2] I felt like I had drawn the pirate and even the correspondence school didn't think it was any good.

In the Day Room of the 1/34 there was a table near the TV where they arranged magazines and comic books, like in a dentist's waiting room. Absentmindedly leafing through a *Sergeant Rock* comic one day, I saw an ad for a place called The Joe Kubert School of Cartoon and Graphic Art. It was a school that taught comic book art, commercial illustration, and graphic design. It looked interesting and it was in New Jersey. I had never considered being an '*artiste* artist' or a fine artist, but the notion of a commercial artist or narrative artist appealed to me. As I had not yet sent off my application to Cooper Union I thought I'd get a catalogue from Kubert and weigh my options. The rejection from Cooper Union was deeply depressing and I wondered what I would do now. Maybe Al would hire me to paint cars with

---

[1] I still have some of them. There was a serious art supply place not far from my off post apartment. It catered to the fine arts and illustration students at the university and carried a wide range of professional art supplies. I would go there on the weekends and stare at the various paints, pastels and illustration boards planning grand projects just as I had done in *Ben Franklin's*.

[2] They never did send back my picture. I'm sure they just threw it in the garbage.

him. I could spend the rest of my life as a body knocker. After I returned home I wasn't especially enamoured of the jobs I was doing. I came across the Kubert catalogue again and took one more shot. I decided that if I didn't get in there that was a sign that 'artist' was also a job I wasn't going to have. I sent off the application with the idea that if this fell through I would just reenlist.[3] Henry asked me if he could help with the tuition, which was twenty-five hundred dollars a year, but I said no. I would pay for this myself. He had paid for too much already with nothing in return for his investment. I scraped together half in cash then took out a loan from a bank for the rest. Fortunately, my application was accepted.[4] My plan was to continue to work at Welco for the summer, then to go to Kubert once the school year began in September. I was assigned to the freshman cohort at the Joe Kubert School for 1983. I liked illustration and had been experimenting with the comic book form. I was not a huge traditional comic book fan, however. I was more in the Creepy and Eerie and Heavy Metal vein. As usual, I just decided I would make it work somehow.

Stan Lee and Joe Kubert

As I had been fired from Welco I now had the summer off. Before I started at Kubert I thought I should try to get some comic book work under my belt. I put together a portfolio and made an appointment to see someone at the West 50th Street headquarters of Marvel Comics in Manhattan. I didn't think my work fit their style, but what the hell? I was just going to walk in. That strategy had worked for me in the past. Just walk in like you own the place. I stepped into the elevator for the ride up. It was crowded and several people were already in the elevator car.

One by one, people stepped off onto their floors until it was just me and an older guy. I looked over at him and was astonished to see it was Stan Lee, the driving force and legendary face of Marvel Comics. Unsure what to do, I smiled, nodded, and said, "Mr. Lee," in that way you do so the other person knows you're simply saying hello and not starting a conversation. He looked at me, saw I was carrying a portfolio, and gave me a look that was half a step away from dismissive. Without changing the already annoyed look on his face he nodded slightly and grunted what I guess was a hello. The doors opened and he stepped out without ever looking back. I followed and walked up to the reception desk. Mr. Lee disappeared into the warren that was their offices. I told the receptionist who I was and who I was there to see. The guy who I was there to see came right out and looked at my portfolio without ever inviting me to his office. He made a few positive remarks, and then said I still needed to work on my ink lines. That was it. Interview over. "Thanks for coming," he said then he was gone. I got back in the elevator and left. As the elevator doors closed there was a big comic book lettering bubble over me that said "Kapow!" So, among my many accomplishments I can say I was snubbed by Stan Lee of Marvel Comics.

Joe Kubert was a famous comic book artist from the same generation as Stan Lee. He did Hawkman for DC Comics as well as Sgt.Rock and many others. DC was Marvel's big competitor. In the 1970s he purchased a huge, old, Victorian mansion in Dover, New Jersey and opened an art school. He talked a bunch of his old comic book friends into teaching there. I showed up at the three-year program school in 1983 and went into first year group three which had its homeroom up in the mansion's attic.

---

[3] Serving in the US Army was the easiest job I'd ever had.
[4] I didn't realise until later that they pretty much accepted anyone who could pay the tuition.

My classmates included the Canadian Grant Miehm, along with Jack Pollack, who kept the cremated remains of his dog in a little box in his art supply carryall and was the first person I ever knew who carried around his own human skull. He called it Edgar, as in Edgar Allan Poe. Alec Stevens, Bob Vasilief, and guys from all over North America were there. Many, including Grant and Jack, went on to long careers in comics and advertising as illustrators, designers, and editors. They were an odd, but creative bunch. It was a weird crucible of creativity. Ideas were bounced around, critiques done. Suggestions made. Twenty -five of us being squashed into that attic room created a sense of close quarters that produced ingenious ideas and finished work.

For example, not really wanting to do an assignment where we had to design then animate a character, Bob Vasilief created Raizin. Based upon the California Raisins commercials then popular, it was just a large black blob with no details. Another student, when the assignment was to create a four page self-contained comic story did it about a guy who accidentally kills himself, in an homage to the late Vaughn Bodē (1941-1975), through auto-erotic asphyxiation. He titled it Scarf Ace.

There were only one or two women students at Kubert. In fact, very few girls went to Kubert until many years later. There were not many professional female comic book or cartoon artists. At the time. A few exceptions being Trina Robbins, Wendi Pini, and others. As with so many industries in America, comic books were mostly done by youngish, immature men. In the twenty-first century, more brave and talented women began to enter the comic's field and they went mostly into the avant-garde / independent, and new wave halls of comics. Some of them came to Kubert, but they faced the same resistance there as they did in the industry. Women who did try to do mainstream comics were often hounded by the mostly insecure fanboys who dominated the field: and still do. Eventually, the growing popularity of fantasy board games such as Dungeons & Dragons and then the advent of electronic gaming opened up as a place one could ply their talents as artists. A good bit of the misogyny that existed in comic books transferred to gaming with similar results.[5]

There were several very good teachers at the school including Tex Blaisdale, Jose Delbo, Hy Eisman, and John Belfi. Joe Kubert himself taught the narrative art class. He tended, however, to focus on the students who already looked like stars. The rest of us were just a rabble to him. My favourite teacher was Ben Ruiz. Unlike the other teachers he never really had a career as a comic book artist but was an incredible illustrator and teacher. Ben taught life drawing.

One of the things I loved about Ben was that he was always challenging students to think more carefully about what they were doing. When each assignment was due we would place them on an easel, and the class would critique them. Invariably, he would ask a student about a piece and what they thought. If the student liked the work they would say it was 'good.' Ben would then ask, "What is good?" That would flummox the student because we had all become accustomed to being vague about how we described things. He expected students to point out specific elements the creator had done which did or did not fulfil the assignment. We were only capable of reacting viscerally to an artwork. He was training us to look more deeply and learn to articulate more rigorously, what we were thinking. He also gave students a hard time for being clichéd or unoriginal. He would love to point out how a

---

[5] Years later when I taught at Kubert there was an incident where several guys were making fun of a young Indian woman in their class. Joe Kubert called a meeting of the faculty to discuss it. I said he should expel every guy involved. He didn't want to lose that much money so nothing was done to address the issue. The young woman dropped out, and I left the next year.

student created a scene which appeared over and over again in comics or movies or animation. He was constantly pushing us to be as original as possible. He taught us concepts such as 'form before detail' and 'horizon of the form.' My work vastly improved because of his nit picking.

Once a student was rapturously explaining a series of comic book panels he had designed and drawn. At one point one of the prominent characters was no longer there. Ben asked what happened to that character. The student said in an offhand way, "Oh, I killed him off." Ben then launched into this dissertation about characters in a narrative. "Why kill him off?" he said, "Did you think about it? Did he have a family? Who do you think you are killing off a character?" Again, it was all designed to get us to think more carefully about what we were doing.

One day outside before class began I ran into Ben and we began talking. I told him I was thinking about designing a monster from an alien planet for a new homework assignment. Without the slightest hesitation he said, "Don't forget, monsters don't come from other planets, they come from our hearts and souls." It was an idea I had never considered. I wanted to ask him to elaborate, but another student just showed up and they began talking. I never forgot that line. It would go on to influence all my scholarly work on the subject of monsters.

As the year went by you could tell who was serious and who was not. The serious students had focused and were taking in everything we were being taught and applying it. You could tell by their work how much they had improved. You could tell who was going to have careers in comics or advertising or commercial illustration or animation. You could also tell who the pure fanboys were. They were the ones who just liked comic books and being around them, but were not really serious about their skills.

I learned a great deal at Kubert and I enjoyed the various quirks and idiosyncrasies of my classmates. When Blade Runner premiered at a local theatre, we all went to see it together. I had already seen it, but it was fun to see for a third time. We, of course, spent the rest of the school year discussing it in class and deconstructing it in detail. We had to do an assignment where we designed a Packman-like video game. I made mine a Blade Runner theme. Detective Decard must negotiate his way up through the abandoned building to reach the roof and be rescued by a flying police car. Along the way, you are chased by a series of Roy Batty's.

The classes would be forty-five minutes or so of instruction and critiques of work; then we had studio time to actually work on the assignments. We loved talking about comics and commercial art, pop culture, movies, and music. The studio sessions would begin with lots of talk and joke telling, but then it would slowly quieten down as everyone focused on what they were doing. The avant-garde musician, performance artist Laurie Anderson had just released her breakout album, *Big Science* with the single '*O Superman*'. Sometimes when the quiet had gone on for too long someone would inevitably start singing in a low voice, "ha, ha, ha, ha, ha..." over and over again. Then someone else would chime in, "Oh superman..." Slowly it would get louder as more of us joined in. Then we'd have impromptu battling imitations of Harrison Ford as Deckard.

"Sushi...that's what my wife called me...cold fish."

A lot of time was spent talking about comic books and movies. The underground comic, Teenage Ninja Mutant Turtles (TMNT) had only just begun to circulate and we talked about it. (TMNT) still had some years before it became a toy and movie juggernaut. We loved that the turtles were created as a spoof on traditional superhero comics: something that went largely unnoticed by the later legions of fans. There were EERIE and CREEPY comics' bastions, and everyone loved Heavy Metal. One old science fiction movie was a particular favourite *When Worlds Collide* (1951) that was one of the first big budget end of the world films. It depicts the race to complete a space ark to save mankind before two rogue planets, Zyra and Bellus, crush the earth. When deadlines in our homework assignments loomed, someone would inevitably yell out, "Three days to Zyra, waste anything but time!" mimicking one of the iconic lines from the movie. If it was a really tight deadline the refrain was, "One day to Bellus, waste anything but time!"

By the end of the school year I had come to realise that despite how much I enjoyed going to the Kubert School and how much I enjoyed the students and faculty, it was time for me to move on again. I had this built-in mechanism that after a certain amount of time forced me to pack up and leave. I had been living with my parents and using the money I had saved in the army, but I needed to get my own place. I received my certificate for the first year then went out and searched for an apartment and a job.

The Grand Union

The first job I managed to talk my way into after leaving Kubert was in the in-house advertising department of a grocery store chain called The Grand Union. They had a night shift and needed advertising paste-up artists. The work was easy, and on the night shift there were interesting characters around and not much pressure. The pay was middling, though. I kept doing freelance work for other clients in order to keep some extra money coming in. While I enjoyed the year I spent at Kubert, I felt I wasn't learning the things I wanted to learn. I knew I was not going to get hired to do superhero comics. My work just wasn't in that style, and quite frankly I had no interest in doing it even if I had.

I was so bored working at the Grand Union that when Grant Meihm called me from Dover to see if I wanted to go into New York City to go to Forbidden Planet I dropped the phone and jumped into my car in one motion. Grant and Jack Pollack took the train from Dover to Newark where I picked them up. We then headed through the Lincoln Tunnel to Manhattan.

Having spent all our money buying hard to find graphic novels and other rarities (I purchased a hardcover first edition of John Willie's *The Adventures of Sweet Gwendoline*) we headed home. We decided to drive uptown first to drive around the MET (Metropolitan Museum of Art) as Grant and Jack had never seen it before. Once satisfied, we headed downtown to the tunnel entrance. Driving along the edge of Central Park we came to a stop at a red light. As we stood waiting for the light, we talked about comics. As we did I looked to my left and saw the actress Diane Keaton standing at the corner also waiting for the light to change. I've always had thing for her and since I figured I'd never get a chance again I rolled the window down and said, "Excuse me Miss Keaton, can we give you a ride?" She looked over and saw me and Grant, and in the back seat Jack wearing his Air Force dress uniform jacket and compass around his neck. God only knows what she thought seeing this odd crew in the gloss black firebird with the chrome mag hotrod wheels. She smiled and said, "Oh, no thanks, I'm okay." Just then, the light turned green. I said, "Okay!" Smiled back and we drove off.

I tired quickly of working at the Grand Union and so began searching for more advertising work. I had a decent portfolio of that type of material now and so I went looking for freelance assignments. They came readily and I did paste-up, design, and illustration.

Meeting Lisa

Advertising in those days was still pre-computer, except for the typesetting. Ads and pages were put together by hand. A typesetter would produce text on sheets of coated photographic paper. The 'artist' would then cut up these bits and assemble a board with the page drawn on it according to a previously created layout. Artwork was produced in the same way: drawn by hand in black & white ink lines, photographed then placed into position as per the layout. All these bits were then glued down to the board in the proper location using hot liquid wax or rubber cement. As you were pasting these bits down, the people doing it were called paste-up artists. It was mind- numbingly boring work with little in the way of creativity, but it was better than filling bulk gas cylinders. The ease of the work was one draw, the other was that in the New York/New Jersey metropolitan area there were dozens of shops where this was done, so if you were even slightly competent you could find work. I bounced from one studio to another which was the norm. Then I found work at a place called Venet Advertising. They had accounts with several large department and grocery stores for whom they did newspaper ads. They had so much work they too had a night shift. I found a place on the night shift and proceeded to work at putting together grocery store ads in a little cubicle.

I found an apartment in Lyndhurst which was on the top floor of a small house. The owners, an old Polish couple called the Dudecks, lived downstairs.[6] I'd get home from Venet about 5 a.m. and then watch MTV until about six or seven then try to sleep a little. I'd spend the rest of the day creating artwork for my portfolio, and trying to figure out what to do. I hated the job at Venet, but I needed to work. I'd do any job to keep from having to move back in with my parents. My heart was never in any of these positions, however.

I got a job down in Darlington

Some nights I don't go

Some nights I go to the drive-in, and

Some nights I just stay home...[7]

Still holding onto my adventuring academic fantasy, the year after I left Kubert I saw that Rutgers University had a degree program in New World Archaeology. It couldn't seem more perfect. With fantastic images of myself exploring ancient burial mounds in my head, I called the department and spoke with someone. After a discussion of what they offered and what I wanted to do it seemed a good match. They suggested I contact admissions, which I immediately did. I explained to the woman at admissions what I wanted to do: I wanted to enter as a New World Archaeology major. I even had, I told her, college credits. She asked what credits and from what school and I told her I had done a year at Kubert. "Oh," she said with a distinct tone I knew wasn't good, "that's a trade school, we don't accept their credits."[8]

---

[6] When she heard I had this apartment, Al Malet's cousin Marie, who was married to a Vietnam vet named Wren-shaw—who everyone referred to as The Wrench—gave me her old living room couch. Al and I stuffed it into the back of my Firebird, with four feet of it hanging out. Al climbed in the back seat and held it while I drove gingerly to my new place. Somehow, we managed to drive across Kearny and Lyndhurst without incident.
[7] Bruce Springsteen. "The Promise," 18 Tracks (1999).
[8] Having no one I could talk to about what going to college was like, I never realized during this period that there were differences between the types of schools. I naively thought that a place like Kubert or RISD were little different from a university. All I ever thought about was what I wanted to study and learn. That one school might be 'better' or 'worse' than another never crossed my mind. The details always escaped me.

She then suggested I take a few classes part-time. That sounded okay. She then told me classes were thirty-five hundred dollars each. I explained there was no way I could afford that. She began talking again, but it was all just droning. All I heard was, "kids like you don't go to college." I hung up with her still talking. Thus ended my career as an archaeologist. Then I did something I hadn't done since high school; I bashed my head against the kitchen cabinet door of my apartment at the Dudeck's house a couple of times in frustration. All I ever wanted was to do something good with my life: something worthwhile, but fun. It seemed every time I came near it, the thing blew up in my face and laughed at me.

I spent most of my time at Venet drawing on my desk instead of doing the paste-up jobs. At about midnight a gut truck would show up at the back door and people would get sandwiches. I didn't interact much with the other employees. I didn't really want anything to do with them. One night in the break room, however, I was leaning against the wall with my head trying to be somewhere else when I heard someone say, "You look like you could use a drink." It was the future DocBotz. I gave her the slow head turn, just as she flashed the cutest smile I had ever seen. It was all over. We started dating and it quickly dawned on me she was special. She was an artist and an artist's model as well, and had been looking for the same work as me. She enjoyed old books and history. An old friend of hers, Dennis 'Deno' Tartaglia, had suggested Venet to her as a possible source of work.[9]

I can't even begin to explain how important Lisa is to my life. If it wasn't for her, my life would have been very different. Regardless of my dreams to do so, I never would have become a professional historian or writer without her support. She was the only one who understood what I was after. She was Velma Dinkley, Trixie Racer, and Lieutenant Ellis all in one. A smart, cute, adventurous and funny girl who wouldn't hesitate to run off with me to chase monsters or ghosts. She understood my desire to be a writer and historian, and wouldn't make fun of me for being a nerd, or tell me I wasn't smart enough. We have hunted fossils together, searched libraries together, gotten the car stuck in mud together, laughed and cried together. Though she wasn't into trucks or machinery, she was someone who instinctively understood and appreciated the meaning of the Alvis Stalwart. She was the first person, since my encounter with the high school guidance counsellor, I told of my dreams to be an historian. As William Shakespeare once said of Ann Hathaway, Lisa "saved my life."

I had always wanted someone to be with who enjoyed adventuring as much as I did. Someone who likes art and books, and creativity: someone who would walk the world with me holding hands and poking at things. That wasn't easy to find. The women I had been with were fine, but none of them had that special something. I wanted someone who wouldn't say, "ewwww!" to dinosaurs or archives. In the years we have been together, we have had our rough patches. There are certain things she does that drive me a little crazy, and there are things that I do that drive her very crazy, but, overall, we have managed to live a good life together. What helps is that we have similar interests and understand the life of an academic. In the end, we both know we would defend each other no matter what. I would spend my last penny on her because I know she would spend her last penny on me.

Uncle Sam Again

When I left the regular army I swore to myself I would never join the National Guard or the Reserves as was common. Then reality set in and I wasn't making much money. I went

---

[9] We all eventually became good friends, including Deno's soon to be wife Sheila. From then on we always made the joke that Deno brought us together.

down to the Army Reserve Center at Camp Kilmer in Edison, New Jersey and enlisted in the active reserves. I chose Kilmer because they were the closest to where I lived. They had no armour or Cav outfits, but they had a basic training unit, the 78th Training Division (Jersey Lightning). Since I had been through NBC school I was readily accepted and became the unit's chief chemical warfare instructor. They even changed my MOS from the original 19E to 54E (chemical warfare). It wasn't a lot of money, but it was easy money: one weekend a month and two weeks a year in the summer. The worst part was I had to get my haircut again. I hung out with them for two years. We did our deployment at Fort Bragg, North Carolina teaching new recruits. As usual, I became bored. I left Edison and headed over to the Morristown armoury where they had a National Guard artillery unit. The 3/112 Field Artillery was more like what I did as a regular. It was part of the New Jersey National Guard's 50th Armoured Division. As I had armour vehicle experience, they put me into the FIST (Fire Support) platoon. I took command of an M113 cookie box outfitted as a fire support vehicle. Because of its simple and uncluttered design, the M113 was a versatile machine that had an unusually long life. It was made into variants as diverse as personnel carriers, command vehicles, mortar scows, anti-tank rocket carriers, anti-aircraft guns, and engineering vehicles. First introduced in the early 1960s it saw extensive service in Vietnam on through to the various Gulf Wars. It is still in service with militaries around the world. This was the vehicle I saw clattering down the street as a child during the Newark riots.

For our two week deployment we road marched up to Fort Drum, New York on the Canadian border and commenced to blow stuff up. The first half of the deployment were field manoeuvres. They assigned us to follow an infantry unit around and in close conjunction with the battalion commander, called in simulated fire support missions on enemy positions. The second half consisted of live fire exercises where we called in fire missions to the batteries of the 3/112 who then actually fired live rounds at the designated targets. The 3/112 was a battalion of 155mm self-propelled guns. For one of the live fire missions, we manoeuvred our cracker box under simulated combat conditions to a point where we could see the receiving end of the range. It was scattered with what was left of dozens of old vehicles used as targets and craters. There were also concrete bunkers that had years' worth of artillery shells dropped on them. Oddest of all, were the large numbers of plastic, man-sized targets simulating "infantry in the open." They stood silently and uncomplainingly riddled with shrapnel and machine gun bullet holes. When we reached the part of a little hill with pine trees that overlooked the range, we manoeuvred the track so that just the nose poked out of the briers. We set up and began calling in fire missions to the battery. This setting up included sitting on the roof of our track sunbathing while calling in fire missions on the radio. The track was outfitted inside with maps and communications rigs. The fictional target for this exercise was the field headquarters of Muammar Gaddafi who had been in the news a lot at the time as a leader of worldwide terrorism. Not long after the Iranian Hostage Crisis, Ronald Reagan tried to bomb Gaddafi without success. As a result, various Middle Eastern dictators were making noises about destroying the 'Great Satan'. With Middle East violence growing this is what we were training for. It was expected that when actually deployed it would be against Arab terrorists rather than the Russians. Our unit commanders also expected this to happen sometime soon. We troopies never took it too seriously, but in the back of my mind I thought, great, I made it through being a regular, now I was going to go off to war in the National Guard.

For the first exercise it was a beautiful, clear warm day. We had several of those short-legged beach chairs. This allowed us to sit on the roof of the vehicle with the radio microphones on long extensions coming up from inside the vehicle so we could call in the map coordinates to the battery which was a mile or so away, and out of our sight. For us, it was all very relaxed and almost vacation-like. We could see the targets through our binoculars, find the spot on the map, work out the numbers then call in the fire mission, all without having to move that much. Around noon, a mortar platoon pulled into position about fifty yards from us. They rode in cracker boxes too, but the back open bed of the vehicle had an 80mm mortar mounted in it. We watched as they went through their setting up protocol: gun commanders barking orders and the men with frantic and practised precision preparing to fire. It was fascinating watching the three teams working. The gun commander would yell out the coordinates we gave them, to be repeated by the gunner. The tube would swing into position as the gunner cranked the elevating and azimuth wheels. Once in firing position, the loader would take a round from the interior mounted ready rack and place it halfway in the opening of the tube. While holding the large round the loader would yell, "half load!" The commander would then repeat, "half load!" Then "fire!" The loader would let go of the round. With that motion everyone in the track would turn away from the tube and bend down so as to avoid the flash. As the round slid down inside the tube and hit the bottom it struck the firing pin. This set off the propellant charge causing it to explode, and shoot out of the tube to fly to the target. They worked in three volley sequences. When the bigger cannons of the 3/112 fired they made a loud, sharp, bang sound. The mortars made a somewhat quieter, more muffled sound as it launched: "Fire!" fump, "Fire!" fump, "Fire!" fump. As the round was relatively slow, if you watched carefully, you could see the round shoot out of the mortar and arch up into the sky before it disappeared and then dropped onto the target. After calling in a mission, we just sat and watched the boom-booms.

In between the fire missions, we had a cassette deck/radio on. Around noon the First Sargeant drove up with lunch. He dropped a cardboard box at the back door of our vehicle and drove off. It was not the usual C-Rations, and some excitement crept in. We took out bags of potato chips and juice boxes, and retrieved the dozen sandwiches lining the bottom of the box. We eagerly took out the wax-bag wrapped sandwiches. Opening mine, I stopped. I couldn't believe it: ham and cheese. They were all ham and cheese![10]

RISD

Finishing my first year at the Kubert school, I realised I was never going to get work as a comic book artist. I had also discovered something called scientific and technical illustration. It would allow me to combine science, history, and artwork in a way I had always wanted. I did some research and found out this was an actual job that people did for a living. I also discovered that there was a guy named George Venable, a renowned entomology illustrator, who worked at the Smithsonian Institution. I found his contact information and gave him a call. I asked him about how to get work as a scientific illustrator, and what kind of a career it was. He was helpful, but a bit standoffish, as if I had told him I wanted his job specifically. He did tell me about a program I should look into. The prestigious Rhode Island School of Design had a certificate program in scientific and technical illustration that, if one applied themself, could be finished in two years of full-time study. After talking it over with Lisa, we hopped in the Firebird and headed up to Providence to interview with the director. I brought my portfolio and he seemed genuinely impressed.

---

[10] When I returned home from this expedition there was a message on my answering machine from the supervisor at Venet. Despite the fact I had told him I was going on this trip and employers were supposed to not be able to fire people for it, the message said because I hadn't come to work for two weeks I was fired. Lisa said I should sue, but I didn't care. I hated that place and everyone there. Once again, with a light heart I picked up and went on to the next job. I started getting more freelance work and found other shops like JJ Michaels and WT Quinn where I did the same work as I had done at Venet.

RISD was the oldest art school in America. It was highly regarded. I didn't care that the Scientific and Technical Illustration program was only a certificate and not a degree program. All I cared about was that it taught the things I wanted to learn. When I told Henry I would graduate with a certification, he thought it was a good idea. The fact that he and Lisa approved made it much easier for me to go. The classes were fascinating and taught everything from perspective drawing to mechanical design to biological and medical illustration. It had an amazing 'Nature Lab' that was in an ancient building on the corner of Waterman and Benefit Streets, and contained a collection of stuffed animals, fossils, shells, and skeletons. In one corner was a collection of specimens in jars of spirits, while in another was a rhinoceros skull. Along with the dozen or so human skeletons—some of which dated back to the founding of the school in the 19th century—there was an entire Zebra skin on the wall. It was an incredible atmosphere that fostered creative thinking and improvement of one's drawing skills. I spent every moment I could there filling notebook after notebook of sketches, line drawings, pastel and watercolour works.

Since I was rather on the poor side, I could not afford a pricey apartment. I checked in with the student housing office and found a boarding house run by a middle-aged woman named Mrs. Tankard. She rented the rooms of a Victorian home in Providence off Elmwood Avenue to students from the many schools in town. The bottom floor apartment was occupied by a sullen, thirty-something guy who acted as an on-site house manager. He was so lazy and incompetent he would not turn up the heat in the winter and would get annoyed if you asked. I eventually saw how I could bypass the lock on the thermostat in the entry hall and turn up the heat myself. The locked, clear plastic box that covered the heating control had four, one-inch long slits in the bottom of it to allow air in. I took a long, thin knife and was able to slip it through the vents just enough to come in contact with the metal wheel which was used to set the temperature. By gently moving the knife, I could turn the metal wheel. That way when the temperature dropped and he, or Mrs. Tankard, refused to raise the heat I would quietly go down and set it myself. No one ever discovered that I was doing this. Since what I was doing did not scratch or break the plastic box, no damage was done. To everyone who lived there it happened as if by magic.

I quickly came to like Providence. In the mid 1980s it was in one of its darker periods with crime and a population of street people. Still, the large student population gave it a funky vibe that I enjoyed immensely. I spent most of my time on College Hill, which is where RISD and Brown University were. I eventually found a job doing the newspaper advertising illustrations for a local department store chain called Apex. Again, it was easy work and as I had a car, I could drive to the store in Pawtucket in fifteen or twenty minutes. I worked there the better part of a year until I went back to New Jersey for a few days to see Lisa and my parents. I stayed an extra day without letting anyone know, then I just showed up for work as usual. The department was run by a straight-laced, sixty-something guy who's claim to fame was that he had been a designer for Lord & Taylor in the 1960s. Everything he knew about advertising he had learned by using a Lord & Taylor style guide which he carried with him the rest of his life like a magical spell book. He had hired me because they needed an illustrator. We initially got along well. I was quick and thanks to my training at Kubert could draw anything they wanted in camera ready line drawings. As time went by my free and easy ways grew on his nerves. My staying away an extra day was all he needed as justification. When I walked in that morning the other people in the department looked at me like I had killed someone. My reaction was to say, "what's the worst they can do? They can fire me."

That's what they did.

I was told by security to clear out my things. I had my portfolio with me in my cubicle, and so I loaded it with everything I could cram into it: art supplies and even merchandise I had been drawing. I waved goodbye to everyone, smiled and left happy. Before I went back to my apartment I stopped off at the comic book store in Pawtucket a few blocks from the Apex. Then I went next door to a tiny greasy spoon diner that served the most delicious 'Saugy Dogs.'; a proud invention of 19th century Rhode Island entrepreneur Alphonse Saugy, these were essentially smallish, steamed hot dogs. The variant I loved was the chilli version with that red onion sauce on them. They were inexpensive and you could get a bag of half a dozen of them for just a few bucks. I was going to eat well that night.

After the fun of doing the big walk out, I had to find some employment. One night, while walking around College Hill, I passed the BioMed building of Brown University. On the ground floor there was an office with the lights still on. As I passed, I noticed that there were posters of dinosaurs on the walls. I stopped and pressed my face against the glass. There were fossils and books and all the things I had in my boarding house room. Except for museum stores, I had never seen a room so decorated. I went around to the door on the front of the building, but it was locked (it had a slide card pass key lock on it). I was determined to find out what was going on here. I came back the next day and waited until I saw someone go in. Luckily, it was an older woman struggling with some bags. I smiled and said, "Oh, let me help you?" She said thanks and I was in. I wandered around trying to find the door to that office. I found it and knocked, but no one answered. The nameplate on the door said, 'Dr. Christine Janus.'

I came back a few days later and finally found Dr. Janus. A mammalogist of English birth, and as I would later learn, worldwide reputation as a scientist, Dr. Janus readily chatted with me when I explained I was at RISD and working on scientific illustrations. I showed her some of my work that she liked. She had a paper coming out on fossil mammal teeth and asked if I was interested in doing some illustrations for it. She gave me a box of fossil horse teeth and a lot of instructions from which I produced a series of pencil drawings. She looked them over and made corrections. As I knew how to produce camera-ready art, it was easy for me to turn the pencil drawings into ink versions. She accepted them, and my career as a scientific illustrator of fossils had begun. She also paid me enough to pay my rent at the boarding house so as not to get tossed into the street. I did drawings for a number of Christine's publications and even found a few other faculty members at Brown who also needed drawings. When Lisa came up to Providence, I introduced her to Christine and they got along. We have all remained friends ever since; Lisa and I have stayed at Christine's house and she at ours in New Jersey many times.

While there, Christine hired me as a lab assistant for her classes. That meant I helped prepare the specimens for each class. I found an unused lab coat in a closet that said 'Department of Anatomy' on the back. I took it and wore it to class. Part of the course in mammal morphology was for the students to do a series of dissections. I would put out all the surgical equipment and prepare the room. During one dissection session there was a Lamprey in a jar. The Lamprey and Hagfish are some of the simplest creatures alive, and thanks to them looking like a penis with teeth, the most revolting. As no one wanted to do it, I sat down and dissected it. Later, an Emu from the Providence Roger Williams Zoo died and Christine acquired it. We dissected that too. It was still warm when we began cutting into it.

A few years later Christine married Dr. Jack Sepkoski, another palaeontologist of world reputation (when he passed away in 1999 his obituary appeared in the New York

Times).[11] They invited us to the wedding party held at the Brown University Faculty Club. Both Christine and Jack knew everyone in the world of palaeontology and many of the biggest names in the field were at this event. At one point we met Dr. Ian Tattersal of the American Museum of Natural History. He could not have been nicer; Lisa and I were nobodies, yet he talked with us for some time. We met him several more times over the years and he was always gracious and friendly. Then, as I wandered around I saw a little gaggle of people talking. One of them was Dr. Stephen Jay Gould, one of the men who helped develop the notion of Punctuated Equilibria, an idea that revolutionised evolutionary biology. I slipped into the crowd and listened. At one point someone said something that I knew some small fact about. I spoke a little bit. Dr. Gould looked at me, gave a bit of a dismissive glance, and without speaking, turned and walked away. So, along with Stan Lee, I can say I was snubbed by Stephen Jay Gould.

I graduated from RISD in 1986. I was proud I had managed to do the certificate in scientific and technical illustration in the two years I had set for myself. We headed back to New Jersey. Lisa and I found an apartment together in Lyndhurst over a bar. We both began taking freelance advertising and illustration work. I did a series of projects for magazines like Scientific American and others. I did work for both small advertising agencies and tiny ones. I also took my portfolio around to various publishers. Taking a chance, I went, cold, to see the people at Prentice Hall. Fate smiled as I had walked in just when they needed someone to do all the illustrations for an upcoming book on environmental science. They were desperate, and I turned on my best charming act to the middle-aged woman who was the acquisitions editor and they gave us the job. Lisa and I had to go into overdrive, as the project required over a hundred illustrations, mostly charts and graphs. Environmental Science: the way the world works (1993) turned out well, as far as we were concerned.[12]

While we were finishing the environmental science textbook, Christine Janus told us she knew a palaeontologist at the University of Rhode Island who was working on a textbook on dinosaurs. It was, in fact, the first college textbook on dinosaurs specifically designed from scratch as a textbook. It was a Cambridge University Press project. Lisa and I headed back up to Providence. We met with the co-author Dr. David Fastovsky at URI. We showed him our work and he liked it. They already had someone to do a brace of full colour reconstructions, but they needed someone to do the charts and graphs and black and white line drawings. We then met with the Cambridge editor. All went swimmingly and we were given the contract. I put a huge amount of effort into the drawings and am still happy with them. Then Cambridge told us the person doing the colour renderings was not working out and would we like to do those as well? Now we would get all the artwork and all the money.

I was very happy with what we did for *The Evolution and Extinction of the Dinosaurs* (1996).[13] Apparently, no one else was. A few years later when Cambridge put out a revised edition of the book, we were not asked to work on it. Indeed, they scrapped all the artwork I did and had the well-known British dinosaur artist John Sibbick re-do all my drawings. In most cases, he simply copied exactly what I did.

[11] Carol Kaesuk Yoon, "J. John Sepkoski Jr., 50, Dies; Changed Field of Paleontology," *New York Times* (May 6, 1999).
[12] Bernard J. Nebel and Richard T. Wright. *Environmental Science: the way the world works* (Prentice Hall, 1993).
[13] David E. Fastovsky and David B. Weishampel. The Evolution and Extinction of the Dinosaurs (Cambridge University Press, 1996).

Kean College

The life of a freelance artist is precarious. You are constantly hustling for work. You rarely know where the next job is going to come from and so you scrounge looking for anything that will pay. Your behaviour becomes like that of a stereotypical New York City cabbie: you race wildly through the job you have in order to line up the next one. I had started taking freelance work from an agency in Boonton, New Jersey that supplied artists to various companies. In 1990, they landed me a job as an industrial designer with AT&T in their Middletown, New Jersey complex. I had sweet-talked my way into a contract position on the back of the technical illustrations I did while I was at RISD. It was fun, but as a contract worker I was told not to expect being given a resident's position, certainly not without a college degree. To cut down on the commute we found a garden apartment closer to Middletown. At AT&T it was made clear I needed a degree to get anywhere there. I began asking around to see what the resident employees had as credentials. I had a one-year certificate from Kubert and a two-year certificate from RISD, along with a portfolio of work. I learned that was clearly not good enough. I needed an actual four-year degree from a college or university. A guy in the AT&T graphic arts studio told me that Kean College in nearby Union had something called the EPIC program. It was designed to help older people who had never gone to college become students. They also had an Industrial Design program. I went to see them wary from my experience with Rutgers. To my surprise, not only was I not brushed off, I was welcomed in. I went to see the Chair of Industrial Design, Dr. Tim Reigel (no relation). We had a nice chat, I showed him some of my RISD work and that was that. I enrolled and began taking classes' part-time as an Industrial Design major.

Going to a conventional liberal arts college like Kean was different from the two art schools I had gone to. All the work in those classes involved drawing and painting and graphic design: things that came easy to me. Now I had other things I had to do. It wasn't as easy, and I still wasn't sure if I should be doing this. I was a thirty-year old freshman. I felt a little out of place. I was the only person in my Intro to College mandatory one credit course, for example, who had fired a heavy machine gun, driven a tank, and who could field strip a .45 auto while wearing a gas mask, in the dark, in fifteen seconds.[14] Intro to College was run by an upper class student. The idea was to have experienced students help new students. One day, our student teacher went around the class and asked everyone to explain something they knew, but other students might not know. One kid had worked in a florist shop so explained how to put cut flowers in a vase. Another, how to work a fryer at a fast food joint. When my turn came I thought for a second then began to explain how to treat someone who had just been gassed with VX nerve agent. I explained the symptoms: shaking, blood coming from the eyes and the importance of stabbing them in the leg with the Atropine injector in just the right way before they convulsively coughed out their lungs. After a few seconds I realised the entire class was staring at me mouths agape.

My college experience was not that of the image favoured by pop culture. Not only was I some years older than most of my classmates, I had to work full time. As a result I never really had the chance to hang out and party with my fellow students in those ways expected of college students. However, I went to a few on-campus events that featured interesting guest speakers whenever possible. The most interesting was Dr. Deborah Lipstadt who was in the news because of being sued by David Irving for calling him a Holocaust denier. I was

---

[14] In the twenty-first century, that sort of thing changed. There were more and more veterans from the various Gulf Wars who were now attending Kean.

spending most of my free time—when I wasn't with Lisa—in the library. I had a goal and I was going to achieve it no matter what. The army had ingrained in me the importance of "completing the mission." I focused on completing the mission. I wasn't the only 'non-traditional' student, in fact, colleges like Kean attract older students who are more focused on their education than hijinks. I had to get a degree so I could be hired as a resident by AT&T.

Then I was fired by AT&T.

The communications giant went through a major downsizing and part of it was being broken off to become Lucent Technologies. They let over three hundred people go from my facility in one day alone. Luckily, I was used to being a freelancer so I could recover quickly. There were people let go who had been with the company for decades who were not so adaptable. AT&T didn't care. I resumed doing freelance work. Then I was asked by my former teacher at the Kubert School, Mike Chen, to come on as an instructor there. I had received instructor training in the Reserves, and I did want to be a professor. This was sort of close to that, and I needed the money, so I accepted the offer and joined the faculty at Kubert. I would be teaching Basic Drawing and Life Drawing.

It no longer made sense to continue with the Industrial Design degree especially considering my poor performance in the maths classes, but I didn't want to drop out. Then I thought an Art History degree would be the way to go. At RISD I would show up on campus early for my classes. To kill time, I would go into the RISD library and read. I found a copy of the massive, two-volume biography of Thomas Eakins by Lloyd Goodrich. I always loved Eakins' work. I would then read all the art history books they had. I enjoyed that so it seemed right. On the next Kean registration day, I stood in line to change my major. This was in the last days before computers took over everything. In the gym there were dozens of tables set up with a huge mass of students lining up like cattle at each one to register for the next semester's classes. The din was considerable. I needed to change my major and then register for the upcoming semester. When I finally reached a table, after standing in line for 45 minutes, I told the faculty member who was at that table that I wanted to register and change my major. He asked me what I wanted to change my major to and I said art history. He looked up at me with an incredulous face and said, "Why art history? You can't get a job with a degree like that!" I blurted out that I really wanted to be an historian. He waved his hand dismissively and said, "I'm going to change you to pure history." I thought, "okay, now I'm a history major." It seemed cool to just say, "you're a history major." It turned out this faculty member was Dr. Larry Zimmer, chair of the Department of History. With this chance encounter, I would spend the rest of my life from that moment forward, associated with this department.

The Department of History at Kean College in those days was a bit of a wild west city. The faculty was made up of mostly old, white men who had been there forever and who had, with few exceptions, not published much, but only taught. That was not unusual given the status of the school. Kean began operations in 1855 as the Newark Normal School. It was established to prepare teachers not researchers. It was part of a French concept then sweeping the west called L'Ecole Normale, Normal School. It worked on the notion that to prepare individuals to be teachers, but not researchers, required a different approach. Over time, however, the school prospered and went through several iterations. It became the Newark Teachers College, then Newark State College. In the 1950s the ancient Kean-Livingston family offered Newark State the large parcel of land they owned as part of the original colonial era Livingston estate on the opposite side of Morris Avenue in Union, New Jersey. The school moved and became Kean College. By the mid-1990s when I was a student there it

112

transformed again into Kean University as its instructional programs grew to include graduate education.

Many of the senior history faculty like Larry Zimmer, Arnold Rice, Robert Mayer, and Martin Siegel disliked each other intensely. One day I had to go to the department for some paperwork. The department's offices were then in Willis Hall. They were cramped and close. Willis always felt to me like an above ground nuclear fallout bunker (Willis was demolished in 2019 and the spot turned into a little park). As I walked down the hall I became aware of heated talking, then outright yelling. I walked in just in time to see Martin Siegel and the new Latin American scholar screaming at each other. I never learned what started it all, but it may have had something to do with Dr. Siegel insulting a new man's work. In his fiery Latin way, the young professor yelled in accented English, "How dare you disparage my work, you've never published anything! I read your dissertation, it was shit!" I left and came back later.

Luckily for me, there were other faculty members I could work with. Dr. Mary Lewis in particular had a huge impact on my career. She was a classicist who had worked on the digs at Mycenae. She was the first person I ever met who had a laptop computer, and knew how to use this weird new thing called the internet. There was also Jim Jandrowitz, the occasionally volatile Vietnam vet, who all the students feared. As a vet myself I got along with him quite well. He did not have a doctorate, but he was one of the best pure teachers I ever knew. In addition, of course, there was Frank Esposito. As a scholar of Native America and historian of New Jersey, Frank Esposito and I got along well. I took several of his classes and he helped show me how to utilise the Chicago Manual of Style. Years later we wrote The Secret History of the Jersey Devil together.

I still had an important decision to make: was I going to try to be a real historian or just play act at it? I was at the proverbial crossroads. Unsure what to do, I took Mary Lewis' four thousand level archaeology class, The Ancient City. I had taken her two thousand level class, Introduction to Archaeology and done well. I told myself that if I did well in this four thousand level history class then I should probably continue, if I didn't I would drop out. It was a fascinating class. Dr. Lewis showed us slides she had taken herself at various archaeological sites around the Mediterranean. Pictures of her standing next to the Bull murals, and the bust of Sir Arthur Evans were inspiring. She could make you feel like you were there. I was hooked. All those fantasies and dreams came back. It felt right. For a final project we had to pick an ancient city on which to write a paper. I chose Jerusalem. I had learned how to do cut-away drawings of vehicles at RISD, and had done reconstructions of extinct animals for Christine Janus, so I thought it would be fun to do a cut-away reconstruction of Solomon's Temple to go along with my text. I had been reading the flurry of speculative books that had come out about 'mysteries' and ancient architecture and weird theories about ancient astronauts and holy blood lines. I thought it all sounded a bit fantastical, but it brought me to more scholarly work on Biblical history and archaeology.

I went through the Old Testament and worked out the proportions for Solomon's Temple as it appeared there. I then did a perspective drawing of the temple including a cut-away of the interior showing the Holy of Holies and the Ark of the Covenant. I didn't have access to any computer drawing programs, so I did the entire thing by hand the way I had learned at RISD and Kubert. You only had so long to complete this, therefore I did it as a black and white line drawing. Along with an accompanying text, I thought I had done well. I nervously turned it in and waited for Professor Lewis to give her critique. It was a bit nerve wracking. She called me to her office. I sat as she looked at my report and drawing. She looked at it carefully and made a few "hmmm" sounds. Without looking up she asked if I was planning on becoming a professional historian. No one had ever asked me that before. I said, "uh, yes." I was suddenly sixteen years old again in my guidance counsellor's office. I waited for her to tell me "well, kids like you don't become historians." Then she looked up smiling. "Good, we could use someone like you in this field." I wasn't sure how to react. It was the first time someone had ever said something like this to me. Finally, I said, "okay, great, thanks." Following our discussion, I had to go outside. I had to sit on a bench for a few minutes to compose myself. I had gotten used to people telling me I was no good and had no future. I always just expected it. It was a bit shocking to me when the opposite finally happened.

That was it. I knew that no matter what happened from now on I was going to do this. I drove home as fast as I could. I couldn't wait to tell Lisa. When I did she was so happy she threw her arms around me and hugged me and told me how proud she was of me. She, of course, never doubted I would be doing this. I never had anything, but doubts. I still didn't have a clue on how to proceed, but I knew nothing was going to stop me from proceeding. I knew there were shards of glass cemented into the top of the wall, and that to climb over I'd get cut and lose blood, but I didn't care. I was going over. I'd bandage the cuts with napkins and duct tape later.

With the encouragement of these people I seriously began to think about graduate school. My desires to be an academic were always intellectual and verged on fantasy. Being an historian was something I wanted since I was a kid, but it had been shown to me by numerous parties that this was little more than a pipe dream. I had long since come to grips with the idea that my scholarly interests would never be more than a secret hobby. While Lisa knew of and encouraged my dream, I never seriously thought it would happen. For me, being an historian was going to be a nice idea I would go to from time to time like visiting another country in my head. Now, however, things were getting serious. It worried me. Worried in the way you get when you get too close to a dream. How was a dyslexic, former Doggie, from the Ironbound ever going to become an intellectual, a book writer, a scholar? Before, I could keep it all safely at a distance. I'd never really had to confront this, and so I'd never really had to risk losing it. Now, that risk had become significant. I would have to sink or swim. My book collecting and my attempts at writing were my secret world, like the mediaeval garden at St. Cecelia's and the Alvis Stalwart. Accept for Lisa, I never let anyone know they existed. Now the opportunity was here. I had a choice. I could say no then have to spend the rest of my life wondering, what if? or, I could go for it. If I did the latter, I ran the risk of failing and would have to spend the rest of my life knowing I really wasn't smart enough and that Sister Louise was right all along.

I chose to go for it.

I made an appointment to see Dr. Mark Lender, Kean University author, historian, former armour Cav officer, and at the time, university provost. After my encounter with Mary Lewis, I told Jim Jandrowitz about my plans. Jandrowitz had been an infantry Marine in Vietnam. I felt I could talk to him and he would understand. He did. He told me to go see Mark Lender. I made an appointment and soon was sitting down in front of Dr. Lender's desk. Before I could say a word, he looked at me and said in his usual gruff way, "Jandrowitz told me you were coming. Why do you want to be an historian?" No one had ever asked me why? I took a breath and I started talking. When I was done I sat back. Again, I expected the worst. He looked at my transcripts then looked at me. "Well," he said, "I guess we are just going to have to get you into grad school somewhere."

114

After some more discussions with Mark Lender I made the decision to do the modern history of science. I first wanted to do the history of mediaeval science, that way I could study the Monstrous Races: the Scipodii, Cynocephali, and other weird and wonderful mediaeval creatures. Then I found out all the languages I'd have to know and that put a bit of a damper on it. I liked the idea of knowing many languages, but the aptitude needed, I feared, was beyond me. Luckily, Mark knew Dr. David Kohn at Drew University who was an important Darwin scholar. The few science classes I had taken at Kean before I switched majors frustrated my teachers as all the papers I wrote in those classes turned out to be on the history of the science the class was supposed to be about. In addition, I was fascinated by the history of evolutionary science, and of course my odd, but ill-formed interest in monsters. I went to see Dr. Kohn. He seemed impressed that I knew that Darwin was buried in Westminster Abbey. After some more discussions with him I applied to the doctoral program at Drew. I had applied to about ten different grad schools and while I was accepted to several of them Drew offered what I thought was the best overall package. I wouldn't have to move, they gave me a 75% tuition reduction (which later rose to 90%), and they had David Kohn. In May of 1995 I graduated from Kean and the following September I entered graduate school.

Drew University

Drew University began before the Civil War as a Methodist Seminary, around the same time that Kean was originally founded as the Newark Normal School. The joke was that Daniel Drew, the school's original founder and benefactor, did so to help insure he achieved salvation after a life of shady living. By the later 20th century, it had become an ecumenical institution, which while it still housed a thriving Methodist Seminary, had taken a more liberal stance towards the world and welcomed all denominations to study there. I entered the Modern History and Literature graduate program.

I met people I would be friends with well beyond Drew. Lisa had finished her MA in Media at The New School then entered the history grad program the year after me at Drew. One or two of the female students were consciously there to find husbands (I didn't think such a thing even happened anymore). One guy was from the Czech Republic or somewhere in the Balkans. He was a philosopher and attractive in that very low key, very hip and smarter than you sort of Euro way. He could quote Derrida and Foucault.

Lisa entered with her own cohort. This included Frank Wyman, the lawyer turned historian of disabilities, turned back to lawyer. Through Frank we not only met his vivacious and energetic wife Debbie, but their 13-year-old daughter, Alice who would become mine and Lisa's beloved God Daughter. Irish born Brid Nicholson and I would be classmates then colleagues at Kean. Wyatt Evens, former Army Ranger Captain, later joined the Drew faculty. Alisha Coleman-Knight joined the faculty at Washington College in Maryland. Matthew Beland became a librarian at Drew, while Chris Anderson eventually took up a position as divinity, special collections curator at the Beinecke Library at Yale, and then at Princeton.

The Drew graduate history program had begun as Nineteenth Century Studies, then became Modern History and Literature. The Drew campus was quite bucolic and woodsy, in fact it was called the 'College in the Forest.' Many at Drew thought of themselves as being a kind of Junior Ivy League school. It was not unusual for kids whose parents wanted them to go to Yale or Princeton, but who did not get in there, to come to Drew as a backup. As a working class kid who only ever saw such places on TV or in pictures I liked the atmosphere of the school. It was very 'collegey.' Kean was a good school, but its appearance at that time was more like an industrial park.[15] Drew had cool mediaeval style buildings, a large, well-appointed library, and lots of trees. The graduate school was run out of Bowne Hall, a two storey, gothic-style building that went up in the 1920s. It had a grand entry staircase and Great Hall that was modelled on ones at Cambridge and Oxford (and which years later reminded people of 'Hogwarts').

The first thing I had to do before classes even started was to prepare for my language exams. Drew required all doctoral students to pass at least two foreign language exams in order to graduate. I had been told by several people at Kean to get ready for this and so I took an intro to French. Drew offered language exam prep classes over the summer so I quickly enrolled in the one for French. The exams were four hour ordeals in which you had to translate a page from a text—you did not know which one ahead of time—which required no more than three mistakes in order to pass. I finished the four week prep course then sat for the French exam. The language exams were held in the Great Hall of Bowne Hall. Everyone who was taking a language exam had to show up so that the thirty or so students taking the exams that day all did different tests. You could bring a dictionary, so I bought one of those giant-sized beasts I had always seen in book stores and wondered why anyone would purchase such a thing. I turned in my test and thought I had a chance of passing. I was wrong. I had made four mistakes. I would have to do the test again. I was totally depressed. I never expected that my career would be derailed by a language test. I managed to talk myself off the ledge and started studying so I could take the test again.

It was time for classes to begin, so I'd have to put off the language test until the end of the semester. My first semester I took the history of science, American intellectual history, and this thing I had heard of, but was not quite sure what it was: historiography.

I took the French exam again, and again had four mistakes. It was now my third and final try to pass the French exam. By now my dictionary was packed with extra pages. At the appointed time I sat in the Great Hall. I was handed my test text. It was a page on sadomasochism from Foucault. If that wasn't bad enough, just as the time bell rang and we began, it seemed every lawn mower and leaf blower on campus suddenly appeared under the open windows of the Great Hall. I ran the clock out completely, but miraculously managed to pass with just three mistakes. It was a huge weight off.

In the back of the student union at Drew they had a snack bar. I enjoyed going there after a long day of work then classes and then library study. I could sit there at 7:30pm eating a personal sized Pizza Hut pan pizza with Lisa or Brid or other classmates. It was relaxing and inspiring as we discussed our work. As an undergraduate, I never had the opportunity to do such a thing with classmates. As I write this I can't remember the names of any of my undergraduate classmates at Kean.

As cash strapped grad students we were always looking for ways to save money. One way to do this was to take assigned readings out of the library instead of buying them. The first week of every semester would see a stampede of students to the library. As soon as you had the reading list the land rush was on. Another way was to scour the campus looking for events that had food. You'd wait until the event was more or less over then quietly slip into the back of the hall and take leftover food from the refreshment table before food services came in to clean up. Lisa and I had many happy meals of sliced turkey sandwiches with creamy pasta salad (a university event staple) for dinner. Occasionally, if the event was high

---

[15] That would change drastically in the 21st century.

116

enough up the ladder of social importance—usually something involving the Board of Trustees or university president or other VIPs—there would even be deserts of some type. That was the Holy Grail. Word would quickly spread and students would descend like vultures on the refreshment spread once the top predators had had their fill.

I also continued to pick up freelance illustration work. I found a studio in Manhattan that made postage stamps for small, Third World countries in Asia and Africa. Places like Chad or Tanzania had tiny postal services, but they engaged this company to make exotic stamps for them. These were mostly sold to stamp collectors. I did a series of stamp sets on topics as diverse as dinosaurs, military aircraft, and even UFOs.

Despite the hectic nature of graduate school, I finally began to feel like all this was real. I finally began to think that I might be on my way to becoming a professional historian; that I might actually be able to do this as a career. I no longer had to keep my reading and researching a secret. I had people around me who I could talk to about this and not be laughed at or ridiculed. The one thing they all had in common was that they all seemed much smarter than me. I knew facts, but I didn't know abstract historiographical concepts yet. Things were about to get very abstract.

Post-modernism

As I did the paperwork and registered for classes for my first semester as a graduate student it seemed almost easy. The full-time requirement was three classes per semester. As an undergrad I had been doing five classes a semester. When I showed up for the first week, my very first class was 'historiography.' I had a vague notion already what this was. Historiography is not the study of history, it is the study of the study of history. You look at what people have written about history rather than the history itself. The professor was the Francophile Dr. Thomas Christofferson. The required reading list was twelve books. The Introduction to American Intellectual History was by Charles Wetzel. He had eleven books on his required reading list. Finally, David Kohn's 19th Century History of Science class had the shortest reading list with only nine books. You were essentially expected to read three entire books per week. That first semester in graduate school I read more required books than I had read in my entire undergraduate degree.

The graduate history curriculum at Drew had a good bit of post-modern sensibility to it. This was the result of faculty predilections, not some overarching school philosophy. Some of the faculty and students embraced this wholeheartedly, others not so much. I found it fascinating watching people argue over these ideas. I found some of it pointless, but other aspects made sense to me. One of the central notions of post-modernism is that there are no 'final' answers to anything: no final solutions, only a never-ending conversation. There were always different ways to see things. As long as you made use of the facts and evidence, different interpretations were allowed, even encouraged.

In questions of meaning, post-modernism could be a challenge. In the end, I think, post-modernism posited that everything we think we know about the universe is a construct that humans create to keep back the realisation that all is chaos. It undermines the notion of structure—regardless of what Saussure said. Humans want to think there is structure and meaning to the universe. Post-modernism says there is no such thing. That anything we see as a structure, or anything we take as meaning, is not out there, but in our heads. It is artificial. This is what generates in some people such a revulsion and outright hatred of post-modernism. Humans like structure and certainty. It is difficult to accept that all is meaningless. There is no right or wrong, no God, no up or down, only a lost and lonely existence (if we exist at all).

117

The universe cares nothing for us, and nothing we do really influences the universe at all. I had already begun to think such things in Saint Cecelia's, but not quite like this. This was way beyond what I had ever thought, but it somehow resonated. It didn't make sense, necessarily, but it didn't repulse me either. Watching the faculty and other students discuss and argue over these things was stimulating even if I rarely understood what they were talking about. One week we had to read Derrida's *The Post Card*. It made me feel like a chimp trying to figure out the right button to push in the cage to get a banana, and getting it wrong every time.

One of the unwritten realities of historical research is that the people, places, and events that are written about the most are the ones where archival material exists. History is, in large part, a study of the written record. It makes sense then that those topics with a written record are discussed and examined. That is why criminals—whether common, political, or religious—try to destroy the record that shows their crimes. This is why archives are so important. They contain the written record of facts and evidence.

When it came time for me to decide the topic of my dissertation, one of the first questions I asked was where are the archives? I chose Henry Fairfield Osborn for several reasons. Initially, I was drawn to him because he represented an interesting position between science and religion. He was a quirky character who's life included religious and political controversies and dinosaurs (I didn't think they'd let me do my dissertation on monsters). Finally, there were extensive archives of his papers and correspondence that were accessible in collections from Boston to Washington, DC. I did not want to spend the next ten years working on my dissertation, as I knew some people who did. With my course work complete, my language exams over and my comprehensive exams behind me I could start on the book. I gave myself two years to complete it. I have always been proud of the fact that I did complete it in that period.

A Return to Comic Books

In 1989 I was let go from AT&T along with several hundred other workers. As another example of how lucky I have been with my career, just after that I was approached by Mike Chen of the Kubert School and asked if I was interested in doing some teaching there? I had, by now, established a fairly respectable career as a freelance artist and so could bring to the students my experiences of advertising, illustration, and design in the real world. Joe Kubert didn't pay very well, he could be tight with money, but it was steady and our rent wasn't too high at the time.[16] The issue with Joe Kubert was that he didn't want to provide health insurance to the faculty. As a result, there was no such thing as 'full-time' for a teacher. The most he would give you was three days a week, with two classes per day. By this time the school had grown out of the mansion and so Joe bought the old Dover High School building. The high school didn't have the Victorian charm of the mansion, but it provided a larger space. I began teaching Life Drawing and a class called 'Methods and Materials.' The latter being a general introduction to drawing using the basic tools of an illustrator that meant learning to draw in black and using brushes and dip pen nibs.

It was funny to me that the students, Kubbies, were just like my classmates when I

---

[16] The high school was always in need of repair and Joe would only do the bare minimum. The halls were dingy and once he decided to have the hall repainted. He hired a thirty something Hispanic guy to do the painting. Joe paid him minimum wage and then bought the cheapest pain he could find. He also would not supply a ladder for the man to use. As he was only about five feet tall he couldn't reach all the way to the ceiling with the paint brush. So, when he was done we saw he had painting the wall up as high as he could reach and that was it. In addition, he painted around all the framed artwork and pictures that hung on the walls. It was funny, but I never blamed the guy.

was there. Some of the faculty from when I was there as a student were still there. Tex Blaisdell for example. A new host of teachers were there as well. The portrait cartoonist, John Troy, and I became friends. He had a deadpan wit that could have you rolling in the isles. Judy Mates was there and everyone was in love with her. Greg Hildebrandt, who along with his brother Tim, was famous for his book covers and work on The Hobbit and Star Wars, taught several classes. Every day during the lunch hour, the teachers met in the faculty lounge to gossip, complain, and to make fun of Joe and his funny ways.

I enjoyed teaching the life drawing class as I could spend time showing the students about human anatomy. The life drawing studio had large, tall windows to let the light in. In the centre of the room was a raised dais the model would stand on. I would lecture for thirty minutes or so on an aspect of anatomy then the rest of the period was spent with the students drawing from the model. They were always having trouble getting live models.[17] Several of the women who modelled—I was not the one who procured the models—also did other things in a human interactive sort of way as well. One of the more memorable models was a guy in his mid-thirties who really enjoyed nudity. During the breaks the models would put on robes and sit in the corner of the classroom reading, having their lunch, or just relaxing until the sessions resumed. This one model, however, loved to go strolling around the corridors with his robe flapping open, making no attempt to cover up. The students took to calling him 'Naked Dave.' Another male model was in his early twenties and a bodybuilder. He was always nervous about being naked in class, but I guess he was desperate to make some extra money. He wasn't too bad at holding the pose, except for the fact that he often became aroused during a posing session. The students, who could be as brutal to other people as they were to each other, called him 'Woody.'

Teaching at Kubert was fun and not particularly difficult. All the classes were during the day, and since my Kean and then Drew classes were all at night I could pull it off. I also brought my freelance work with me to class. I could show students what actual assignments looked like, then work on them while they worked on the class assignments. I did this for several years. In the middle of every August, Mike Chen would call me to see if I wanted to work the upcoming year and what classes he needed to teach. Then in 1997, he called in July. As soon as I heard his voice on the phone, I knew I had been fired. It had nothing to do with my teaching skills or conduct. After a certain number of years working, Joe would have to give you a raise, and he didn't want to. In the parlance of such things I was not actually fired, I was simply not invited back. Again, fortuitous timing came into play. It was around this time I was getting the work doing the postage stamps so I still had money coming in. Also, shortly after, I was offered a research Fellowship with a quirky group of religionists in Boston.

---

[17] It was only after some weeks of dating Lisa she told me she had worked as a live model at various schools and art societies around the state to make ends meet. This included the Kubert School. Therefore, in the end my friends Grant Miehm and Jack Pollack saw Lisa naked before I did.

119

Chapter 6
An Incident in New York City

The only thing I've ever been good at was finding things

- Jack Taylor

I was inching closer to the career I wanted. I had finished all of my required graduate course work, had passed my language exams, and had taken my Comps. Now, all I had to do was to write my doctoral dissertation. David Kohn wanted me—as he wanted all his grad students—to specialise in Darwin's botanical work. I found anything to do with Darwin fascinating, but I had other plans.

Henry Fairfield Osborn

I have always been drawn to the odd, the strange, and those things outside the humdrum existence of everyday life. I wanted to be an historian of science, but I didn't want to work on mainstream science history. First, an army of incredible historians much more gifted than I, with better pedigrees, and access to the primary source material, were covering a lot of it. I didn't think I could have anything new to say about Darwin, or the history of biology or Benjamin Franklin. Second, I wanted something different. I wanted something that could unite the strands of thought that had been entwined in my head for years. One of the great advantages I had coming up academically the way I did was that I never had anyone telling me the 'right' materials to look at.

My imagination roamed over a vast area of scholarly and popular material, both professional and fringe (works that some advisors would be aghast at). I wanted to somehow link all these things I had been reading about since sitting in the Kearny Public Library and dreaming in the secret alley at Saint Cecelia's. I wanted to think outside the academic box. A more strictly controlled education, of the kind I later learned of from many of my international friends, would likely have scrubbed all that out of my thinking. I was lucky enough to never have had anyone say to me, that's not worth studying, or don't waste time with that nonsense. Nevertheless, I felt I couldn't come out and say, "I want to write my doctoral dissertation on monsters." Finally, I came up with an alternative that I thought would be more academically acceptable yet still feed my needs.

The life of Henry Fairfield Osborn became the focus for my doctoral dissertation for several reasons. He was a fascinating character who straddled the world of science and religion. He was involved in politics and dinosaurs. These were all the things I wanted to work on. Appealing to my natural laziness, his archival material was readily available. Osborn was one of these guys historians love because he didn't wipe his behind without saving it. There were large caches of his letters and other manuscript materials at the American Museum of Natural History in Manhattan and right across the street at the New York Historical Society. In addition, the New York Public Library and the Princeton University Library also had his materials.

So, I could immerse myself in this huge pile of stuff without having to travel too far.[1] Finally, there was only one major book on Osborn: Ronald Rainger's excellent *An Agenda for Antiquity* which came out in 1991.[2]

When I applied to graduate school, I did so planning to engage with it as a serious and central part of my life. No one had to tell me that part. I vowed to focus on it exclusively. I had to take the terrifying step to go from 'safe' hobbyist to 'risky' professional. This was the only way towards achieving the goal I wanted. I asked Lisa if she thought this was worth all the cost and effort? We had a long talk and she asked if doing this would make me happy and fulfil all those dreams I had been talking about. I said I thought it would. She smiled and said, "then you have to do it no matter what." It was like we were in an aeroplane and I was about to do my first skydive and wasn't sure if I should. The look she gave me was one of such support, I just turned and jumped out the door without the slightest hesitation. If Lisa thought I could do this then I could. Once I had made the decision I was all in, my commitment was total and unwavering. I would allow nothing to get in the way of it. No one told me I hadn't gone to the right schools or made the right connections or that the job market was awful and that no one was going to hire me. I was either going to become a university professor and scholar, or I was going to be the world's best-educated body knocker. So when the school gave me a set of instructions for how to do this, I launched right in. Having no experience with such an endeavour and with no one to talk to who had done it recently, I reverted to how I always did things: I set my sights on doing whatever they asked as long as in the end I was awarded a PhD. If that meant going full-time, spending hours in the library, and writing at all hours of the day and night, so be it (though to be honest, I liked the idea of doing that). If I had to suffer, I'd suffer. If I had to do two language exams, and had to do classes in a certain order, and had to fill out this form or that form, and be here for this meeting or that, I was going to be there. I didn't question, I just did it. It was a crazy, stupid, unrealistic dream (that's what everyone but Lisa had always told me). I knew I was standing on a dangerous edge, especially financially. In the end, if I had to, I would duct tape my hands with napkins from the mess hall, ignore the pain, and grab the chin- up bar again.

> TonightI'll be on that hill because I can't stop
> I'll be on that hill with everything I've got
> With lives on the line where dreams are found and lost
> I'll be there on time and I'll pay the cost.[3]

As I began to get to know my classmates, I saw that some of them were hard-core and working on a goal not unlike mine. Their attitudes about work were similar to mine. On track, they were not going to let anything slow them down. I found them inspiring. Others had been at this for five or even ten years already. They took classes part time and didn't seem to be in any hurry. I did not want to be a ten-year doctoral student. I had plans. I wanted this to be completed as quickly as possible so I could get on to the next step. They inspired me to

---

[1] One of the things most people do not know about the writing of history is that you can only really write about people and events and places that have extant records. The lifeblood of historical research are primary materials: letters, records, writings, and other such original sources. The people and events that are written about the most are those that have large collections of surviving primary sources. You can't do this using Wikipedia.

[2] Ronald Rainger. An Agenda for Antiquity: Henry Fairfield Osborn & vertebrate palaeontology at the American Museum of Natural History, 1890-1935 (Tuscaloosa: University of Alabama Press, 1991). The very first time I gave a paper at a professional conference, the History of Science Society meeting in Boulder, Colorado in October of 2001, Ronald Rainger was in the audience. I didn't see him sitting there in the back until I stepped behind the podium. I did get a little nervous. As I talked, I thought his face looked like he enjoyed what I was saying.

[3] Bruce Springsteen, "Darkness on the Edge of Town," 1978.

work even more feverishly. Despite an almost complete tuition remission award, I couldn't afford to keep taking out loans.[4] Other students had lower remission levels so had to take out more loans and run up even more credit card debt. Intellectually, graduate school is a full-time job. Working full time is difficult which makes it harder to survive. Many of my classmates struggled financially, and those with kids even more so. I was lucky (once again) because as a graphic artist I could take some work from clients that didn't require me to be in an office every day. I could go into Manhattan and get some illustration work doing postage stamps or advertising illustrations. They were easy to do and while I was not making a huge amount of money, they just barely kept the werewolf from the door. As a freelancer, I was also used to having to constantly hustle for work. Plus, Lisa was working and we had no children to worry about, although she then entered as a doctoral student as well. We both sacrificed and went into debt, but we felt it was all worth it. We would be able to achieve our goals and dreams, and the best part was we could do it together. As long as we were together everything would work out. Once, years before, Lisa and I decided to go to Washington DC to see the major retrospective of the work of Georgia O'Keefe. We scraped together a little money and drove down. It was great fun and just before we left I bought her a stuffed Tyrannosaurus doll with the last five dollars I had. When we arrived back home she gave me a little card she had bought. It was one of those two by three inch cards you attach to the outside of a present to show who it's from. It was a cartoon drawing of a pair of smiling dinosaurs, a large one and a smaller one. Inside on the blank part she wrote, "Things are always easier with your pal by your side! Love, Lisa."

Years later I learned of the hardships others had gone through to acquire their degrees and I realised yet again how incredibly lucky I had been, and how lucky I had been to have Lisa by my side.[5]

I looked over the schedule for the program: two years' worth of classes, then write the dissertation. I decided I would complete my dissertation in an additional two years (once again my naiveté worked to my advantage). With that settled in my mind, I put the time out of my head and forged on. The course work required a huge amount of reading, far more than I had ever done before. It made my head hurt, the word 'spinning' wasn't quite as bad as it had been, but I had to do it. After two years, however, I was ready to tackle the dissertation itself. I knew the first place I had to go to was the museum where Osborn had spent so many years. Another thing that helped me cope was that as I had been thinking about this life for a very long time, it all seemed like a grand adventure. I could ignore how perilously close to utter ruin we were, because both our lives had been on the edge of utter ruin before, so this was nothing new. I could enjoy the fact that I was on a train into New York to look inside the archives of the American Museum of Natural History, and it was so very cool. I never knew if any of my classmates felt the same way. As usual, I didn't discuss such intimate matters with them. I was afraid I would be seen as the dumb, poor kid who naïvely wandered into somewhere he shouldn't have been.

When I first arrived at the central archive at the American Museum of Natural History they had a squad of little old ladies there filing things and making catalogue entries. They were delightful and I often spent the first half hour of each visit chit chatting with them around a table as they cheerily did their work and drank tea. I began going through the material and saw there were other archives in the museum that had his letters. Once I had

---

[4] It took me ten years to pay off my grad student loans.
[5] I have had this card on my desk ever since.

123

finished with it, I began spending time across the street at the New York Historical Society going through the collections there. I then swooped down on Princeton and their Osborn collection. I churned through as fast as I could knowing I couldn't afford to take forever. It went well and I scribbled and copied furiously until my hands cramped up. As there was such an enormous amount of material, all of it in chronological order, the book practically wrote itself.

Agnes, and the life of an adjunct

Having received my MA, I started looking for teaching work. Being an adjunct was fun and it gave me great teaching experience. Adjunct teaching, however, did not pay well. At the time most colleges in the area were paying between $2,500 and $3,000 per section if you only had an MA. For a time I was teaching six sections at three different schools while attending classes full-time. I worked as an adjunct at Middlesex County College, Morris County College, (who fired me after one semester for being a day late on my grades), and Fairleigh Dickinson University.[6] The best way to become a skilled teacher is to do it as much as possible, and adjunct teaching allows for that. When I joined the 78th Reserve Division in Edison in 1984, it was as an instructor. As a result I had to go through a rudimentary, teaching techniques class. The underlying philosophy of army teaching is that you walk in and immediately dominate the class. You took charge and you made sure the trainee/students knew that you were in charge. That has always followed me. As time went by, I realised what an important thing it was to look like you were in charge of the class. Students can always sense when a teacher is nervous, doesn't know their material or is unsure of themselves. The army taught me that once that control is lost the teacher can never recover. I brought that idea with me when I started adjunct teaching at community colleges and then university teaching as well. In the service, when they said to dominate, they meant it literally. As an army basic training instructor, I could yell at the trainees or even kick them in the ass. That was perfectly acceptable behaviour. In a civilian classroom, however, that was obviously not going to go down well, but you still had to take control.

Spending so much time adjunct teaching allowed me to hone my technique. As a rookie college teacher, you get dropped into a class with little preparation. None of the schools I worked for knew that my only teacher training had come from Uncle Sam. I had some preparation, but most new adjuncts did not. Regardless, when I was given an adjunct assignment I was simply told the class and the time and to go do it. I had little supervision. This helped me figure out what worked and what didn't. Day after day, you're in the classroom and you have to be in charge, you have to know the subject. The students have to know that you know what you're talking about. I learned my chops. I learned how to deal with

---

[6] One day, about halfway through the first semester I taught at Fairleigh Dickinson University as an adjunct I entered into a conversation with an aged, distinguished, white-haired gentleman in the faculty lounge. He saw I was new and still working on my doctorate, and he thought it would help the new man understand what we were doing in higher education. It started very well, and I thought it might be one of those times to remember as I learned at the wise old and charming knee of Yoda. We sat in comfortable chairs taking our ease. The only thing that would have made it more wonderfully stereotypical would have been if we were snifting brandy. The conversation came around to "why we were here." He proceeded to explain to me with all the assuredness of an expert so secure in his position he never thought anyone would ever disagree with him, that the be all and end all of historical studies, "the subject all others bow to" was diplomatic history. I gently disagreed. I naively gave some reasons why I thought other areas, such as, say, the history of science, might be vital to the historical project. I saw he was not appreciating my resistance so I just gave in (what did I care?). When we finally parted, he did so a bit miffed that I had not genuflected before the authority of his *éminence grise*. I only learned later that he was the most senior member of the history faculty. When the time came some weeks later to apply to teach the next semester, I was told I was not a good fit. I never taught at Fairly Ridiculous again.

disinterested students, students who couldn't quite grasp the material, students who sat in the front row and were a bit over-eager. It was sink or swim. They leave you in a room with twenty-five or thirty students and you're expected to teach them something. I experimented quite a bit, with technique, voice, dress, jokes, everything.

Adjuncting for me was to be a temporary and learning experience that would, hopefully, lead to a residency job somewhere. Consequently, I applied to every job that came along. I kept a special folder with copies of cover pages I would adapt to each school. I then would write the date and the name of the school I applied to on the outside of the folder. By the time I stopped doing that, I had over forty school names on that folder.

One day, I received a letter from what I thought was the Church of Scientology. As I often do because of my eyes, I was about to crumple it up and throw it away. Why would Scientology be sending me their crap? Then I hesitated and looked at it more closely. It was not from Scientology it was from the First Church of Christ Scientist, the Christian Scientists in Boston. I had totally forgotten about this because the job I applied for was for the 'Mary Baker Eddy Papers Project.' The letter said they wanted me to come in for an interview.

Lisa and I jumped into the car and headed for Boston. The Christian Science Church had been started by a woman named Mary Baker Eddy. Born into a relatively comfortable family, Mary Baker Eddy (1821-1910) was, in many respects, an extraordinary woman. Born and raised in New Hampshire, she had a complex relationship with her father and bouts of various medical conditions. She married and as she was about to have a child, her new husband died in a yellow fever epidemic in the Carolinas. This left her alone and desperate. She headed north where she had a bad fall on the ice in Lynn, Massachusetts. The injury to her back was thought to be so severe she might never walk again. Determined, she read the Bible intensely and, she claimed, saw hidden ideas in the text about self-healing. Her back issues cleared up as a result of her discoveries.[7] Convinced she had been healed by prayer and God, she began teaching her technique. Calling her method Christian Science, she argued that sickness and injury were illusions that could be eliminated by correct prayer. Her following soon grew, the cash rolled in and after a few years, she was wealthy enough to build a church and spread her teaching around the world through ubiquitous 'reading rooms'. By the time of her passing, the First Church of Christ Scientist was thriving. By the late twentieth century, the church was a force to be reckoned with as a source of good works. The Church's board of directors decided it was time to turn their vast archive into a library 'for the betterment of humanity'.

The Christian Science Church now had a huge collection of nineteenth century manuscript material, and a new, more liberal board of trustees who wanted to make the collection more visible and available to not only church members, but the outside world. They also had a lot of money and wanted to pay well for a series of fellowship positions for historians, librarians, archivists, and museum people to whip the whole thing into shape. It sounded like a great opportunity: access to a magnificent, important, and hardly-touched collection, a good paycheck and a chance to work in Boston. The interview went well, and they asked me back for a second. Consequently, they offered me the position as a Senior Researcher.

It would be a major shakeup in our lives. The fellowship duration was one year with a

[7] Though many said it was because of the Laudanum the doctor gave her.

possibility of a second. I decided I'd go up alone at first, rent a small apartment in Providence, and see what happened. Lisa remained in our apartment and continued with her freelance work, adjunct teaching, and grad school. I joined a unique team of scholars: Ed Rafferty, Marylin Costanzo, Chris Millard, Heather Gunsales and others. They were all young and hungry to build careers. We all saw this Fellowship as a launching point. At MBE, as we called it, our job was to take this enormous collection of 19th century, primary source material and organise it. All of us Fellows were hired at about the same time. I was, in fact, one of the last to show up. The rest had been there for a few weeks already. It was one of those cosmic moments where a dozen or so people were brought from different places, thrown together, and then immediately hit it off. We began hanging out from the start and making jokes about ourselves, but especially the people we worked for.

It didn't take long for this new project to become known throughout the ranks of Christian Science. Our presence was not welcome outside the library or the board. Indeed, there were people inside the library who did not like the idea of us being there at all. One of the issues with Christian Science in general is that, unlike say, the Catholic Church, Judaism or any other major religions, there was no tradition of scholarship within its ranks. There were no Christian Science philosophers or early church Fathers or historians to examine and argue doctrine or theology. Everything in the church was built around the cult of the personality of Mary Baker Eddy.

What Mrs. Eddy said was all there was. Nothing else mattered. You didn't question her or her teachings. No one examined the distrust of medicine, for example, because once Mrs. Eddy had said medicine was bad, all discussion ended. As a result there were very few church members who had higher degrees in history, philosophy, archives or museum work. The best they could muster was a sprinkling of middle-aged women who had been grammar school literature teachers with maybe a master's degree in English or education. This is why the board decided to go outside the church for this project.

We scholars, non-church members all, now had access to the entire secret archives of the church. A collection of Catholics and lapsed Catholics, Jews, atheists, and even a couple of practising Pagans, could examine with impunity all those deep, dark secrets, and church papers that, up until then, even church members could not look at. There was a long tradition of keeping the archives hidden, even from church members. Mary Baker Eddy—we used the code name *Agnes*—was a complex woman and a virulent anti-Catholic. She often referred to Catholics as 'Zeros'. She was also addicted to Laudanum (the liquid painkiller that was a mixture of alcohol, honey and opium popular with mystics and Romantic poets). She could be nasty, vindictive, cruel and petty. The very antithesis of the public image of her as a loving maternal character. We saw it all.

Many church members were outraged that the board let these outsiders get so far into the collection when they themselves were restricted from seeing it. There were a number of occasions when we would go out as a group for lunch along Massachusetts's Avenue where we would be accosted by angry church members who wanted to tell us how much they didn't like us. A shadowy group, formed in direct reaction to us, circulated a newsletter where they could blow off steam at the sacrilege of having us touching Mrs. Eddy's letters. This may have been run by the former head librarian. From what I gathered, the Board fired him just before we arrived because he had been a vocal opponent of the entire enterprise. We found this controversy incredibly silly, but they were serious.

Just before we arrived in 1998, Welsh author Gillian Gill had released *Mary Baker Eddy*.[8] She had previously written a biography of Agatha Christie and later Florence Nightingale. She was one of the few non-Church members who had been inside the archive. Just how she managed to acquire this access may have been that she came along just as the Board was considering this whole new adventure in public transparency. The church loved Ms. Gill and her book. They even brought her in to lecture us on how to 'properly' deal with Mrs. Eddy's life. Gill's book, while based upon the materials in the archive, had the distinct whiff of hagiography about it. That's why, I believe, they liked it so much. I think part of the reason we scholars, as outsiders, were so reviled was in part owing to the fact we did not deify Mrs. Eddy the way they did. To us, she was a fascinating subject of historical study, not an emissary of God.

We were organised into three person teams in the library. A senior researcher, a junior researcher, and a church member. Each group dealt with a different part of the collection. I was on the correspondence from church members to Agnes. My junior researcher was Chris Millard, a very bright, hardworking young guy, and a musician, who later went into library management. I was writing my doctoral dissertation so I managed to put all the work off on him while I concentrated on my thesis. Eventually, the woman church member working with us, found out what I was doing, went to the board, and tattled. That was the beginning of my falling out with the church. I didn't care at that point. I did not want to stay there any longer than the Fellowship anyway.

I found the church members fascinating. We worked in the 23-story main church administration building across the square from the magnificent 19th century neo-gothic 'Mother Church.' On the 22nd floor, we could look out the windows and directly down into Fenway Park that was just a few blocks away. The members could not drink alcohol so whenever we didn't want them listening to our conversations, we would start talking about going out and getting drunk after work or about visiting a doctor. Rumours were rife that some of the church members in the library and archive had taken it upon themselves to unilaterally remove any sensitive materials that in their personal judgement made Mrs. Eddy look bad. We were constantly on the lookout for papers going missing. A number of letters and scrapbooks 'disappeared' because, it was suspected, the church members working on them had made the decision to protect the memory of Mrs. Eddy by destroying them (this without even consulting the Board).

Providence

Accepting the job at MBE meant I had to live up there somewhere. Having lived in Providence while attending RISD, I had good memories there. It had the additional attraction of being more affordable than Boston. Finally, the Massachusetts Bay Transit Authority (MBTA) ran a commuter line back and forth to Providence. I found a studio apartment at the housing complex called Nicholas Brown Yard and moved in the Labor Day weekend of 1999.

I was rather fond of Providence. It had a certain mystical quality to it. The antique houses, horse steps, and narrow lanes of College Hill especially beckoned to me. When I lived here in the mid-1980s, I lived across town in the somewhat depressed area called Elmwood. Now, I had found an apartment that was ideally located so that the moment I stepped out the

---

[8] Gillian Gill. *Mary Baker Eddy* (Da Capo Press, 1998).

door I was on College Hill. I had read H. P. Lovecraft's *The Case of Charles Dexter Ward*, in high school. This disturbing tale of a magician's attempt to achieve evil immortality was a travelogue to the very streets I could now walk down. Lovecraft himself walked these places, as did Edgar Allen Poe.

As I was here by myself for the first year of the job at MBE I spent all my time not in Boston, but writing my doctoral dissertation in Providence. I could walk the streets of Providence for hours thinking about my writing. I always carried a notepad with me and when the mood struck me I'd sit down on a low wall or set of steps or lean against a tree and scribble furiously. I wrote large chunks of my dissertation this way. On days I wasn't at MBE I'd go to the Providence Athenaeum to write or to just sit and think. It turned out they had a first edition of Roy Chapman Andrews' *New Conquest of Central Asia* that I needed to read for my dissertation. I read large chunks of this physically impressive tome with its many fold out maps and photos of camels lumbering slowly across the Gobi Desert. On occasion, I thought I saw the shadow of something pulpy and squid-like down an ancient dark alley.

Founded in 1836, the Athenaeum, or the Ath, occupied a wonderfully neo-classical building on the corner of Benefit and College Streets. It became for me, what it had become for so many others, an oasis of scholarly quiet in a world of screaming idiocy. Edgar Allen Poe supposedly spent time reading there, as had Charlotte Perkins Gilman. Its interior had a catwalk as a second floor. There were stacks there that created niches where they put little desks and chairs so that each niche could accommodate one person. This made it very cosy as you sat at a desk surrounded by books in your own little world. You reached this upper level by a series of enchanting but precariously steep, narrow staircases. My favourite niche was the one where the desk there had come from the original Rhode Island State House. Attesting to this, there was a small plaque on the Victorian desk, which was just large enough for one determined scholar to sit at. Ringed around the main floor were a series of marble statues and busts of philosophers. They always seemed to look at me while I worked. I would ensconce myself, sit, think, and write. Years later on the faculty of Kean University I would take the train to Providence for the week of spring break, or for a week during the summer to be by myself. I would take a room at a hotel then spend every day sitting in the Athenaeum writing. Sometimes, just sitting and thinking.

On my Providence walks I would come out of Nicholas Brown Yard and directly onto Benefit Street. It raised up a bit to a pinnacle where it flattened off then headed down again to Narragansett Bay. The houses dated back to the nineteenth century, some to the sixteenth. They were ancient by North American standards. I fantasised about what it would be like living in every one of them. After writing my way down Benefit Street I'd go to a bar or restaurant on Weybosset Street. The College Hill area was the centre of student life. It teemed with funky bars, antiques shops, restaurants, and bookstores: all of which appealed to me. After leaving Weybosset Street, I'd begin the climb back up the hill. I'd then cut over to Thayer Street, then over to Prospect then back to the apartment.

There were also several good book stores such as Myopic Books and, in particular, Cellar Stories . The joke about Cellar Stories was that it was on the second floor of a building downtown. Cellar Stories was one of those used book stores that bibliophiles dream of: funky, but not disgusting, and very well stocked. They even had a rare book section. I found a first edition of Delabarre's book on the Dighton Rock there. To enter the rare book section you passed through a portal where they kept the trashy paperbacks from the 1950s. They had them in those little plastic bags to protect them, thumbtacked to the wall. Pulp lesbians, action men, and science fiction stared down at you. Long after we moved away, Lisa and I would sometimes travel back to Providence. We always made it a point to go to Cellar Stories. Somehow, the owner always seemed to remember us.

And of course, there was East Side Pockets. One of the best little restaurants I've ever eaten at. East Side Pockets was run by a family of Coptic Christians from Syria. They made falafel, tabouleh, tender chicken pita wraps and spinach and feta pie. It was incredibly delicious and yet affordable. Everything was made fresh and assembled right in front of you. You stood in line, that sometimes ran down the block, and then you stood before the counter. It became a Providence legend that the first thing the guy behind the counter said to you was, "Hot sauce?" Then you pointed at what you wanted and shuffled to your right as he put it all together. You wound up around the side of the counter at the cash register. There were times in later years where we had to drive up to Boston for something or other, and we would detour to Providence on the way home just to load up on East Side Pockets.

During the first year of the Fellowship, Lisa would occasionally come up to see me. Normally, she would drive the journey, four hours one way. Once she came up by train. There was a train station downtown that Amtrak and the MBTA operated out of. It was fairly new and well laid out. You had to go down an escalator to get to the train platforms. The area, while technically underground, was still open to the sky in several places. When the train left the platform in either direction it only ran a hundred feet or so before it was out in the light. When it was time for Lisa to go home we went to the station and I stood on the platform holding her until the train pulled up. After hugging and the usual departure sweet-talk, she boarded the train. I stood on the platform watching as the train began to pull away. As other people, who had seen their friends and loved ones depart, began to walk away back to the escalator I walked along with the train. Eventually, I was the only person there as I walked all the way down the long platform until I was prevented from going any further by a safety barrier. I stood there watching as the train became smaller and smaller until it disappeared down the line. After it was gone, I stayed standing there for a minute. Finally, I turned and walked back to the escalator and up and out of the station. I still wasn't any good at goodbyes.

Someday when you leave, it will be forever.

MBE was an easy job. Standing on the same platform on which I saw Lisa depart, I'd take the train from Providence to Boston and walk the ten minute distance to the archive. The work was not stressful, in fact, it was interesting. The collection was, and still is, a major insight into 19th century America, chronicling not just the role of the church, but the role of women. Coupled with my fascination with American religious history, it afforded me a unique primary resource. Unfortunately, most of the church members involved saw it only as a way to glorify the memory of Mrs. Eddy. Anything else, for them, was a waste of time. Once while looking for something else, I came across the diary of an early church member who had served in the Civil War. As I leafed through it, I saw that he had made a series of drawings of things he had seen. These drawings included the Battle of Hampton Roads. He had been an eyewitness to the fight between the USS Monitor and the Rebel ironclad the CSS Virginia (considered a pivotal moment in naval history). He described it and produced several quite skillful drawings of it. Excited, I brought this to the leadership's attention. I explained what a rare thing this was. There was no mention of this man's experience, certainly not this drawing, in the historical record. It was a major find. The collective reaction was, meh. Since it did not directly impact upon the glory of Mrs. Eddy, it was deemed unimportant. From here I knew that no real historical work would ever be done on this collection.

The first year at MBE was fun, but during the first part of the second, I began to realise that my enthusiasm had waned. I had finished writing my doctoral dissertation and I was prepared to defend it. I was a bit torn. The job was interesting and easy and with Lisa, who had by now moved up to live with me, we loved Providence. I was beginning, though, to feel I belonged back in the classroom. Anyway, I felt I was never really going to be allowed to research the collection the way I felt it should have been. I began applying for teaching positions.

The PhD Defence

One day, on the way into work, I stepped off the commuter train at the Boston South Station and climbed the long stairs as usual to the street level. When I reached the top I suddenly thought I had dropped my wallet. I turned around in the crowd to check my back pocket. I saw I had not dropped it, it was right there where it was supposed to be. Relieved, I went to turn around again and continue on my way, when I looked down the stairs to the platform I had just come from. Another train had pulled in and the mad rush of commuters were climbing the stairs towards me. I saw the looks on their faces. They seemed odd: they were blank, without love or humour or dreams. They reminded me of the monsters who would sit in the darkened booths of *Lancers*. It was like seeing into an abyss. I knew I had to do something. This job at MBE had been good for my career, but it was clear that it was time to go. It was time to take Lisa by the hand and head out. It was time to run again. The old fear, the terrible old need to flee and move forward, had seized me.

By the spring of 2001 I had finished writing my dissertation. Now, all that stood between me and being called 'Doctor,' was to defend it. A date was worked out, I took a couple of vacation days from MBE, and I headed back to New Jersey. "How do you think William James would have reacted to the evolutionary work of Henry Fairfield Osborn?" This was the question Charles Wetzel asked me at the end of my doctoral dissertation defence at Drew University in April 2001. It was not just the last question of the defence, it was the last question on earth I expected to be asked of me.

I walked through my PhD like a wide-eyed innocent. This despite the fact that I was turning forty, had been around the world several times, and had stared down the commies on the Iron Curtain before I began. I was the first in my family to do such a thing. I had no history to look to. I had wanted to become an historian ever since I sat on the rug of the living room floor on Saturday mornings dreaming of being Jonny Quest. Now that was about to happen. When they said it was time to do my defence I just showed up ready to go.

I had three on campus readers: David Kohn as my primary, the aforementioned Charles Wetzel, and the American religion scholar Donald Dayton. My fourth was the legendary historian of biology Garland Allan (on a phone link). We all met in Mead Hall, Drew's beautiful, nineteenth century showcase building. The defence was held in an antique-filled side room which upon one wall hung a large portrait. The subject had a greying bristle haircut, moustache, and a general air of seriousness that inspired the students to call it the 'Stalin Room.' I dressed smartly for the encounter. I wore a high-collar dress shirt with a vest, and polished my shoes: my very own 'professor' style I still wear to this day. The thing about dissertation defences is that they are like graduation speeches, you have to get it right, but they are forgotten five seconds after they are finished.

I sat across from my board of readers, a large, heavy, polished oak, nineteenth century table between us. I had no notes or cheat sheets, just me. It was not unlike the sergeant's board or a PNCO or BNCO committee I had to sit for in the army.[9] They started right away. I tried to be concise. I only stumbled once or twice, but recovered and clarified my position. They asked questions and follow-up questions. It went that way for the better part of two hours. We were allowed to invite spectators, but I wasn't having any of that. I preferred my failure to be apocryphal rather than eyewitnessed (every time a person went to their defence a rumour mill automatically generated about what went on). I answered as well as I could without looking like I was trying too hard. It all seemed to be going well. I started to get relaxed. I could see the light at the end of the tunnel.

Then Wetzel sucker punched me with William James.

I have no recollection of what my answer was: Though I do remember saying "Ugh" in a painfully drawn-out way. Apparently, whatever I said was acceptable because Dr. Wetzel smiled, leaned back in his chair, and folded his fingers behind his head the way he always did in class when he was happy with something you said. There was a brief pause, and it was over. There were smiles all around, lots of backslapping, and "well done Doctor!" talk. After a minute or two of official form signing and saying goodbye and thank you to Garland Allan on the phone, we all headed off to a local restaurant for a congratulatory lunch. I had made it. I could now be called a doctor of philosophy. I wanted to call Lisa, and then my parents. The air seemed just a bit sweeter and cleaner.

Because the school was paying, I had the lobster ravioli.

Max Planck

Shortly after my defence, one of my job applications paid off. I received an invitation for an interview with a small engineering college called the TCI College of Technology located across the street from Penn Station in Manhattan. When I was asked to interview for the job at TCI, I came down to New Jersey and stayed with M&D. I took the New Jersey Transit train into Manhattan to Penn Station. When the doors opened, I was hit by that muggy, July New York underground heat. I instantly knew I was home. The interview went well. By the time I returned to Providence there was already a message on my answering machine asking me to call. I did and they offered me the job: which I took. I then learned I had been picked to attend the prestigious summer Fellowship at the Max Planck Institute for the History of Science in Berlin. That year's topic was human evolution.

I was on a roll.

Originally known as the Kaiser Wilhelm Institute, the Max Planck Institute in Berlin, Germany was a world recognized leader in scientific research. They also had a history of science division which held regular seminars and research fellowships. The August 2001 seminar was to be about human origins and so I had applied. I did not think I stood a chance, but I applied anyway. When I was chosen it was quite a shock. There would be a dozen or so students and six or eight established figures in the field. The first week was just us students and the organisers of the Fellowship. We would read a series of papers and then comment on them. In the second week, the old pros would arrive and we would have a series of discussions from there. It would all culminate in a big panel presentation where the seniors would give

---

[9] These are the military boards one must sit before in order to be promoted to sergeant then tank commander.

papers, but be introduced by the students.

The guest speakers included Martin Rudwick, whose book *Scenes From Deep Time* (1995) was a hot topic of conversation. One of the star guests, Pat Shipman, whose book *The Man Who Found the Missing Link* had just been released, wound up on the end of some odd criticism. A prolific and award winning author working out of Penn State University, her book looked at the life of Eugene DuBois, the man who discovered the hominid fossil known as Java Man. She received opprobrium from some of the seminar members—particularly the senior ones—because she wrote the book almost as a novel. I thought it was an interesting experiment. She used primary sources to create scenes between characters with dialogue she created based upon the known correspondence. She clearly stated that this approach was experimental and might not be to everyone's taste. Regardless of this caveat, she was accused of not being a proper scholar. It made for some tense moments. I thought it was mostly because she was a woman doing it.

Despite the awkward moments, The Max Planck Seminar was a great experience and I met several people with whom I became friends and would stay in touch with for years after. Holly Dunsworth, Olof Ljundstom, Anna Mearker, and others went on to star careers. I knew Olof and I would be friends from the end of the first day when we were coming back to the hotel, which was right around the corner from the Kurfürstendamm, the famous and fashionable shopping street (the Berlin version of New York's Park Avenue or LA's Rodeo Drive). We saw there was a small, but very high-end hobby shop across the street. We both wound up kneeling in front of the glass display window looking at a cut-away model of Captain Nemo's submarine, *Nautilus*. With our noses against the glass all we could do was say, "Whoa!" Unfortunately, it was closed at the time. The Institute had put everyone up in the Gates Hotel, a three-star establishment on Knesebeckstrasse in the Charlottenburg District. It was named after Bill Gates though I'm not sure why.

In the years I had been in West Germany I never went to Berlin. Now the Wall was gone and Germany had unified. From my interest in military history, I knew that the Battle of Berlin, which occurred in the closing days of the war, had been one of the most horrific of the entire war. It was once referred to as the most destructive battle ever fought in a city. There were places around town that still had battle damage from 1945. There were places in the walls of buildings that had the tell-tale pock marks of bullets. They were intentionally left in order to remember. At one location there was a large building which had a basement. At the bottom edge of the building there were those low, wide basement windows you often see in such places. It was an old building and the frames of the windows were made from heavy, but ornate, stone and concrete sections. You could see where thick iron bars had been set into the frames as an early form of security precaution. All around this one window that faced down the long street there were large chunks and chips missing out of the masonry. The evidence suggested that German soldiers had turned this basement window into a street level bunker— probably with a machine gun and maybe a Panzerfaust. The advancing Russian infantry and armour had to neutralise this position before they could proceed down the street. As a result, a ferocious firefight had ensued with the Russians firing in and the Germans firing out. Bullets ricocheted all around as both sides fought desperately. Eventually the Russian troops would have taken this position. Then they would have had to fight the next one, then another after that, and then another, and another until the city was captured and the fighting –and the war— came to an end. There would have been dead and dismembered bodies and blood everywhere. The rattle of guns, explosions, the squeaking of tank tracks, and the screams of wounded and dying men and women reverberating through the air. Now, shoppers walked by laughing and talking. The engine sounds were from taxis, cars, and delivery trucks, not T-34s or King Tigers. I wondered how many residents and tourists realised what the dents and dings in the walls meant.

As always, I enjoyed wandering around and looking at things. As it was August, it was hot even at night. Sometimes I'd go around with fellow historians and sometimes on my own. The entire time I was there, I kept hearing the theme song from 'The Third Man' playing in my head. Even today, I cannot hear that music without thinking of Berlin.[10]

One day we went walking to a wide square. There was a superficially innocuous memorial to the past. There was a hole in the pavers, which had a thick Plexiglas top so you could see down into a space about two feet across and about three feet deep. At the bottom of this shaft was a pile of books. Indeed, the entire space was lined with books, all painted white. The seemingly bland installation belied the fact that this was the spot where the Nazis first burned books in the 1930s.

Later, Holly Dunsworth and I went to the Pergamon Museum where all the famous Greek statues were. The *Ishtar Gate* was impressive for the deep blue ceramics. I wandered around looking at the incredible collection looted from the ancient world. I leaned over what I thought was a museum balcony railing and took in the broad view of the lower part of the museum with the various exhibits and people milling around the large open atrium entryway. Taking in the site I suddenly realised someone was yelling. Just as I was getting annoyed because the yelling was ruining my reverie, I realised I was the one being yelled at. What I thought was just a museum balcony turned out to be a part of the famous *Altar of Zeus*. I put up my hand as if to say, "sorry!" and climbed down.

Later, to enjoy the day, Holly and I went and sat on the broad steps outside which led up to the museum entrance. We started to complain about how we were disappointed that the fellowship was not spending enough time on human fossils (most of the discussions were about anthropology rather than paleoanthropology). Then we had ice cream while complaining about Steven Jay Gould, and I told her my story of getting snubbed by him.

While we went to a number of museums in Berlin. My two favourites were the Virchow Museum and the *Körperwelten* exhibition of Dr. Gunther Von Hagens. The *Body Worlds* exhibition was already controversial. Gunther Von Hagens had developed a way of injecting cadavers with a plastic resin which allowed them to be posed. Rather than just figures standing around he had them doing things like playing chess and riding a horse, which was also embalmed. It was touted as a serious scientific undertaking, but that was undermined a bit by having the final exhibit in the walk through experience, a room full of deformed babies in jars. I still thought it was fascinating. In later years he expanded his collection to include figures playing basketball and dancing, and added a gorilla.

Rudolf Virchow was a pioneering German physician/teacher who created a collection of medical specimens so that students could see body parts and anatomy outside a body or see the effects of disease. The collection also included deformities and broken bones and similar materials. The idea was a big success and influenced the creation of similar collections around the world including the Mutter Museum in Philadelphia. During World War II the Virchow

---

[10] Yes, I know. The Third Man takes place in Vienna not Berlin, but let me have this.

Museum was hit by allied bombing and part of the collection incinerated. It was rebuilt after the war though as was done in a number of locations, part of the battle damage was retained so people would remember. The entire Max Planck trip was a fascinating and informative experience for me on many levels.

The other good bit of news that came along at this time was that my first book was about to be published. While working on my dissertation at MBE, I came across a small ad in the back of the journal of the History of Science Society, *Isis*. It was from the British publisher Ashgate. A respected scholarly press, Ashgate was looking for manuscripts on the history of science for a new series they were putting out. I thought, what the hell? I sent them a short proposal. As a grad student one of our professors, Dr. Johnathan Rose, would give little seminars on how to get published. He told us that when you approach a publisher trying to get your dissertation published; don't tell them it's your dissertation. So, when I approached Ashgate I never mentioned that it was my dissertation. I wasn't expecting anything to happen. I just did it to say I was trying. I had received so many turndowns from schools for teaching jobs and I took the same approach with publishers: send it off and don't expect it to work.

To my surprise they responded enthusiastically. They asked for a more detailed proposal, which I sent. They liked that too, and asked for a sample chapter. I only had three chapters written and only one of those was complete. I sent that to them. They then asked how long it would be before I had a finished manuscript. I had no idea what to say. I took a walk around College Hill to think. I estimated, with no experience in writing a book, it would take me eight months to finish. I assumed they'd say that was too long, but they said that was fine, and why don't I take fourteen? Then they sent me a contract. I was dumbfounded. I went walking around College Hill again for a couple of hours thinking about it (I didn't tell anyone at MBE). Finally, I sat on the steps of the Athenaeum in the pitch dark and signed it on my knee. I felt like Bruce Springsteen signing his first record contract on the trunk of a car in the parking lot of a New Jersey diner at 2am. The next morning, I put it in the mail then I called Lisa and told her. When it came time to do my defence, I never told the committee that I already had a contract to publish.

The only thing I had to do now was to finish. I went into writing overdrive but I didn't own my own computer at the time. The one we were issued as grad students at Drew University by now had conked out so, I wrote everything out longhand on yellow legal pads at night, then typed them up during the day on my work computer. A genuine sense of fear set in. I had reached this point mostly on Newark style bluff and guile. I had stepped out on the stage figuring nothing would happen, but they called my bluff. If I didn't make it work it would be more confirmation that I was not smart or good enough to make this work. After about eight months or so—I had been right all along about the time—I finished the manuscript and sent it to Ashgate. Then the editing process began. Again, as I had no prior experience with any of this I had no idea what to expect. Luckily, they did not make any structural changes, only some syntactic changes, typos, misspellings and few others. The thing that stands out is that there is a point in the story where I mention the words 'Gila monster.' The editor had no idea what that was and insisted I had confused it or spelled it wrong. I had to explain, without sounding testy, what it was. Finally, she said okay, but I'm convinced she never really believed me. With all the editing done, I enquired about the cover. They said they didn't have one yet. As a graphic designer, I wanted to do my own cover. I had an idea. They said to send it along and they'd think about it. So, I worked up a colour rough using construction paper and printing out text at MBE and glueing it all together. I wrapped it up and sent it to them. I have no idea how they made the decision, but they liked what I had sent them and the cover of

Henry Fairfield Osborn: Race and the Search for the Origins of Man turned out pretty much as I had designed it. They scheduled it for release in early 2002. Returning from Berlin, I was elated: starting my first resident faculty job, and having my first book about to come out. The life I had dreamt of since I was a kid was now here. What monsters could possibly intrude now?

9/11

I got up early for my first day at TCI. I had put all my materials together the night before, and planned on going in and teaching the hell out of that place. Lisa sent me off with a hardy, "good luck!" and a smooch. I headed to the Chatham train station to join the morning commute into Manhattan. It was 8am, Tuesday, September 11, 2001.

Riding the train, no one had any inkling that as we watched New Jersey go by, hijacked jetliners were on their way to destiny. About halfway through the trip people started saying they were hearing strange reports on their Walkman radios about a plane crash in Manhattan. Then someone said loudly, "A plane has crashed into the World Trade Center!" Even with such news no one yet thought it was a terror attack. We all assumed it was a terrible accident. Then they started saying another plane had crashed into the World Trade Center. I thought, maybe a plane had hit one tower then bounced off and hit the other? The buildings were close to each other . Then the train came to that part of the line where it heads out over the Meadowlands and you can see the Manhattan skyline. We all could see those now terrible twin columns of oily, evil, thick black smoke. There was no doubt. This was no accident.

Oddly, the train just kept going. We passed through Market Street Station Newark, then headed out over the Meadowlands. You could see the burning towers getting closer, but the train just kept going. As we finally arrived at Penn Station, New York, the conductor announced over the loudspeaker, "There seems to be something going on downtown, so please be careful." I went to the nearest pay phone and called my mother. She hadn't been watching the TV news so I told her to put the set on, and that I was alright and not to worry.

As I walked I thought to myself, 'I'm supposed to be an historian, I'd better make notes and watch what's going on around me so I can write about it someday'. I had an appointment at TCI with the Dean of the Division of Arts and Sciences to discuss the first day of class which was supposed to be the next day, September 12th. I went in for the meeting. The place was quietly chaotic. We were supposed to open for the school year the next day. The president of the college was meeting with senior staff and faculty. That's when I walked in. Everyone stopped, turned and looked at me. "Uh, hi, I'm Doctor Regal, I'm supposed to be starting here today," I said a bit sheepishly.

The college president insisted we didn't just stand around. We couldn't go downtown and volunteer to help, so we did the only other reasonable thing: we went to a restaurant for lunch. About a dozen of us walked a few blocks and crammed into a restaurant. Obviously, all we talked about was what was going on. It seemed bizarre to me we were doing this. I don't think it had really sunk in what had happened. It was hard to comprehend. When the meal—that the school paid for—was over, we went back to the college. Everyone who had access to one was glued to a radio or television.

By the afternoon people who had been downtown in the thick of it, and who had started walking north away from it, were beginning to reach midtown where we were. They were all covered with grey ash. They walked silently. It reminded me of those stories that came out of Hiroshima about crowds of injured people walking silently out of town after the bomb went off. There wasn't much noise at all. Not even many emergency vehicle sirens. They had all already headed downtown. Those fire engines, police cars, and ambulances that had not been destroyed when the towers fell were not going anywhere soon. They walked as if in a parade of ghosts.

By the late afternoon New Jersey Transit, PATH (though the PATH station under the World Trade Center had been destroyed), the Long Island Railroad, Metro North, and the MTA began sending trains out of town. They abandoned the regular schedule and trains started pulling up to the various platforms. They packed them full with as many people as they could then sent the train on its way. No one had any idea yet if it was over or if more attacks were coming. We had heard, by now, of the attack on the Pentagon. They wanted to get as many people off the island as quickly as they could. As soon as one train pulled out another was immediately brought up and that one filled to capacity and sent off. It went on like that into the evening on all the commuter lines and subways. It was like an army of steel worms wiggling their way out of a burning tree trunk. From across the street in front of TCI I saw the crowds getting a bit thinner so decided to take the chance and go into the bowels of Penn Station. Port Authority officials were directing people, and there was little sense of chaos or pushing or screaming. It didn't take too long and I was on a train. I then realised that it was about the same time of day that I would have been heading home anyway. The train disappeared into the long tunnel under the river that connected New York to New Jersey.

Coming home out of Manhattan, the Dover train made all its usual stops. Not many people talking, all just sitting there in stunned silence. Then I noticed at each stop there was a biohazard team with state troopers, local police and fire units in full protective gear standing on the platforms. They were there ready to decontaminate anyone who was covered in dust. I was lucky, I didn't have any visible dust on me so when I disembarked at Chatham I just walked home.

That's how 9/11 ended for me.

An Incident at the NYPL

Everyone was in shock from the 9/11 attack, but life had to go on. TCI began classes the following Thursday. Incredibly, the majority of students, faculty, and staff showed up. Once it was seen that the attacks were over, the commuter train lines went back to a normal schedule. Weeks went by and the city settled down into a weird form of its normal routine. Fall turned to winter. It was a chilly day in Manhattan with light flurries falling that I sat in the third floor portrait gallery of the New York Public Library. I loved to go to the library to sit and think and write. There was a crowd of people walking around slowly, looking at the art hanging on the walls. I had just received the contract for my second book, *Human Evolution: A Guide to the Debates* and I was making notes for how to organise it. I was on my lunch break from TCI. It was February of 2002.

As I scribbled into my notebook I became aware of someone standing over me. I looked up to see the smiling face of a young man in his early twenties. He was wearing a suit. Not a very expensive or trendy suit, but one he had clearly spent, on what was for him, a lot of money it seemed. And he was proud of it. "Are you an American?" he asked. His demeanour and accent gave away his West African origins: Sierra Leone, or Senegal or Nigeria maybe.

"Yes," I replied.

He then gestured with a sweep of his hand to the paintings on the walls, "Who are those people and why are their pictures hanging here? I thought this was a library." The walls of the large third floor reading room, across from the cavernous main reading room, were covered in classic 19th century life-sized portraits. Thick oils on canvas, heavy, imposing frames, crafted by masters. Images meant to flatter the sitters and impress the viewers with their seriousness and importance. I explained to him that they were members of the Astor and Lenox families. The fabulously wealthy benefactors of the library who had given of their wealth so that this cathedral to learning could be built.

"Why did they do that?" he asked with a certain incredulous look.

I told him that they felt that they were obliged to use their wealth to make the city a better place. By building a free public library, those in the city not as fortunate as they, who could not go to the finest schools, or to school at all, could still have access to the knowledge of the world.

He resumed his upward gaze at the faces from long ago. I was about to resume my scribbling when he turned back to me suddenly and flashed his big smile. "That's what I'm going to do!" He turned back to the pictures. "That's what I'm going to do!" The second time more to himself than me. "I've just arrived here!" He grabbed my hand and shook it vigorously. "Thank you, Sir, thank you!" He then briskly walked off, disappearing into the crowd.

The entire incident took maybe sixty seconds. I had never seen him before, and I never saw him again. Sitting there it struck me, "We win!" I thought. The rubble of the World Trade Center was still smouldering, but new immigrants were still coming here any way they could, and still wanting to follow the American Dream. Despite everything, this young man was not just going to become an American, he was going to do something to make not only himself, but America a better place.

America was built by immigrants, maintained by immigrants and improved by immigrants. That's what makes America great. For their efforts we insult them, we arrest them, we spit on them, we call them rapists and criminals and bad hombres, and do whatever we can to make their lives miserable and to keep them out. We make up foolish arguments about 'illegal immigration' and argue our ancestors came to America in a somehow different or better way than they do today. Yet, these newcomers make the country great anyway, and continue to do so. Some day in the future I'll see a news report about a proud immigrant man from West Africa who, despite being labelled an illegal, built a library somewhere in America. He will not remember me, but I'll remember him.

TCI

One of the things that I loved about working at TCI was that our students were predominantly new immigrants—many would probably have been labelled 'illegals' by anti-immigrant bigots. They worked hard and studied. They did the reading even if their English reading ability was not as strong as it could be. My colleagues at TCI fell into two categories: the deeply committed and those who should have been committed. It was often called an engineering school, but it was really more of a mechanic's institute. I don't say that in a

137

derogatory manner. Since its opening by Guglielmo Marconi in 1909 the school was, by design, one that would train technicians to operate the electrical equipment of the future. It had kept pace with the times for decades, but then ran into a wall. That was due, in large part, because the technical faculty were all mechanics who were teaching only the things they knew. The problem was they learned that material in the 1970s and hadn't progressed since. More than a few times, I sat in all college faculty meetings and suggested we start teaching the students robotics. This was the wave of the future and we should be on board. There was no reason, I argued, that TCI could not fashion itself—without too much effort—in a kind of two year MIT. Where we had been teaching students air conditioning repair, we could now start teaching them robot repair as well. This put me squarely on the shit list of the tech faculty. Most of them did not have higher degrees, none of them knew science or even advanced technologies. The few that did were looked up and down by the old school wrench turners. Part of their resistance to moving forward was that they were incapable of teaching new technologies. They knew nothing about robotic hydraulics or kinemetrics. They could not even teach the fundamental principles of mechanics. The students only learned about the laws of thermodynamics, for example, if they took my history of science class. As a result, most of the veteran tech faculty I surmised, resisted upgrading because they feared they would lose their jobs.

My best friend at TCI was Professor Robert Fuhrman. He was the classic New York bohemian. An artist, author, and sometimes an actor. His cinematic claim to fame, for which he was regularly chided by his friends, was a major role in *Hotdog: the Movie* (1984) - a coming of age skiing movie. Under the gruff exterior, was a man deeply dedicated to teaching and helping his students pull themselves up. We would often end the week sharing a few pints at the *Molly Wee* pub around the corner. The *Molly Wee* only hired new immigrant Irish girls as waitresses. When the great blackout hit on August 14, 2003, Robert and I went to the *Molly Wee* and after a while ended up sitting in the pitch black on the curb on 33rd Street drunk as skunks talking Hegelian philosophy and Shakespearean sonnets (which is odd as I didn't really know Hegelian philosophy). The bars had lost their refrigeration and were giving beer away for free: I may have solved the riddle of the universe, but I don't remember. When Robert died in 2009, he was one of the few people I knew personally for whom I mourned and for whom I missed when he was gone.

When I started at TCI there were no separate humanities departments. There was one large Division of Arts & Sciences into which everyone who wasn't an engineer was placed. When I was hired it was along with another historian (we were the only two) named Phyllis Kohn whose speciality was the Soviet space program. After just a few months the woman who was then Dean of Arts & Sciences was fired for having an affair with a student. This was the same person who had taken me to lunch shortly after I had arrived and began telling me how she wasn't sleeping with her husband and was looking for a new partner. I left that particular meeting feeling very weird; simultaneously hit upon yet worried about my job, so I was quite happy when she was let go. For a new Dean they chose a far more qualified candidate and promoted Phyllis to Dean. They had also removed the department Chair, who was Robert Furhman, though he was not fired. Then one morning I was at my desk in my office in the basement when I looked up and saw Robert Furhman and the college president standing there. They took seats in front of my desk and looked at me very seriously. Robert said that he was stepping down as Chair and that he could think of no one better to assume that position than me. I was being offered the position of Chair of the division after only being there for a semester and a half. Since I was still the most naive man in the world, I said thanks but no thanks, as I had a new book I was working on and that I didn't think I was qualified for the position. He then explained there was a major reduction in teaching load and a raise in pay. When I still hesitated, the college president finally spoke. He leaned forward and looked at me over his glasses. "You don't seem to understand Dr. Regal," he said rather sternly, "either you take this job or you're fired." My response was, "Well, you know. Maybe being chair would be good for my career?" They both leaned back in their chairs and smiled in the way that co-conspirators do when their plan comes together. They stood up, congratulated me, told me to start moving my things to the Chair's office, turned and left. I was left there wondering what the hell had just happened. In the short time since I started at TCI I experienced the 9/11 attacks, been hit on by my Dean, found out my father was dying, had my first book come out, received a contract for my second, and now had been promoted to Chair of my department. I remained Chair until I left in 2007.

My nemesis at TCI was Jenny Greenblatt. She had cerebral palsy or some other similar affliction when she was young which left her as an adult with a crippled leg and some difficulty walking. She made up for this condition by being a huge pain in the ass to everyone around her. She had a master's degree in Liberal Studies. Such degrees are not taken seriously by scholars. The curriculum consists of a hodgepodge of art, literature, and nebulous non-technical classes. She fancied herself as an 'artist' and a 'writer' yet she had produced no art and published written work. She had little in the way of knowledge about anything, yet claimed she knew everything. When I arrived at TCI, they wanted to offer studio art courses. As I had such experience from working at Kubert they asked me to create several drawing classes. I readily agreed. Ms. Greenblatt was furious that the newcomer was allowed to do this as she had lobbied for years to be allowed to create a drawing class, but had been turned down by the administration as 'unqualified'. She was at best a mediocre teacher. As chair, students often told me they thought she was awful. She was the teacher students hoped they didn't get.[11] She treated the students with as much contempt as she treated her colleagues. Once, when as Chair, I said some offhand remark she didn't like, she called the police and told them I had threatened her. A couple of uniformed officers arrived, and she gave them all the gory details in breathless exuberance. When she was finished, they looked at each other, rolled their eyes, and told her they would look into it. They left disappointed, no doubt, for what they thought might turn out to be an interesting investigation into a major assassination plot, turned out to be nonsense. I was never contacted again by the authorities or even the school administration over it.

TCI occupied two facilities at the time. The main building was on the corner across from Penn Station and the Post Office, with several floors of a high rise office building a few blocks away. Our two floors were on the eighth and ninth. Several elevators and staircases serviced the building. One semester, I had a student in my USII class who was blind, with a Seeing Eye dog, and who was confined to a wheelchair. Despite this, he made it to every class in the large building and never complained, not once. Jenny Greenblatt refused to teach classes or come to department meetings in the building because it was "too difficult for her to get up to the eighth floor." We had a large office in the 34th Street building occupied by a dozen or so faculties. When the administration promoted me to chair of the Division of Arts and Sciences I also had my office in that building. I took dark delight in always having department meetings in the 34th Street building because I knew Ms. Greenblatt would not attend. It gave me special glee knowing that we were paid an hour's salary for every meeting we were required to attend. Since she refused to attend, she did not receive the pay. There was nothing she could do about it.

---

[11] She was so disliked by students some of the crueller ones called her 'Hip Hop' because of the way she walked.

TCI, which began in 1909 as the Marconi Institute that later became the RCA Institute, was always scrambling for students. We never had more than 1500 at a time. 9/11 had hit us hard as well. The school always seemed on the verge of closing. Lisa and I bought the Webster house in 2003 during a brief moment of financial stability at TCI.[12]

Creation Convention

On a Tuesday in January 2005, I was in my office at TCI when my phone rang. It was a producer for the recently launched 'Liberal' radio station, *Air America*. I had been listening to it, primarily because one of the hosts was the actress, comedienne-turned-political-activist Janeane Garofalo. I had been a fan of hers since I saw the Medieval Times scene from *The Cable Guy*. The producer said, "Janeane saw your book on evolution controversies and wondered if you'd like to come on as a guest?" I tried to contain my excitement and remain cool. I said that I'd be happy to. As it turned out, the studio where *Air America* broadcast from was right up the street from TCI. They asked if I could turn up that Friday; I would be in the last slot of the week. I took the next couple of days to decide what to wear. I went in at the specified time and sat in a little anteroom just off the recording studio. At the commercial break I was led into the studio and introduced. I took my seat and pulled on a set of headphones.

Janeane's co-host, Sam Seder was on vacation and sitting in for him was actor Justin Theroux. The interview went well. Janeane had clearly read my book, and was quite knowledgeable about the subject. The producer had originally told me I would be on for one segment—roughly twenty minutes, but they kept me on for the rest of the show; almost an hour and a half. I didn't make any gaffs or goofs and she seemed to like me, even calling me a genius at one point. I had never been on the radio before. In fact, I had never been interviewed in my life. It was to be my first media experience. One of the things she wanted to talk about most was the Christian evangelical response to evolution.

Having included a chapter on religious fundamentalism in my Human Evolution book, an opportunity to observe anti-evolution up-close presented itself a few months after my star turn with Janeane. The Christian fundamentalist group *Answers in Genesis* organised an anti-evolution 'conference'. Masquerading as a scholarly event, it was, in reality, a three-day festival of obscurantism, anger, and self-righteousness. I decided I should go down and participate. It was held over several days in July 2005, at Liberty University in Virginia. The dates are meant to coincide with the anniversary of the Scope's Monkey Trial. They wanted you to sign up for the entire program, so I told the woman on the phone I could only manage one day and I would need accommodation. She immediately sounded sceptical, but in the end relented. I rented a car and drove eight hours one-way to get to the campus. It was boiling hot, but luckily all the buildings were air conditioned.

The panels they presented were a hodgepodge of pseudoscience and pseudo history. The best part about it, from my point of view, was that the presenters who talked about genetics and fossils had no formal training in any of it. It was just a bunch of religious fundamentalists trying to explain how science was bad and evolution was wrong, all the time having little idea of what they were talking about. The two they had who were the closest to being actual scientists were Dr. Don Batten - a horticulturist, and Dr. Georgia Purdom - a

---

[12] The school was eventually sold to Touro College, one of our rivals, in 2016. The name TCI was retired.

biochemist. Batten tackled the fossil evidence. He argued that one need not know anything about anatomy to know that evolution was a sham. He claimed that the *Ardipithicus* remains, recently found in Ethiopia, represented the first "suicide bomber". As the infamous 7/7 bombings had just taken place in London it seemed especially creepy and inappropriate. His audience, however, roared with laughter at the reference. Dr. Purdom tried to explain to her large audience all about DNA and how it had nothing to do with evolution. Despite a PhD in biochemistry, Dr. Purdom ended her talk by showing a PowerPoint slide that said, "God said it, I believe it, and that settles it."

One of my favourite parts of my time there was strolling through the parking lot looking at the vanity plates. One said 'NOEVO' while another said 'ALL4HM.'[13]

Conclusion

Seven years had gone by at TCI and I felt I had reached the end of the line there. Moreover, I began to worry about how I could help my students. While some of the faculty were excellent, there were those who didn't want to do any more than they absolutely had to. Some regularly worked to undermine not only faculty, but also the students for reasons I was never able to discern, most likely jealousy. Also, TCI had a student population made up of local kids from mostly disadvantaged circumstances. They all worked hard to try to turn their lives into something better, but many were weighed down by extra emotional, economic, and cultural baggage. I had been growing weary of working at TCI. I had become one of the teachers who students ran to when in trouble. I helped them with advice and guidance as much as I could, but I had been trained as an historian not a social worker. I even helped a few financially with a ten or a twenty here and there when they couldn't afford lunch or bus fare to get to school. I wrote letters of recommendation for the ones who were going on to other schools and jobs. After seven years, I was feeling exhausted. What was I supposed to say, for example, to an eighteen-year-old, distraught girl on her third child who asked me what to do, now that her father had called her a whore and thrown her out of the house? There were some problems I was just not equipped to solve, no matter how much I wanted to.

Luckily my old alma mater was looking to hire.

---

[13] I wrote an article about this experience for the Fortean Times, "Dem Ole Dry Bones," 202 (October, 2005): 57.

The Alvis Stalwart. My first vehicle of escape.

Me, my father, and our first dog Fuzzy in the Ironbound, 1965.

Sherman, named for Sherman and Mr. Peabody.

Me and Dreamboat Annie II, 1981.

Hunting Werewolves on the Iron Curtain 1979.

Hunting Werewolves at the Museum of Natural History, Oxford.

Dr. Lisa Nocks, historian of robots, Shelley scholar, author, adventuress, and my best friend.

Chapter 7

A Theory of Monsters

If I see but one smile on your lips when we meet, occasioned by this or any other exertion of mine, I shall need no other happiness.

— Mary Shelley, *Frankenstein*

When I was ten years old, I heard there was a bust of Christopher Columbus in a park along the Passaic River in Kearny. Sculpted by artist Michele Salvemini (who passed away in 2020), it was installed in 1967. One sunny day, as I was just beginning my career as an historian adventurer, I rode my bike to see it. I thought they had put it there because it was the spot where Columbus made landfall in 1492. I couldn't figure out why Columbus would have wanted to sail on the Passaic with its chocolate milk consistency and colour, but what did I know? I didn't like the look on the statue's face as he stared at the traffic on Passaic Avenue. Also, it seemed they made his head weirdly big. In 2020, during the great toppling of Columbus statues, competing groups began petitions to both tear down and protect the bust. As of this writing, he's still there.

After I graduated from Kean University in 1995, I went off to graduate school, then on to the Fellowship at Mary Baker Eddy, then Max Planck, then the residency at TCI. With the Osborn book published, I went looking for the next project. The publisher ABC-CLIO released a book by Michael Ruse called *The Evolution Wars: A Guide to the Debates* (2000). Ruse was a prolific science writer whom I admired (and who had reviewed the Osborn book favourably). I liked his book and it gave me an idea. I contacted ABC-CLIO and asked, "why not a book specifically on human evolution controversies?" To my amazement, they agreed. I put together a proposal. They liked it and sent me back a contract. My second book would be *Human Evolution: A Guide to the Debates*. Over the next few years I was offered the chance to write a new introduction for Darwin's autobiography, then a book on the history of radio, which I managed to finish just as I was getting ready to move on from TCI.

Then Kean beckoned again. One of the people who had most helped me as a student, Mark Lender, was now chair of history at Kean. He wanted to expand the department and add several tenure track posts, one of which was for the history of science. For this application I called out all the stops and cashed in every IOU I had. I was like a guy at the poker table who pushes in all his chips, then takes off his watch and throws it down, and just to be sure, tosses his car keys on the pile as well. I asked for letters from David Kohn, Garland Allen, Kevin Downing the editor from ABC-CLIO, even Olof Ljungström. I had a preposterous ten letters of recommendation from both national and international references. I wanted to blow the hiring committee away. I didn't even want to consider what would happen if I didn't get the job.

Keaneana

Dr. Mark Lender was an historian, former armour officer, and an old-school style, machine politician. He started at Kean College in 1982 as a Grants Officer then moved up the career ladder. As a result, he knew everyone and everything. He knew how to get things done. He knew how to walk into someone's office, and after an amiable chat, walk out with what he

147

wanted. He had been provost before he took over from Larry Zimmer as Chair of history. He knew how to talk to people.

I sent in my application, made the proper animal sacrifices, and now had to wait. Once the job went public, over one hundred people applied for it. After a few weeks, I was asked to go in for an interview. I felt I had at least one friend there, my former grad school classmate at Drew, Dr. Brid Nicholson, who had been hired at Kean the year before. On arrival, I was sent to the CAS building to a conference room. To prepare, I sprayed the covers of the three books I had already published with furniture wax so they would shine when I put them on the table in front of the hiring committee. Mark Lender was there, as well as Christopher Bellitto, Sue Gronewold, Dennis Klein, and Rob Mayer, but not Brid. The questions began: Why do you want to work here? Why are you leaving TCI? What's your research all about? Then Bob Mayer, who was well over six feet tall, a kind of hulking figure, spoke. His provenance at Kean went well back into the bad old days. When he retired, I discovered he began at Kean College the same year that I began high school. He hadn't said anything the entire interview then suddenly sat forward and asked, "What would you do if a student was getting unruly in class?" Without thinking—I probably should have given it more thought—I said, "I'd tell them to shut up!" I felt like Ralphie after he blurted out that he wants a BB gun for Christmas. Dr. Mayer just raised an eyebrow, let loose, what for him, was as close to a smile as you'd get, and said, "okay." He never asked another question.

When it was over, I packed up my things and went home. A week later they asked me to come in and give a guest lecture. That went well, and so now the waiting game began. On a Friday, several weeks later, Mark called me. The moment I heard his voice I heard the echo of eternity. I heard the voice of God. It was either going to be good news or I was going to go stick my head in the oven with the gas on. He began by saying, "I've got bad news." My heart sank as my life passed before me, and I headed for the kitchen. He then explained how the faculty had tallied who they liked and who they didn't and had a vote. I had made it to the final cut. In the end I received a unanimous vote with one exception. Mark wanted a totally unanimous vote. "Give me a couple of days," he said. I spent the weekend in a permanent sweat. Finally, he called back. "Okay, you want the job?" I began to explain that since I had several books out and had already proven myself in a residency job at TCI maybe I should start with tenure or at the Associate level, or maybe with a higher pay level. In the classic Mark Lender way, he allowed me to give my speech then said, "Listen, no to all of that, the school will not go along with any of it, do you want the job or not?" I said "yes", to which he replied, "okay, and that I'd be hearing from HR sometime soon". Finally, he said, "I'll see you at the end of August for orientation." and hung up. It would be a good summer after all.

After I received my PhD, I told my father that I was applying to several schools for a job. He asked me, "have you just asked if they have any positions available?" He had even looked through the *Star-Ledger* ads for me to see if there were any jobs labelled 'professor,' that I could apply for. He was trying to help me in the only way he knew. He was the kind of man who wanted, in his own closed mouth way, to be a good dad. He felt it was his responsibility to look after his kid and do whatever he could to help (it didn't matter that I was forty). As a construction worker, he knew nothing of the inner workings of academia. He assumed it was like any other job: You went up to the foreman and asked if they were hiring. I smiled and said I would do that. When I did get my first resident faculty position at TCI, I told him I had followed his advice and it worked. It made him happy to think he had helped me, which of course, he had. He passed away before I had been offered the job at Kean.

The year I began at Kean as an assistant professor for the history of science, almost forty other faculty members had been hired by the university: three in the Department of History alone. They were heady days. Joining me in history were Jonathan Mercantini and Elizabeth Hyde.[1] The days of history faculty screaming and backstabbing each other in the halls were now over. It had become what Mark Lender had set out to make it: a department of young—well, youngish—faculty go-getters who had their eyes on the future; who would become publishing machines; who would engage with the community; who would teach the hell out of their students, and become scholars of international stature. It would be a faculty using cutting edge technology inside the classroom and out.

It became apparent to me immediately that this was quite a crew. A group who would not only make a name for themselves as scholars, but who would help rather than hinder each other. Many academic departments and programs, not just at Kean, but around the world, can be hotbeds of infighting and pointless intrigues. I think what allowed us to avoid so much of the university department drama was that we all shared, more or less, a similar vision of the department's and the university's future. We all wanted it to become a place that students wanted to attend. We all wanted it to be a jewel in the crown the way Mark Lender envisioned. Also, while each faculty member had a wide knowledge of history over multiple disciplines, and could certainly teach almost any class we offered, our specialties did not clash. Whereby I did the history of science, technology and medicine, Brid Nicholson did women's history, military history, and Irish studies. Dennis Klein did Jewish studies. Beth Hyde was the Francophile who specialised in the history of gardens and gardening, Jonathan Mercantini was a colonial America scholar, Christopher Bellitto was a classicist, but primarily Church historian. Frank Argote-Fryre did Latin America, Sue Gronewold did the history of Asia, Larry Zimmer did British history, and Robert Mayer did military history and psychohistory. Jay Spaulding did the Islamic world and Africa, while Mark Lender did the History of New Jersey. Frank Esposito did New Jersey, but his specialty was Native American history.[2] No one else on the faculty was interested in monsters.

It was in the late 1990s, that things began to change in the Kean College department. Mark Lender took over as chair and was determined to turn a dysfunctional department into a jewel of the university. He brought in an Asia scholar, Dr. Sue Gronewold, and classicist and church historian Dr. Christopher Bellitto when Mary Lewis retired. Also, this was when Jewish studies specialist Dr. Dennis Klein joined. Eventually, Frank Wetta, Xurong Kong, and Abby Perkiss joined. Xurong Kong was a Chinese national who did her graduate work in Asian literature and poetry at the University of Wisconsin, Madison. While at Kean she became a US citizen and wrote an important book on the Silk Road. Abby Perkiss had, along with her history degrees, a Juris Doctor degree and so taught our history of law classes. She would do amazing work in the area of new and experimental ways of classroom instruction.

Despite him being several years older than me, Frank Wetta and I got along quite well. We often bought each other drinks at Suspenders. Originally from Louisiana, he was incredibly smart and had published a shelf full of books on military history and pop culture. He had a great deal of university experience and, in fact, had been provost of Ocean County College before he was hired to be the department's on-the-spot man at Ocean. He was a bit on the politically conservative side and we often gave each other a hard time over our political views, but it was never mean spirited and always done with a smile.

---

[1] Jonathan eventually became Dean of the College of Liberal Arts, while Beth became department Chair, then Associate Dean.
[2] Within a couple of years Mark Lender retired as did Jay Spaulding. Larry Zimmer passed away.

A Cryptid of My Own

Following the human evolution book, Greenwood Publishing asked me to write an encyclopaedia of pseudoscience. They sent me a cheque and I began. Very quickly, other needs called me away and I forgot about the encyclopaedia. Then five weeks before it was due, I came across the contract and realised that in all that time (almost a year and a half) I hadn't worked on it at all. I let out an expletive laden scream and started in. I began typing furiously. I wrote about everything, monsters included. A few days before the deadline, I had completed the manuscript. It was the fastest book I had ever written.

With this experience behind me, I thought it would be fun to finally do something entirely focused on the history of cryptozoology. I wanted to go looking for monsters again. I was also increasingly drawn to the question of amateur investigators and their relationship to professional scholars. As I had written a chapter for the human evolution book on the ancient American burial mounds, I thought a book on amateur archaeology should be my next project. With this idea, I suddenly saw myself back in Kearny as a nine year old at the entrance to the Hudson County Park and my fantasies about lost civilizations. All these things appealed to me. That has always been one of my scholarly problems; I am interested in a wide variety of topics and want to write about all of them simultaneously. I became one of those people who usually has two or three major projects (and a couple of minor ones) going on at once. It dawned on me then how I could get a lot of this into one book. While I had yet to come up with a way of articulating this clearly, I felt an interdisciplinary approach to monsters was needed. I was not going to look for monsters in the woods, I was going to track them down in libraries.

In 2004, I determined my next project would be tentatively called *Darwin and the Monsters*. This was a project I had seriously considered as my doctoral dissertation. I didn't submit it because I didn't think they'd let me write about monsters. It was to be a grand examination of how most of the great biological researchers and writers, back to antiquity, had seen monstrosity as part of the understanding of generation and ultimately evolution. As I prepared my notes and research materials, I decided I would do a chapter on the origins of modern cryptozoology. Whilst working on it, I encountered Dr. Grover Krantz. I remembered him from appearances he made on the Leonard Nimoy series *In Search Of* as well as *Arthur C. Clarke's Mysterious World*. Grover Krantz had recently died, but his estate had donated his voluminous papers to the Smithsonian Institution. I was on a train down to Washington DC as soon as I could get on one! The material went to the National Anthropological Archive in Suitland, Maryland. On my first visit, I spent several days there going through the collection.[3] Krantz was a major player in the world of cryptozoology and so the collection contained extensive materials from other important figures in the field. Commonplace in such situations was that, as I went through the folders I saw that other collections in the Smithsonian had similar materials on everything from the skulls of giants to the Minnesota Iceman. I also saw that I was the first person to look at this material. What I had envisioned as a chapter in the Darwin book rapidly expanded into something more extensive.

Most people who pursue monsters do so in dark woods, caves, and fields. I always instinctively knew they were missing the real action. The real story of monsters was not in swamps, but in libraries and archives. This is where I would pursue them. I realised the Krantz material cried out to be a book of its own. As I went through the Krantz collection, the world

---

[3] I went back several more times over the next few years.

of late twentieth century cryptozoology sprang to life. Letter after letter, notebook after notebook made these characters live. The adventures, the arguments, the petty jealousies, the back-stabbing, the envy and all the other parts of the human experience climbed out of those archival boxes. The idiosyncrasies and foibles of these legendary characters came to life in all their bare-knuckled glory. I knew this book had to be all about this. Darwin would have to wait a bit.

While scholarly and learned people had been interested in, and wrote about, monsters all the way back to the ancient world, the modern field of Cryptozoology began in the mid-twentieth century with the work of Bernard Heuvelmans and Ivan Sanderson. Both trained academics, they simultaneously coined the term cryptozoology in the 1950s. They were joined by more trained scientists like John Napier, Grover Krantz, and others. By the latter part of the twentieth century, most of the academics had fallen away once it was seen that reports of monsters such as Bigfoot, the Loch Ness Monster, and the Minnesota Iceman were shown to be hoaxes and misidentifications. This allowed for the rise of the amateurs and outsider authors. It was this relationship that fascinated me. These characters seemed to me as tragic as anything Shakespeare ever wrote about. They were people doggedly pursuing something they thought was there, but that everyone else told them wasn't.

I have always been drawn to the idea of biography. In the later twentieth and early twenty-first centuries, however, biography as a form of historical investigation fell out of favour with scholars. This stemmed from the fact that in the nineteenth and first half of the twentieth century, history in the west generally and, particularly in America, was all about the 'great white men' of the past. Modernist historians argued that history was the result of a few white, elite, Protestant Christian men using the power of their will to bend and mould and to make history into what they wanted. The best way to tell those stories, they reasoned, was through biography. History was seen as triumphalist Whig history. With the advent of postmodernist historical thought, the 'great white man' theory was rejected by the new generation of scholars. As a result, biography was now seen as an old-fashioned way to write about the past. Then, along came the 'New Biography' movement. This argued that biography could still be a valid form of historical storytelling if it was used to examine larger ideas, and focus on a larger pool of possible subjects. Being someone who always liked biography I thought I would tackle Krantz that way. He was a white male, but he was also at the centre of the world of cryptozoology. I felt I could use his life's journey to tell the wider story of the history of monster hunting. I would use a smaller story to tell a big story.

As I delved deeper into the world of cryptozoology and monster hunting, I saw that there was an enormous amount of archival material on its history. Cryptozoologists, including authors on the subject it seemed, knew little of this material. In addition to Washington DC, I researched in Philadelphia, New York, Boston, London, Cambridge and Oxford. All these places gave up their many cryptozoological secrets. While there were shelves full of books and articles on cryptozoology, it was not a topic that was much written about by mainstream, academic historians. Most writers on cryptozoology, and other such fringe subjects, tended to be believers: their work was an attempt to prove that monsters, ghosts or UFOs were real. These works tended to be sensationalistic and concentrated on 'mysteries' (21st century television still takes this approach on these subjects). Others were pure sceptics and debunkers who wanted to show how foolish these beliefs were and that they had no basis in any reality. I didn't want to take either of these approaches. I wanted to examine the history and to tell the stories of the searchers, but based upon the primary sources, not third and fourth-handed rumours and baseless myths, repeated a thousand times. There was the possibility that academia might not consider anyone who did as being serious. At that moment, however, I never thought of any of this. As usual, I didn't consider any adverse reactions. All I knew was that this was what I wanted to study so I just headed off in that direction. If there were to be negative consequences on my career, I'd deal with them later.[4] I realised that here at Kean my interest in monster history would be accepted and that I'd be able to get research funding. The department, and the school, would appreciate my work.

The Farahi Years

The president of the university when I joined was Dr. Dawood Farahi. Born in Afghanistan and coming to America as a young man, Dr. Farahi stood as a self-described model of the American Dream: an immigrant who worked hard, went to school, and rose to be the president of a large state university. Being on the faculty at Kean for twenty years prior, he took office in 2003, and immediately began a program to transform the school. He said he did not want to be the president of a glorified community college. When I was a student at Kean, it looked and felt like an industrial park. By the 1990s, what had been state-of-the-art facilities and 1950s modern buildings, had fallen on hard times. Large tracts of dirt zones—that turned to mud in the lightest rain—gave the place a gloomy feel. The faculties were terrific, but the physical school was drab. Farahi was determined to change all that. He started on a construction and beautification program together with an academic expansion program that transformed the university. He purchased the nearby Pingry School across Morris Avenue and rebuilt it, turning it into a modern learning centre,[5] and he built a new STEM science building on newly purchased land. Along with new buildings and improved grounds, he hired dozens of new faculty. When I joined there was a genuine air of optimism. I personally felt supported by a robust administration.

That began to change with the Middle States inspection of 2010. Colleges and universities in America have certain standards they have to meet in order to remain open and receive government funding. For a state school like Kean, which receives operating funds from the state and federal governments and whose students are dependent upon state financial aid, it is a major concern. Without government funding Kean would not be able to remain open. The way that was decided was that every ten years the school would go through the civilian version of a military Inspector General's review. This was conducted by the independent Middle States Committee. The school would put together a detailed report of what they have been doing, how they meet all the criteria, how courses are put together, where the money goes, and what the future plans are. It requires a lot of effort on the school's part. The Middle States Committee then inspects. The entire process, while gruelling, is meant to ensure the school is performing well and is, in fact, designed to help the school improve. We almost failed.

Accusations and incriminations soon began to fly. The administration blamed the faculty for not working hard enough. The faculty countered that they had done everything required and more, and that it was the administration who had half-assed it, expecting to coast through.[6] At a series of awkward, public 'Town Hall' meetings with the President and the Board of Trustees, it was made clear, on both sides, who they thought was to blame. A number of faculty and students pointed their fingers at an administration that had not really taken the

---

[4] It was only years later that I discovered that there were scholars today looking at this concept of fringe science, especially in the area of pseudoarchaeology.

[5] One of the Pingry School's claims to fame was that a young man named William Halsey graduated from there. He went on to international renown as Admiral 'Bull' Halsey, hero of the Pacific during World War II.

[6] When I was at TCI, we too went through the Middle States. The administration and faculty rallied together and we passed with flying colours. It was barely a blip in our lives.

entire process seriously. We would get one chance to redeem ourselves. A follow-up inspection was scheduled for the following July. If we did not pass that re-inspection, the school would lose its accreditation. That in itself would not close the school, but it would eliminate state funding for students which would be a de facto closing in essence and we'd all be out on the street. Efforts were doubled to pass the final inspection. All this, of course, made it into the press. There were forces out there who hated the school, hated Dr Farahi (he had a penchant for making enemies), and hated even the very notion of state-funded education. Exacerbating the tension, Dr Farahi threatened to sue the Middle States. Harsh words flew in the media. When July arrived and the re-inspection began we were all on edge. Lisa and I were in the UK for our summer research trip. Sue Gronewald was in Vietnam, and Chris Bellitto was in Italy.

With the final inspection complete, Middle States, who were very aware of what was going on, held a public forum on campus to announce their findings and final determination. In the morning, while we were in Canterbury, I received the email about the final determination. I was in a computer coffee shop within sight of the legendary Cathedral, and I saw the heading of the email. I immediately broke into a sweat. I nervously opened and read the message. All around me teenagers were playing video games and downloading music: my life was hanging by a thread over the pits of Hell. The Middle States Committee's public forum was heavily attended and there was an air of great tension. Tens of thousands of peoples' careers, futures and even lives were on the line. Amidst the sweaty stink of fear, the Middle State's Committee calmly gave the results of the re-inspection. Their report showed we had met all the criteria and our accreditation was renewed. I slumped back in the uncomfortable plastic and metal chair and simply stared for a minute or two at the screen. Contrary to what the papers had said, Kean University had never lost its accreditation, but we almost had. However, now we were safe and could all get on with our lives: at least for ten years until the next inspection came along.

With the Middle States debacle behind us, at least for the time being, the feelings and attitude at the school had changed. The administration, and particularly Dr. Farahi, had changed to a much more adversarial attitude towards the faculty. Dr. Farahi had a good bit of George Steinbrenner in him. Like the infamous owner of the New York Yankees, he could slap you on the back on Monday, tell you how great you were, what an asset to the university you were, and ask if there was anything he could get you. Then on Tuesday, he could slap you on the back of the head and tell you what a sorry failure you were. He once sent me an unsolicited, hand-written note telling me how much he enjoyed reading an Op Ed I wrote for that week's *Star-Ledger*. The year after I achieved tenure, I ran into him in the STEM building as he was showing around some VIPs.[7] I always tried to avoid running into him, but sometimes it happened too suddenly for me to either dive into some bushes or flatten against a wall like an octopus and take on the colouration of the bricks until he passed by. This time it was a situation where I had to go up to him. I did what I always did when I ran into the university President: I smiled and said "Good afternoon, Mr. President." He congratulated me on getting tenure and I thanked him. He then made a point of reminding me it was all due to him, and that he was in charge. "I gave you tenure."

Following the Middle States debacle, the faculty and the teacher's union was now the enemy as far as the administration was concerned. Every chance they had, they let us know it.

---

[7] During this period it was typical for it to take several tries for faculty to achieve tenure and then separately for promotion.

Even the Department of History, a group Farahi had shown favour to in the past, was now a foe. Every chance he had he would remind us that if we didn't raise enrolment in our program he would eliminate the department.[8] They put in place a number of new requirements, which while it was claimed, were all for improving the school and the quality of student experience, were clearly meant, first and foremost, as punitive against the faculty. Mandatory faculty improvement weeks during winter break then again during spring break were instigated (designed to keep faculty from travelling to do their research). In one infamous faculty improvement seminar, we were lectured by the local fire inspector on how to properly clean fireplace chimneys.[9] The required number of faculty office hours was raised to twelve a week. Faculty had to be in residency four days a week. Funds were cut for the acquisition of new books for the library. Most insulting of all, faculty now had to fill out timesheets for every pay period. As a result, a world class faculty, writers of books and articles of consequence, discoverers of new ideas of how the cosmos works, whose faces were familiar to watchers of CNN, local news, television documentaries, and media around the world, now had to fill out timesheets as if we were minimum wage workers who stocked shelves for a living. It would not be until he retired in 2020 that this animosity began to subside.

Teaching Monsters as Therapy

Historians are not ahead of their times, they are right where they should be. It's everyone else who is behind the times. Along with being a history writer and researcher, I love being a history teacher. There are many lines of thought about what teaching is or should be. I have always tried to understand what it was I was doing, though the frantic nature of teaching—especially as an adjunct—did not always allow for sober contemplation. The only formal teacher training I ever received was from the army. When I joined the active reserves, the unit I signed up with in Edison, New Jersey was a training unit, the 78th. They spent a lot of time practising how to lecture on various topics to a company of trainees in the open, in the rain. You had to behave as if nothing was happening, as if it were a sunny day. When I entered civilian classrooms, I naturally just kept that approach. In the army you lectured with little or no expectation of a student asking a question. If a student was not paying attention you could yell at them, make them do punishment push ups or even kick them in the ass. I wasn't going to be able to do that now.

For me, teaching was not just the act of professing knowledge to students, it was a personal form of therapy. It was also part performance art, part religious ritual, and part life coaching. I never liked teachers that came in and sat down at a desk and ran the course from there. I almost never sat down in class. In fact, I paced back and forth as I talked like a caged animal. For me, at least, lecturing was a contact sport. My weakness was that I've never been as good at getting the students to talk and engage with the material. I have great respect for my colleagues who can do that so effortlessly. I relied on lecturing.

When I did the *Air America* interview with Janeane Garofalo, we had a long

---

[8] This was a serious threat. He had already disbanded the Philosophy Department a few years before, and just before he retired he eliminated the Art History and Music programs. There was also a rumour that he had plans in 2019 to go through with his threat and fire half the Department of History. No names ever cropped up and I'm not sure if it was genuine or a rumour, but it was not beyond his experience to do such a thing. If he had, it would have been for little more than spite. He could be generous and simultaneously cruel and vindictive.

[9] At first, sitting in Wilkin's Theatre, we looked at each other as if to say, "is this a joke?" But, it was not. We had to sit through an hour-long presentation. There were several ironic aspects to this. First, there was not a single fireplace on campus, and certainly not in any faculty offices. Secondly, if there were, we as faculty would not have been authorised to clean them. That would have been done by specialist chimney sweeps. It was just punishment.

conversation during the commercial breaks. We both felt we discussed our personal lives in our public jobs more than we should: that we gave away too much of ourselves. We also felt that doing that, as uncomfortable as it might be, was the way to help the audience engage with the material. I have always felt that students respond to stories about people. Stories of people doing things help the students find a connection to what they are studying. I often used stories from my life to illustrate the material at hand.[10] One of the things that surprised me when I taught in China, was that I quickly realised that half of any given lecture I do is referring to pop culture. In China, however, the students were not versed in that culture so few of my asides or jokes made any sense to them. I had to learn quickly to add more material in order to fill the class time. As I grew older I also saw that the pop culture I grew up with was now ancient history to my young students.

In the end, teaching is a performance art. At least, if you're doing it right. It's little different from stage acting or stand-up comedy. It may actually be more difficult than stage acting. An actor on stage or in a film has a set amount of dialogue to learn and recite. A teacher is ad-libbing almost all of what they are doing. If you do the same class often you can start to rely on the transmission of certain facts and evidence, but you still wind up presenting it differently each time.

You have to be at the top of your game every time. It doesn't matter if you've given this lecture a thousand times before; the students, or the audience, in front of you have never heard it. You have to do it as if your life depends on it: as if this is the one you will be remembered by. You have to be ready to come back day after day, week after week, year after year, and be as fresh as a daisy. You have to be ready every time. It doesn't matter what is going on in your personal life. It doesn't matter what is going on with the administration or your dean or the college president. It doesn't matter what's going on in the world. You have a responsibility. You are the one who has to hold the line. You have to be there on time, be enthusiastic, and be ready to go. In your worst moments, you have to be able to reach down and find the will to do it again. You have to be able to put the entire world out of your mind during the class. All you can think about is the material of that class. It's like standing in a downpour and acting like it's a sunny day. This is something non-teacher critics of teachers always get wrong. I always know when I hear someone disparaging teachers for "not working hard enough" who has no idea what the job actually entails. Few of the critics of teachers could ever do the job themselves. Teaching is exhausting. It is physically and mentally draining. Running a two-and-a-half to three-hour class is like running a marathon. If you're doing it right you should need a nap and a drink after.

My Rock Star Period

When I was a kid my mom told me she'd get me guitar lessons. I was very excited, but when the instructor showed up at the apartment with an accordion instead of a guitar, I was a bit crestfallen. In typical Betty style, when I asked where the guitar was she said, "Oh, you'll like this better." I liked the sound a lot, but the instructor was a bit odd. The instructor had a studio over the Lincoln Theater. The lessons were the instructor and me and two or three other kids all with accordions strapped to our chests. We would practise rudimentary lessons, all of us squeaking out of rhythm with each other. I quickly lost interest and stopped going. I would have to wait before I would learn how to make music, however imperfectly.

---

[10] Some of the stories I've told in this autobiography I have told in class.

Lisa's sister, Terry, and her husband, Lou, were professional musicians. Lou was from Brooklyn originally and they lived in a high-rise apartment there on one of the Ocean Avenues. They had been in bands and toured. Then they bought half a duplex on Staten Island that had a large basement. Every once in a while they would invite people over for day long jams. A friend of theirs, Chris Moore, was a music aficionado, but not a musician. He was a successful optometrist. In the 1990s he would rent out the dance hall above *The Shillelagh Club* in West Orange for a special Halloween dance concert. I had been slowly trying to learn to play something so I could do more than just watch the jams and the Halloween shows. I thought a mandolin might be just the trick. It was small, relatively inexpensive, and, I hoped, relatively easy to learn to play. With some help from Lou I learned to play the parts from the Joan Osborne song, 'St. Teresa.' That would be my first public music performance. It went well, though Lou's electric guitar turned up to eleven—as usual—walked all over my acoustic parts. I still had fun. I played in the next few Halloween shows, but then Chris Moore was no longer able to sponsor the parties so they ended.

I had always loved the sound of the accordion, regardless of my experience with lessons, and so in my late forties I decided to go get one. *Sam Ash* was having a sale so Lisa and I went over. They had several, but my eye fell upon a red *Carlo Robelli*. As no one wanted accordions at the time I was able to get it at a reduced rate. Once home I immediately began practising. Lisa always told me I should take lessons, but my schedule was such that I knew I'd treat it like going to a gym. My preferred way of playing was to switch on my MP3 player and play along, as always, by myself.

At some of Terry and Lou's jams I met Rob and Elle Landsman. They were also Staten Island musicians. A lovely older hippie couple, they had created a group called SIAMS (Staten Island Acoustic Music Society). They had been able to get the owner of a local community bookshop and coffee bar called *The ETG Café* (Every Thing Goes) which had a small stage for music and spoken word performances. SIAMS was doing shows at ETG and I was invited to participate.

At first the SIAMS *ETG* shows were wonderfully democratic. The shows always had a theme linking all the music. The most popular were the Beatles shows and the Bob Dylan shows. Singers would volunteer to sing this song or that and a house band, made up of Rob and Elle, Terry and Lou, Kevin Johnson, myself and others, would be the backing band. A week or so before each show the band, a sort of acoustic version of the famous 'Wrecking Crew' would assemble at Rob and Elle's (they lived just a couple of blocks from the ETG Café, which itself was just a block or so from the Staten Island Ferry) and rehearse. I enjoyed this a great deal. There was a wide range of musicians from highly accomplished pros, like Terry and Lou, to amateurs with more heart than skills, like myself.

One of the SIAMS regulars was Frank Gialombardo. As he played a twelve string guitar, he liked being called 'Twelve String Frank'. Later he changed that to wanting to be called Frank Grail. Frank at first was always a solo act. He would often be given the opening slot at the SIAMS shows. He was an enthusiastic singer and musician. I appreciated him for that.

One of my favourite SIAMS moments was during the Beatles show of 2017. Carl Croce, cousin to the late singer Jim Croce, was scheduled to perform with his good friend Joe Patratis. Carl had been in failing health for some time. His various medical issues were compounded by his morbid obesity. Despite this he was a great guitar player and an accomplished singer, and a good guy. I was scheduled to perform that night with Frank Grail. I was sitting there by myself in the audience section waiting for everything to begin.[11] Carl and Joe arrived and he sat next to me. We exchanged pleasantries. After a bit he asked if I wanted to sit in on his set. Joe Patratis was one of only three people in the SIAMS world who played the accordion (the other was Dave Stoler of *Joan Cadell and the Midnight Choir* who played SIAMS on a regular basis). My reply was, "Uh, yeah!"

When Carl and Joe's set came up, they climbed the stage with me in tow. All I knew was that they, like everyone else that night, was going to perform some Beatles' songs. Once the tuning and amps were plugged-in and they were ready to go, Carl turned to me and simply said, "I Saw Her Standing There," then turned back to the mike and immediately started playing. Luckily, I was familiar enough with the song that I just started banging away with them. A guy as big as Carl bouncing up and down very animatedly on that little stage had the whole thing rocking. We crashed to an ending and the crowd loved it watching two old guys having a great time singing about a seventeen-year-old girl.

Then Carl turned again and said, 'Eleanor Rigby.' That has always been one of my favourite Beatles' songs. They did it relatively slowly, more of a lament than the original. About half way through, Carl turned to me again and gave me the "take a solo" nod. I did, and I managed to do so without hitting any bad notes. When done, another round of applause. Then Carl said to the crowd "that was great, thanks Brian for being kind enough to join us. We didn't even get to practice and it sounded that good!" He didn't have to say that. He didn't even have to invite me, but he did. A few months later his medical issues caught up with him and he passed away. I'll always be grateful I was able to play with Carl Croce on his last public performance.

China

When I was fourteen years old I saw the movie *They Came to Cordura* (1959) on the late show on Channel Five. When I wasn't watching monster movies I was watching movies based on some historical event. This movie was about an incident during the punitive expedition of 1916 to try to capture Poncho Villa. I became enamoured of the period and the romanticism of it, and started reading everything I could on the subject. I refused to eat anything other than frijoles for weeks. I've always done this sort of thing. I'd get fixated on something then, ever the scholar, I'd read and watch everything I could find on it. Then I saw *Fifty-Five Days at Peking* (1963) and I became fascinated by Chinese history. I wondered what it would be like to visit these strange and exotic places. As was often the case, the library came to my aide. The Kearny Public Library had "how to speak Spanish" books and I started reading. They had one in Chinese as well, but I quickly realised that was going to be beyond me. Once again, my aspirations had far outstripped my abilities.

When I enlisted in the Army, part of the deal I agreed to was that I would get to pick my first duty station. This was a result of me enlisting for an extra year and getting the signing bonus. I didn't think much about it at first, but then a plan came to me. Watching the news

---

[11] Coming from New Jersey I had to leave early to get to the show on time (usually 7:30pm Saturday nights). Added to that, the parking on Staten Island, especially around the ETG was awful and filled up very quickly. That meant I had to leave the house at 5:30 to ensure I'd get a parking space by the club instead of having to park a mile away and schlep my equipment to the show. That meant I was always the first person there and so would sit around for an hour waiting for things to begin.

with Pops once, there was a segment on China and Nixon and global relations. I noticed that in China there were American troops on duty. Remembering this, it hit me, I'll choose China as my first duty station. This was going to be sweet. When I told Henry about my idea he said it was fine, but just "no matter what you do, don't volunteer to go to Korea."

Around three-quarters of the way through tank school, recruits were issued their dress uniforms. It's thought that, by then, any recruits who are going to drop out or fail out have done so, and so the remaining cohort will be graduating. The other thing that was done at this point is recruits would receive the first duty assignments. You stood in line in a large suite of offices and waited for your name to be called. When I heard mine I practically ran to the desk and stood at attention waiting for the lieutenant to tell me to "stand as ease" and sit down. I was genuinely excited.

"Okay, private Regal, where do you want to go?"
"Sir, I want to be stationed in China."
He looked at me like a dog looking at a piece of plastic fruit.
"No, you can't go to China."
"But, but I'm supposed to be able to pick my first duty station."
"You can, but you can't go to China. We don't have troops in China. You can only go where the US Army has troops."

I explained about what I had seen on the TV. He thought about it for a second then said, "Oh, what you saw were US Marine Embassy guards." His attitude was such that he was talking to an idiot. I was so disappointed. He then asked if I wanted to go to Korea, "That's close to China," he proclaimed. Remembering Henry's advice, I said, "no." I also did not want to be stationed in the US. I wanted adventure, not a 9-5 job. I didn't enlist to do that. I enlisted to see the world. He thought a bit more then said, "How about Germany? It's good tank duty, a little dangerous, but the girls there are hot and they are all blonde and have big tits."

That didn't sound too bad. I said okay and signed the paperwork.

It would take some years, but eventually, I did get to go to China. Around the time I took my position at Kean, they had been in negotiations to open a campus in China. President Farahi, during some of his travels, had met some big wigs from the Chinese board of education. The decision was to create a joint US/China project in the ancient port city of Wenzhou. With a population in the nine million range, Wenzhou was a sprawling urban area with that very Chinese combination of the ancient and modern. At first, the agreement was that Kean would open a satellite operation on the campus of Wenzhou State University. That didn't quite work out, so it was decided Kean would build, from scratch, a totally independent University on the outskirts of town.

By 2014, the campus was still a construction site, but classes were being held and students enrolled. It all seemed to be going well. While some Kean programs, such as communications and computer science had majors available at Wenzhou, history did not. However, in order to graduate the students had to take the HIST1062 Worlds of History course to satisfy part of their General Education requirement. The plan was to use adjuncts, but who would want to go all the way to China to adjunct a couple of classes? Kean was not interested in offering a tenure track history position so that attraction was not there. Also, for a semi-permanent lecturer it was hard to find people. Again, to up and go to China for years if you were not Chinese didn't seem a viable option. For the winter session of 2013/14 they asked for a volunteer to go for the four week assignment. Jonathan Mercantini, who by now was Dean of the College of Liberal Arts, asked me directly.

I didn't want to go: I liked the idea of going to China, but the idea of a fourteen hour one way flight did not appeal to me. I tried to convince myself by watching *Fifty-Five Days at Peking* again, but it didn't help. I was genuinely torn. I wanted to go, but the prospect of that flight was a real negative. I had trouble with the six-hour flight to London, what was a fourteen-hour flight going to be like? Also, my mother's health was deteriorating—we eventually had to move her in with us—and I didn't want Lisa to be left alone with her if there was an emergency. Also, Lisa herself was having issues at her job and with her health. After a few months of gentle, but persistent pressure, I accepted the offer. I talked it over with Lisa and she said I should go. So I did. I would teach two classes for the four week winter break semester. One of HIST1062 and one elective. I chose the History of Medicine.

I boarded the plane and found myself in the middle seat of a middle row. I had managed to be given the least comfortable seat on a plane for a fourteen-hour flight. Making it more uncomfortable, the flight was delayed two hours out of Newark so we arrived late to Shanghai thus missing our connecting flight. The three Kean people, myself, Fred Fitch and Wenli Yaun (who was a Chinese national) from the Communication's Department were not even seated together. They scattered us around the plane. Somehow, I was still alive when we touched down in Shanghai. Then we boarded a commuter flight, *China Eastern*, for the trip down to Wenzhou. We arrived around 2 a.m. local time.

Fortunately, the people at the school had figured out what happened and there was a van ready and waiting to meet us. We drove through the murky early morning Chinese air. China had, by then, developed notoriously polluted air. Their rush to catch up with the West led to shortcuts being taken, environmentally. While the air was especially bad up north around Beijing and Shanghai in the south at Wenzhou it was not quite so awful. Poor Fred Fitch, however, spent the first three days of class locked in his hotel room sick with respiratory issues. Luckily he recovered. I never did have an issue though you could clearly tell the air was a bit thick.

They put the three of us up at the *Ex Palm D'or Hotel* in downtown Wenzhou. Said to be the first boutique hotel in China, the *Palm D'or* was a very nice three-star establishment with Italian style wall murals and other Western touches. It sat on the corner of the busy intersection of Minhang and Guihu Roads. As I was unpacking in my room, I saw that Lisa had secretly placed DVDs of *A Charlie Brown Christmas* and *The Grinch That Stole Christmas* hidden in my socks as a surprise so I wouldn't be too lonely. They were my two favourite Christmas cartoons. We Skyped all night talking.

It was Christmas Eve, a few days after we arrived. We all went out together for dinner. We went to a great little Indian restaurant a few blocks from the hotel. It was fun having Indian food for Christmas in China, though I wished Lisa could have been there with me. Walking back, it was almost midnight and I still had a little energy. Someone said there was a funky little bar a block or so from the hotel in a quiet neighbourhood. Some of us trooped over. It was a small establishment but it had people in it, and the owner seemed happy about suddenly having four Americans walk in. After the first drink, I saw there was an old accordion and a ukulele on the wall. I thought about it for a minute, and then took down the accordion (which was missing some keys). It seemed obvious what song I should play, so I did *Fourth of July, Asbury Park*. Everyone turned to see what I was doing though I'm sure no one knew the song.

Odessa

Among the other faculty members at the Wenzhou-Kean campus was a classicist also named Brian. He had his wife and two children with him. He had spent the last few years taking teaching jobs all over the world. Where I had joined the army to travel, this Brian earned a doctorate then went traipsing around the globe as a school teacher. I had to admit, it was impressive. He had been teaching at a school in Afghanistan, but left when it became too dangerous, and was hired by Kean to teach in China. He was also legally blind. He and I hit it off immediately. One day during the break between the morning and afternoon class sessions, he asked me if I wanted to come to a local bar for trivia night. I said sure. He said he would come by the hotel at nine that night to pick me up. Just before nine, I went down to the main entrance of the hotel to wait. The street was busy with traffic and people. All the holiday lights gave it an extra sense of life.

As I stood on the corner of this very busy street, I noticed that people were walking by and staring at me. Despite the fact that Wenzhou had a long history of interaction with the West, and that there were quite a few foreigners in the city, it was still a bit of a surprise for most Wenzhouize to encounter someone like me. Coming around the corner they saw this tallish, long, grey-haired creature, in a leather trench coat suddenly standing there. They would stop and stare for a second. The four weeks I spent in Wenzhou, I was constantly being stared at. It was also common for people to take out their phones and snap a picture. A number of times people even asked if I would pose with them for pictures. I must be in at least a dozen Wenzhou family photo albums. I thought to myself, this must be how Bigfoot feels when humans see him in the woods.

Just then, a tiny cab came to a screaming halt in front of the hotel and I could see Brian in the back waving at me. I climbed in. The cab driver, a middle-aged, Chinese man, looking exactly as you'd expect a Chinese cab driver to look, turned around to us. He flashed a huge smile and said in broken English, "Where you go, gent-mins?" Brian said, "Odessa." The driver, who probably knew every single store and bar in this city of nine million, said, "Ah, Odessa!" knowingly. He stomped on the gas pedal and he sped off. After a short and careering ride through the teeming streets of Wenzhou, where there were a couple of moments I think the driver seriously contemplated driving up on the sidewalk, we pulled up to a side street that was a shopping lane. The two of us tumbled out of the cab and managed to land on our feet. I said the only word of Chinese I was sure of, "Shu, shu" (thank you) to the driver. He let out a loud laugh, said, "Shu shu" in return and screamed off into the night.

We went down a few stairs and there was Odessa. It was a nightclub. Originally opened by some Ukrainian émigrés—hence Odessa—it was a popular place for the expatriates that lived in town. We went in and I immediately heard the accents of Russians, Australians, and British. It had a wonderfully funky internationalist feel. I expected to see Humphrey Bogart sitting at the bar. Brian had somehow talked his way into a job there running the Tuesday trivia night for the foreigners (it was also popular with hip young Chinese).

I told Brian I was a little hungry and he said excitedly, "Oh, you have to try the food here." "First," he said, "let me introduce you to Superman." We walked over to the bar, and as we did, the bartender, a very tall, thin, thirty-something Chinese guy practically ran at us. "Brian!" he called out. Brian replied, "hey, Superman!" I later learned that his actual name was Bohia (elder brother). He insisted, however, that everyone call him Superman. He loved everything about America. He even demanded the kitchen make hamburgers and fries, which he called 'American Fries.' He was incredibly happy, energetic, and smiley. I'm not sure if he owned the place or was just the head bartender. They had *Tsingtao* beer on tap, and ice cold. The burgers were delicious. They had a special kind of Chinese chutney they put on them. The fries were made to perfection. I went there several more times during the four weeks I was there, but really just for the food. I was never much of a trivia person. Sitting in Odessa, I looked around and tried to imagine who the international spy was. Then I realised, it was me.

Driving in China

In America, we like to think we have the craziest drivers anywhere. We have some doozies for sure, but you could not be more wrong. Now I know better, I've spent time in Wenzhou, China. The people of China are quite nice and never became impatient with me and my horribly limited Chinese (in a way that few Americans would be to a visiting Chinese person unable to speak English). Wenzhou is a big bustling city where it seems every building is either being torn down or built new. It seemed bricks were the most important thing in town. Everyone seemed to be employed carrying bricks, making bricks, installing bricks or removing bricks.

What struck me most was not the eager ambition of almost every citizen, not the national embrace of consumerism and the future, not the love of Capitalism or the intense work ethic: it was the traffic. I only wish I could explain the astonishing philosophical approach to operating motor vehicles the Wenzhouneze have, but I don't have the epistemological chops. At best I can try to describe it.

It's like every vehicle on the road is a stereotyped New York City cabbie, and they are all trying to get to their destinations RIGHT NOW! They bob and weave through traffic like an NFL running back heading for a game winning touchdown. Should a driver hesitate, every other driver will immediately begin pulling around them at the same time. If that means driving on the sidewalk or into oncoming traffic, so be it. The morning rush is something akin to the chariot race from *Ben Hur* only more dynamic. Swarms of cars blend and flow in ways reminiscent of schools of fish.

Along with the cars and trucks—which are loaded to ridiculous heights with cargo of every kind—there are the scooters. They are inexpensive to own and operate and whether loaded with a family of eight or half-a-dozen full-sized rolls of living room carpet they are everywhere driving just as fast and as crazy as everyone else. Because they are electric, you can't hear them until they are on top of you. At night their operators see no reason to drain the batteries by turning on headlights, or their running lights, or even having reflective stickers. Pitch black in the dark they infest the streets like a ghostly army of wraiths from the underworld moving stealthily, and with an unnerving silence, amongst the living.

Traffic cops are everywhere backed up by hoards of white-helmeted, yellow-jacket-wearing *Xie Jing*—traffic helpers—whose job is to keep the exuberant chaos moving rather than enforce traffic laws, which are treated more as casual suggestions rather than concrete rules of behaviour. Despite seeing enough traffic violations on any given day to fund a US state for a year with fines, I never saw a single car pulled over. You park anywhere you can squeeze in, and that means anywhere. 'Car Talk' is the language of the horn and how people send signals to one another.

161

That's not to say the laws are not enforced. There are wracks of cameras at each corner which flash at every violation with the rapidity of a disco. From these photos, the tickets are sent out in the mail. The most astonishing thing about driving in Wenzhou is that no one ever seemed to get mad or crash into each other. As long as you kept a six-inch space between yourself and everyone else, anything went. Serious traffic accidents are rare and road rage was all but non-existent.

Mr. Lin

The entire Wenzhou-Kean project began with talks between various heads of education systems. The Kean man in charge in China, Robert Sirrasa, was also the de facto go-between for faculty/student/administration relations. As Fred, Wenli, and I were sort of special guests—only being there for four weeks—we were seen as somehow VIPs. A dinner was arranged for the three of us to meet with the head of the Party's education office. His name was Mr. Lin. We went to a fancy restaurant/events centre a few blocks from our hotel. It was one of those big places for weddings and special events. They brought us to a smaller, more intimate space upstairs. The three of us, along with Bob Sirrasa, were situated at one end of the large round table with a large lazy Susan in the middle. Various lesser VIPs and school administrators sat around the table. Then a hush came over the room and everyone stood up. Mr. Lin had arrived. He took his seat between myself and Fred Fitch at the VIP end of the table.

Mr. Lin, from what I gathered, was a very, very high official. He was basically the head of the department of education for the entire region. When he came in we all stood. He was a forty-something man, lean, well dressed, but not formally. Introductions were made and we sat down to eat. After a while, Mr. Lin stood, and through an interpreter, made a short speech about international relations, and how he knew the relationship with Kean would be fruitful and bring great fortune upon us all. There was polite applause and I went to sit down. Then Robert Sirrassa looked at me and motioned with his head to stand up again. "Doctor Regal," he said, "how about a toast?" Mr. Lin, standing next to me, raised his glass of wine and smiled at me. I picked up my glass and began to speak of international friendship and how I was sure that the relationship between Kean and China would be fruitful and bring good fortune upon us all. There was an interpreter whispering my words to Mr. Lin. He smiled broadly and seemed genuinely happy with what I had said. Robert looked at me with a wry smile and nodded gently as if to say, "well done!" I had saved international East-West relations. Now we could eat.

After a wide range of delicious food and ample amounts of wine, Mr. Lin stood and said his goodbyes. With that, the evening was over. We all started to leave. I hesitated for a moment to ask someone something. As I finally walked out the door I saw, up ahead of me, several men in tuxedos pulling Fred Fitch into the next room. It was a much larger banquet hall where a wedding party was in progress. There is a belief in China that if someone or something unusual should appear at a wedding it brings extra luck to the marriage. When the father of the bride saw Fred, a middle aged, white haired Caucasian suddenly walking by it was an omen and they hijacked him. The crowd was happy. A few more toasts for good luck. Fred was patted by everyone as if he was a magical talisman. Now we could leave.

With the four weeks of the Winter Session adventure at an end we prepared to leave. The students in both of my classes insisted we take group photos together, as well as individual pictures. There was lots of hugging. Then back to the airport for the fourteen hours home. I hoped I made a difference in their lives. I hoped this entire enterprise helped make Chinese/American relations better.

Arriving back in Newark, remarkably, my bags came out first from the carousel. Fred said I didn't have to wait, I said I would. I pointed to the spot near the check-in counter where we had joined up four weeks before. "We started together over there," I said, "we should finish together there." He and Wenli seemed to like that idea. I saw Lisa standing there, smiling, and waving.

Conclusion

It was some years after my encounter with the monster trying to get into my room before I took to studying them seriously. In 1973, when I was thirteen, I asked the librarian at the Kearny Public Library if they had any books on monsters. I had just been looking at a book on how to become a private detective. I was so intrigued it almost derailed my plans to become an historian. I thought it was very cool that private eyes called a pistol a Gat (from Gatling Gun). The librarian looked at the private eye book, made a face, thought about it briefly, and sent me off to a corner of the library. On the shelf, I found a copy of James B. Sweeney's *A Pictorial History of Sea Monsters and Other Dangerous Marine Life* (1972) which had only come out the year before. Sweeney filled his book with a treasure trove of original artworks and photographs. It seemed very grown-up to me. I looked at it for hours. I rode my bike to the library many times just to sit by myself on the floor in the corner and read it. Enthralled, I began reading other works in monster lore. It seemed like I was the only person in the world who was interested in this material. I didn't realise it at the time, but with that book, my career as an historian of monsters began.

My work on the life of Henry Fairfield Osborn brought me back to the world of fringe science, creationism, and monsters that I had found fascinating since sitting on the floor of the Kearny Public Library. These fascinated me more than the usual realms of the history of science. I resumed my reading into 'mysteries' and 'unexplained' phenomena which had begun for me some years before. In 1989, I read *Holy Blood, Holy Grail* by Michael Baigent, Richard Leigh, and Henry Lincoln. This controversial work argued that Jesus had married Mary Magdalen, and that a secret society had formed to preserve that information. This society, The Priory of Zion, continued to exist into the present. It seemed a cogent argument supported by citations and a scholarly attitude. It was about this time that I began taking history classes at Kean College. As I waded through texts on classical history, mediaeval history, and began to learn the methods and techniques of professional historical inquiry, it struck me that my original appraisal of *Holy Blood, Holy Grail* might be a bit off.[12]

Although I found the premise fascinating, and that it asked some important questions and told a captivating story, in my still amateur opinion, Baigent, Leigh, and Lincoln took too many things at face value. They were a little too quick to accept the statements of shady characters. My professors were teaching me the importance of primary sources, of sober consideration of facts, and of a general scepticism of outrageous arguments based on flimsy evidence. The positive side of all this was that *Holy Blood, Holy Grail*—and a number of other outsider publications I was reading at the time—made me want to study history further. I wanted to learn all the other parts of the story: could such accusations stand up against known

---

[12] As an adult, my dyslexia lessened. It never went away, but I felt the effects less.

facts and evidence? As such, my encounter with such books helped me become a better historian. This attitude helped me deal with monster sighting reports as well as the endless conspiracy theories about UFOs, Area 51, anti-vaccination belief, and a host of others. This also convinced me that these topics were worth researching, but had rarely been examined by trained historians. It made me think this might be my niche: proper historical examinations of fringe ideas particularly cryptozoology. While there were many excellent books on the main aspects of science history, there was another angle.

As I read more and more of contemporary, high-end writers on evolution history such as Peter Bowler, Steven Shapin, Simon Schaffer, Janet Browne, James Moore, and my doctoral advisor David Kohn, I saw that the field tended to concentrate on a number of specific personages and periods. There were legions of incredible studies of Darwin, and Newton, and Einstein, of the Renaissance and Early Modern period, and others out there. These topics became the objects of study for a number of reasons. First off, they are obviously important players who made significant contributions to human knowledge and advanced our understanding of how the universe works (in the twenty-first century a wider set of dramatis personae—both famous, obscure, female, and non-Western—have rightly become the objects of study as well). In addition, these people and institutions left behind copious letters, correspondence and other materials needed to study them. Finally, the Darwins, Einsteins, and Royal Societies of the world can be considered, in a vague way, winners.[13] Their White, Western, Protestant, male, Christian orientation also helped put them in the front of history. While they may have encountered roadblocks and resistance to their work, ultimately, they succeeded at what they were doing. The meta narrative was one of success and progress. What I saw when I looked at the history of fringe thought, was a world not being studied academically in part because scholars saw UFOs, the paranormal, alternative American discovery narratives, and monsters as unworthy of study.[14] Historians of science tended to view these topics as not for them because they didn't think these pursuits constituted 'real' science. These fields, it is sometimes argued (including by myself), contributed little or nothing to modern science or medicine. This made them, for lack of a better expression, losers. There was no grand narrative of success. As such, they had nothing to teach us. I disagreed. I began to think that a study of fringe thinkers that never broke out of the fringe basement because they had not been able to prove their arguments and assertions could still tell us something. I felt the losers had as much to teach us as the winners. That is where I pointed my career.

I wanted to approach the topic a little differently. There were many excellent books on the history of human evolutionary biology. Many tended, however, to focus on fossils and genetics in a fairly narrow way. I wanted to bring in other threads of the story. My approach to writing about history has always been to try to see the wider view by bringing in divergent areas. As such I included chapters on race, gender, artwork, and psychology, as well as the stories of fossils. Along with these topics I made the decision to include monsters as well. I had seen how such legendary evolutionary pioneers as Darwin, Huxley, and Richard Owen saw the study of monstrous creatures as part of the study of human development. It was my first tentative step towards writing a history of cryptozoology. Grover Krantz would be my guide.

---

[13] I know these terms can be vague and problematic, but I use them here as a shorthand to make a point.
[14] Academics, while they are uninterested in modern cryptids, are very interested in medieval monsters. There is, in fact, a huge scholarly literature on mediaeval monsters and their meanings.

Chapter 8

On the Trail of the Jersey Devil

I don't collect telescopes, microscopes, and globes for their historic value
I do it in case we get lost
I might be able to find you again.

I love writing and have always tried to write my books—and articles and Op Eds—as an exciting, or at least interesting, narrative. Readers may not always agree that I pull it off, but that's what I have always tried to do. In the end though, I will do it anyway. If you told me no one would ever read a word I wrote, that no one would care, I'd still write. If I'm happy with what I have written, if I've learned something, that's really all that matters to me.

Anarchy in the UK

Having decided to launch myself into the world of monster studies, I wanted to do a thorough appraisal of the literature in the field. I wanted to do a historiography of monsters. One of the things that has always annoyed me about the world of monster hunting was the narrow-minded vision of cryptozoologists. They became hyper-focused on monsters and rarely looked away from that term to see what was related. I wanted to see how all this fitted into wider history. I knew from research experience, and my training as a historian, that there are always related veins of material, and of thinking, that are just a step or two off from what you were looking at. Cryptozoologists, in general, rarely learned to look a little to the right or left of Bigfoot. If they did, they would see much more in the shadows.

As I worked up the historiography of monsters, the dates of publications grew older and older. I saw that there have been authors writing about monsters way earlier than the twentieth century. Aristotle, Ovid, Lucretius and other classical authors wrote about them. I saw the names of Ulisse Aldrovandi (1522-1605), Fortunio Liceti (1577-1657), Gaspar Schott (1608-1666), and others. They wrote heavily-illustrated books on monsters. I had to see these. As I searched library catalogues for these works, I kept coming across references to the Bodleian Library at Oxford University in the UK. I realised I would have to go there.

In 2007, Lisa and I went to the UK for the first time. It was for our first British Society for the History of Science (BSHS) meeting. I took a chance and I submitted a paper proposal to this venerable English institution. It was to be about the life of Grover Krantz. To my amazement, they accepted it and put it into the conference line-up. Lisa and I had been to many places around the world individually, but now we wanted to travel overseas together. We wanted to walk the halls of the historic world, while holding hands. Neither one of us had ever been to the UK, so this seemed perfect. Held in Manchester, we decided to take extra time after the meeting to go to London: I had left TCI, but was not going to be starting at Kean until September, so we had a window of opportunity. I finally had an entire summer off for the first time since the mid-1990s. As a result, Lisa and I could head off to England for a couple of weeks for this international conference. We came to like the BSHS meetings because they tended to be smaller than some of the gargantuan assemblies of the American Historical Association (AHA) and others. The BSHS had a more intimate feel. Some of the members were a bit snobbish because of their academic pedigrees, especially some of the younger ones, but overall, we felt welcomed and made many friends.

One of the movers and shakers of the BSHS was historian of science Dr. Joe Cain. An American who had gone to England years before, Dr Cain rose to Head of Department of the program of STS at University College London (UCL). We found out about him through a Drew classmate, Dawn Digrius, who had worked with him. She said he was the guy all Americans who go to the UK should know. I contacted him by email and told him I was going to be in a panel at the BSHS meet. He had a reputation for being helpful to early scholars trying to get started. He turned out to be a great guy who helped Lisa and myself more times over the years than we'll ever be able to repay him for.

It was not the first paper I had ever presented to a scholarly audience. The first had been at the History of Science Society meeting in 2001 at Boulder, Colorado not long after 9/11. Manchester was my first paper on monsters. No one told me I should have a PowerPoint presentation (I didn't know what PowerPoint was yet), no one told me to read my paper. We arrived at London Heathrow and caught a train to Manchester then a taxi to the university. It was all a great big adventure. At the check-in, they handed everyone special commemorative 40th anniversary BSHS/Manchester umbrellas. I'm still not sure how they knew it would be raining, but it was, so the umbrellas did come in handy. We went to several panels on the first day. That evening, the university bar was open and most people from the conference were there, and we mingled.

My panel was the next day. I arrived early to the classroom where my panel was being held. As the room was virtually empty, I just sat there quietly in the front row waiting for the panel to begin and for my turn. As people came into the room, Joe Cain, who it turned out was the moderator for this panel, came over and introduced himself. He asked me if I had a slideshow. I said I didn't. Then he asked if I was going to read my paper? Again, I just said, "no". Smiling that smile of his, he then asked good naturedly, "So, you're just going to dazzle us with your sheer brilliance then?" I smiled and said, "yes".

The room filled, and the panel began. Joe did the intro and then the first and second speakers did their fifteen minutes. They had PowerPoint presentations and read from their notes. Then I stood up. I was still not exactly sure how these things went. I looked at Joe and he nodded as if to say, "go ahead". I did what I always did. I just started talking. For fifteen minutes. About Grover Krantz, and monsters.

When it was over, and people were milling around talking as they do, Joe came up to me and shook my hand. "Wow, you really did it. I thought you were joking! Well done". We've been friends ever since. At the end of the conference, while everyone was heading off to other places, Joe Cain found us and suggested we should go to see his lecture on scientific jokes at the Darwin Theatre at UCL, a few days from then. Of course we went. Joe gave a funny and insightful lecture on how scientists will sometimes put hidden jokes in their writing. Following his talk, there was a reception in the museum. This was a couple of years before the museum moved up the street to a new, larger facility, and when it still had that wonderfully cramped, Victorian feel, where the exhibits were right there next to you with little separating the viewers from the viewed. I spent some time talking with people, sipping wine, standing next to a fully articulated tiger skeleton, whose head and snarling teeth were just inches away from my own. When the reception was over, Joe insisted we go with the group who then trooped a few blocks over to an Italian restaurant called *ASK!* It was a chain, but the food was good and it was only a short walk from the museum and the Tavistock hotel, where we were staying . I wound up sitting next to Grant Museum manager, Jack Ashby. I figured I was never going to get another chance like this, so I leaned over and said, "So, Jack, when do I get to give a talk here?" He swallowed a mouthful of pasta and said "what would be the title?" Without hesitation I said, "Crackpots and Eggheads". With even less hesitation, he replied, "Great, can you do it next July?" I smiled and thought to myself, "Did that just happen?".

We had discovered the Tavistock Hotel online. We wanted to visit London after the Manchester conference. I Googled "bed and breakfasts in London" and it came up. I thought it was a typical B&B, small and intimate. When the cab dropped us off at the main entrance, I thought there was a mistake. This was not some cosy little place; an old house turned into a B&B. It was a full-on, twelve-storey hotel. One of the reasons we chose it was because it was appropriately priced and well located in Bloomsbury. It was a short walk to UCL, the British Museum, Charing Cross Road, with all of its rare book stores, and musical instrument shops, the West End, and even Piccadilly Circus. The rooms were clean, well-staffed, and they had air-conditioning (something not widely available in London because the weather never really became that hot for that long). One of the things we loved most about the Tavistock (we would stay there many times over the years) was that the price of your room included breakfast in the cafeteria downstairs. They had a large dining room on the ground floor (in later years it was turned into an Indian restaurant in the evenings). Every morning, they laid out a traditional English breakfast: bacon, sausage, eggs, baked beans, tomatoes, toast, and all the trimmings. We loved it because it was a fun and relaxing way to begin each day. Lisa and I would sit and eat and plan and scheme and be happy to be together, to be in love, and to be in London.[1]

The year, my first as a resident faculty at Kean, went by as I prepared for my talk at the Grant Museum, a place where T.H. Huxley and Richard Dawkins had spoken. I hadn't even finished the manuscript for the book, and I was now committed to giving a talk on it. Unlike the Manchester BSHS talk that only went fifteen minutes, I would now need to be able to fill almost an hour.

A day or two before the show, I was contacted by a British history of science radio show called *Naked Science*. They had heard about my upcoming talk, thought it interesting, and wanted to do a show on it. They interviewed me in a back room at the museum just before my talk. This was the first radio interview I had done since Janeane Garofalo on *Air America* three years before. It was fun doing it, and I didn't gaff too much. When it was over, I stood up and walked right out onto the stage. The house was packed. I couldn't believe it.

Jack Ashby introduced me. My PowerPoint was already up on the screen and I started off. I did what would become my usual forty-five minutes on Grover Krantz and the history of monster hunting. Then came the Q&A. People asked a number of good questions, then we were done. A round of applause and everyone stood up to leave. As is usual in such cases a few people then take the guest out for dinner just like the year before with Joe Cain. We ended up at the same Italian place, *ASK*, up the street that we had all gone following Joe's talk. As we were about to walk up the isle of the lecture hall and outside a man in his mid-thirties, who was now standing in the middle of the isle, said to me, "Can we ask you a question?" I said of course. He then stepped to the side. His son was standing there behind

---

[1] Also, the staff seemed to be the same every year we went there. The concierge who greeted and seated you was the same man every time.

him. He was about eight or nine years old and dressed in a little brown suit. He stepped forward and asked me why the Yeti seemed to look different from Bigfoot? I answered his question and he smiled and said in his little hesitating voice, "thank you Sir. I really enjoyed your talk." He had clearly practised what to say. I thanked him for attending, shook his little hand and handed him one of my Kean University business cards. His father smiled, also said thanks, then said to his son, "Okay, let's go." They turned and walked up the aisle and out the door holding hands. I was suddenly hit with this weird feeling. I felt like somehow some strange cosmic rift in the time space continuum had occurred, and I had just encountered my own nine year old self. I had even had the same little brown suit.

The Bodleian

The one thing I wanted to do while we were in London was to visit the legendary Bodleian Library at Oxford. There was a train that went to Oxford from London and was only a forty-five minute trip. Lisa and I headed there. We hadn't been able to make reservations to use the collections though: that would come the next year. Upon our arrival at Oxford train station, we walked up Botley Road to George Street and to Broad Street and to the college district. Along the way we saw the building of the Oxford History Department and became very envious. We passed the *White Horse* (the model for the Prancing Pony in *Lord of the Rings*) across the street from the *Museum of the History of Science* and decided to go there for lunch. Right onto Catte Street and we arrived at the entrance of the Bodleian.

Walking through the ancient double doors reminded me of the door to the secret garden at St. Cecilia's, only better. Through this narrow space we entered the quadrangle. Your first reaction is to look up at the towering walls and carvings that seem to go to the sky. Oxford is a theme park for historians regardless of what periods of history they study. We hadn't been able to line up research time yet so we decided to take the tour. When I walked into Duke Humfrey's for the first time I thought that I'd been there before. I've never believed in past life experiences, but if I had lived one, then I had lived it there. I felt immediately comfortable. I had fantasised about a place like that since sitting on the floor of the Kearny Public Library. Everything about it appealed to me, to both of us. We fell so in love with it we later rebuilt our house to mimic Duke Humfrey's. In later years, we watched the TV series *Lewis* (known as *Inspector Lewis* in America) obsessively, just to see all the places we had been to and what we wanted to be reminded of.

Later in the day of our first visit to Oxford, we saw there was a ghost tour of town.[2] We went as part of a group of about thirty people. We walked around with the guide telling us about this ghost story and that spectral appearance. It was silly of course, but good fun. The guide was professional, but not dull the way some tour guides can become after telling the same story a thousand times. The crowd got into it. One of the bonuses of this particular tour guide was that he finished the tour at the entryway to the Turf Tavern. As part of the entry fee for the tour, you received, only at the end of the tour, a coupon for a free sample at the Turf.

As I did when I first saw Duke Humfrey's, the minute I laid eyes on the Turf Tavern I knew I wanted to stay there forever. I took Lisa's hand and enthusiastically dashed in the door. As I did, I forgot about the notion that one of the defining features of genuine Tudor architecture are the low ceilings with thick oak beams. I was one step inside and not knowing to duck down a little smacked my head on one of the ceiling beams. I yelled, "oww!"

---

[2] There are actually several. I strongly recommend you take one.

Immediately inside this door was the bar inside the tavern. The cute bartender smiled and said, "You're an American aren't you? You guys always hit your heads the first time here." I presented our two coupons for free beer samples, and she gave us an extra one to make up for my still aching head. You could choose any beer you wanted for your sample. One was 'Black Boar.' It sounded like fun. She pulled us each one and it was black as ink. Tasting it, I couldn't believe how good it was. We had several pints. Before we took the train back to London, I made sure we bought every picture book and history of the Bodleian we could get our hands on in the library book shop.

The next year we returned with the specific intention of doing research in the Bodleian's collection. I contacted the head librarian, Richard Ovenden, and explained what I wanted to see. Instead of treating me like the nobody American I was, he extended every courtesy and even ensured the books I wanted to see would be waiting for me. Upon our arrival, we went to the office where they issued passes and filled out the forms. When all was ready, we headed over to the library. Passing though the short tunnel, we emerged onto the quad. Now officially able to enter the building as bona fide researchers we passed through the gate and into the staircase that led to the upper research rooms. We climbed slowly wanting to savour every step. I ran my hand along the ancient railings in the stairwell. The railings were held up by barley twist balusters. The Bodleian was established in its earliest form in the 1300s. Duke Humphrey, who was Henry V's younger brother, donated the original set of books and manuscripts to the collection in the 1470s. The library as it stands today, first opened in 1602. The hands of thousands of students and researchers, famous and obscure, over the centuries have held these railings. Scientists, astrologers, historians, authors, and alchemists climbed these stairs polishing them to a high shine. Arriving at the level of Duke Humfrey's reading room, I stepped through the door onto the floor. Immediately in front of me was the section with the books still chained to the wall, and the upper level catwalk. The ceiling, painted in alternating green and red squares, gave the effect of a starry sky. Every Harry Potter fan knows this area as the 'Restricted Section' of the library at Hogwarts. I have been in other ancient and historic libraries since this, but as my first, the Bodleian will always hold a special place in my career. I have written parts of every book I have published since then with material from its collection. We fell in love with Oxford as well. We loved exploring the various historic nooks and crannies of the city. One day, we stood together in front of the Shelley Memorial off the High Street. Holding hands in front of the marble statue of a dead Shelley on the beach where he drowned, we took turns reciting some of his poetry.

I went up to the guard at the entrance and showed him our reader's cards. He smiled and let us in. I walked slowly down the central aisle that connects the Arts End with the Seldon End, looking for a stall that did not have anyone sitting in it. I wanted to stay there forever, just me and Lisa and the books. There were several times we went to Oxford over the years to do research when all I really wanted to do was sit there. I went through all that time, expense, and trouble to come to this place and sit in this chair and simply 'be' in this space. I thought about the famous people who had sat there before me, and who would sit there after me. I've met several people over the years who attended Oxford as students. I would ask "it must have been great to be able to go to the Bodleian every day?" The reaction was often, "uh, well, to be honest, I don't think I ever went in there my entire time." I would have to try to hold myself from saying, "What? What the hell is wrong with you?"

There was a rule in those days forbidding picture taking inside Duke Humfrey's. There were posters around warning about the adverse effects of flash photography upon ancient parchment. I had a digital camera and while I wanted to take pictures of some of the material I was working with, I wanted to get a couple of shots of me sitting there. Unfortunately, the camera had a power zoom lens that retracted and extended as you turned it on and off. It made a buzzing sound when it operated and I didn't want the librarians to hear and possibly make me leave. To get around this, I quietly opened the window in the stall I was sitting in. I leaned out with the camera and turned it on. The buzzing of the lens motor was drowned out by the outside sounds.

So far, so good.

I took a few pictures of the early printed books on werewolves I was working on. Once or twice someone walked by, but since you could hear a pin drop in that space, I was able to shield what I was doing. Once finished, I leaned back out the window to turn the camera off. That's when I noticed a group of Japanese tourists in the courtyard looking up at me. I'm sure they wondered what this strange person was doing leaning out the window of one of the oldest libraries in the world fidgeting with a camera. I looked down at them for a second then smiled and waved. They smiled and waved back, and I leaned back in and closed the window.

Lunch with Peter Bowler

Over the years I've had a number of research adventures. In 2013, I was in Cambridge using the library to go over Darwin's personal copy of Étienne Geoffroy Saint-Hilaire's book on monsters. It's heavily annotated with Darwin's ideas about monstrosity. I was planning on having lunch at *The Anchor* pub where *Pink Floyd* supposedly started. As I was walking down the hall to leave, I came around a corner and literally ran into Peter Bowler. He insisted he buy me lunch in the library cafeteria. I had the courgette soup and a chicken baguette. He told me about his latest book, *An Interview with Charles Darwin* (2014).

It was not the first time we had lunch together. In 2009, Lisa and I were able to attend the big Darwin anniversary conference in Cambridge.[3] It was the 150th anniversary of the publication of *The Origin of Species*. All the world's important Darwin scholars were there to speak: James Moore, John Van Whye, as well as Peter Bowler. and even my doctoral advisor, David Kohn. One of the people we read in graduate school, Peter Bowler, was at my talk in Manchester. He was an incredibly gracious man and fun to be around with. He never treated me as anything other than a colleague. He even agreed to write a chapter for my book, *Icons of Evolution*. We ran into him one day during the break of the Darwiopalooza and Lisa and I ended up sitting on the grass with him outside the conference venue eating box lunches; which for some reason contained fresh strawberries.

As there was so much material available, the book on Grover Krantz raced along. When I thought I had written enough of it, I began to approach publishers. A few were interested and in the end, I went with Palgrave-Macmillan. Amazingly, they really liked it. With a contract in hand the book came together quickly. It almost wrote itself. That's what a thorough survey of primary sources and correspondence collections will do for you. I was lucky because I had several people I could ask for advice. Joe Cain, once again, came through for me. He read my text and said I needed to address the notion of leisure-time pursuits. The monster hunters, he rightly argued, were not professional scientists and so were doing their

---

[3] I liked to refer to it as the Darwinopalooza.

monster hunting as a pastime rather than a job. This opened up a new way to look at the material.

When I began the book that became *Searching for Sasquatch*, I felt I should contact people who knew the main characters. I approached several of the leading lights of cryptozoology. I explained what I was doing and asked for their insights and if they had any private papers or materials I could make use of. They all responded positively. They said they were happy that an academic historian was finally going to write about them. When the manuscript was just about finished, Palgrave wanted releases from the people whose unpublished materials would appear. This is standard procedure for such things and, usually, is never a problem. There is a form letter that the subjects sign saying they allow their materials to be used. As I had been having such a positive experience with them, I never thought there would be an issue.

I was wrong.

Most of the people involved readily signed the releases (in the end there were not really that many). A few, however, changed their rosy dispositions towards me. This was because as part of the release procedure, the publisher used the final title of the book: *Crackpots and Eggheads*. This prompted a couple of my correspondents to pull out of the project. They were offended. One told me no one in the world of cryptozoology would ever buy the book because of the title. The other, a major player in that world, that everyone would know, was so incensed he sent me an email typed in caps and even different day glow colours. He called the book stupid, an insult and that I should be ashamed.

My reply to all this was to say that I had not made up those words. I took them from both the public and private writings of some of the legendary originators of modern cryptozoology. I simply used phrases to describe cryptozoologists that had been originated by cryptozoologists. It didn't satisfy them. After telling me how wonderful I was for writing this book, they now hated me for it.

In the end, the people refusing to give their permissions didn't change anything. I had more than enough material from the public domain and various other archives to support my argument. It would have been nice to have been able to use that material for some special flavouring of the narrative, but I was able to get by without it.

The summer of 2010 saw the book ready to go: except for one last thing. I have always wanted my work to be telling a story. In the late twentieth and early twentieth century, storytelling in history had fallen out of favour in some scholarly circles. Storytelling was something only popular authors did rather than serious scholars. While I have always appreciated hardcore, scholarly writing, I have never really been very good at it. I always want to tell the story. I always did my work as narratives. Having grown up on movies and music and science fiction novels, I have always constructed my work—whether a full book or an article—as having a structure with a beginning, a middle and an end. I was influenced by the structure of poetry and pop songs. Everything I've ever learned about writing a compelling narrative came from listening to Bruce Springsteen and Al Stewart records.

Having completed the text of the monster book I needed an opening. I wanted a beginning that would sum up everything about what I was trying to say with the book in one or two sentences. I couldn't find it, and it was making me crazy. Lisa and I were in the UK again that summer and we were in Oxford working at the Bodleian in our usual favourite seats in Duke Humfrey's (I in a stall and Lisa at her favourite large desk in the Arts End). Reaching a frustration point, I told Lisa I was going to take a walk to clear my head. I ended up walking around a bit then wound up at the Turf Tavern.[4] Heading in, I remembered to duck down so as to not hit my head on the low beams again. There wasn't much of a crowd yet so I went to the bar in the middle of the labyrinth that was the building and ordered an Old Speckled Hen. I had to be satisfied with a Golden Hen, but it was okay. I sat at one of the little tall tables against the wall. I love the atmosphere of places like that; The ancient irregular stones of the walls; the polished wood of the bar; the multiple pull handles of the different taps with their colourful pump clips attached to them so you can see which tap is which beer. Henry would have enjoyed this place too, I think. I sat there watching the world go by. It reminded me of all those times as a kid sitting in all those Ironbound bars while my parents drank. They were not quite as old as the pubs of Oxford, but they served a similar purpose.

Sitting there in The Turf, I felt comfortable and at ease. I felt so relaxed I almost fell asleep leaning on my hand. I was thinking about what the Sasquatch book was supposed to be about. What was I trying to say? I had my grand thesis, but how to start it off? I had told the story of these people: the weird moments, the discoveries, the fights, the friendships, the grand hopes and the bitter disappointments that made up their lives. I had written a book about sad, lonely people who superficially were chasing monsters, but who were really chasing their own dreams.

Then it hit me.

I wanted a line that would sum up everything I wanted to say about cryptozoology. In that relaxed atmosphere—feeling, just for a few moments, that all the weight of all the responsibilities that hung on me like stones had lifted momentarily—my head cleared. That was it. They dream of finding this thing. They built their entire lives around finding it. Some had sacrificed everything in their strange, crazy quests. What did they have to show for it? My eyes opened, and I frantically began scrawling in my notebook.

"This story tells of dreams that do not come true."

Eccentricity

In early 2011, Stephen Johnston, head of research at the Oxford Museum of the History of Science, was putting together a summer speaker series on 'Eccentricity and Natural History', and asked me if I would like to speak about monsters. The Cambridge historian and Simon Forman scholar, Lauren Kassell, would also be one of the speakers over a period of a few weeks. In the end, I was the first in the line-up to speak - July 19, 2011. Several days later Dr. Kassell spoke, then cryptozoologist **Jonathan Downes** was the guest speaker.

The impressive building that housed the Oxford University Museum of the History of Science had originally been built in 1683 as the Ashmolean Museum. It quickly became a focal point for science in Oxford. Now, public lectures took place in the large basement display room. The room had originally been an alchemical laboratory and anatomical theatre. You could almost still smell the various potions that were mixed there. The museum contained

---

[4] I've done some of my best writing just walking around, going nowhere, but thinking. I wrote large chunks of my doctoral dissertation walking the streets of College Hill in Providence where H.P. Lovecraft walked. I've always carried a little pocket notebook with me for when a brainstorm hits.

one of the world's great collections of scientific instruments. On the top floor, was the collection of astronomical devices; a room filled with rare, antique astrolabes and armillary spheres. As the sun streamed in, the light would reflect off the highly-polished brass machines which allowed their original users to imagine travelling the cosmos the way Sherman and I did with our metal filing cabinet spaceship. In the basement exhibits room, where I was to speak, the museum had a piece of chalkboard written on by Albert Einstein during his visit, as well as several large, early electric generators. Another case held a collection of small, original glass vials of Deuterium: the heavy water used during WWII by the Nazis to try to build an atomic bomb.

The museum staff produced an advertising poster for the series, but also one specifically announcing my talk. The poster was a single, large black footprint containing the announcement. They turned this into a 3 feet by 4 feet billboard that hung on the entrance gate to the museum. Being centrally located on Broad Street in Oxford, the museum was passed by hundreds, if not thousands, of people every day. Individuals, students, and the ubiquitous groups of visiting school kids that swarm Oxford in the summer, passed by the gate and the poster.

Since Lisa and I were there in Oxford for a few days, while she was in the Bodleian doing her research, I went to the *White Horse* pub, directly across the street from the museum, and with my pint, took a seat in the front window. I just stared at the poster and people-watched. Enjoying the moment, I noticed a middle-aged couple standing at the front wall of the museum reading the poster. I jumped up and ran out the door of the pub. Being a centuries old Tudor building, the ceilings were quite low and, as I rushed out, I hit my head on a beam. Undaunted, I dashed out into traffic and, after almost being run over crossing Broad Street, I sidled up to the couple as unobtrusively as I could. The woman said, "Hey, this looks interesting," to which the man replied, "Yes, and it's tomorrow night." Standing next to them I said, "Yeah, this does look really interesting!" They smiled and walked off. [5]

For my talk, it was a hot July night. The basement had no air-conditioning yet there was still a standing-room-only crowd of about sixty people. I didn't care about the heat, all I cared about was that I was in this place giving a lecture on my research. In the back, Lisa watched and smiled. It was very nearly close to heaven. It seemed strange and exhilarating to think a kid from Newark, who had been told by so many people that he would never be smart or intellectually successful or amount to anything, was standing in this place giving a lecture to a packed house.[6] Stephen Johnston gave me a very nice introduction and I stepped up to the podium and uttered into the microphone, "Okay, let's talk about monsters!"

The Jersey Devil

I enjoyed driving to Kean University along South Avenue, because it allowed me time to think. Driving and thinking has always worked for me. This road was a long, major artery. As I drove back and forth, day after day, I noticed there was a collection of middle-aged men who jogged up and down the street. There were at least four of them. I don't think they knew each other, I think they just liked running. Some could run quite quickly while others were just speed walking, but they were doing it nonetheless. I noticed them at all times of the day and night, and in all weather. One guy, in his forties I guessed, had a striking page

---

[5] They did actually attend.
[6] Betty was very proud when I told her. I only wish Henry could have been there so he could see how far his Estwing geologist's hammer and the little box of rock and mineral samples had taken me.

boy style haircut, and walked with a distinctive gait where he threw his hands up into the air swinging his arms as he went. Another, older man, did more of a shuffling walk and always looked like he was about to keel over. You had to give them some respect for doing this with such regularity. They reminded me of those people in Lancers I thought were lonely monsters.

In the Fall of 2012, New Jersey had a visitor named Sandy. She laid waste to large swathes of the region. One of our big oak trees fell on our neighbour's house. It did some damage, but fortunately not too much and no one was injured. One house a block away, was flattened by a huge tree. Another had its attached garage sheared off by a falling tree trunk. With the power out, the neighbourhood descended into pitch black. As Lisa and I lay on an improvised bed in the ground floor living room, all we could hear were the crunching of falling trees and the intense howl of the wind. It sounded like there was some huge, reptilian kaiju stomping around outside. Despite this, no one was injured. Other trees fell and blocked the street so no one could drive out of the neighbourhood. The next morning people began coming out of their houses magically armed with chainsaws and we had a block party to cut the trees out of the street. Naturally, many power lines went down and we were out of electricity for over a week. Gradually, however, the power came back on, trees were removed from houses, and people recovered.

When things returned to something near normal, I had a conversation with Frank Esposito. As one of the longest serving historians at Kean, Frank Esposito had seen and done it all. He was even interim college president a few times. I had him as an undergrad for US history and we became friends. He was a terrific researcher and scholar and had a good sense of humour. With his short, squat build, and distinguished greying, short-cropped hair, he always made me think he looked like the Kennedy son who had gone into academia instead of politics. When I was offered the job at Kean, he was first to call and congratulate me. When he decided to finally retire, I was the first member of the department he told. In our post Sandy conversation, I complained about all the awful TV 'documentaries' that discussed the Jersey Devil. We decided it would be fun to write a book on the Jersey Devil legend together.

We set down to do a proper historical examination of the legend, ignoring mythology, in order to look for genuine history. We quickly realised that the story of the Jersey Devil was not that of a monster, but of a man named Daniel Leeds. We scoured the libraries and archives of the northeast and were able to find a large amount of primary source material that had almost never been looked at.

Realising the story of the Jersey Devil was also a Quaker story, it didn't take long to see there was a trove of material in England. I visited the Friend's library in London. In New Jersey, the first place I went to was the Quaker Meeting House in Burlington. It was the original building put up, with Daniel Leeds's help, in the 1680s. Lisa and I visited and they obligingly let us wander around the meeting room. Being hand-made, the pews reminded me of St. Cecilia's Church. The ancient wood held many secrets. I then noticed that many of the pews had carvings and initials cut into them by parishioners as they sat through the meetings. I searched frantically hoping I would find a set of initials that said DL. Either I didn't see them or they had never been carved. I was a little disappointed, it would have been amazing to find such an artefact. We did search for Daniel Leeds's grave. We spent some time just slowly stepping from one grave marker to the next in the nearby Anglican Church (Leeds had converted from Anglican to Quaker then back to Anglican). We never found it though we knew it was there somewhere. We searched for his father at the Shrewsbury Meeting but didn't find him either. In London, I located the site of Daniel's mother Mary Leeds, or at least the graveyard where she was buried. Unfortunately, the graveyard, though still owned by the Quakers, was no longer an active cemetery. If there had been any headstones there, they had long since been removed or stolen. What was once a solemn graveyard was now a trash and broken-bottle covered lot. I knew she was down there somewhere, the official City of London records said she was, I had no idea exactly where. After a bit, I paid my respects and left.

The Quakers of Burlington had travelled to the New World in 1675 on board a little wooden ship named *Shield*. After crossing the tempestuous ocean, they found the mouth of the Delaware River and cruised it north as far as they could go. When the ship began to scrape the river bottom, they made a hard right turn and rammed it into the beach. This is where they would build their community. This was the moment the Jersey Devil was born. The ship was left there and, over time, was cannibalised for building materials. The Meeting House that still stands in Burlington has parts from the *Shield* built into it (though I am not sure which bits). One day, I drove down to Burlington again and went to the riverside. After looking at various maps and comparing the texts, I thought I knew roughly where the good ship *Shield* would have been beached three-and-a-half centuries before. The town had built a modern 'riverwalk' at the spot. I stood at the railing for an hour staring into the brown water, hoping I might hear the voices of those forgotten people. Maybe hear them sing their Quaker songs. All I heard were the calls of the river birds and the lapping of the waves. I wondered how many people strolling along this concourse today, walking their dogs in the sunshine, jogging, holding their beloved's hands, yelling into their phones, ever suspected what history lay just a few feet below them.[7]

Daniel Leeds was not only the first author in New Jersey, he was its first censored author. After the first almanac came out, the Burlington town Fathers took issue with it. They thought it was just too preoccupied with the occult. They decided to destroy his attempt to bring science and erudition to the wilderness of New Jersey. They managed to destroy most copies—though they were sure to pay Bradford for the loss of business, yet they did not reimburse Leeds—except for the ones that had been sent back to England for the edification of Quakers still in London. A copy, along with a fragment of another copy, ended up in the collection of the British Library in London. I travelled to the UK, amongst other reasons, so I could see it. Sitting there in the large British Library reading room, I waited for this document to be brought to me. After a while, I could hear the tell-tale squeaking of a library cart being rolled in my direction. The librarian proceeded to place a large, heavy scrap book on my desk. Leafing through it I passed many important, rare, and interesting bits of ephemera: newspaper ads, small pamphlets, and bits and pieces of history. I would have liked to have stopped and looked at each one, but I had an important engagement with an almanac. Finally, I arrived at the next to last page before the Leeds almanac. Turning one more page there it was. All this time, all this research, all this thinking and puzzling and here it was. As it was printed on rag paper it looked like it was brand new despite it being on the top side of 230 years old.

I always tell my students that even with so much primary source material having been scanned and available on-line for research, there is nothing like holding an original document or artefact in your hands. It is as close as we can come to time travel. It gives you a visceral connection to the past that the digital age, as useful as it is, simply cannot.

As I sat there in the large, grand, British Library reading room, looking down at this

---

[7] I thought it might be fun to put together an operation to find the Shield and maybe recover some of it. After three-and-a-half centuries, all that is likely to remain might be parts of its keel sunk into the cold, preserving mud.

innocuous object, really just a seventeenth century version of a newspaper page, I became unexpectedly emotional. Daniel Leeds had travelled across the Atlantic by boat to reach America, to reach New Jersey, so he could write this document. I travelled from New Jersey to England by jet liner to be able to read it. This document had been held by Daniel Leeds himself. It was held by William Bradford as he printed it. It was held by others of the period. Was it held by someone as they hid it so it would not be burned like the other copies? Daniel Leeds had risked everything to come to America in 1677. He had risked everything to try and bring enlightenment to his neighbours. He risked everything on the idea that he could make his world and his society a better place through scholarship and learning. For his troubles he was rejected, cursed, insulted, threatened and had his work destroyed. He was called 'Satan's Harbinger' because he dared to say that facts and evidence and history and science were valuable and important. As I sat there I felt even more strongly that I had to tell his story, and indeed, that monsters were relevant for the 21st century.

Satellite Sky

One of the crucial things for an historian is to work with original manuscript material. These sorts of primary sources are, for me at least, the most important raw materials we have for studying the past. It can give you an immediate connection to the past. Once, while working on the Darwin and the Monsters project, I was able to view the working notes of Edward Tyson as he dissected his 'Pygmy.' Tyson was the first Westerner to study the anatomy of a primate. In the 1760s, he managed to get a hold of a juvenile primate. Later scholars think it was a chimpanzee or a bonobo. His work led to the first detailed scientific description of a primate, along with detailed drawings of its anatomy. No one in England had ever studied one before. Westerners were familiar with primates, but none had been able to investigate them anatomically. It was brought to England by some sailors, but the creature died soon after its arrival. Tyson managed to acquire it and set about dissecting it. The unfortunate, baby-sized beast was laid out on his dissecting table and Tyson went to work. As he did he made careful notes of what he was doing. These pages came into the possession of the Royal College of Physicians in London. I now held these notes in my hand. I imagined Tyson looking into the eyes of this poor, hapless creature, taken from its family and brought so far away only to die alone. Did Tyson think of that? Did he feel any sympathy for it? I thought I could smell the creature's blood on the notes.

One summer in the 1990s, Lisa and I spent the weekend on the Jersey shore at Wildwood. On Saturday evening, we went walking along the quieter end of the amusement boardwalk. There was a band stand and a little brass band was playing patriotic summer music. We watched and listened for a while, and when they finished we walked further down the boardwalk. It was hot and despite being a few yards from the ocean, it was still muggy. Now that it was relatively quiet, we sat on a bench and stared up at the stars. The music was replaced by the gentle crashing of waves on the beach. We sat quietly just enjoying it. Suddenly, Lisa said, "Look at that light, is that an aeroplane?" I looked up and saw what she meant. It was small like a star, but was clearly moving quickly across the sky. After a moment we both realised it was probably a satellite crossing over at the edge of space. We watched for a little while longer. She took my hand and we sat there staring up at the heavens. It was one of the best moments of my life. I realised how lucky I was to know her.

In April of 2016, I headed, once again, to the UK. I had been invited back to the Oxford History of Science Museum this time to talk about the life of Sir Richard Owen and his unintentional position as grandfather of cryptozoology. Lisa didn't accompany me as she had just been diagnosed with cancer. I didn't want to leave her, but she insisted I go as I was scheduled to give a talk. It was not easy going without her.

Again, the museum staff produced a wonderful advertising poster that they hung on the gate outside for the crowds to ogle. Our friends, An and Mark, now residents of Oxford (she worked at the Ashmolean Museum of Art and he at the Oxford Museum of Natural History) graciously came to the talk. We really liked them because we seemed to have a lot in common. We originally met them through Joe Cain. There are certain people whom I want to be able to say I had drinks with and talked about museums and history in an Oxford pub. They are on that list. The Mexican journalist and science writer Alejandra Arreola-Triana was there also. She had contacted me via Twitter, and it had just so happened that she was in Oxford the same day as my talk. By an odd coincidence, there was a Tom Cruise movie shooting in Oxford that week. He was working on a remake of *The Mummy*. There were film trucks and equipment all over the school precinct. They were filming just a block or two away from the museum including on the night of my talk. Despite the attraction of the fabled Tom Cruise, I still had a standing-room-only crowd for my second talk at the fabled museum.

After the talk, we went over to a trendy restaurant on the High Street called *Quod* to have dinner. I invited Alex and her friend to come along. Alex readily agreed, but her friend wanted to go see the filming and see if she could meet Tom Cruise. As An and Mark and I sat chatting and having a wonderful meal—paid for by the museum and Stephen Johnston— Alex's phone began to ring. She picked it up and spoke for a moment, "You're kidding!" she exclaimed. It was her friend calling. She had met Tom Cruise. She even sent along a selfie of her and the actor to prove it.

Working diligently, Frank Esposito and I had finished most of the Jersey Devil manuscript by that summer. I still had some tinkering to do. I obsessively tinker with my manuscripts, trying to get the phrasing and layout the best it can be. Thinking about the hardships Daniel Leeds went through, I encountered more personal difficulties. Lisa was put on a number of different drug treatments and even surgery to remove cancerous nodes from her windpipe. That began a period of ups and downs as her condition improved and worsened then improved again. We were also trying to sell the Webster house and had received a number of offers. Each time, however, after the usual ton of paperwork and expectation, the buyer would pull out: either they couldn't get a mortgage or they had changed their minds. The house I once loved more than most people I've known, had become an albatross around my neck. Another thing to lay awake at night worrying about. Once in the UK, I was notified that yet another sale had fallen through.[8] So, I was upset and depressed, which only made my worries over Lisa's condition worsen.

On the U.K. trip, as usual, I had taken a few extra days so I could do some research at the Bodleian. On my last night in Oxford for the year, I decided to walk over to the Eagle & Child pub for dinner. Research always helped me forget the crap that was going on in my life. While I immersed myself in ancient texts, all seemed right with the world. Eventually though, the real world comes back whether you like it or not.

I sat alone in the Eagle & Child, scribbling notes as always trying to ward off the news about Lisa's condition. Sitting there in the very spot where J.R.R. Tolkien wrote *The Lord of the Rings*, and where C. S. Lewis wrote *The Lion the Witch and the Wardrobe,* should

---

[8] I did eventually manage to sell it in late 2019.

have had me elated. The pub served a chicken and mushroom pie to die for. I was washing it down with a pint of Abbot Ale. The pub was crowded with people talking and laughing. I sat in the middle of it all by myself. There was a group of three older Chinese women tourists sitting at the table next to me. They were speaking in Mandarin, looking around the room, and pointing at the various antiques and pictures on the walls commemorating The Inklings. I was still depressed.

I've felt alone and on my own most of my life. The idea that Lisa could die left me feeling more alone than I have ever felt. The idea of a world without her was too much to take. I've always been able to shrug off anything, even the worst news. I shrugged off being told I would never accomplish anything with my life or get into college. I shrugged off falling out of a helicopter, and the death of my father. I shrugged off almost failing out of grad school. I shrugged off 9/11.

Not this!

I had worked hard over the years to build this life; the life of an adventuring scholar. When Lisa and I met, we built it together. This was what I had dreamed about: to be sitting in an ancient Oxford pub, having a drink after a day of research and writing at the Bodleian, after having given a standing room only talk at the Museum of the History of Science. This was the world I had begun to build the day I walked away from Tappan Street. Yet, the notion of this world existing without Lisa made it all seem pointless. I drank several more pints (more than I usually do) and headed back to my college room. Walking along those mediaeval streets I had come to love, made it all the more poignant. I dreaded the day I would call your name and you do not answer. I did the only thing I could. The only thing that could bring me in off the ledge.

I went to work.

I left the Eagle & Child and walked along the cobbled stone streets that Newton, Boyle, and Hook and so many others had walked along. Oxford streets that had known the footsteps of so many historical personages, and now knew mine. Once, when I was in Germany I was up in the tank park doing some repairs in the turret of *Dreamboat Annie*. By the time I was finished, I climbed out of the loader's hatch to see that everyone had left to go to the dining hall for dinner. It was about 5:30pm and it was getting dark quickly. Being lazy, instead of climbing down off the tank after I locked it up, I stood on the fender and jumped down. It was early February and freezing cold. I landed on the outside toes of my left foot. The instant I hit there was an electric pain that shot through my foot and up my leg. My toes were numb from the cold and I had now just hit them with a hammer. When the lights stopped flashing, I hobbled down the hill to the barracks. I never went off sick. I never had a doctor look at the injury. I just walked it off. I had clearly damaged the nerves in my foot. From that time on, I have felt that pain, especially in the winter. That pain, like that in my knee from when it was hit by the baseball, has walked with me ever since. It walked with me across Europe, across Manhattan, to every part of the United States, up and down the Jersey Shore, around London and Berlin, to the streets of Wenzhou, China. It walked with me that night in Oxford.

I came to a stop at the Catte Street entrance to the Bodleian. They had locked the ancient carved entry doors for the day. These doors reminded me of the door that led to the secret garden at St. Cecilia's. As I couldn't go in, I just plopped down on the curb right there, took out my notebook and began to write. Nobody paid much attention. It was Oxford after all, and weird, long-grey-haired, guys sitting on the curb scribbling into a notebook, would not raise any eyebrows. I wrote about how I thought Daniel Leeds might have felt when all his good work had been taken away from him. When I looked up, two hours had gone by. Writing helped me cope. It kept me from killing myself.

> I am not to speak to you
> I am to think of you when I sit alone or awake at night alone
> I am to wait, I do not doubt I am to meet you again
> I am to see to it that I do not lose you.[9]

In November 2018, the NBC television network contacted me. They were putting together some promotional projects for the latest Harry Potter related movie, *Fantastic Beasts: the Crimes of Grindelwald*. They wanted me to come to Radio City Music Hall to record my comments on the J.K. Rowling world and the history of alchemy. I went over and entered the fabled building that had contributed so much to television and American history. I had been told to sign in at the desk and they would tell me what to do. The guard led me to the elevator and pushed the right button to take me up to the studio where I would do my thing. He said someone would meet me. The doors opened, and I stepped out onto the floor expecting to meet the woman who had originally contacted me. There was no one. A few people walked by busily on this errand or that, but no one approached me. After a minute or so, I went exploring. It was exactly as you would expect. Equipment jammed into the corridors with lots of people milling about. I figured at least someone would approach me to ask who the hell I was and what I was doing there, but they didn't. I walked past a large make-up room with chairs, a huge mirror and all the accoutrements. I walked a little further and went through a pair of open double doors. On one door it said 'studio' so I thought this might be where I was supposed to be. I found myself surrounded by the weighty hanging curtains I remember from my high school's stage. Enveloped in the heavy drapery, I had to push and fumble my way through. Suddenly, as if the waters had parted, I found myself on a stage. It was the stage of the *Tonight Show*. There was no one around, it was in the morning so Jimmy Fallon wasn't there. I stood on the stage where Johnny Carson and David Letterman held court. After looking around briefly, I walked up the aisle between the seats to the back door. Detouring over, I wandered back into the first corridor and managed to find the studio I was supposed to be in, as well as the people who had asked me to come over in the first place. With the filming finished, I realised the real adventure had been roaming, completely unchallenged, in the halls of one of the most historically important television studios of all time.

When I started studying the history of monsters and science and alchemy, I thought I might be able to use them to make a place for myself in academia where few others were. Later, however, I realised I wasn't sure what I was trying to do. Besides attempting to tell a story I thought no one had told before, what was the point of standing over Mary Leeds's grave or holding a fifteenth-century book on werewolves in my hand while sitting in the same chair as Montague Summers, or getting teary-eyed in the White Oak bar reading the private diary of Nellie Horsford? Did I have some meta concept for my career? Did I need one? I have approached life this way since I was a kid: I decided I wanted to do something and so I pursued it but never really giving a lot of thought to the long-range implications or consequences or reasons. I guess I always felt that way; if I just ignored the bad things they might not happen. As long as I was happy, that was all that mattered. The problem was, bad things always happened, no matter what.

---

[9] Walt Whitman, *Leaves of Grass* (1855).

It's easy to think it's just amateur writers in the field of paranormal or mystery studies, who go off on wild excursions without any sense of historical reality or research ability. While you do find quite a bit of research incompetence out there, other fields of history can exhibit the same deficiencies when the authors are outside the academy (not all of course, I've read some very good historical work done by non-academics). One of the things professionalisation of historical research does with its degrees, accreditations, institutional affiliations and peer reviews is to help keep down the nonsense. Non-members regard all this as some kind of elitist gate keeping when, in reality, this is what helps produce high-quality writing and research by insisting on higher standards. But, what was the point?

One of the things I quickly noticed about the academic world of professional historians of science was that their view of monsters seemed odd to me. While academics had long ignored cryptozoology, there was a considerable amount of scholarship on Medieval and Early Modern monsters. There were, in fact, a long line of canon works on the subject. Stephanie Moser's *Ancestral Images* (1998), David Williams' *Deformed Discourse* (1999), Knoppers and Landes' *Monstrous Bodies* (2004), and a number of others had great respect, and rightly so, but no one was writing about cryptids. Except for me and the outsider authors, that is.

The rule of thumb seemed to be, if you're a Sciopod you were worthy of scholarly study, if you were Bigfoot you were not. I wanted to buck this trend. I foolishly thought, in my wildest fantasies, that my Sasquatch book might break open the field of modern monsters and cryptids for other academics to follow. When that didn't happen, I thought my Jersey Devil book surely would. When it still didn't happen, I gave up thinking I'd have any impact upon the field. I reverted to my old tactic of turning away from the idea and I continued off on my own, for no reason other than I enjoyed this work. I wouldn't quite give up on academia of course, I still gave talks and presented papers, but any notion of my monster work meaning anything to anyone but myself I abandoned.

To be honest though, by 2020 and 2021, I had grown tired of cryptozoology. There seemed to be nothing but nonsense. There were a few people doing some interesting work such as Charles Paxton and Darren Naish, but they were trained scientists who did not call themselves cryptozoologists. Richard Freeman in the UK, was doing some interesting things concerning the Orang Pendek, but other than these people there wasn't much going on. Some of my favourite cryptozoological moments came from having drinks with Darren Naish at the *Hoop and Toy* pub in London and with Richard Freeman at the *Shakespeare* in Bristol. You can't sustain a field where the best parts are ragging on true believers while downing pints.

The traditional, untrained, amateur investigators (who self-identified as cryptozoologists) were still doing the same old things: running around the woods, setting trail cams and finding nothing. In almost a century since the Abominable Snowman, and since then Graver Krantz, Rene Dahinden and the other members of the Golden Age, nothing came along except fakes, frauds and hoaxes. With my Sasquatch and Jersey Devil books I felt I had said all I had to say about the topic. I was invited to be on a number of television series to talk about the Jersey Devil and other monsters, but they never seemed to move very far beyond saying, here is this or that monster and here are some people who claim they had an encounter with them. Every time I tried to talk TV producers into doing something different and more interesting, they would smile wearily and say, "yeah, that's great," then do nothing. I heard the same story from historians and archaeologists trying to get the networks to try some actual history and archaeology instead of the same ancient alien and monster in the woods nonsense.

There was plenty of drama, suspense, and controversy being found by real historians and archaeologists. No one, but themselves, seemed to understand how amazing history really is. I once stood at the Quaker graveyard in London hoping to hear Daniel Leeds's mother call out to him. Then I stood on the sidewalk outside the historic Quaker Meeting House in Burlington, New Jersey, waiting for the ghost of Daniel Leeds to come along. Television producers have yet to realise this theory of monsters, no matter how much we try to explain it to them.

Chapter 9

Monsters in the Promised Land

No happier joy I hope or ask
than thus to sit with loving eyes
and watch the bed where Báli lies.

– Hanuman's speech, *The Ramayana, canto XXI*

As a kid growing up in the Ironbound, every bigoted, white, schmuck dreamed of getting out of the city. As the Black and Hispanic population expanded in the mid-60s, riots ensued and white flight swiftly set in. The place they all wanted to move to, it seemed, was Toms River, New Jersey. I heard the refrain constantly at all the family functions and in all the bars my parents dragged me to. I was surrounded by drunken adults saying, "I'm gettin' out, I'm movin' to Toms River." A growing suburban town at the head of Barnegat Bay, south of Newark, Toms River was close enough to the shore attractions without being beachy, and just about exclusive enough and non-urban enough for residents to think of themselves as better than everyone else. Burned by the British during the Revolution, Toms River became, by the post-World War II years, a kind of toney enclave for more well-off, upwardly mobile, aspiring working class and lower middle class people looking to escape city life. During these years, it took on an almost mythical quality as a kind of promised land for whites, who saw themselves as superior to people of colour and poor working whites, and who didn't want to live around 'them' anymore. Uncle Billy moved to Toms River.

I've never been one much for belief in promised lands. The whole idea seems suspect to me. A promised land is somewhere preordained for you usually by someone else. It's a destination that, once reached, you never leave. There are few places I could imagine staying in forever. I always want to be able to go forward, to find out what is next. In a way, for me, a promised land is a trap. If I were to wind up in heaven or some such place, I'd be the guy staring out the back window wondering what's out there beyond.

When I went into the army I realised one day that all the shaking, fear, and anxiety attacks I had experienced as a kid had vanished. Monsters didn't scare me anymore. My fears started to return, however, after the first year at MBE. Up until that point, I had no real responsibilities in the world except to myself. I lived a devil-may-care attitude to life. If I lost a job, so what, I'd find another, no problem. If a girl broke up with me, no problem, there were others. When Lisa and I got together, and it looked permanent, I still didn't feel the pressure of taking care of her. She was pretty good at taking care of herself. Halfway through the second year of my Fellowship at MBE, things started to change. The board of directors of the Christian Science library found out I had been writing my dissertation on company time. They found out because the Church member on my team squealed. I was not worried about losing the job as such. I had reached a mental point where I wanted to leave anyway, but the loss of the paycheck without another one already lined up, affected me. How was I going to be able to keep a roof over Lisa's head? Would we have to leave Providence? I started having sleepless nights. When the job at TCI came along I felt better. I cashed in my meagre retirement fund— which would just cover the cost of moving and the security on a new apartment in New Jersey—and we headed out.

183

Returning that August from Berlin, the prospect of starting my new teaching position helped a great deal. Then along came 9/11 and the bottom fell out. Though I was never in any direct danger that day, I began to realise later that it had indeed bothered me (several of my relatives were actually at ground zero that day). On the streets of Manhattan, for the first year or so after, every time an aeroplane flew overhead or a firetruck or emergency vehicle screamed by, my nervous system tightened up. The monsters returned to my dreams.

This went against everything I imagined about where I'd be by now. I thought that when I received my doctorate, I would find a faculty job somewhere and assume the life of a globetrotting researcher and writer of books. I did do that, but there was something wrong. I thought that by achieving the promised land, the anxiety attacks would end permanently. I had achieved all that, yet the anxiety attacks only increased.[1]

Is it 'a historian' or 'an historian'?

Historians are weirdos with a great training in how to understand the past. What do they do, exactly? This is a question professional historians and students alike get asked quite often. Most people have no idea. They have gotten a skewed, odd sense of it through pop histories written by non-historians such as Bill O'Reilly or Graham Hancock. Or from popularizers like David McCullough or Jared Diamond. Most movie depictions of historians are wildly fantastical and inaccurate. It's easy for accountants, for example, to say what they do, the same for astronomers, or firemen, or cooks. How do historians answer this question?

In its simplest terms, the work of historians is the careful and thoughtful study of those elements which make up this thing we vaguely call, 'the past.' Those elements are in large part the written record (although artefacts, photos and music form part of it as well). Historians plough through the mountains of paperwork left behind by the human race. We call these primary sources. We study the large and the small, the significant and the seemingly insignificant: the good, the bad, and the ugly. We do go on adventures and we do battle evil doers, but mostly, our time is spent travelling the world to go to libraries and archives so we can read the words of the people we are studying and the data of the events we are analysing first hand. We spend lots of time reading through the details few others look at or even know exist. We read the letters and correspondences, the notebooks, and random scribblings of the past. We follow loud screams, quiet whispers, the seductive promises of lovers, and the inspiring words of heroes. We have heard the pitiless cries of victims in the night, the sharp bark of the evil and the abusive, from earlier today back to the dawn of time. This is an attempt to get some idea of what happened, why it happened, and who did it. We do this so we can learn from it. This is part of why people hate historians. We remind them of all the terrible, awful things they and their ancestors have done, but what they now want to forget or behave as if they didn't happen.

While looking at this material, historians ask questions about it. We look to put our findings into context, and do it all according to the rules and procedures of scholarly research. We look for connections, but we have to be careful when doing so. Humans naturally look for connections and patterns. Anthropologists call this Apophenia. It's like when you see a horse silhouette in a cloud or a human face in a rock formation. This is not a delusion, it is likely an evolutionary survival adaptation to being able to tell friend from foe. There is an inherent

---

[1] I haven't slept an entire night through in so many years I've forgotten what such an experience is like. I usually start off well, but then around two or three AM it hits.

danger in this. Sometimes the patterns and connections we see in the historical record can lead us to new insights about the material, more often than not the images we think we see are illusions. That is why when historians see these connections and patterns we analyse them in detail and continue to search for more data and evidence. This helps us to see if the face is really there or not.

At the heart of the historical process is the tacit understanding that it is done without preconceived ideas. We try to let the facts and evidence guide us to possible answers. Those answers are determined regardless of the political, religious, or cultural consequences they might have. We are always ready, however, to change our position should new evidence come along. The understanding of the past is not static, and it is not about making you feel good about yourself. You don't get to ignore facts because they do not sit well with your own disposition. Knowledge can elevate and it can infuriate. It can challenge the status quo and undermine deeply held convictions. It can unmask criminals and topple empires. It can support the voiceless and accuse the loud and oppressive. Part of the job of the historian is to bring all this out into the open.

The role of the historian in society is to remind us of where we came from, not only as a society but as individuals. This knowledge can help us to make better informed decisions about how to conduct our lives, and how to avoid getting into trouble. When we stick our finger into an electrical outlet, because we thought it would be a good idea, then we get shocked. History helps us learn not to do that again. The historian warns us not to stick our finger into the electrical outlet over and over. Unfortunately, we are not always as convincing as we hope. One of the greatest problems historians are up against is not just a lack of knowledge; it's a lack of memory.

Some learn the lessons we have to teach, others do not. Some simply do not get it, while others know we are right, but intentionally refuse to hear, or even disparage our work. This is often the result of religious or political concerns because historical facts and evidence can be deeply troubling to some. They desire the past to have been a certain way so as to make them feel better about themselves in the present. When the facts of the past do not line up with their desires they try to manipulate and hijack the past for their own agendas. Historians fight against this: we hold the line against nonsense. Part of the reason people dislike historians is because we remind them of the things they and their ancestors did that they'd rather forget happened or try to cover up.

Historians, especially when they come up with a new way of looking at something, are often called 'revisionist'. This accusation is employed when the historian writes something you don't like. 'Revisionist' is used as a derogatory term. In simple terms: all history is revisionist history. It only upsets you if you don't care for the revisions, if it interferes with how you see the world, or if it undermines your political or religious position. Historians are always looking for new sources, new data, and new ways of understanding. When they find them and tell a story in a new way that is revising the body of knowledge. That is how history works. It is not static and unchanging, only Holy Scripture is unchanging. Historians do not write Holy Scripture.

Being an historian can sometimes be disheartening, but that cannot stop us from doing our jobs. We fight to preserve facts and evidence; we fight to preserve rationality no matter the cost. We fight the evildoers. In the twenty-first century, we need historians more than ever. Historians do not just know the facts, they know how to analyse and interpret them.

In that way, historians work to save the universe. It is also a hugely fun and satisfying endeavour.

    That's what historians do.
That's how you answer that question.

The Job Market

I am extremely lucky. I beat the odds to get where I am. Just being good at this was never enough. Every year, university graduate programs around the world crank out hundreds of history doctorate holders. While in the twenty-first century there has been much discussion of 'alternate paths' for PhDs—ways outside of academia that doctorate holders could find employment—everyone wants that traditional university tenure track position. Whether they say it out loud or not, that's the goal. That's the dream. We don't go through all the trouble, blood, sweat, and tears, and money, to get a job with a corporate cubicle. Even if it pays better, that's not what we got into this for. We got into it so we could be in a university history department. So we could research our areas of interest and publish books and articles on it. We did it so we could have that nameplate on our tiny office door. We did it to teach, we did it to hear students call us 'Doctor' or 'Professor.' At least, that's part of what motivated me.

The problem is that the number of such positions that become available is far lower than the number of people who want them. Schools like Oxford, Cambridge, Harvard, Princeton, Berlin, the Sorbonne, and dozens of others, turn out PhDs with those coveted pedigree names attached to them. There is a glut of such scholars in the world. The top 10% of prestige jobs go to these people. Whether they are brilliant or mediocre, the name of the school carries significant weight. Then the lower ranked schools gobble up the others. Lower ranked schools want to be able to put on their brochures that Professor X is from Oxford or Harvard. Then you work your way down the ladder. As you do, the odds of you getting such a job continue to dwindle. I've known plenty of top scholars, with incredible brains and even important publications, who have to survive by being adjuncts. It doesn't matter how good they are, they will never find resident faculty jobs simply because there aren't any available.

The odds are stacked against someone trying to do this. To do this job one must 'need' to do it. If you are not from an elite school you have huge obstacles in front of you. You have to have a kind of blind, stupid, crazy aspect to your persona. You have to be willing to keep going when everything else in the world tells you to give up. You have to have a fire in your belly to do this job. You have to be willing to embrace the rejection, the ridicule, and the dismissive attitude. You have to be ready to eat it and keep going. The difficulty is even greater for female scholars, and even greater still for scholars of colour. Even with this level of determination, there is no guarantee.

When I applied for the job at TCI, I later found out that I was one of over seventy people who had applied for the position. Despite its small size and intellectual inconsequence—it was essentially a glorified vo-tech school—a lot of people were desperate for that job. I was proud that I had landed it on my own merit. Like MBE they didn't know me in any way other than the C.V. I sent them. When I applied to Kean I had Mark Lender, the man who wouldn't let me change my major to history at Kean until I explained why I wanted to do it. He had written me letters of recommendation to grad school and had introduced me to David Kohn. So, when I applied for the position at Kean I felt I had a friend. Again, though, a huge number of people applied for that job. There was no guarantee of anything, Mark had told me that point blank, "Don't think you're going to just waltz into this. If I think you are half-assing it for an instant, I'll tell the committee to not consider you. And, if the committee are unanimous in wanting someone else, I will not interfere." With everything Mark Lender said, he meant it.

The History of Science

The field of the history of science tends to focus on winners and progressive success stories. I do not mean that as a critique. Most of history is like that. The success stories of how obstacles were overcome in order to discover how the universe works are important. How scientific methodologies were worked out, and how scientific institutions were built are important stories, and necessary to the understanding of the human experience. More synthetic works look at big ideas such as how race and gender and socio-economics impacts on how science has evolved. The historians who pursue things like institutional history, and who sit and count up how many telescopes were manufactured and who actually published the first papers on electromagnetism, do a hugely important service as well.

My professional career as an historian of science has been digging through dusty archives in order to write about the losers not the winners. I count up the shattered remains of broken dreams. The world I investigate is populated with people running around looking for the little bits of junk they think will prove their wacky theories about the 'true' shape of the Earth, why are there still monkeys, how Leif Erikson discovered America, or why Bigfoot is real. Rarely do they prove anything even remotely. They finish a life doing this, then die and lapse into an even deeper level of obscurity. At least until some jackass, like me, comes along to dig them up the same way they dug up their theories and ideas. I try to learn something from their sad, lonely, tragic lives so that others can as well. Some day in the future some jackass will come along and look into my sad, lonely, tragic life and the cycle will begin anew. That's what history is: an endless cycle of people chasing after one another, trying to find out the secrets of the universe. We are dogs chasing their tails around and around until exhaustion causes them to collapse and their dead bodies are pushed unceremoniously off into the culvert by the side of the dirt road of life.

While I have never considered myself a debunker, I have spent my career explaining the history of people who believed in the paranormal, monsters, ghosts, race science, anti-evolution, anti-vaccination, and UFOs: all those things some collectively refer to as 'Woo.' I am not the only one doing this of course. In the second decade of the twenty-first century, a growing cadre of historians, archaeologists, anthropologists and other scholars began to fight back against the evil that is the lies, obfuscations, misinformation and the twisting of history that manifests in the pursuit of power and profit. That is part of the job of a scholar as well.

What is a proper scholar? If an 'historian' is anyone who studies the past then we must differentiate the layers. There is a category we might call hobbyist historians. They have little or no formal training, just a passion for the past. They watch a lot of television and read a lot of popular books. Some might even consult scholarly peer-reviewed journal articles (this is the life I was almost consigned to). With no training in modern techniques of scholarship, they tend to follow a kind of instinctive approach: they look to great men, great battles, well known figures, and 'do' their history in a manner reminiscent (whether they recognize it or not) of the 19th century modernists. They search for 'truth.' A subset of this group are the genealogists. These people look to uncover the history of their own families.

A Life Online

In my senior year at Kean College, Dr. Frank Esposito stopped me in the corridor of Willis Hall one day and told me the New Jersey Historical Society (NJHS) in Newark was looking for an intern. He explained that such an entry would look good on my C.V. I went along with his recommendation and I was interviewed. Since the job didn't pay anything, and I was eager, I was asked to come on board as part of the library staff. I started out sorting newly acquired materials that had yet to be catalogued. I found it fascinating, and when I started grad school I stayed on. They were happy enough with my performance that I was hired as a paid, part-time employee. What helped, I think, was that I was willing to work on Saturdays. The library was opened every other Saturday, but few wanted to work that shift. I did, because I knew that no one in charge of anything would be around and I'd have a free run of the place.

The NJHS opened in 1845 thanks to a number of wealthy, civic-minded, Newark patrons with a love of the past. Initially, its home was in Trenton. Then it moved to Newark. With money from department store magnate Louis Bamberger, it moved to a magnificent, purpose built, multi-storied building of marble and iron with, what was then, a state-of-the-art vault in which to keep the most valuable materials. This stately home, at 230 Broadway, was where I first came to work for them. In 1997, they moved again, this time to an equally beautiful building in downtown Newark, across from Military Park and just down the street from the new NJPAC Theater, and a few doors down from the old Robert Treat Hotel.[2] This new home had originally been the Tudor designed, and exclusive, Essex Club.

The move was always explained as taking up a prime position in the centre of the downtown area that was beginning to be revitalised. In reality, the neighbourhood around the Broadway building was deteriorating. They had closed and stopped using the beautiful, main entrance directly on Broadway and were sending patrons to the rear entrance where the parking lot was. It was not unusual to find homeless people sleeping in the storm drain at the back of the building in the morning.

My job at the society library was to assist researchers. On Saturday mornings, our primary patrons were local genealogists. These were mostly older people who wanted to tell the story of their family history. Some did this out of the belief that some famous person was connected to them. They wanted to be able to say that George Washington or Benjamin Franklin was a relative, or that they were related to Winston Churchill or Marie Antoinette. Many were children of immigrants proud of their heritage. Some were Mormons who wanted to find 'unclaimed' dead people who they could posthumously baptise as Mormons. I always had a mixed opinion on the 'Genies' as we called them. They were nice enough, but they always wanted to explain to you, in excruciating detail, their family stories that were little more than birth lists and who begat whom. These tales, though important to the individuals, held no interest for anyone outside their immediate family.[3] Many were just lonely people trying to keep their brains from turning to mush: something I appreciated. I did find the 'Genies' a bit tedious. As they recounted the stories of their unremarkable ancestors, I took to responding by smiling and saying, "Hmmm, really? You don't say? Very nice." That would usually be enough to placate them so I could go back to what I was doing. I always seemed to attract the little old ladies who were trying to prove that they were related to Thomas

---

[2] The hotel was eventually taken over by Best Western, but they kept the name Robert Treat.
[3] Just like this autobiography.

Jefferson. They would call me over to the table they were sitting at, and ask me questions. They were often so physically tiny I would need to kneel down on the floor next to them as they talked. As they left they would stop at my desk which was next to the entry portal to the main library space, and thank me. They would then shuffle out and take the elevator down to the main floor. It was good training for the public engagements I was expected to do as a resident faculty member at Kean.

With the advent of social media in the 21ˢᵗ century, my career—as it did for many scholars—took on a new aspect: jousting with angry idiots in cyberspace. Online, I learned a whole new way to think about my role as an historian. I had always taken a strange pride in being the weirdo in any group I found myself to be in. It helped give me a sense of individualism, as well as a buffer against the world of muggles. It gave me a certain identity. In the interweb, I had entered a field full of crazy people. For most of my life I had been the weirdo in the crowd, now I was surrounded by them. Gradually, focusing on the history of the paranormal and pseudoscience, a new set of eccentrics have entered my orbit. As a scholar dedicated to researching the history of such topics, I angered some of the people who viewed my work. Every book, article, Op Ed piece and most of my social media work has brought hate mail of one kind or another. I have been accused of being a shill for Big Pharma and the Deep State. My credentials have been questioned, as has my patriotism.

In the midst of the Corona/Covid-19 pandemic, I wrote an Op Ed about selfishness and white privilege. I titled it, *Karen Wants to go to the Salon*. I used the then pop trope reference of 'Karen' as a foil for my discussion. A 'Karen' became a comical stereotype of a white, middle-class woman who is upset about some minor slight or inconvenience she has suffered and wants something to be done about it. Her rage often ends with her berating a low-level employee of a store or restaurant while demanding to "see the manager." I've always received hate mail for my Op Eds, but this one seemed to have touched a particularly tender chord. Within a few hours of the piece going online, I had an inbox full from mostly outraged readers, wanting to tell me a thing or two.

Many of the respondents took issue with my mentioning of white privilege. They also seemed to read into my words as meaning that anyone who wanted to go to work during the pandemic lockdown was a bad person. Not only did I never say that, I didn't mention work at all. My point was that we shouldn't be so selfish in a time of crisis and should do those simple things like wear a mask and gloves and stay six feet apart from each other which could save large numbers of people's lives.

One of my favourite aspects of writing Op Eds was that the angriest responses always seemed to confirm the thesis I had put forward. If I said people are awful I would get angry messages. Comments like these are the sweet elixir that regenerates the drowsy creation. One of the central ideas I write about is how, within the realm of amateur investigators, there is a strain of thought that says academic, 'professional' scholars are suspect because of their training. They are not as smart as the amateurs. There is a real streak of jealousy there. I have met plenty of gifted amateur investigators, Some have real chips on their shoulders. They rejoice in being able to catch a scholar who is unaware of some tiny detail. It thrills them to be able to say "I bested the so-called scholar!" It has always given me an odd sense of satisfaction when an angry letter or tweet fired at me, conforms to this. Studying this effect in historical figures and then seeing it in action right in front of me always helped prove I was on to something.

189

The debate about whether historians and other scholars should engage with promoters of pseudoscience and other nonsense, whether online or in person, is an important one. It's easy and tempting to wave it off and say, "we shouldn't encourage idiots." Increasingly I saw it as a question of "what choice do we have?" There is so much disinformation, genuine confusion, and outright lying going on that needs to be confronted. Who else has the expertise to do it if not scholars? If the professionals don't do it then the amateur theorizers and untrained, but emphatic evildoers will become the face of 'history.' If we don't do it then history will get hijacked by pompous windbags like Bill O'Reilly, Dinesh D'Souza, Brian Kilmeade, and all the other nincompoops of the apocalypse. All of them full of righteous, conservative anger and invective, but with little knowledge or experience. It winds up as something like, the government and Donald Trump sponsored '1776 Commission', whose total brief seems to be to fight against 'Leftists,' 'Globalists,' and the 'Woke' while sounding like a detergent commercial strapline: *Makes whites even whiter!*

Most academic historians and other scholars traditionally kept their fighting about history within the historical community. They argued and disagreed over the excruciating minutiae of the past: the meaning of past events, the analysis of data and primary sources. They tended to stay away from public encounters with civilians, especially over controversial subjects. With the advent of social media—especially after the election of Donald Trump— that began to change.

One of the more visible practitioners of this was Professor Kevin Kruse of Princeton University. His profile in all this came from an encounter he had with the political pundit, and ersatz intellectual, Dinesh D'Souza. An outspoken conservative, Trump supporter, and convicted criminal, the Mumbai born D'Souza, with no training as an historian, took on the role of 'honest historian' by arguing that the true purveyors of racism and ethnic bigotry in America was the Democratic Party. He often, and loudly, trumpeted the fact that Abraham Lincoln was a Republican. Therefore, he argued, Republicans are the real party of anti-racism and individual freedom. Kruse rightly pointed out that while Lincoln was a member of the Republican Party in the mid-nineteenth century it was a time when the Republican Party was the party of liberal progressives and abolition. The non-existent Democratic Party, about to come into being, would be the party of right wing conservatism, racialism, and pro-slavery. He also pointed out that as the years went by, the parties switched their affiliations and concerns. The Republican Party became the party of the wealthy, the powerful and ethnic bigotry, while the Democratic Party evolved into the party of the poor, working people, and civil rights. All this, as Kruse pointed out to D'Souza, was a well-known and widely discussed part of American history. Many works citing the regressive and bigoted side of the Democratic Party, adherents who were known as Dixiecrats, were written by progressive authors. Rather than acknowledge the subtle, and nuanced aspects of history, the conservatives like D'Souza preferred to rant over such things to benefit their side knowing the majority of their followers would never check.

My focus on pseudoscience and pseudohistory brought me the attention of lower ranking villains and their henchmen. As a result of my Op Ed writing, public speaking, and social media content on controversial topics such as abortion, climate change, evolution, the efficacy of vaccinations and others, I received hate mail from anti-vaxxers, anti-maskers, political conservatives, climate change denialists, equal rights opposers, gun nuts, history white-washers, and even pro-Columbus supporters. If historians do not do this, what good are we? What is our job? Is it only to examine history or to defend and argue it? The social media phenomenon of the twenty-first century forced historians to consider their place in society in ways unlike any before.

This is not about being selfish 'gatekeepers', (a derogatory term suggesting that 'professionals' are a cabal of baddies, who protect their privilege and fight against dissent of any kind) as is often the accusation. If you think historians are a dodgy bunch trying to preserve a specific view or way of studying the past, it shows you really have no idea what professional historians actually do. We fight to preserve facts and evidence, even the uncomfortable ones. We fight so that the reality of the past is widely known. When we discover some unusual or controversial material we can't wait to tell everyone, to write papers, and to publish. That's how we build careers. We also love to fight about it and argue about its meaning. Arguing meaning is a large part of the historical endeavour. Historians can sometimes feel swamped by all the spurious ideas—not just legitimate misunderstandings, but outright fraud—put forward by unscrupulous writers and pundits and bogus historical pontificators.

What many non-professionals have always failed to understand is that history, especially the history of monstrosity, is not just a great piling up of facts alone. Historians do spend a lot of time in pursuit of those facts, and their writing is built upon this effort. They chase the painful minutia of the past through texts, correspondence, diaries, and other written works, as well as through artefacts, in order to get as close as they can to people, places, and events. However, these facts and pieces of evidence are vetted for authenticity, placed in a wider context, and analysed for meaning. They are not just lined up like a grocery list. Theories are constructed to organise these facts and make sense of them so historical understanding is created. Nevertheless, history is still contentious. Historians often disagree with each other over the analysis of evidence, and to the conclusions drawn. History is never complete, there is never a final solution. As new evidence is evaluated or old evidence is shown to be faulty and discarded, the analysis and meaning can change over time. This work is done by individuals, by groups, and always as part of a wider community. As much as the facts themselves, the relationship between the communities of investigators also had a powerful impact upon the question of who discovered America. The lack of contextualization of facts, and the willingness to accept dubious evidence with little or no vetting exhibited by many amateurs, has been at the root of the resistance of professionals to take their work seriously. The online stuff also had me thinking about my role as a writer, and what things would mould how I approached writing.

The Hanging of Susanna Cox

In an effort to help my interest in science as a kid, my father bought me one of those junior geologist rock collections with the fragments of rocks and minerals glued down on a piece of cardboard. I loved that thing and would play with it for hours. He even took me to a local rock and fossil show. My mother insisted I put on my little brown suit with a tie. As we walked around looking at the tables, there was a stone plate with a large fossil fish in it. Two feet long and in magnificent condition, this creature once swam the shallow seas of Montana. Everyone was admiring it. Suddenly, the Old Man says, "it's nice and all, but it's so old!" It was one of those needle record scratching moments and the whole place came to a halt. That was his sense of humour. I got it, although I'm not sure if anyone else did.

My parents also wanted us to learn there was more to the world than what was in the Ironbound. They would take us on long drives out into the countryside or down to the Jersey Shore in the summertime. Once, we packed into the new car, a 1966 Mustang, and drove up to

New London, Connecticut to visit the submarines.[4] These trips helped in reducing my anxiety attacks. I loved sitting in the backseat staring out the window as the world went by.

As a union crane operator, my father didn't get a vacation. If he took time off to take the family somewhere, he didn't get paid for it. He did it anyway because he felt we should see things and that it would improve our lives to get out of the city once in a while. The summer before he bought the Mustang, we loaded into the car and headed to the wilds of far off Pennsylvania to go to the Pennsylvania Dutch Country Summer Fair at Kutztown. Most of what I remember about it was lots of straw with cows and chickens running around. They had displays and music and farmer's market style stands selling all sorts of food. It all had that great smell of newly mown grass, which my mother had to tell me was the smell of newly mown grass. I discovered an ambrosia of the gods the Mennonites called 'shoofly pie.'

They also hung a woman right in front of me for killing her kid.

It was a beautiful summer's day and Pops said let's go see the hanging of Susanna Cox. I had no idea what that meant, but he seemed oddly enthusiastic about it, whatever it was, so naturally, I wanted to go as well. We headed over into a big field where a crowd was gathering. In the centre of the field was a wooden structure of a type I had never seen before. It had steps going up to it. It was a gallows. Then I noticed there was a young woman in a period outfit standing on the gallows with a rope around her neck and a black hood over her head. Then a man began to tell a story. In 1809 a young immigrant woman named Susanna Cox was accused of killing her child. Thanks to language barriers and prejudice, she was found guilty, and hanged at Reading. She became, in fact, the last woman executed in Pennsylvania. Her story became a *cause célèbre* after her death when it was discovered she was likely not guilty. Her story was retold down the years as that of a folk hero.[5] The organisers of the Kurtztown Festival were so adamant about remembering her story, they worked it into the festivities. That's when I came along.[6]

As I watched and listened, I didn't really understand what was about to happen—I didn't realise it was a dummy. It looked so lifelike. I never imagined it was fake. Suddenly, the narrator grabbed the gallows handle, gave it a yank, and with a very loud bang, the doors flew open and she fell to her death. The noise was so loud it scared the hell out of me. I started shaking and hid behind my fathers' legs, crying. He scooped me up and tried to reassure me it was all just play-acting. I think he also suddenly realised this was not turning out to be the fun he had hoped. To make up for it, he bought me an extra shoofly pie, and on the way home we stopped at *Roadside America*, a huge model train set open to the public. For months afterwards, whenever I heard a door slam, it made me jump as it reminded me of poor Susanna falling to her death.

I had no way to articulate how I felt about this thing I had witnessed. I tried to draw a few pictures of it. Then I tried to write a narrative under my crayon drawings. That might have been the moment I started to be a writer.

---

[4] The one time my father splurged on himself was when he bought a 1966, maroon, Mustang hardtop. He even bought an aftermarket horn that made the sound of a horse neighing. Everyone in the neighbourhood was jealous, especially Uncle Billy.

[5] Sutter, Earnest, and Corrine. *The Hanging of Susanna Cox*: The True Story of Pennsylvania's Most Notorious Infanticide & the Legend That's Kept It Alive (Stackpole: 2010).

[6] The festival is still held, and they still do the hanging

On Being a Writer

In its simplest terms, a writer places words down on a surface in a certain order to communicate an idea. We associate this act with a profession. Even as I write these words, it seems strange to me to be calling myself a writer. Growing up, writers were almost mythical beings, even more so than Bigfoot. In fact, I would have been more surprised to meet a writer on the streets of the Ironbound or Kearny than a hairy anomalous primate. Writers existed in another dimension. I never knew anyone who knew anyone who knew anyone who was a writer. They appeared on talk shows on our little black and white TV. They sounded so very, very smart as they chatted with Dick Cavett, Mike Douglas or Johnny Carson. While I always wanted to be a globetrotting, adventuring, historian and writer, I saw myself more in the Tin Tin mode.[7] I did make small efforts to write stories early on, and my letters home, while I was in the service, were excuses for me to get creative. When I wrote to my parents or to Al or Mike or Carol, I did so as if I was writing a novel. Still, the job of writer seemed even more unobtainable than that of historian. Part of the reason I pursued a career as a commercial artist first of all was because that seemed an understandable way to make a living. You could draw things for publication. Henry understood this aspect. To my father, an 'artist' was a vaguely untrustworthy, bohemian type, sitting around in a loft making 'art' when the inspiration moved them, living off their parents. They were dreamers who rarely ever made a living. My father constantly instilled in me the importance of earning a living. I had to be able to take care of myself financially. No one was going to take care of me but me.[8] There was no family fortune to inherit. When I explained what a 'commercial' artist was to him, the penny dropped. To him it sounded a bit more like real work. I was raised to believe men used their hands to dig, or hammer, or fight, not create: certainly not write. They did real work. Hands were for making a tough living, for giving another guy a bloody nose. Showing him I could earn a living by producing art and selling it, helped ease his worry. He had greater difficulty in understanding how a writer would earn a living. I don't think he ever really understood my career as an historian, but he saw I was happy and had a job. That was all he asked for.

I had no one encouraging me to be a writer until I was an undergrad. Then I was really encouraged to be an historian, not necessarily a writer. In graduate school, in my mid-thirties, the closest I came to a compliment was from my graduate advisor, David Kohn, who once said, when looking over a part of my dissertation, "Some diamonds are rougher than others." I just wanted it that badly. In the early stages of my writing ambition, I had no one to encourage me to write, mostly because I had learned not to tell anyone about my plans to be a writer in the first place. My parents encouraged me in a general way, but we didn't talk about it. When Henry got me that little typewriter, his reason was that he thought it would help me with my school work, not that I had expressed any outward signs of wanting to be a writer.

To this day, despite a shelf full of books and articles, I still feel self-conscious about calling myself a writer. I've always felt more like an intellectual mechanic than a philosopher. I come from a community of men who were not Ferraris or sports cars. They were not sleek, fast, and stylish with blemish free surfaces. They were not meticulously maintained, kept in fancy garages and pampered. They were more like dumper trucks or half-tracks: meant for work, slow and plodding, covered in dents, with chipped paint, bullet ricochets and with

---

[7] Tin Tin is supposed to be a journalist. This was the excuse for him to do all his adventuring: he's tracking down a story. Despite being referred to as a journalist, in the entire run of the *Tin Tin* stories he never submits an article or has a story published. Eventually, Herge dropped any pretense of Tin Tin being a reporter.

[8] My father was not selfish. He would give me anything he had, and did. He just didn't have much in the way of money to give.

broken parts held together by wire and duct tape. They stayed parked out in the open, in the rain and the snow, the heat and the cold. Despite my hands being cracked and calloused and having a few scars like my dad and all the other men I knew growing up, it still seems an almost pompous thing to do. To say, "I'm a writer."

I was one however.

Everything about your life impacts upon the way you put those words down. Every incident, every person you've ever met, loved, hated or envied: they are all there. It is a common misconception that scholarly historical writing is devoid of personal input. Historians, we are told, collate and analyse facts alone in a dispassionate way. That's what my professors told me. The reality is that while we do indeed try to examine the past as accurately as possible, we are human like everyone else. Our feelings and attitudes get involved. Mine certainly always have. I saw Henry Fairfield Osborn as a pompous, self-important, conflicted old man who tried to do the right thing. I was annoyed by Grover Krantz. I felt bad for Daniel Leeds. It upset me that in the end Nellie Horsford turned out to be a bit of a bigot.

A student once said to me that I only write about "pathetic losers." I prefer the term "tragic," but the sentiment is the same. I have always been drawn to people who take on seemingly pointless endeavours, put huge amounts of energy into them, and then wind up never completing the things they set out to accomplish in the first place. To me these types of characters can teach us as much about the world as those who have been successful in what they were trying to do.

I have always had to work hard at writing. I still struggle, I am still unsure of what I'm doing. I still suffer from imposter syndrome. I have presented scholarly papers at Princeton, Oxford, Berlin, and dozens of other places around the world, and yet I still feel self-conscious while doing it. I imagine people sitting there, people with much more distinguished pedigrees than myself, who are wondering what the kid from Kearny is doing there.

"How did he sneak in?"
"Someone get him off the stage!"

In order for me to take on a writing project, I always have to find some personal hook to start. The subject has to appeal to me, and I need to be able to identify with it in some way. I don't have to like the people or events involved, but I have to have some kind of affinity with them. I have always preferred the structure of a biography. I think people relate more to stories of other people rather than to abstract ideas.

When I write, placing words on a piece of paper is neither the beginning nor the end. It's actually more of a middle stage. I begin by reading and thinking, then thinking and reading. Writing requires a lot of sitting around. Thinking is just as important as researching. I write my notes in longhand on yellow legal pads. That way, I can cross out stuff, make notes and think about the words. I tend to scribble notes as I think of them. I do this on pads or scraps or placemats or anything handy I can write on. My desk is often covered in little bits of paper I've made notes on. I treat the words like sculpting material. Once written down, I can look at them, rearrange them, add to or eliminate them. I constantly rewrite. I am forever reworking ways to make the words clearer or more explanatory. It's like reworking a pencil drawing. You add, erase, and change until you get what you're looking for. I have an image in my head of what I want, but getting that onto paper isn't always straightforward. It takes work and perseverance. This isn't mathematical, despite what Leopold Von Ranke said. History is not done like an engineering equation. Beyond the need to follow the Chicago Manual of Style and do the citations and bibliography correctly, the writing of history is a creative endeavour. We must base our work on facts and evidence in the form of primary sources, but the way we arrange those facts and analyse that evidence is the creative part. As a result, I work and rework my words. If it doesn't feel like it's working out, I rip it up and start again.

A student once asked me why I write? I replied in all seriousness, that I did it because it's impossible for me not to. All my life, I have felt a compulsion to put down ideas I've had in my head: either by drawing pictures, writing words, or trying to express things through adventuring.[9] When students come to me and say they want to be historians I always ask them, "Is this something you have to do?" What I mean is not that you have to do it because you need a job, but because you can't imagine being alive unless you do: that you have an inner compulsion, a crazy, stupid, unexplainable need to do it. Sometimes, this compulsion amounts almost to a pathology that psychologists call hypergraphia. For me, the act of writing involves where I do the writing. The setting is as important to me as the ideas. In addition to the libraries listed above, I have written large proportions of my books, including this one, at a number of pubs around the world including: *The Grasshopper* in Morristown, *The Harp* in Metuchen and *Suspenders* in Union - all of which are in New Jersey; in Oxford, England at *The Turf, The White Horse, The Eagle and Child*, and *The Kings Arms*; in Providence, Rhode Island at *Harry's* (one of the few places in the US, outside of New York, to have Old Speckled Hen on tap) and in New York at *The Shakespeare, The Playwright's Pub*, and *The White Oak*, amongst others.

While I'm thinking in my contemplative mode, I will listen to music. I go for tunes that are inspiring me while I'm in the moment. There is no rhyme or reason as to what I listen to. Sometimes rock-n-roll, sometimes classical (never Country & Western - that does nothing for me). It helps me form images. I don't think in words, I think in images. Sometimes I'll go driving, nowhere in particular, just driving. It helps clear my head. I've always done my best work with a clear head. History writing is a creative act not a mechanical one. Suddenly, I'll drop out of the contemplative mode and enter the productive mode. I'll start writing feverishly. The next thing I know is that I've written several pages. Then the editing begins. Sometimes when you write, other people read it. Sometimes they like it and sometimes they don't.

Monsters on TV

Until *Searching for Sasquatch* came out, the only media appearances I had made were with Janeane Garofalo in 2005 and then *The Naked Scientist* podcast out of the UK in 2008. Then things got a little weird. For the 2009 Darwin Day-Palooza for the anniversary of *On The Origin of Species,* I came up with what I thought was a novel, but light-hearted, approach to evolution. For that year's BSHS meeting, I sent in a proposal arguing that the process of natural selection, as a way of understanding the world, undermined and ultimately led to the disappearance, or at least the lessening of belief in, mythical creatures such as werewolves in favour of the belief in Bigfoot. Rather than expecting people to take this too seriously, I meant for it to be a creative and tongue-in-cheek idea. To my delight, the BSHS accepted my paper.

---

[9] Not through poetry though, I just don't have the skills.

At the time, the evolutionary ecologist turned journalist, Henry Nicholls, was acting as public relations man for the society. He sent out a press release announcing the conference and listing a few of the more interesting papers. He had included a reference to mine. The next thing I knew, *USA TODAY* contacted me about it. They ran a short article on my work in June of 2009. Then *SCIENCE* ran a blurb and it wasn't long before articles on my little funny idea appeared in German, Italian, French, and Polish. The attention was odd but amusing. It certainly did wonders for my promotion application at Kean. It also prompted Blake Smith to invite me to be a guest on his new podcast, *Monster Talk*.[10] What followed was a run of media appearances on podcasts, radio shows—including one in Ireland—and publications as wide-ranging as the *Times of India, Wired, The Guardian*, and *The Wall Street Journal*.

All this led, in turn, to what was probably my most unusual media appearance. In 2011, I was approached by the television game show series, *Who Wants to be a Millionaire?* They had seen my work and created a question based upon it for their show. They told me what they were doing and wanted to make sure they had phrased it correctly. They said they couldn't tell me when it would be used, since the way the show worked depended on compiling each contestant's set of questions from a large pool of questions that were picked randomly. Time went by and I forgot all about it. Then in class one day in April 2012, a student came in somewhat excited. "Did you know you were on TV yesterday?" she asked. I assumed it was a rerun of the series I had appeared in for the Science Channel. "No," she said, "*Who wants to Be a Millionaire?*" The question posed was:

"According to historian Brian Regal of Kean University, the spread of the evolutionary theory of Charles Darwin led to a decrease in the belief in which mythical creatures, A. Fairies, B. Werewolves, or C. Ghosts?"

My happy surprise at the silliness of it all was tempered by the fact that the contestant who drew the question decided to pass on it. I had been so close to stardom!

After the Sasquatch book was released, I began getting more interest from media sources. My first introduction to the area, commonly referred to as 'cryptozoology', came as it did for many people of my generation, through the Leonard Nimoy hosted series, *In Search of*. Originally airing in 1977, the programme approached a number of paranormal and 'mystery' related topics such as Easter Island, the disappearance of Emilia Earhart, Atlantis and monsters. The series producer was Alan Landsburg (1933-2014) who achieved fame as the creator of various documentary films about similar topics, including the highly regarded series *Biography*. This series took its material seriously and explained the phenomenon and the different schools of thought concerning its validity. They talked with the people involved and didn't talk down to the audience. I first saw Grover Krantz on this series. It was also the first time I ever saw the Paterson Film.

By the 1980s, the success of *In Search of* and others spawned more such series as TV networks saw there was an audience for history and science related material. By the end of the 80s, however, reality TV had arrived. This was, in part, fueled by the TV writer's strike. Producers of programmes saw they could make an entire TV series by employing would-be actors who were willing to be locked in a house with others so they could fight and argue with each other and behave like children. The producers now had no need for writers to create content: just leave some people together and they would act out on their own. They saw that with a relatively small outlay of money, a reality TV series could generate large profits. It wasn't long before this approach was applied to paranormal subjects. Shows such as *Ghost*

---

[10] It was the Halloween show, October 29, 2009. I went on to do his show several more times.

Hunters and *Finding Bigfoot* had groups of clueless enthusiasts running around trying to solve mysteries.

Not every cryptozoological TV series was quite so shamelessly sensational. It wasn't long after my *Searching for Sasquatch* book came out that I started getting approached by TV producers. At least two or three times a year I'd get a call. They usually went like this:

"Oh, man, we loved your book! You'd look great on camera!"

To which I'd reply, "well, okay that sounds fine, but I don't want to be made to look like a fool."

"Oh, no way, we totally understand. This will all be done respectfully. You'll make good money and your profile will be transformed!"

"Great, but I will not wear night vision goggles and wander around the woods at night."

"Uh, okay, we'll get back to you."

And they never would. As soon as they heard I refused to act like a buffoon like the protagonists of paranormal shows, they were no longer interested. The problem with television and anything even vaguely cryptozoological or paranormal is that the most important thing producers want is a spectacle. They tend to dismiss actual recorded history in favour of the sensational. They feel that the only way people will watch is if you have 'investigators' stumbling around in the dark with night vision goggles yelping, "What the hell was that!" every time they hear a twig snap. On each occasion I was asked to do a show, I'd say I was interested, but I would not wear night vision goggles while I stumbled around the woods in the dark. That was usually enough to end the conversation.

There was a major disconnect between television producers and the people who genuinely knew the most about the odd and eccentric topics they wanted to make shows about. By the twenty-teens, there were many younger, traditionally-trained, academics who were interested in the history of the paranormal, as well as a growing coterie of archaeologists willing to buck the nonsense being spread about ancient cultures by charlatan authors and TV personalities. The problem arose from the academics wanting to do actual history, philosophy, and archaeology, against the insistence of the TV producers wanting to do what the scholars rightly considered nonsense. It was all too easy for the untrained, speculative writers such as Eric Von Daniken or Graham Hancock, neither of whom have any academic credentials, to attack scholars as stodgy supporters of the status quo, who hide the 'real' evidence of alien visitation or ancient lost cultures. It is deeply frustrating to people who know the actual history of the world, to see this unproven, speculative, material being foisted upon the public when we know so much of how the world really works, and how much more fascinating and exciting actual history is. In 2020, I was approached by the CW network to be a guest in a documentary talking about werewolves. Plans were made and dates set. Then...nothing. It reminded me that I once went all the way to the Bodleian Library in Oxford to look at an original seventeenth century book on werewolves.

Not Knowing How to Talk to People

As any educator will tell you, teaching is about more than just communicating content knowledge. You often wind up becoming a social worker, guidance counsellor, advisor, and even a parent. Sometimes it's easy, and sometimes not so. There have been times when students came to me for emotional help as well. I left TCI for that reason: I had no idea how to help some of them. Their problems were far beyond my abilities to assist. You want to solve all their problems, but that's impossible. My great inability has always been not knowing how to talk to some people, not knowing the answers to their problems. My father always seemed to know what to do or say. I never seemed to know.

You begin to realise that some of your students see you as much more than just an instructor. You can profoundly affect their lives for both good and ill.[11] At times, even the older, more 'mature' students can see you in that light. I've had students who were combat vets from Afghanistan and Iraq. They were looking for someone to help them deal with university life and work. They came to me because I had served as well, but my service—at its worst—was nothing compared to theirs. How could I help them? How could I do that? I would always be as professional as I could, and try to help them, knowing I could never really help them the way they needed. I'd be able to understand, lend a sympathetic ear and guide them to the professionals who were trained for such things and who could do a better job. Then I'd go into my office and hate with a burning fire towards the ones who sent them off on these fools' errands in the Middle East. It's like seeing someone in a lake drowning. You throw them the lifebuoy, but you can't throw it far enough. All you can do is hope they can grab a hold of it. I hated myself for not being able to help them more. In the end all I could do was stand on the corner and watch.

I have not slept well since the turn of the century. I have rarely slept an entire night. I have been constantly awakened by weird, depressing dreams, restlessness, and physical insomnia. I can get up and go down to the kitchen and have a bowl of cereal or plop down like a broken robot on the couch and stare at the TV until I finally fall asleep. What makes the experience worse is that I will usually begin to fall asleep around nine at night. I will become completely sleepy. It is all some kind of cosmic tease. Each night I think that I'll sleep well. Then I will nod off, but after three or four hours I will be wide awake again. The anxiety can be terrible. It makes me think there must be something wrong with me. Maybe I have a condition, in addition to my dyslexia, that no one has noticed.

Alice

Sometimes, people come into our lives out of nowhere. Maybe it's a kind of cosmic blender or one of those spreaders on the back of a DPW truck throwing salt into the wind. That's how Alice came into my life. I met her one night when her parents, Frank and Debbie, invited Lisa and I to have dinner with them at their club. I always liked the idea of "having dinner at the club" so I was sort of excited. Lisa had recently met Frank Wyman when they began as grad student colleagues at Drew University. Consequently, I met Frank. He was a former corporate lawyer who decided to leave the law to study history. I've always liked Frank. He was a bit quirky, but he was incredibly intelligent and had a dry sense of humour, which appealed to me. His wife, Debbie, was very likeable also and full of positive, frantic energy. She was one of those people who appears to be heading in five different directions simultaneously. Her energy was invigorating. She could walk into a room full of strangers and

---

[11] In 2004 I first began to realize I couldn't or at least shouldn't tell my silly little army service stories in class anymore. At TCI there was a kid in my US II course. He was a recent immigrant from Russia. He may have been a Kazakh. He was intensely handsome. He should have had a career as a fashion model. He came up to me one day towards the end of the school year all excited. He couldn't wait to tell me. He had just enlisted in the US Army, in the armored cavalry. When I asked him why the hell he had done it, he said it was because of me. "Those stories you told in class were so exciting! I want to be a good American so I joined." In the way my father did to me when I was seventeen, I tried to talk him out of it, but there was no arguing. I later found out they sent him to Iraq where he was killed.

come out knowing all of them and having all their phone numbers with plans to meet. The Wymans were one of the few couples I could stand to spend any length of time with. They were low maintenance and always bubbling with ideas and stories. They even taught Lisa and me to play Mahjong. Therefore, the prospect of having dinner with them at their country club was just fine.

We arrived at the club, and the Wyman's were already seated at a table. As we joined them, I saw a young lady sitting there with her eyes just peering over the edge of the Harry Potter book she was reading. Frank said to me, "this is our daughter, Alice" (Lisa had already met Alice on the Drew campus when she accompanied her dad there one day). Our eyes met. I said hello, and she said hello back. She was thirteen. I smiled and she gave me the most endearing little smile back, although I think she thought I couldn't see because of her book. It was all over. It sounds a bit overly grandiose, but in that cosmic instant a connection was made that, to this day, I can't really explain. When Lisa and I bought the house on Webster Place the Wymans were the first people we invited over, after my parents. Alice immediately surveyed our book collection on the first floor, then headed upstairs to my office to peruse my artefact collection. After a little while, she came bounding back down the stairs just as I was coming out of the kitchen, and practically threw herself into my arms. "Would you be my Godfather?" she blurted out. Lisa then came out behind me and Alice immediately and just as enthusiastically, asked her, "Would you be my Godmother?" How could we say no?

Of all the people who appear in this autobiography, Alice is the most problematic for me to write about. It was genuinely difficult for me to find the right place to put her in this story. She occupies an oddly intimate spot in my life. I have somehow managed to turn her into both a daughter and a girlfriend. The only person in the world who means more to me than Alice is Lisa. Over the years, Alice and I have told each other things and shared emotional issues we have never told anyone else about. I have never really been sure how to handle her emotionally. Though I never saw this in her (and I have told her this), she and her parents were convinced she was mildly autistic. Alice has the ability to be simultaneously filled with self-doubt, and able to see things others can't.

After graduating from Drew with a degree in psychology, Alice spent several summers travelling the world, largely by herself. She was intelligent, capable, and full of energy, but couldn't quite figure out what she wanted to do with her life. We were once having lunch in a pub and, during a lull in the conversation we were having about the various points on the 'autism spectrum' about which I was sceptical, she put her hand on mine and said, "You know, you're on that spectrum, too." I looked at her and said, "Uh, what?" She smiled, "It's okay, I know how to see these things." She then proceeded to explain and point out a number of my behaviours that I'd never even thought about. It actually made sense—my inability to know how to behave in certain situations, my aloofness with others, my ability to totally disconnect myself from those around me—and she explained something about myself that I had never understood; my never knowing how to talk to people. Her apartment was full of Manga and action figures, and comic books.

At that same lunch that was at a place called 'Spirit' (which unfortunately went out of business during the Covid lockdown), I ordered the Caesar salad with chicken. They made a really good one. This was during a period when there had been a bit of a scare about leafy greens being contaminated, especially romaine lettuce, and many restaurants were not serving it. When I asked for the Caesar salad, the waitress said that since they didn't have the romaine, was it okay to make it with iceberg lettuce? I said yes, then quipped, "Ah, the fall of the

Romaine Empire!" The waitress didn't get it, but Alice gave me the slow head-turn and said, "Why aren't you on TV more?"

A Fully-Fledged Scholar

It dawned on me one day that I had finally achieved the goal of becoming a professional writer and historian. I had finally made it. I had a tenured position as an academic at a major state university, as tenuous as it was. All those dreams and fantasies had come true and I hadn't even noticed it happening. In the United States, it is common that a resident faculty member is eligible for tenure after five years of service.[12] Every year you have to submit a portfolio of your work and accomplishments. For the first four years this was to justify 'reappointment.' The department's promotion committee looks at it first. They then recommend it to the university's promotion committee. The university committee looks at your portfolio then decides if you should be kept on for another year. The fifth time you go for tenure, the department committee recommends you to the university committee who then recommends you to the university Provost who recommends it to the university President who finally recommends it to the university Board of Trustees. I received tenure in 2012. In every college and university in America, when a faculty member achieves tenure, they are automatically promoted from Assistant to Associate Professor. The idea is, if you deserve tenure, you deserve promotion. Kean University, however, was different. We had Dawood Farahi as president. He had separated out tenure from promotion so you had to apply separately for it. Very few, if any, were promoted as they received tenure. Chris Bellitto was promoted the year after he achieved tenure. He deserved it, and he was well received by the president. I applied for promotion every year after I received tenure. Every year I was denied. In fact, virtually everyone who applied was turned down. The president had decided to only promote one or two people a year rather than everyone who was eligible. It was his way of controlling a faculty he did not trust. It was one more thing that generated resentment for the administration within the faculty. Every person who applied for promotion, regardless of their department, was more than qualified for the step up in rank. Adding to the frustration, the administration was vague about what accomplishments had to be attained to rate promotion. Personally, I was growing increasingly disaffected. How many more television shows, how many more books and articles did I have to have published to warrant a promotion? How many more times did I need to be invited to speak at Oxford to prove I had an international reputation?

I know several excellent faculty members—not only in history—who simply gave up and stopped applying for promotion. They thought it was a waste of time. I refused to give up. My feeling was, at this point, that I no longer needed to prove why I should be promoted, the administration needed to prove why I didn't deserve it. I was going to shove my one-foot thick portfolio into their faces each and every year. They were going to have to look at this and continue to say I didn't deserve to be promoted. Finally, in 2016, I was promoted to Associate Professor. Many in the department were also finally promoted, as they should have been years before. I was happy, but still annoyed that it took so long. I was annoyed that the administration took such an adversarial attitude to the faculty: the thing that the entire university hung on.

By 2020, I had spoken at conferences around the world. I had spoken as part of

---

[12] Depending on the school it can be anywhere from five to eight years.

panels and as an invited one-off guest. I had appeared in several television programs and had a shelf-full of published books and articles, both scholarly and popular. People asked me to be on radio programmes and podcasts. I had written countless Op Ed pieces (I was even an invited speaker at the 2018 New York Comic Con). Then one day, I received an email from a grad student at the University of California at Berkeley. They were working on a project about monsters and pop culture and wanted to ask me a couple of questions. "I am writing to you," the email began, "because you are one of the world's leading scholars on the history of monstrosity." I had to read that several times. "...world's leading scholars". Were they writing to the right person? In 2019, I submitted a paper to the New England Historical Association Fall conference in Rhode Island. After having received confirmation that my paper was accepted, I received an email from a young Brown University historian who was going to chair the panel. He had seen my name in the papers accepted list, and then browbeaten the committee into letting him chair the panel that I was to be part of. He was a fan of my work. "When I saw your name," he said, "I knew I wanted to meet you and be part of your panel!"

It seemed something had happened, over the course of the previous twenty years, that I hadn't noticed. I was so focused on creating a career I didn't realise that I had already done so. I guess I was now this person: the person I had dreamt of becoming sitting on the living room rug watching Jonny Quest. I didn't feel like a respected senior scholar, though. I still felt like a kid from the Ironbound, that everyone said was stupid. I still felt like I was hiding my 'hobby' of researching the past and writing stories that I hid in my drawer so that no one would see them and laugh at me. I had somehow become this character. How was that even possible? It's easy to deal with fantasies when you think you'll never actually live them. The more desperate we are to achieve something, the more painful it is when we don't achieve it. For all those years, it was easy to live with my fantasy of becoming a university professor. I accepted deep down inside, I would never actually attain it. It relieved a huge amount of pressure. That way I could never fail at it. I could enjoy it without the risk. I no longer had that safety margin. I had become Jonny Quest. The guys in the frog suits were now looking at me.

There was a problem. It hit me one day that I didn't know what I stood for. It's relatively easy to determine what the people I write about stand for. I could wend my way through the corridors of their lives and work out their philosophies, their loves, their hates, and their inner demons. When it came to myself, it was not so easy. What was my purpose? I was so busy trying to create this career that I'd never considered why I did it. Besides wanting to go on adventures, get away from everything I knew, and wanting to be a writer and an historian, I had no idea what the purpose of my career was. Was just doing something that made me happy enough of a purpose? Becoming an historian was everything I ever wanted, everything I never had. I had been going along all the while on adrenaline and putting on a brave face.

I was in China somewhere when I realised I wasn't as brave as I thought I was

That the monsters might be winning
I'm not sure how it happened
It hit me suddenly standing on a busy street corner in Wenzhou
A lot of stuff came back to me at the same time
Stuff I thought I had put away long time ago
Then my mother died.

It was a combination of things that did it. I had been taught from the beginning that I was supposed to be brave and honest and true. I tried to act that way, but I had my doubts. I finally understood that what may have looked to others like strength or confidence was all a show, all a bluff, a façade. It was all a manifestation of a deeply held fear of everything I had developed in childhood that I thought I had overcome, but I hadn't. I have let so many people down over the years, by not being what they needed me to be even when I tried. I reacted to my failure by moving forward to get away from them, and leaving them behind. It wasn't very nice, but it was the only way I knew how to survive. I guess that's why I've always preferred to be alone. If I was alone, no one would count on me or expect me to be there to save the day I couldn't save anyway. There was one last thing that clinched it.

Saying Goodbye to Betty

In October of 2017, my mother Elizabeth had been living with us for a year. Lisa had been incredibly accepting of this when she really didn't need to be, and did her best to help me deal with the situation. Betty didn't try to be difficult, but her deteriorating body and mind had other ideas. To be as comfortable as possible, we set her up in the small TV room on the ground floor. On the wall, I hung a painting I had done years before, of my dad as explorer Roy Chapman Andrews. The day she moved in, she asked me to put channel seven on the TV for her. This was the local New York, ABC station. I did, and for the next year she never changed it. I tried to get her to watch other channels, but she steadfastly refused. The TV was on 24 hours a day. She would just sit there and watch. I would get up at 5am and make her breakfast, then get Lisa to wake up, so I could get myself ready for the day. The nice thing about the room was it had a large picture window that looked out over our garden. As time went by, her condition deteriorated. Once, I took her to physical therapy but, despite working with a lovely and understanding young physical therapist, it didn't go well. Betty didn't like it and so we never went again.

Sometimes, she would slide off the couch—she refused to sleep in a regular bed so Lisa bought her an embroidered divan to sit and sleep on—and wind up on her back on the floor. Instead of using her energy to push herself back up onto the couch, she would push herself randomly around the floor, out into the hall and sometimes even into the kitchen. Once when we came home we found she had wedged herself between the wall and the toilet of the half bath off the kitchen. We brought in state health advisors and they gave her a series of tests to see how her cognitive abilities were. They asked her to draw a clock with the right time. She could barely draw a circle. They asked her some other questions like, where are you, who is this, and others. As I sat there watching I kept telling myself it was not an adequate test or, she can't draw so of course she couldn't do the clock thing. They were all just lies, I told myself, to try to keep from the realisation that she was suffering from dementia and it was getting worse rapidly, and that there was nothing I could do about it.

Not only could she not draw the time, she lost the ability to tell the time. She thought three in the morning was three in the afternoon. When she called, I could always tell what was wrong. If she called out, "Bri?" I knew she wanted something. If she called out, "Brian!" I knew she was in trouble.[13] Finally, in October of 2018, she had made herself so dehydrated—despite our best efforts to get her to drink water and eat properly—she could no longer control her limbs or stand up. An ambulance took her to Overlook Hospital. The doctor and attending

---

[13] For years after her death, I'd suddenly snap awake at three in the morning having heard her call out, "Brian!" I knew it was in my head, but it still woke me up in a panic thinking she had fallen. Then I'd realize it was a hallucination.

nurse said she needed to be institutionalised. I felt such relief, then guilt at my relief. She went from the hospital directly to an elder care home. I visited her every other day, but each time she looked worse. We had already filled-out all sorts of paperwork in preparation for this, stating that she did not want to be forced to eat or fed intravenously. Back when she was still coherent, we talked about what to do and she was adamant. She went downhill with astonishing speed. In those days in the nursing home I could see her drifting away just as my Godmother Marion had, just as Aunt Wanda had. At one point, when I sat with her in the nursing home day-room during a visit, it suddenly struck me that she had no idea who I was. She was on the little ship of dreams, and she wouldn't be back for a while. It only took a week from when she entered the nursing home.[14]

It was a very nice early fall day in October when I went to see her. The nursing home was in Cranford on my usual drive to and from Kean. I went in and she was asleep in bed. I placed the little holiday pack of shortbread cookies down on the table next to her. All my adult life she would tell me how much my dad loved shortbread cookies so I, and then Lisa, would get them for 'him'. In classic Betty style, it turned out my father never liked shortbread cookies at all, she did. She couldn't simply say, "I like shortbread cookies, can you get me some shortbread cookies please?" She could never tell you anything directly. If you asked her the time of day she would launch into a story about how when she was a kid there was a clock in the town hall.

Two days before, when I had visited, she was sitting in a wheelchair in the activities room with other people. Now she was in bed. I pulled over a chair and sat looking at her. She looked dead. Her skin was a pallid yellow and she didn't move. "Ma…" I said quietly. She didn't respond. She must be dead, I thought. Then she did move ever so slightly. She was still alive, but very close to the end. When Henry went the family was there. Now, it was just me.

My mother had been slowly suffering from dementia for some time, although I really didn't notice. In 2016, her niece, Maureen, died suddenly. Betty and Maureen had been very close. Maureen, who was Marion's daughter, was always happy to take her to dinner or to the movies or out shopping. Her death hit my mother harder than we realised at the time. She could no longer be left alone. I received several calls from neighbours in Kearny saying they had just found Betty walking around the neighbourhood. They helped her get home. One time a neighbour smelled gas. Betty had left the oven on. I concluded the only course open to me was to move her in with us. We had to arrange for a health care worker, but I could only afford to have them come three times a week to look after her while Lisa and I were at work. It was a rough year as her behaviour became increasingly erratic: saying she saw people outside the window, putting her pants on over her head, and cutting her clothes "so they would fit better." She began to refer to Lisa, whom she had known for over thirty years, as "the lady who lives upstairs." Several times, she referred to me as her husband rather than her son to health care workers who just smiled knowingly. I never knew, once we went out, what we would return to find. She would either be sitting normally watching TV, or on the floor wedged against the toilet, or she'd be dead. Those were the three possibilities I faced.

Looking at her in the nursing home bed, I didn't know what to say or do. My head

---

[14] After she died, I cleaned out the TV room. I found a pile of the vitamins and medications we had been trying to get her to take under the couch. There were medications and vitamins in all the pots of the plants that were in the room. She had also hidden little packets of food around the room and behind books, "in case something happened."

was like a rock. It didn't work, it didn't think, it was just there. I wanted to do something profound, something magical, something I could remember fondly and say, "well, I did this." But, there was nothing. I've never really known what to say or do in any number of emotional situations. People have always interpreted that as disinterest or dismissiveness, and hated me for it. Staring at my mother in a nursing home bed, I started to get that uncomfortable feeling once more. That primordial desire to flee that I have always been afflicted with. I stood up to go. I couldn't stand the idea of her dying right in front of me. I'd had enough of that with Henry. I was about to turn to leave when I said to her, "It's okay Ma, it's going to be alright. You'll see Henry soon." I turned and walked out of the room into the main visiting area. Heading down the hallway, I walked faster and faster as I neared the main entrance. I had been reduced to my core self, a lonely ten-year-old with no one to turn to. All those years as a kid that I thought I had erased or at least put somewhere, came crashing back down on me as if they had never left. I didn't even have the *Alvis Stalwart* to save me as, ironically, Betty had been the one who had thrown it away years ago. I walked quickly down the hall towards the exit. I passed all those sad, lonely, bewildered old people there in that place: some were in beds, some were in wheelchairs, some were already wandering ghosts who hadn't realised it yet. Some were just standing there, lost and alone, slowly disappearing. All of them were waiting to die like Betty. Part of me wanted to go back and wait until the end. A real, considerate son would have done that. "You were a soldier! You stared down the Commies on the Iron Curtain! You could go back and sit next to your mother as she died." But, I couldn't. I will hate myself forever because of my cowardice at that moment.

I didn't go back and hold her hand. I left her to die alone with no one she knew around her. In fact, no one at all around her. I left her as alone as I had left myself. Hating myself, but still unable to go back. I wanted to go outside and bash my head against a tree. To bash it until there was nothing left to bash. When I arrived home wondering what I would tell Lisa, the phone rang. It was the nursing home. "Dr. Regal, your mother has passed." My response? "Uh, okay, thanks. Is there any paperwork I need to fill out?"

I called a local funeral home and made arrangements to have Betty cremated. We had agreed that was the way to go. We had cremated Henry and his urn rested in our living room next to the fireplace. Mr. Dooley, the undertaker, was professional and compassionate without being cloying. A lifetime career in a family business had given him this power. He wasn't pushy in the way I expected when I called. He gave us exactly what we wanted (and could afford) and Lisa and I were satisfied. We then went to the funeral home office and paid for everything. The walls had framed historic black and white photos of the Dooley family business back to the nineteenth century. It was all relatively easy and painless. I handed him my credit card and it was done. I wouldn't have to do a thing, not lift a finger. They picked up her body later that day and brought it to the funeral home for preparation.

We went back the next day. After finishing the paperwork I asked Mr. Dooley if we could see her one last time. I hadn't thought of this until that very moment. He said yes, and to just give him a minute. He then led us down some carpeted stairs into a small viewing room in the basement—I had secretly wished he would lead us into the operating room so I could see what it looked like. The space had a living room-like feel designed to suggest warmth and family. A place we all remember or at least wanted to remember as 'home.' Weirdly, it did look just like the living room of that crappy tenement I grew up in. If there had been a painting of a toreador on the wall I might have begun to freak out. It had the soft hush of a finished basement recreation room. It was not a formal viewing, it was just a stupid kid whose mom had died suddenly, and who had snuck into the funeral home to see her one last time. The funeral director was a decent sort, so he let me see the body. There she was on a gurney with a white shroud tastefully covering her so only her face was shown. Lisa stayed a moment then quietly left. As did Mr. Dooley.

I noticed how unreal she looked. She was pretty much in the same state I saw her in the morning before when I visited her, but she was asleep or comatose or something and she didn't respond when I sat there and told her everything would be okay and that we loved her. Now she had a waxwork look to her. Her right eye was closed, but her left eye was just slightly open. She seemed smaller than usual. I wondered if she had felt her life was worthwhile. She had told me many times, in her own awkward way, that she was proud of me. She wasn't a bad person, or at least no more or less than anyone else. Her life had made her who she was. I've known plenty of worse people. She had always supported me, as did Henry. She had her little pleasures like watching the Yankees, and eating cheese and drinking wine. Not great indulgences by most standards, but they were hers. In the end she did not rage against the dying of the light, she embraced the darkness. She was ready to go and she went. And that was that.

With a few exceptions, everyone she knew was already gone, all her family, all her friends. She had no monuments, no great achievements, not even a footnote mention. I satisfied myself with the idea that she was now in heaven with Henry and Sherman and God, and whoever else was wherever she had gone: if she had gone anywhere. I didn't believe any of that, but she did, so if it made her happy for me to even fake belief, then I would.

Then of course I thought about myself, even in that moment, I thought about myself. Why was I not distraught? I was sad, but not overwhelmed. The emotion I felt most strongly was relief. I thought with genuine relief that there was not going to be a funeral. I had such bad experiences with my family as a kid at family functions like birthdays, and christenings, and funerals that I was enormously relieved I wouldn't have to go to one for Betty. I left my father's memorial as soon as I possibly could, I practically ran out the door just to get away. All I ever wanted to do with my family—well, okay with everyone I ever spent time with except Lisa—was get away. To run away and go somewhere else, even from my dead father's funeral. Now with Betty gone I could enjoy the selfish exhilaration of being set free from any more family obligations. Here in the basement living room of Dooley's Funeral Home I didn't have quite that need to flee, but I didn't, however, know what to think. Was I a horrible person? Had I become some kind of monster? What do you say to the corpse of your mother? You're supposed to do something; you're supposed to say something profound. I had nothing, nothing. Mr. Professor with the shelf full of books and articles, who spoke to public crowds for a living, had nothing. I felt ashamed as I always did. Did I do enough for her? She always did things for me. My parents had given me everything they had, I had given them very little in return. I touched her shoulder and quietly said "I love you." At the last second, I touched her foot through the shroud then I left, walking back up the carpeted stairs leaving that quiet room hoping not to show any emotion in front of Mr. Dooley and Lisa. I would never see my crazy mother again. Out in the car the first thing I said to Lisa was, "well, where shall we go to eat?" It was raining lightly. A few days later, I picked up her ashes and put them next to Henry in the living room.

Conclusion

I've never been afraid of dying. My fear is that I'll outlive everyone. Left like some relic on the back of a shelf in an obscure museum, or an old book in a library that no one reads, or an overgrown statue like the ones in St. Cecelia's hidden garden. I have to admit that, being able to walk anonymously down a street knowing that no one cares who I am or who even cares about me, does have its appeal. High school taught me what it was like to be invisible. Not having to "be somewhere" at a certain time or having a scheduled meeting with someone, beholden to no one, may be the best part of the entire growing old scenario. Total anonymity is both frightening and appealing. When I first thought of writing this autobiography, a part of me asked, "Why would you do this? Why would you want anyone to remember you or your deeds and adventures?" It is, I think, the great conundrum afflicting people like me: we want to be forgotten, but we also want to be remembered.

One of the things proven correct in my life is that no matter how much you anticipate something, no matter how well you think you've figured out what's going to happen next, it's never what you thought. After eight years of the Barack Obama administration, many thought we might be on the verge of a new golden age: a period in American history full of hope and possibilities. Sure, there was still racism and inequality and sexism in America. The world was still tainted by terrorism. Dictators still concocted their horrible deeds, but there seemed a chance to make it right.

Then the monsters really came along.

Chapter 10

Dangerous in the Days of the Coronavirus

Life, which you look for, you will never find. For when the gods created man, they let
death be his share, and life withheld in their own hands.

– The Epic of Gilgamesh

In 2008, a black man named Barack Obama, was elected President of the United
States. It seemed to usher in a new era of optimism, peace, and prosperity in America. On the
night of the election, Alice, who was then a student at Drew University, telephoned us late to
tell us how excited she and all her classmates were that he had won. While Obama certainly
was not, nor could ever be, the saviour some had hoped for, he ran his administration on an
upbeat, serious and inclusive note. He understood what the office of President was all about.
He understood the leadership role it carried. He understood it wasn't about him, he knew he
was president of all of the people of the United States, not just those people who had voted for
him. He set to work reducing the huge war deficit George Bush had created with his disastrous
adventure in Afghanistan and Iraq. He began programs that cut the high unemployment rate in
half. He put through a health care program, commonly called Obamacare, which while it too
was not perfect, did make health insurance available to millions of Americans who had none
before. When some tragedy occurred, like a school shooting, he was there on the spot,
comforting the victims. There are rolls and rolls of video tape showing him with victims. You
could see his grief was as genuine as the people he consoled.

Then came the election of 2016.

Having grown up in New Jersey and New York, I and many others, knew Donald
Trump was a pathetic joke: a pathological liar, racist, adulterer, accused sex pervert, con artist,
narcissist, incompetent negotiator and a poor businessman. He was a buffoon not to be taken
seriously. As such, people here saw his campaign in the same way they saw him: as a joke.
The optimism generated by Barack Obama had come back to Hillary Clinton. She was seen as
the person who would continue the Obama age of growth and prosperity. Young women in
particular, found inspiration in someone who seemed like she was about to become the first
female American President. When Lisa and I went to vote at the local school, we saw crowds
of people excitedly voting for Clinton. Parents brought their children into the voting booths so
they could say they were there. An air of excitement pervaded the experience. People were
laughing and joking. It was clearly another historic occasion for progress and decency.

By that evening, however, that optimism had turned brutally to a sense of foreboding
and outright fear. We left the TV on with the returns, as we fell asleep. I woke up to a terrible
anxiety attack. All evening the reports were coming in that despite the popular vote going to
Clinton, Trump had garnered the Electoral College. When I saw that Pennsylvania had gone
for him, I knew it was all over.

Trumpism

It is often said that bad people have good in them and good people have bad in them:

that no one is ever really all of one or all of the other: that few people were genuine monsters. Donald Trump showed this was not a hard and fast rule. He had no redeeming qualities. None that I ever saw. He was petty, cruel, vindictive, and narcissistic to the point of absurdity. He was clearly incompetent, and enjoyed hurting people. He especially enjoyed hurting poor people, the sick, and the suffering. In classic bully style, while he enjoyed kicking people when they were down, he was too cowardly to attack the wealthy and the powerful. He loved dictators, he gravitated towards them, admired them, and wanted to emulate them.[1] Every decision he made hurt the American people. In his entire Presidency, not a single thing he did benefited the country, only the super wealthy, his shadowy benefactors, and of course, himself first and foremost. He had no idea what the role of President meant. He acted the entire time as a petulant eight year old. He could give Nero, Stalin or Hitler a run for their money. Those who voted for him, did it less because they thought he would be a superior president, but more because his behaviour unleashed their own secret and not so secret monsters. A wave of amateur politicians were swept in along with him. These individuals rejected the notion that the primary job of an elected official was to look after the well-being of their constituents: to pass laws and legislation that benefits the people. Instead they saw their jobs as attacking those they didn't like, and exacting revenge on their opponents, while of course, filling their own pockets with loot. They voted for Trump as a symbol of their hatred and fear rather than for him as an individual. Trump showed that the monstrosity exemplified by the Scipodii, the Beast of Bodmin, the Mothman, or Bigfoot was nothing compared to that of horrid humans.

There was the palatable feeling that we had been driving along uphill into clear skies and bright sunshine, then suddenly the car drove off a cliff and plummeted into darkness. The sheer speed at which the country fell startled us. His followers saw this as a positive rather than a negative. Their lava-like, race-based fury was stoked by Trump's endless platitudes about patriotism and Christianity: red meat which they gobbled up ravenously, but in which Trump did not believe, but had contempt for. His perpetual smirk was not for his opponents—who understood what he was doing—but for his masses of followers who thought he was being honest with them, and for the Christian fundamentalists who thought he was chosen by God. They thought he believed the same things and hated the same people they did.

I saw people with giant Trump flags attached to their cars and especially large pick-up trucks. The myth of the Trumpian acolyte was that they were poor and angry over their economic failures. The vehicles, cars, trucks, and even boats, and their penchant for expensive firearms showed the 'economic anxiety' idea to be as hollow as everything else about Trumpism. When groups of these people arrived together—they often ran in packs—flags fluttering, like an angry and hate-filled Renaissance Fair. Trump supporters were not just happy their man had won, they were intensely angry that they had won. Despite the victory they were still mad at, well, everything. They never really seemed to enjoy their victory. They seemed to know deep down something was wrong. That only made them even angrier. Trump's mostly white worshippers felt they had been wronged for years. Though their slogan was "Make America Great Again", what they really wanted was to get their revenge on the world. He was going to be their God of payback who would lead them to triumph over their

---

[1] I am not a psychologist so I do not have the training or expertise to diagnose anyone (this autobiography is an awkward attempt to diagnose myself). It seems, however, that Trump's childhood was such that as a response to the cold and loveless way he was treated made his adult life one long attempt to destroy the world and make it pay. He knew he was a coward, unintelligent, and incompetent, and so worked hard to cover it up. Hence, the constant boasting that he was the greatest at everything.

enemies, both real and mostly imagined. His weird and obviously dyed yellow/orange hair and painted skin gave him the distinct image of the Golden Calf from the Bible.[2] To hammer this home, Christian Fundamentalists actually constructed a model of Trump for use at a Republican rally that had its skin coloured shiny, gold. They had clearly missed the irony.

The Plague Years

As if this wasn't enough, in 2020 a little known disease called the Coronavirus suddenly became world news when a number of people died from it in Wuhan, China. Media hype soon had people in the US and other countries stocking up on food and water in anticipation of a Hollywood movie style, planet-ravaging plague: at least those who didn't see it all as a "hoax perpetrated by the Left." The expected, incompetent reaction of the Trump administration—lies, falsehoods, lack of specialist analysis and guidance—was for many the ultimate metaphor of the Trump administration. At first Trump and company said there was no virus, that it was all a hoax by 'Leftists' to discredit the magnificence which was Trump. Then when it was beyond such foolishness, he blamed the Chinese, he blamed liberals, he blamed governors and he blamed Barack Obama. Donald Trump was the sort of person who when seeing the sunrise, would claim it was his doing and everyone should thank him for doing it. When he saw the coming of the evening, he complained the Sun was going down in order to make him look bad. As to the skyrocketing infection and death rate he famously said, it would be over in no time with very few sick or dead. He then said, "I don't take responsibility at all."[3]

By March, Italy had all but shut down, China had large numbers of cases and was quarantining major parts of its population, airlines were cancelling flights, conferences were being postponed, and schools were closed. Kean University decided to close just as the Spring Break ended and was scheduled to remain closed. While the death rate was relatively low at first, as compared to other diseases, that number rose with frightening speed. The closing mania—which eventually extended to restaurants and bars—came from the notion that the disease spread most rapidly in large crowds where people were in close proximity to each other. Faculty were expected to continue to provide educational services during the closing. In our department, Beth and Brid were on the job quickly rallying faculty and students, and providing quick-start training in the use of *Blackboard* (the online teaching transmission system that Kean, and many other schools employed).[4] The Fall 2020 semester and the following Spring 2021 were held online. The new Kean President, Dr. Reppolet, a seasoned administrator, took charge and led the school in a way that impressed many on a faculty who had been browbeaten by the former incumbent.

The Waterproof Classroom

In 2009, the Kean University student Christian association, brought in a pair of speakers to 'debate evolution' to campus. When I saw the adverts around, I thought that, as the

---

[2] One of the more fascinating things about Trump was how the right wing conservative world of Evangelical Christianity embraced him. During the 1980s and '90s American Evangelicals argued that the anti-Christ was about to appear. Where they once argued the Pope or some Arab dictator was the embodiment of evil mentioned in the Book of Revelations, they now saw a somewhat different character. They began to argue that the Anti-Christ would be a fabulously wealthy, fast-talking businessman from New York who would lead the world to oblivion. When Trump appeared they paradoxically embraced a man they had been warning about for years. Once they did accept him as their saviour—and many spoke of Trump as a Jesus like character—all the talk of the business man Antichrist evaporated.
[3] Donald Trump, March 13, 2020.
[4] I always felt Beth Hyde had the potential to rise to president of the university.

resident specialist in the history of evolutionary thought, I should attend (though I was annoyed they set it for 9pm, a time I'd normally be home preparing for bed). My plan was to be discreet, to slip in the back of the hall and observe. I showed up intentionally a few minutes after the advertised start time, to better facilitate my undercover intentions. As I quietly pushed open the door to the classroom, I saw that there was not going to be any quiet observation on my part. There were exactly four people there: the two speakers and the President and vice-President of the student group. I went and sat in the back of the room after all four stared at me on my entrance. The two presenters were men in their early fifties wearing polo shirts. I have no idea how the student organisation found these two. It's possible they themselves approached the students. Their slide presentation included materials with graphics in the style of *Answers in Genesis* (AIG) a notorious Christian fundamentalist, anti-evolution, anti-gay group, but it was never made clear if the two men represented AIG or were just using their graphics. As to the 'debate' there wasn't much of one. The two presenters simply stated that evolution was wrong and evil and that everyone can see that God created everything.

They used images, many of which I was familiar with, using fake fossils and other boilerplate, anti-evolution ideas. Eventually, I couldn't take the "there's no evidence of evolution" routine and I spoke up. Then one guy said with great confidence that, "Carbon dating doesn't really give you an accurate date." I asked him if he could explain what carbon dating was? He began to stammer. He answered by showing a picture of an infamous fake fossil humorously called the 'clock in a rock.' "How do you explain this?" he asked. I began to explain calcification. He then showed a picture of what he called a photo of a 'thunderbird.' Anti-evolutionists have picked up on cryptozoology as some sort of burn on evolution: if Bigfoot is real then there is no evolution. "How do you explain this?" he demanded. "Well," I said, "first off, that is not a photograph of a thunderbird. It's a painting of a pterodactyl created by Charles R. Knight in the 1940s." At this point, he was really upset. I decided to leave them to their 'lecture.' I got up and left. One of the two students who attended came after me in the hallway. "Professor! Thanks for coming. That was awesome." He seemed to genuinely mean it.

One of the things teachers in general, and university professors in particular, have to deal with in America is the perception that they are all overpaid, underworked, liberals who indoctrinate their students into un-American and un-Christian ways. The ones who are the most vocal about insulting professors are usually the ones who know the least about it. In reality, America's university and college classrooms are filled with sharp, smart, tough, and dedicated professors who put in more work in a week than the average politician, pundit, and random civilian critic does in six months. These people have held the line for years, and will continue to do so despite the name calling, the dismissive attitude, and the envy. The average working week for a professor is between fifty and sixty hours, even more at the community college level. After listening to some fool go on about how the high salaries of professors is scandalous, I smile and wish that I made that much.

With the advent of Covid, schools around the world shut down for live, face-to-face instruction, everyone went to remote learning. As I had never really used *Blackboard*, I needed some training. My original approach to online learning was to create web pages for each of my courses: something I later learned was rare at the time. On each web page I provided contact information, a copy of the syllabus, a list of required reading, and online sources for useful information pertaining to that particular course. This new reality, however, would require all of us to go digital completely.

It took a while before I became just about comfortable with teaching by sitting in my office at home and talking into a laptop computer. It was like being in a waterproof classroom. Although I was able to make use of *PowerPoint* effectively, I could never quite break the habit of looking at myself in the little box at the lower left hand side of the screen instead of looking into the camera. Over the 2020-2021 winter break while I was experimenting with it, I discovered you could play music in *Blackboard* and the students would hear it. I began opening each session by playing a song. At first I used only instrumental music that wasn't too loud or ragged. I used music of the type you'd hear on the *SPA* SiriusXm channel. Then I became a little bolder. To open one live session for the History of Pseudoscience course—the introduction to cryptozoology lecture—I played the Connie Francis song, *Stupid Cupid*. I also played the theme for the movie *The Blob* for the lecture on Monstrous births in the History of Medicine class. For the lecture on Race Science, I played *Take the Skinheads Bowling*. For the lecture on the Civil War for the 1062 Worlds of History, I played *Marching through Georgia*. This made it all a little more fun. The students understood why we were doing this, and at Kean, at least we had very little trouble from parents of students about not meeting on campus. Where other schools, including nearby Rutgers University, had demonstrations and even some violence on occasion, we at Kean soldiered on. Our community understood that the total immersion in remote learning was not something being done for the fun of it, but as a strategy to save lives, and to keep the school from disappearing. What helped us was good university leadership. It wasn't perfect, and there were glitches and issues, but in the end it worked.

Had there been effective presidential, and Republican Party leadership when the first warnings came out, the country would have fared better. Social distancing would have kicked-in earlier and the nation would have suffered less. Had the President gone on television and given thoughtful, inspiring, and calming words—in the style of FDR's fireside chats—there would have been much less of a run on things like toilet paper, face masks, and disinfectants. People would have been far less resistant to wearing masks and getting vaccinations, once they were available. Still, it would have been difficult and some people would have died regardless, but the impact would have been greatly reduced. Instead, we were treated to a mincing show of petulance, of claiming it was all a hoax, of blaming others, of the promotion of false cures, and general inaction.[5]

The real issue was that the Republican Party leadership stood by and let Trump exercise the worst angels of his nature upon the nation and the world. Trump's behaviour and attitude helped unleash a dark side in people. They could have put a stop to the insanity early on if they wanted. GOP leadership, in the form of Mitch McConnell, Lindsey Graham, Paul Ryan, Rand Paul, and a host of others, refused to hold Trump accountable because they were themselves guilty of the same crimes as he. They too were moral weaklings, and hypocritical opportunists willing to flush the country, and even the world, down the toilet in order to increase their personal wealth and power.

The Period of Empty Highways

Early in the quarantine, Lisa and I took a ride just to get out of the house. We took the scenic route up the Watchung Mountains towards Morristown. This is the route I took to go to the Morristown Public Library. It's a long winding road through farmland and woods. It wends its way through the Great Swamp nature reserve. For me it's a relaxing ride through a

---

[5] Trump once famously suggested people with Covid should be injected with bleach. He thought that would "burn it right out."

bucolic landscape where I get to clear my mind and think. As we drove down Route 22 the normally, heavily-trafficked road was all but empty. Driving through the mountains, we encountered few other vehicles. The plague had even curtailed pleasure driving.

We watched the news as large, angry red splotches grew and spread across animated maps of America and the world. They tracked the spread of the disease. Trump ignored it all because he was afraid it would make him look bad. He feared that, not only because his profound narcissism would not allow for the idea he hadn't done something wonderful, but because he feared it might keep him from being re-elected. He knew that the minute he was no longer president, he feared he could be prosecuted for all of his various crimes.

Trump's lies became the drip of rust corroding our society. It looked horrible, smelled horrible, and did horrible things to the machinery of our existence. Like rotted meat, it attracted bugs, and mould, and rats, and other horrible things from out of the shadows and from under rocks. The level of greedy incompetence shown by the Trump administration and the GOP leadership will be a blight upon American history forever. In years to come, the same conservative religious groups that fight now to keep evolution and slavery out of school books will fight to keep knowledge of the Trump administration and GOP's wrongdoing out of future texts. Watching gun-toting, protesting fools scream about, "opening up the country again." or watching idiots intentionally going without masks or seeing dopes yelling at nurses and doctors, have all helped hammer home a lesson learned long ago: assholes ruin everything.

For historians and thoughtful, honest people, it has long been known that America was a racist country. People of colour, particularly women, have always known this better than anyone. Despite all the genuinely good things about the United States, with all its opportunities and positives, the nation's history has been undermined by racism in its worst and most monstrous form. Not everyone has accepted this or even acknowledged it. The Trump administration, and the Republican Party in general, made me feel like I had wasted my time in the military. Why did I spend those years protecting my country from the Russians only to see those in power ultimately sell it to them? The same tanks my fellow Doggies and I served on in the '70s and '80s to protect the US from the Russians, were handed over as surplus to the Turks who, in the Fall of 2019, used them to slaughter the Kurds to benefit the Russians. Listening to Trump and the leaders of the GOP cosy up to the Russians infuriated me. I heard voices from the past I thought were silenced long ago. What had so many done, all those years ago, for this to happen? Trump and the GOP gave the country away and embraced the Russians.[6] This was not the appropriate embrace of one-time enemies like the Japanese and the Germans after World War II: An embrace was meant to rebuild the world together as friends and allies for a better future. This was an effort to enrich a few with power and money at the expense of the future.

When I was in the service, particularly in West Germany, each and every one of the several hundred thousands of serving men and women from a dozen countries were expected to do something. They were expected to sacrifice their lives in order to keep out the Russians and the Warsaw Pact countries. Trump and the GOP gave the country away and the Russians never needed to fire a shot. Then, during the pandemic, the same fools who complained about

---

[6] Rumours were rampant that the Russians had been exercising a program of entrapping and blackmailing US officials, especially leading Republicans. They offered sex ,drugs and money and the Republicans took them. Then the Russians had enough to blackmail them.

Millennials being weak and privileged, threatened to kill people if they had to wear a cotton mask and not go out to eat for a few months. This was too much for them.

The high death rate (over 600,000 by the time Joe Biden was elected president) came in large part from incompetence on the part of Trump and the GOP. He, and his cronies in government and on Fox News, at first, claimed the virus was a hoax concocted by 'Leftists' to smear the president's reputation. Then they said it was real, but not deadly, then they said it would "go away" by itself, or that the summer heat would make it disappear. This delayed the implementation of protective measures such as mandatory mask wearing and the six foot social distance rule.

Eventually, states like New Jersey, which continued with the quarantine and made widespread vaccination available, began to reduce the number of infected and dead. Broadly speaking, these were states with Democratic governors. The anti-quarantine folk were found to have the backing and involvement of big Republican donors and white supremacist groups. The pro-reopen ranks were almost exclusively made up of Trump supporters who sported confederate flags and swastikas and came toting their assault rifles and cosplay military gear. They threatened and perpetrated violence against the police, elected officials, even school board members and teachers. In the end, those states that embraced widespread public health through mass vaccination and quarantine reduced suffering, those that embraced anti-mask and anti-vax sentiments saw their death rate skyrocket.

As if the virus wasn't bad enough. Then, a middle-aged black man, George Floyd, was accused of supposedly using a bad check for the items he had just bought at a local market in Detroit. The police arrived, and as he tried to explain he had done nothing wrong, one of the cops, Derek Chauvin, attacked Floyd. He wrestled him to the ground, handcuffed him then rolled him over face down. He then proceeded to kneel on Floyd's neck for the next ten minutes. When it was over, Floyd was dead. This wasn't the first time an angry white cop had killed an unarmed, non-resisting black person, of course. This time, the incident was captured on film, up close and personal. The sight of a growling, wild-eyed cop kneeling on the neck of a handcuffed, black man face down on the pavement, his body wedged under the bumper of the cop's Ford, begging for his life, his voice growing fainter and fainter as he died, was simply too much. Protests in Detroit spread around the country. The peaceful protests grew violent mostly at the hands of outside provocateurs. It was later discovered that those doing the fire-starting were connected to White Supremacist and pro-Trump groups. There was also at least one documented case of an undercover Detroit police officer smashing the windows of an auto parts store with a hammer. It took some time, but Chauvin was eventually fired, subsequently arrested and charged with murder.

For better or worse, over the course of the 20th century, the United States had become a totem of contemporary civilization. It brought as much good health, modernization and concepts of democracy as it did death and destruction. With the advent of Trump and the Republican Party, the emphasis was fully on death and destruction. Trump and the GOP undermined every positive aspect of American civilization. I will always hate them for that.

Teaching Online

As a way of combating the spread of the virus, Kean went to total remote teaching beginning with the spring break. Online teaching was nothing new at Kean or to most universities in America. The Department of History wanted to offer cyber classes, but the

213

office of online teaching was difficult to work with. Online classes had to have special paperwork. You couldn't just say you were going to offer a class online. In order to justify having an office of online education, obstacles were put in place to make it intentionally difficult for faculty to design their own courses and for students to take them. Technically, if you designed an online class, you had to receive payment for the effort. Instead of having, for example, the maths professor, who was an expert in their field, design the class they were going to teach, the office of online learning would farm out the course design to someone off-campus. We as faculty never knew who was being paid to design our classes. When I brought this up at a meeting, I said I was uncomfortable with 'mercenaries' writing the online curriculum for these classes when we had an entire faculty of world-class scholars who should be designing their own classes. Using the term 'mercenary' did not exactly put me in the good graces of the Online Education program.

When COVID arrived—or at least when the Trump Administration finally began to acknowledge its presence—we had just gone on Spring Break 2020. The sudden need to turn the entire curriculum to online, changed everything. The administration decided, as had every other school in the country, to cease live education and go over to online. Starting the week we would have returned from Spring Break, we were to give our classes in the cyber world for the rest of the semester. I had never taught online before. I had plenty of opportunities, but never did. It seemed like far more work to run a cyber class than to run a live class. Also, I thought there was too much distance between student and teacher to really do the job properly. Now, however, there was no choice. We all had just been pushed into the pool at the very deep end and had to sink or swim. Due to the lack of preparation time, the administration said that while they preferred the classes to be run on *Blackboard*, because of the emergency, we could use any online method we wanted. This *ad-hoc* approach was a desperate move by the administration to simply get to the end of the semester in one piece. Kean had been using *Blackboard* for some years by now. In fact, every semester, every course being offered had a *Blackboard* page set up for it, whether it was online or not. Many faculty did use it for non-cyber classes, but only to post grades and send announcements to the students. I never used it mostly because I did not know how to. The school was constantly offering training for faculty in how to use it, but I was stubborn and resisted.

To finish the semester, I sent mass emails to all my students. I also sent them *PowerPoint* slides, and for each week, I typed out two-page lectures for them to read. It was a bit awkward, but it worked. By the end of the semester I only had two students drop-out due to family issues with the COVID pandemic. That was a smaller loss than other semesters. All the faculty did essentially the same thing and the entire university made it through the second half of the semester with surprisingly few glitches. By the time the semester ended, Kean University had fared well against the disease. A few students and staff became ill, and luckily survived but, unfortunately, we did have one faculty fatality. No one became sick at the campus. Anyone who did, contracted the disease away from school.

I had already agreed to teach the Senior Seminar for Summer I before the pandemic hit. For this semester, however, I was not going to be able to wing it. The administration decreed that from Summer I on, any faculty member wanting to teach had to go through special online training and create a special 'Conversion Packet' for the class. Any professor not doing so would not be allowed to teach and would be furloughed. I took the brief summer course in *Blackboard* and somehow managed to pass. Though to be honest, I was never contacted and told I had passed, I just wasn't stopped from teaching for the Fall. The two things I was best at in life were tank driving and teaching. In a tank and in the classroom were the places I felt most in control. They were the places I felt most alive. I had left the one behind, but now online teaching was taking the other away from me.

A New Career?

With the advent of COVID, one worry during the summer of 2020 was that students might decide it was too dangerous to go back to school at all. The Department of History had just started to tick our numbers back up and while we still had a way to go, everyone was happy the numbers were going in the right direction. Now we were worried about the bottom dropping out. At sixty years old, I had enough savings to last a year or so if I lost my job: not enough to simply say, to hell with it and retire (Lisa's job at IEEE was secure—they had gone remote as well—but we needed both of our salaries to survive). Once I committed to this, I never thought of what I'd do if I couldn't acquire this career, or if I did and then lost it, what would I do after? I still would have to keep working, but at what? I would want to do something that played on my strengths and experiences. Who was I? I hit upon the idea of becoming a private detective.

I'd had this fantasy about turning myself into a boozy, world-weary, private detective. My trademark would be always quoting the Romantic poets and bits of obscure history to criminals and police alike. I would specialise in taking cases that involved monsters and the paranormal. My 'office' would be in a downtown bar—not too divvy, just enough to be fashionably low rent—where I'd sit and talk to clients or write articles and books waiting for the next job to walk in. Everyone would call me 'The Professor.' I'd dress just like I dressed before for my classes: vest, tie, sometimes suspenders. I'd wear a long, black leather trench coat, and carry an old M1911A1 .45 calibre pistol in a shoulder holster, like when I was in the Cav. The youngish police lieutenant, who didn't like me, would complain about my unorthodox ways. As they were putting the latest Crim into the back of the squad car, I'd be standing there talking about Teddy Roosevelt and the LT would look annoyed and say, "You still carrying that antique hog-leg under your coat?" I'd just smile and quote Coleridge. Then he'd say, "One of these days you're not gonna be able to pass that exam." I'd just smile again, turn, and walk to the bar.

So that was my fantasy for what I'd do if I lost my job at Kean.

With all the disease and political friction, there was still the presidential election to think about. Soon enough, November third, Election Day, came along. Many anti-Trump people assumed that the combination of former Vice-President, Joe Biden and the feisty senator, Kamala Harris would win in a staggering landslide. It made sense, both were respected political figures, and besides that, the Trump administration had spent the previous four years being so totally inept and corrupt it seemed almost easy. They didn't reckon on the depth of racial and religious hatred that motivated the Trump side. It was a record turnout of voters, for both sides. As the day went by, the usual Democratic states fell into line as did the usual Republican heartlands. It had boiled down to several 'battle ground' states in particular, Georgia and Pennsylvania. By late in the evening and stretching into the next couple of days, people on both sides held their breath. Finally, Pennsylvania went to Biden as did the upset state of Georgia. By November seventh it was being announced that Biden had won. When all the final tallying was complete, Biden had won by a remarkable six million votes, the largest majority in the nation's history. Congratulatory messages began to roll in: first from Fiji, then Germany, France, Canada and Israel and then from many others. Only begrudgingly, did any Republicans admit Biden had won. The first was Mitt Romney. For his part, Donald Trump refused to concede. Ever the petulant child to the end, he tweeted feverishly, "I won!" His closet supporters began a chant of voter fraud, for which they had no evidence. They began what came to be known as, 'The Big Lie,' that Trump had won but had the election 'stolen.'

For myself, I was surprised, but very happy. I assumed Russian interference and Republican efforts to purge voter rolls would win out. When it seemed clear that Biden/Harris had won I felt a strange, unexpected joy. I hadn't felt this since the night Barrack Obama became president. Many spontaneous celebrations broke out, not just across America, but around the world. The very planet itself seemed to let out a big, long sigh of relief.

Donald Trump was the offspring of hateful, indifferent parents who taught him, both consciously and subconsciously, that only wealth and power mattered: that the acquisition of wealth and power legitimised any technique to acquire it no matter how criminal or debased. He came to believe he could do anything or say anything, no matter how terrible, and there would be no consequences. His followers, the MAGA (Make America Great Again), saw in him a licence to unleash their pent-up hatreds under the thin veneer of a sick and diseased form of patriotism. They became a legion of minions bent on destruction for destruction's sake. There was little joy, little love, only bile to make the broken and decrepit children, 'Ignorance' and 'Want' seem almost tame by comparison. They had consciously thrown away their humanity and replaced it with a seething evil. They let loose the darker angels of their nature because they hated so much.

Then came the insurrection. Trump riled up his supporters to storm the Capitol building on January 6, 2021, just prior to the inauguration. He wanted them to find Democratic congress people and kill them. He also wanted them to kill his own Vice-President, Mike Pence. As if that wasn't bad enough, the majority of Republican officials wanted to wave all this off as nothing important. Some even claimed that despite the many Trump flags and shirts worn by the insurrectionists, it was not Trump supporters in the middle of it all, but rather it was an elaborate ruse concocted by BLM and 'Antifa.' On January 13, 2021, Donald Trump was impeached for a second time. Seven Republicans voted for impeachment, the same number as voted to impeach Richard Nixon. But then when the real crunch came the GOP sided with Trump. They sided with criminality and pathological lying. They sided with everything I was raised to think was un-American and wrong and un-Christian.

Locked down, sort of

When it finally began to ease up, the Corona virus had killed over half a million people, and that was just in this country. The lockdown, mask wearing and social distancing had helped to keep that down. For many people the lockdown was a genuine hardship. For Lisa and myself, not so much. While everyone was freaking out over the pandemic, wearing increasingly larger face masks and not going near anyone, or not going out at all, Lisa and I tried to remain calm. Since we had been doing repair work on the house, we had a pre-pandemic supply of face masks. At first we did a lot of home cooking, which was nice, as Lisa—and I to a certain extent— really liked cooking. Most of the grocery stores in our area remained open. We also normally kept a supply of toilet paper, canned food and beer and wine in the basement. This was not because we were survivalists, but because we were lazy and if it snowed or there was some other extreme weather event, we didn't have to go outside. There were idiots who were standing in line and fighting over buying ten giant boxes of toilet paper, but we were able to stay out of that nonsense. I was particularly pleased when several of those types were arrested for buying out store supplies then trying to resell them at inflated prices. The pandemic brought out the worst in already awful people. I liked to think that once it was all over, there would be plenty of Trump supporters who would be stuck with huge amounts of surplus toilet paper and hand sanitizer that they couldn't use or sell.

Both Lisa and I were lucky enough that we were able to keep our jobs by doing them remotely. Kean did put all faculty—but not the administration—on furlough for two weeks in May, but I did a half semester section of HIST3990 Junior Seminar, and then HIST4990 Senior Seminar for Summer I, so while I was still upset to lose pay to the furlough, I was able to make up for it so it wasn't too bad a bite out of our finances. Our favourite diner, the Westfield Diner, re-opened and we went regularly. Lisa was vaccinated at the medical centre she went to for her cancer treatments, and by April, the city of Plainfield had set up a vaccination station at the high school, so many of our neighbours and ourselves were now protected. The worst part was that the libraries and archives I needed to visit to pursue my research and writing stayed closed. Other than that, we really did not suffer much. Though I know many people who did.

By now well over half a million Americans alone had fallen to COVID and millions made sick, some permanently. Despite this, the numbers began to slow and even stop in some places. In New Jersey, one of the states hit hardest at the beginning of the epidemic, life began to recover. As more and more people wore their masks and practised social distancing, and as the various vaccines became increasingly available it was clear the nightmare was starting to diminish and enter the end phase. Governor Murphy, systematically and reasonably, reduced restrictions until, by the start of the summer of 2021, most restaurants had reopened, and restrictions were lifted.

Angry parents and rabble-rousers continued to protest against health professionals because they said you should get vaccinated and wear a mask. They assaulted doctors, nurses and researchers. They didn't just attack medical practitioners, they attacked the very notion of medicine and science. They were throwing away a thousand years of science and medicine. In its place they wanted mob rule under the seething veneer of 'personal freedom' (an idea very few of them even understood). They were monsters with an instinctive and primordial hatred of something they were not quite sure of, choking on their own hatred. They attacked blindly in a red foggy rage, spitting the acid of their ignorance. It was a misguided Libertarian desire to be free to behave and to act in any way they wanted, and anyone who dared disagree had to be eliminated. Their children were drowning and they attacked the person trying to throw them a life raft. They made me want to watch them all die in the agony of their own foolishness. They were terrified of dying in a way I wasn't. I didn't want to die, but I wasn't afraid to. I figured I'd ride it out as long as Lisa was still around. I always had this dark part of me that thought the thing worse than dying was not dying when everyone else I cared for had done so. It was the being left behind I didn't look forward to.

In 1980, I was doing my required stint as jeep driver for the company First Sergeant. We all cycled through at one time or another. He had served in Vietnam as a Doggie. He had seen more than his fair share of war and death and despair. He was in his mid-thirties, yet he looked fifty. He was that type of man who gave off--without any of the tough guy play acting, foolish, heroics of those who pretend--the aura of someone you'd follow to hell if he asked. He knew things for real, poseurs only acted like they knew, but never would. We were on an alert and the company had moved into position to face down the hordes of Russian tanks we expected to fight during the end of the world. A fight we were expected to lose. An alert had been called: one of those no warning, here's your ammunition, make sure your gas mask works, serious alerts. It was February, three in the morning, and bitingly cold. Around us, the tanks of our company seemed like ghosts in the snowy mist. I held a loaded twelve gauge shotgun on my lap. In the back of the mutt was a private named Andy Jackson (yes) on the M60. He was even more nervous than I was. He bit his lip and moaned a little. He too wanted to be a real man not wanting to show fear. The machine gun he was manning was trembling subtly, showing it was his nerves alone doing it. Top looked up at Andy and smiled. Then he turned to me and said, totally unsolicited, "You know kid, don't worry about death. If you have to, you can always screw your .45 into your ear and all your worries go away forever." He was dead serious. He was so genuine in his exhausted sincerity, that from that moment on I was never afraid to die. It was life that scared me.

Conclusion

One of the things the Trump era brought into sharp relief for me was that Bigfoot, the Jersey Devil, werewolves and all their kin, are not the real monsters. The Trump administration, as well as other governments in England, France, and Russia, reinforced the idea. An idea that I had begun to suspect ever since growing up in the Ironbound, that the overwhelming majority of people are shits. They are lying, desperate, hypocritical, horror shows who will sell-out their country, their neighbours, even their own families for profit or power or even just for the fun of it. They don't become monsters accidentally, they prefer to be that way. Director Tod Browning had already said this in his movie *Freaks* (1932). The various physically deformed side-show people like the legless man, the Pinheads, and the others were not the freaks of the title, it was the 'normal' people who were the real monsters. Trump showed that monsters were everywhere. They were in the White House and in your house. They were not confined to the dark corners of forests and lake bottoms. And, they would always be with us.

Chapter 11

A Room Full of Monsters

We should set aside a room at the back of the shop, just for ourselves, quite isolated, where, as the principal retreat for our solitude, we establish our true freedom.

-- Michel de Montaigne, *On Solitude, 1580*

In the last century BCE, the Roman lyrical poet, Catullus (84-54 BCE) wrote, "*Qvid est Catulle? Quid moraris emori?*" (What is it Catullus? Why do you not make haste to die?). He is talking to himself, not unlike the way Hamlet speaks to himself almost 1700 years later. Because of events in his life which have drained his sense of self, his desire to go on, and his belief in the future, Catullus wonders why he is still alive, why hasn't he taken his own life yet? He should, he thinks, be gone by now. I personally never thought I'd ever have to wrestle with such questions. Look how wrong we can be.

In the summer of 2019, I was again approached by a television documentary studio about being in a new series on monster history. They wanted me to talk about a wide range of topics. They also said they were willing to travel to New Jersey to film me on the Kean Campus. I agreed and we all met in the beautiful and historic Kean Hall under the stained glass, and commenced filming. We talked about the Minotaur, and the Loch Ness Monster, and werewolves—almost nothing about Bigfoot. While talking about centaurs, I went into what I thought was a humorous rant about why you never hear about female centaurs except for Hylonome (the males are jealous and intimidated by her). To finish, they asked if I had any controversial views on cryptozoology or monsters. I thought about it for a moment then asked, "Should I just go?" The director nodded yes, and I went into a dissertation on how monster history was less about the biology of unusual creatures and more about the history of human fear and hatred. When done everyone smiled, said it was great and how happy they were with what I had said, and that it would be great on TV.

Two years later, when the show finally aired on the Hulu channel, it was very different from what I had envisaged. In the interim, the film makers had come across an odd story about how a Bigfoot allegedly killed some pot growers in California. They completely changed the structure of the series from monsters in general to essentially focus on Bigfoot, especially from the murderous Sasquatch angle. They had never asked me anything about Sasquatch in the filming. So, despite the fact that I am one of the world's leading authorities on Sasquatch history, the only part of my original hour-and-a-half long interview that made it into the series about Bigfoot, is me talking about human hatred and fear (though I was happy they got creative and included the "should I just go" part). Such is the life of an historian of monsters.

I've always suspected that all paranormal stuff like ghosts, magic, numerology and all their related offshoots were nothing more than foolish nonsense. By the time I reached my sixties, however, I had come to the conclusion that cryptozoology wasn't interesting to me the way it had been before. I no longer found magical beasts and those of mythology intriguing. I had never thought any of these creatures were real, in the way believers did, but I did find them worth studying. With the Jersey Devil book I felt I had said everything there was to be said. I had learned over the course of my journey that most cryptids were little more than a skinny adulterer climbing down a fire escape in the middle of the night after scaring some children.

I've always had a certain ability to be alone. There haven't been many people I liked having around all the time except for Lisa. The place where I wanted to be alone the most was in a library. When I was seven we were in St. Cecilia's library and I was sitting in a little wooden chair reading and feeling good about myself for a change. Sister Louise called out to us that it was time to put the books away and head back to class. I didn't notice because I was so absorbed in my reading. She became upset and thought I was "being obstinate" so she rushed over and hit me across the head hard enough that it knocked me out of my chair and onto the floor. The other kids just laughed. I had been reading *The Little House*. I determined that someday I'd have my own library. It was going to be my special place. The St. Cecilia's Grammar School library was not anything grand, but with bookshelves that seemed to go up to the clouds, it was transformative for a little kid. I never wanted to leave. When I had my own library, I would fill it with the books I wanted, I would decorate it the way I wanted, and I would never ever let anyone tell me to leave. There would be no room for monsters unless they were in a book.

My library was to be a place where no one could enter unless I allowed them, and I wasn't planning on letting anyone in, unless it was Velma Dinkley, of course. I felt good surrounded by books. It made me feel safe, calm. I started collecting them early. I had a wooden three level bookcase in my room that my dad bought for me at one of those unpainted furniture places. I put all my prized editions (cheap, dog-eared paperbacks) on it along with the laboratory glassware from the Gilbert display in the *Two Guys*, I purchased with my allowance. I carefully positioned it so I could sit on my bed and look at them. I'd imagine I was in some great international library somewhere. To that end, I began collecting pictures of libraries from around the world. I would stare at them and imagine myself there.

Then I saw a PBS documentary about Shakespeare on Channel 13, where they discussed the First Folio. A few days later, I was on the Ave in Mr. Finger's store looking at the plastic models and weird kitchen utensils. Down in the back of the store there were shelves with books on them. These were mostly new paperback novels by the likes of James Clavell, Herman Wouk, and Jacqueline Susann. There were a few older, used books as well. As I looked at them I saw a Shakespeare First Folio. I couldn't believe it. It was dog-eared and worn, but there it was. An orange dot sticker on the spine said 50¢. I dug frantically through my pockets and came out with the appropriate coins. Carefully, I took the precious tome off the shelf and carried it to the cashier. In the show, they said these things were extremely valuable and had to be handled with care. As I approached the checkout counter, I hoped I wouldn't be discovered. I put the book on the counter and counted out fifty cents in change (I had three cents to spare). Mr. Finger looked at me. He was one of those guys who always looked at you suspiciously, as if he knew you were up to something. I hoped he wouldn't realise what was happening. He handed me a receipt, put the precious object in a new, crisp paper bag, and I walked out carefully. After a few steps of my nonchalant walk, I broke into a run. I dashed out onto Kearny Avenue and almost into a car. The beeping horn and screeching tires only made me run faster. I went straight home and locked myself in my room in order to examine my prize in solitude.

I wanted to learn everything about books: how they were made, how writers worked, how did one get something published? I might as well have been trying to figure out the recipe for the Philosopher's Stone. I didn't know anyone who knew anything about books (I had learned to never ask adults for help so I never thought to ask the librarian at St. Cecilia's). I don't think a single one of the kids I knew had a book in their rooms other than the ones we had to have for school. After a bit of digging, I saw that the publishing information was on what was called a 'title page.' I checked my First Folio to see what the title page said. As I studied it I discovered that my new treasure was not a First Folio, but a paperback copy of *Henry V*. I was disappointed, but wiser.

In high school, I found my favourite spot in the library there. A heavy oak table hidden just a bit by a stack, and a window looking out over the football field, beyond to the Meadowlands and then on to New York City. There was a lot of old polished wood and glass. The tables had decades of students' initials scratched into them. I liked that. It was there that I started reading science fiction and fantasy. Roger Zelazny was an eye opener. Reading his *Guns of Avalon* (1972) in the Kearny High library, was the first time I saw an author use the word 'shit' in his text. I read voraciously there even though the words were still spinning around and gave me a headache, but not quite as much as they once did. I assumed this happened to everyone, so I never asked. It just seemed like another thing to overcome, to deal with somehow. As it did for so many kids, reading became an escape. I read Robert E. Howard's Conan stories, and H. P. Lovecraft. I read the Moon novels, the Venus novels and some of the Mars novels of Edgar Rice Burroughs (enthralled initially by the Frank Frazetta covers), though I never read any of the Tarzan books. My greatest author discovery of this period was Harlan Ellison: a science fiction writer who didn't really write science fiction. He wrote about human relations in a speculative setting. He had a deep insight into loneliness, frustration, and people who don't always understand the world around them, and how they deal with the monsters that harass them. His characters felt the same way I did.

I went into the library whenever I could. However, I never went when certain students were there. I didn't want them to know what I was doing. I had had enough of the ridicule from these people. Reading and research was my private domain. I knew no one else would understand so it was useless trying to explain. Even the few people I thought were genuine friends didn't know any of this. The one exception was Kenny Williams. His dad was a cop in Kearny. Kenny had just read Joseph Wambaugh's *The Choirboys* (1975) that had only been released the year before. He told me about it and so I read it too. I studied the way Wambaugh created his characters and wrote their dialogue to make them so convincing. At the time, an actual serving police officer with the LAPD, Wambaugh's breakthrough novel was *The New Centurions* (1971). He wrote about the lives of police officers often including stories of mental breakdown, drug and alcohol addiction, abuse of power, racism, misogyny or a number of other issues that plagued the department.

All through my time in the service, I kept my scholarly pursuits to myself. When I came home from the service, I resumed my book collecting. Moving into my own apartment allowed me to get a bit more extravagant with my selections. When Lisa came over for the first time, she gained lots of points when, rather than saying, "what's with all the books?" as others had, she said, "Wow, nice books."

In the army, I always carried books with me out on operations and missions. The first time I went with my company to gunnery exercises at Grafenwoehr, I salvaged a metal .50 calibre ammunition box and turned it into my secret library. It was just big enough to hold seven or eight paperbacks with a small writing pad and some pens and pencils. It had a collapsible handle and it sealed when you closed it so water wouldn't get inside. It was common practice for tank crews to keep these canisters, which looked like metal shoeboxes.[1] It was not unusual for a tank to have several of them in the bustle rack or strapped to the grunt rail. They were used to carry tools, nuts and bolts, and other bits and bobs useful on a tank in the field. So my box with my field library never attracted any attention. Depending upon my mood, I'd have some history in there, maybe some dinosaur stuff, science fiction, naturally, or some weird science. There was always at least one Harlan Ellison, some H.P. Lovecraft, and Greil Marcus' *Mystery Train* (his essay on the history of the song, 'Stagger Lee' is still a magnificent job of writing on the history and romance of music). No one ever suspected that the .50 cal can in *Dreamboat Annie's* bustle rack was full of books.

Once, during a winter exercise, the company took up a position to defend a little town crossroad. It was almost ten at night, and as usual, snow flurries were falling. As it was dark outside, we had the interior red lights on so we could have the hatches open, but not attract attention. I was sitting in the loader's position inside the turret, reading and nodding off. I heard someone climb up on the outside of the tank and say something to Sergeant Moore. I recognized the platoon sergeant's voice and sat up, so it wasn't too obvious I was dozing. I still had the book on my lap. Then the platoon sergeant stuck his head inside the open loader's hatch and said, "what are you doing Regal?" "Uh, nothing Chief, just doing radio watch." He pointed at the book. "Lemme see." I held it up. He screwed up his face, looked at the cover for a moment, then gave me a "hmmm." Then he left. The book was *Phenomena: A Book of Wonders* by John Michell and Robert Rickard.

While I was a student at Kean College, I quickly discovered my favourite spot in the Nancy Thompson Library.[2] I found a good seat at the back of the second floor where the bound periodicals were. They had those one-person cubicle desks along the outside wall. It was in the corner with windows that looked out over the back of the library building onto a little copse of trees that separated the library from the basketball courts and Downs Hall. Not many students went to this part of the library, so when I was there I tended to have it all to myself. I could sit in this little boxy cubicle and look out over the woods. When I went there, I'd quickly do my homework, then delve into some obscure historical text that I'd found while browsing the shelves. It made me feel like a real scholar. One of the things that attracted me to Lisa was that she, too, was a book collector and library fan. Where other couples went to night clubs for fun, Lisa and I went to used book shops. We were poor and couldn't afford expensive works, but we found some real discount gems.

Working at AT&T, I had a better salary so indulged some more. When I was offered the Fellowship at the Mary Baker Eddy Papers Project, part of the deal was that they paid to move you to the Boston area. The removal company sent a truck with two Boston guys right out of central casting. They were terrific and worked incredibly hard. The little guy, upon seeing our artefacts said, "this stuff's wicked, awesome!" Most of the boxes they had to load were full of books. When we reached my apartment in Providence and unloaded everything, I

---

[1] It was great fun firing a .50 cal. Our tanks did not use the standard M2 weapon most people know from war movies. We used the special M85 version. It was shorter and did not have the firing handles on the back. That was because it fitted inside the commander's cupola and was fired by a hand crank with a button on it. The ammunition came in these metal boxes—Fifty cal cans—with all the bullets held together by metal links called belts. As the weapon fired, the spent casings and the links spit out an ejection port on the outboard side of the cupola to fall down and clatter loudly on the tank's fender. As it was a large calibre weapon with a relatively slow rate of fire, the M85 made a distinctive 'bump, bump, bump' sound. You could count the rounds. The rate was so slow.

[2] I have a favourite spot in every library I've ever been in.

bought a couple of pizzas and a six-pack for them. As they devoured it, the taller guy said he hoped he never had to move a professor with so many books again.

A couple of years after I started at TCI, we bought the Webster Place house. I turned the walk-in attic into my office/library. Alice called it the Astronomy Tower.[3] When we moved into the Sleepy Hollow house, we decided that the bedroom in the back corner would be the library. We outfitted it with bookcases from IKEA. It worked well. Then came the storm of 2017.

April of that year saw a late Spring snowstorm.[4] I was sitting at my desk in my office at the back of the house next to the library. It had been snowing persistently for several hours in the late afternoon and early evening. Because it was relatively mild, the snow was wet and heavy and since it was Spring, the trees had already begun to sprout leaves. The heavy, wet snow had accumulated to over eight inches. I had done some good writing that day—I was working on the Jersey Devil book—and was happy that the arrival of snow meant there would be no school the next day. I got up and was about to go down to the kitchen when a freight train decided to crash into our house. Our neighbours had a tall, ancient, and imposing oak tree in their yard and the heavy wet snow had caused it to topple over. All three-and-a-half tons of it smashed into our house.[5] As the roof was caving in, I ran and dived on to the floor, sliding into the bedroom as the tree crashed down on the roof at the back of the house. Luckily, Lisa was downstairs. Parts of the ceiling were falling all around mixed in with parts of the tree, and snow and pieces of drywall. Quickly, I crab-walked down the stairs, like that scene in *The Exorcist,* calling out her name. Lisa was safe. I went out the back in my bare feet to see what had happened. The tree had fallen onto the roof of our garage, punched through the roof of our back porch in several places, and demolished the roof of the main part of the house. It had demolished the roof and the cathedral ceiling in the attic. It had also crashed through the attic floor into the library, hitting and almost destroying the bookcase that held our Darwiniana collection. (It also destroyed my mandolin, although I didn't find out for a week because of all the debris now in the library.) I went outside again in my bare feet to survey the damage. Only then did I really see how much carnage the fallen tree had caused. In an instant, I saw in my head a huge bill that I would not be able to afford; months of work, inconvenience, and nothing but endless *agida*. Half-dressed, standing barefoot in twelve inches of wet, ice-cold, snow that was still falling, I started screaming obscenities at the tree.[6]

Eventually, we were able to get a specialist insurance assessor to look at the house. To my amazement, we had taken out enough insurance to fix all the damage. The insurance company set us up with a catastrophic recovery contractor to rebuild the house. A tree surgeon came in and removed the tree: it took fifteen guys, a bucket crane, a heavy lift crane, four more tree surgeon vehicles plus eight hours to get the tree removed. I tried to be physically involved with all the deconstruction and reconstruction. At one point, I helped three little Central American guys wrestle a large bough of the trunk from off the roof. I took a sledgehammer from one of the construction guys and bashed out one of the shattered cathedral beams. They thought I was a little crazy, but I wanted to be able to say I helped with the demolition and the reconstruction at least.

---

[3] A Harry Potter reference.
[4] I'm glad that the whole climate change thing is just a Lefty hoax.
[5] The tree removal people calculated that it weighed that much.
[6] A few days later our neighbour behind the house said he saw the tree fall. He was about to come to see how we were when he heard me in the yard screaming foul language at the tree. He figured I was okay.

It would take almost two years to finish rebuilding the house.

While the reconstruction was going on, Lisa and I came to a decision as to how to proceed. After a year or so, the majority of the rebuild was complete: what was left of the roof had been removed, rebuilt, and re-shingled. The rooms were gutted and insulated, and re-sheet rocked. All new hardwood floors were installed as was new wiring.[7] Now came the finishing touches. Both of us had dreamed, all our lives, of having a really cool library. We realised we would never have another chance like this to build one, so we decided to go for it. While we were constrained by the size of the room and the layout of the house, we couldn't do everything we wanted—like having a turret, for example—but we would have a pretty good go anyway.

We had both fallen in love with Duke Humfrey's library at the Bodleian in Oxford. We took some pictures of the library to show the carpenter, Larry Mathews, who was doing the rebuild. We explained what we wanted to do: we wanted to recreate the Bodleian here in as close a reproduction of the original as we could manage. We knew we couldn't do it exactly like Duke Humfrey, but maybe we could capture the essence of it. We assumed he wouldn't get it, would pull a face and say it couldn't be done. To our great surprise, he listened attentively to what we asked him for and studied the pictures we showed him. Then he thought about it for a second or two and said, "Sure, I can do that. It will be fun!" When it was all done, I had a little metal plate made and screwed onto one of the cedar ceiling beams that read, "Library built by Larry Matthews, 2019."

Lisa found a bespoke carpentry service online that could make custom staircase balustrades for the staircase leading up to the library. She designed them based on pictures we had taken of the handrails and the barley twist balustrades of the staircase leading up to Duke Humfrey's. The carpenters did a good job and Larry installed them. Larry gave the ceiling of our library a similarly coffered look using cedar planks. All the trim was in oak. When all was said and done, a carpenter from Bergen County, New Jersey, who had never been to the UK, and who knew nothing about ancient libraries, had built us our very own Duke Humfrey's, Oxford reading room. The library I had dreamed about since I was a kid, after being beaten up by Sister Louise, had become a reality. The best part was that I could share it with Lisa.

I started looking for chains we could use to replicate the chained books at the Bodleian. We purchased new wooden bookcases with glass doors. Lisa picked out a beautiful round desk with a barley twist pedestal. She also bought two small leather covered chairs. I had seen these in a furniture store. They were comfortable to sit in, and as if that wasn't good enough, they were called 'Professor's Chairs.' They were a bit pricey, so I said we should probably get something more affordable. Lisa however, found them online at a discount and ordered them for us (she often did this sort of thing. She'd see something I wanted, but was reluctant to get it because of the price—I always splurged on her, never on myself—so she would go and purchase it anyway because she loved me and wanted me to be happy). We spent many happy times in the library sitting in our matching professor chairs, sipping whisky, talking about books, and history, robots, and monsters, and all the adventures we had been on and would go on again.

---

[7] Thank God for having a healthy dose of insurance. In the end there was over $150,000 worth of work that had to be done, not counting the $6,500 just to remove the tree.

Collecting Monsters

As soon as I understood that such things existed, I began collecting books on monsters and mysteries. An important discovery of books on fringe thought was, *Phenomena: A Book of Wonders* (1977) by John Michell and Robert Rickard, which Sergeant Rodriguez had caught me reading. They were associated with *The Fortean Times*, an English magazine that I would eventually write a few articles for. It exposed me to new ideas beyond simple monsters. I saw for the first time such Fortean staples as falls of frogs and fishes, strange disappearances, and my new favourite, Toad in the Hole. Every book I could get my hands on that had anything to do with monsters and the strange, I bought. You could capture and hold an entire range of monsters in a library. You could have your own room full of monsters.

As I began work on the Sasquatch book, I knew I'd need primary sources beyond the manuscript material at the Smithsonian. Many of the protagonists in my story, from Grover Krantz to John Green and Rene Dahinden, had published their work already in one form or another. Searches of the internet turned up many first editions from them and other more obscure writers. Our home library shelves quickly filled with outrageous claims and reports of encounters with monsters from Bigfoot to Loch Ness and the werewolves of Michigan. I even found that someone had a collection of books once owned by Grover Krantz. I managed to acquire a few including ones that had some of his marginalia in them.

As my knowledge of the ancient history of monsters increased, I began collecting these works as well. I managed to secure copies of Gaspar Schott and Ambroise Paré. However, important works by Conrad Gessner and Ulisse Aldrovandi, were simply beyond my budget in their original versions. I'd have to settle with consulting them on the shelves at Princeton and Oxford. Living in northern New Jersey allowed me easy access to New York City and its rare book and manuscript trade. Lisa and I would go into the city on book-collecting expeditions. We went to rare book shows and visited archives to view exhibitions of rare books and manuscripts. We especially enjoyed going to the Morgan Library at Christmas time to see their display of the original manuscript version of Dickens's *A Christmas Carol*, and to the New York Public Library (NYPL) on the Fourth of July to see their copies of first editions of the *Declaration of Independence*. Another major surprise for us was when we were invited to the NYPL's annual Christmas gala. They would open various departments and have rare and valuable works for people to look at. Lisa and I had built a life of scholarship, books, and adventure. What we both had been working on for years. We would enjoy it now more than ever. In an age of fake news and the disparagement of knowledge and of the knowledgeable, Lisa and I wanted to save books: that would be our contribution. Coming out of the library, we sat on the steps between the lions—Patience and Fortitude—as it began to snow, just so we could say we did. Then we walked over to the Shakespeare pub for a drink and dinner. It was wonderfully romantic.

Book hunting was another adventure that made life worth living. Towards the end of the first winter after I had joined TCI, I went to The Old Print Shop on Lexington Avenue. First opened in the late nineteenth century, it boasted an amazing collection of prints and rare books. I found a first edition of Edward Hitchcock's *Geology of Massachusetts* (1841). A physically large and weighty book, it still had all the magnificent fold-out maps and artwork inside. I didn't bother to take a bag for it, I just carried it under my arm as I walked back to my office on 34th Street. I was dressed for a 4:30 p.m. class. I caught a glimpse of myself in a storefront window as I went past. It made me feel like a real scholar.

Lisa and I frequented many bookstores in the city. We revelled in the fun of the book hunt. Places like The Strand (where I found many monster books by obscure authors and where Lisa found a copy of Grover Krantz's doctoral dissertation stuffed on a back shelf) and Argosy Books provided great hunting grounds. Lisa and I bought each other many books there. "Oh, I saw this and thought you'd like it," was a constant refrain from both of us. It was great fun, but relatively short lived: the rise of the internet as well as the skyrocketing world of New York rents, resulted in used and rare book dealers, once plentiful on the streets of Gotham, disappearing fast. Institutions such as Traveler's Books, Shakespeare & Company, and Pageant Books (that had featured prominently in the film *Hannah and Her Sisters*) were all gone. They had no choice but to retreat to the cyber world. We understood, but sadly, a piece of our romantic lives was gone. You could find wonderful material online, and there was a wider range of book sellers to choose from, but the thrill and romance of finding something on a shelf in a quirky, cosy, and alluring physical store, was rapidly being consigned to living memory.

The Return of the Alvis

In 2017, to take my mind off things, I got the bright idea to do a little plastic modelling again. I loved doing this when I was a kid and I thought I could recreate the magic, the thrill of the build. That might help me sleep better and maybe not worry about things as much (I was already on medication for high blood pressure and hypertension). Lisa's condition didn't help either. But, what to start with? I drove down to Hobby Masters in Redbank. I had come across this place a few years before. It occupied a large two-storey, bunker-like building. The toys and games occupied the first floor. Scale models and trains were on the second. They carried kits for serious modellers. Tamiya and European imports crowded the shelves. They carried accessories and tools and paints as well. I had gone there several times, sometimes dragging Lisa with me, but usually by myself. In the exact way I did as a kid, I would stare at the boxes of the different kits lined up on the shelves. I'd imagine what I would do with this model or that, or what design of diorama I would make for them.

I had resisted the impulse to buy anything since I had convinced myself I'd never actually get around to building them. They would just sit in the basement while I thought about it. I also had a vague notion that what I was trying to do was to recreate a lost period of my life. I'd had so much fun building and super-detailing my models that while I did, life wasn't so crappy. I'd also had the vague notion that I could never really recreate that feeling. It was a good memory, but that time was in the past. I didn't want reality to come crashing in and ruin my memories, so I never tried to build any plastic kits again. In 2017 though, I had a change of heart. Hobby Masters had all the tools and accessories I'd need, but the tank I was going to build first, was unavailable through them. I wanted to build an M60A1, I wanted to recreate *Dreamboat Annie*.

I found one on eBay and purchased it. I also discovered that someone had a mint-in-box, original Monogram Sturmpanzer 43. I bought that one as well. The Sturmpanzer had all the parts—including those three iconic figures—and the Shepard Paine full colour tip sheet. As I poured over the tip sheet, I was hit by a powerful wave of nostalgia. I was in Ben Franklin's again, and biking up the ave. After a few enjoyable minutes, another feeling came over me. This all made me think of those videos on YouTube where some guy in his seventies is reminiscing about how much fun he had as a kid playing with Lionel Trains. They wax philosophical about their trains and how "kids these days" don't appreciate this stuff from the past. I get the nostalgia, but it also depressed me a little. I'm not quite sure why. This was all just nostalgia: a misguided attempt to recapture something long gone. I packed the Sturmpanzer carefully back in its box and put it on a shelf in the basement and left it there.

I tried to build the M60, however. I started the laborious process of assembling the road wheels and sanding the vacuum-forming seams off them. I assembled the turret. It didn't come with any figures, so I looked for some online. I realised no one made 1/35 scale figures of American tank crews from the 1980s. Then I found a kit of four South Korean tank crew figures that had all the right equipment but the wrong uniforms. I bought those and sanded down the uniforms to be like the one me and the other Doggies wore. I cut, sawed, glued, and puttied two figures to be sitting in the TC's cupola and the loader's hatch. I redid the one figure so that he was sitting on the loader's hatch with one foot dangling down inside and the other propped up on the rim of the hatch, the way we used to. He's also leaning towards the TC, one hand on the cupola and the other one pointing off in the distance. I made the TC lean towards him as if he's listening. I sat there looking at what I had done. I tried to modify all the little bits of plastic to look as realistic as possible. Then it hit me again.

I was wasting my time. This was not going to make me feel any better. It was only going to depress me. So, like the Sturmpanzer, I packed almost *Dreamboat Annie* back into her box and put her on a shelf. They were not going to relieve my anxiety attacks after all. Every once in a while, I'd look at them, but they sat there for years. I finally finished building her towards the end of 2020. My effort was anticlimactic. I took a couple of pictures of it then put it on a back shelf in a closet. I also thought about buying a Major Matt Mason (MMM) figure online. I'd just have it on a shelf, I told myself. I didn't buy it. A mint condition MMM costs in the region of $300.00 and that's a bit steep for me to spend on nostalgia.

As good as the memories of these things were, they were still memories of the past: a past that can never come again. My dread of going backwards reared its ugly head. I had to go forward. The past would be a trap and I didn't want to get caught in it. The one thing I allowed myself, was to get an *Alvis Stalwart*. I almost didn't do that either as they are very pricey when in good condition with the box. Fortunately, I stumbled upon one in good shape with the box on eBay, and it was only $5.00. The seller must not have realised what they had. I quickly purchased it and in a week or so, the trusty *Alvis* was back in my life. I put it alongside its box on the side table in my home office. That way I'd see it every time I sat down at my desk to write.

The Importance of Solitude

One of my duties on the faculty at Kean was to teach both the Junior Seminar and Senior Seminar in History (HIST3990 and HIST4990). These two classes are designed to get the students to think like professionals. All the history classes taught by all our resident faculty were always working on this idea, but the seminars allowed us to focus on professionalisation. Most historians only really get this kind of training once they are in graduate school. At Kean, since we didn't have a history graduate program, we as a faculty made the conscious decision to start introducing our undergrads to these ideas. I, for one, had only vaguely heard of historiography before grad school. That was not unusual for undergraduate programs in the US. We wanted to make sure that our history majors who went to grad school would have a leg up on others, since they would already be familiar with this concept (as well as other concepts such as historical theory and the proper use of citations through the model of the Chicago Manual of Style).

One of the things I added to my lectures was to bring up the idea of the need for solitude in order to be an historian. I explain how important it is to find a place in their lives to study, and think, and write, and ponder: to find or create their own private, special place. It could be temporal or physical.

> I don't write my name in my books, so people know it's mine
> I do it so that when the time comes,
> I'll be able to remember who I am...

Solitude is something we create for ourselves and sometimes it is created for us. I've always had a detached relationship with other human beings. I could never really get close to them, and I never allowed them to get too close to me. It has always been my form of imposed solitude. The rest of the world—even the people who meant a great deal to me—existed in such a way as if I was seeing them inside a glass display case. The world has always seemed a sort of giant museum and I was walking through the halls looking at the exhibits. Some things I just walked past, others I'd stop and examine more closely, but always there was the distance of the railing between me and the exhibits. I could get within an inch of someone, but never really touch them. There was always a barrier. I can't explain why I feel this way, but I always have. Even the people I have loved most dearly have always seemed separate from me. That was the one railing I never figured out how to climb over.

> In my room I travelled
> I visited London and China
> I travelled to Jupiter
> I went alone because there was no one to go with me
> I was fine with that
> I went anyway
> Just to see...

The LHAC

In the spring of 2018, Kean University began building a new history centre. The Department of History became a school leader in research and teaching, beginning with the efforts of Mark Lender bringing in a world-class faculty. President Farahi had a bit of a love/hate relationship with us. On one hand, the history faculty was well known for publishing, media engagement, and teaching excellence. On the other, we had become a source of critique to the administration. Sometimes faculty in other departments would say snide things about us. Our feeling always was that we were just doing our jobs: excuse us if we do it so well, maybe you should do yours as well.

When I first arrived, the President loved the history department. Then, after "The Troubles" of the accreditation debacle, he seemed to turn on us. It may have had something to do with the department being a major critic of the way the administration handled the university, almost losing its accreditation, and thus its life. After a few years of our sterling service, however, we seemed to stumble back into his good graces. It was then that he hit upon the idea of a purpose-built history centre near Liberty Hall. Kean University has always had an odd relationship with the Kean family. Governor Tom Kean rarely visited the school during his governorship. And when he left that office he took a job as president of neighbouring Drew University and behaved as if Kean University didn't exist. In the early years of the twenty-first century the school, under the leadership of Mark Lender as provost, worked out an agreement with the Liberty Hall Museum to finally partner with the department of history in an exchange of archival materials. With the construction of the Liberty Hall Academic Center (LHAC), the department now had a state-of-the-art facility. We even managed to bring Special Collections along with us. Neglected for years in an unused room in the main library, Special Collections contained some real gems. Now it had a purpose-built location on the first floor of the LHAC where it could be properly cared for by archivist, Erin Alghandoor. Faculty and students alike quickly began utilising this important resource. With the new President in Kean Hall, the history faculty began to grow again as well. New people came on board, and we were able to start teaching courses that had lost their professors due to retirement, and to add new areas of historical inquiry. Our second- floor offices looked out over the grounds of the Liberty Hall Mansion, with its carefully arranged garden and orchards that went back to the time of the Revolution. Sometimes groups of deer would wander through along with the occasional rabbits and foxes.

The one thing that didn't change within the resident faculty of the department of history was that I was still the only member who did not have children. I always had trouble understanding parenthood. Why have another child? Wouldn't you rather have more books? I would never actually say this to my colleagues—all of whom I liked a great deal and had a huge amount of respect for as scholars—but I often thought about it. I'm sure they thought, why doesn't he want any kids? What's wrong with him? Part of the reason I never had children, besides the fact that Lisa didn't want to have any either, was because I knew enough about myself that if I had a child one of two things would happen. Either I'd neglect my child for my career, or I'd neglect my career for my child. I never wanted to do either one, so I opted for the no child bit. In a way, however, I did have children: lots of them. Every semester I acquired over a hundred new children in the form of students. They often required as much work as actual children. I lost a few of them over the years to illness, war, and even one to murder. I felt bad about every one of them. There was one loss, however, I felt the worst over: that I could never recover from.

My Best Bet

The single worst moment of my life was sitting on the floor of our little TV room— the same room my mother had lived in before she died—next to the body of my beloved Lisa. It was September 9, 2021. I quietly told her how much I loved her, how much I was going to miss her, and how she was the best person I ever knew. I held her hand and kissed her forehead. I wrapped her the best I could in a blanket from our bed so she wouldn't get cold: she always hated the cold. She had been moaning all night. The hospice nurse was arranging to get her morphine. As the day went along she grew slowly quiet. Then she slipped into a coma. Her condition was such that, on that last day she was losing touch with reality. Just as my Aunt Marion had, as Aunt Wanda had, then my mother had, Lisa no longer recognized me. Around 2:30pm she stopped breathing. She had always listened to me when I talked to her. Now, no matter what I said she didn't hear. Outside I could smell the approach of fall. The birds made those sounds they make to say they were leaving. It made me feel more alone than ever. It was going to be a very long walk by myself.

You are only coming through in waves.
Your lips move, but I can't hear what you're saying...[8]

---

[8] Pink Floyd, "Comfortably Numb," *The Wall* (1979).

She was gone forever, she was dead as earth. The police had left, the paramedics had left. The house was empty and the undertakers were on the way.[9] I didn't want her to, but she had to go. It didn't matter how much she didn't want to go or how much I didn't want her to either. This was to be my last moments alone with her. She was my love and my best friend: my advisor and confidante. She was always on my side and would defend me against anyone and anything. We had many adventures together: we roamed the museums of the world, dug for fossils together, and spent a quiet, misty morning communing with the ancient stones of Avebury. For almost thirty-six years it had been the two of us against the world. Our superpowers were each other. Without her love and support, I would never have become an historian and writer.[10] I trusted her implicitly and knew she would never lie to me. She helped curb my worst impulses and helped me become a better man. With her I always knew where I was. Now, I was lost. It was a loss that pained me worse than anything I had ever experienced. It wasn't fair. She still had so many things to do, places to visit, books to write, relics to poke at, conferences to attend, adventures to go on. She seemed perfectly healthy just a few days before. I let out a low moan. Only later, did it remind me of the broken hearted werewolf crying in the depths of the Black Forest I once heard while I stood on the turret of *Dreamboat Annie*. As the undertakers carried her out, I touched her body one last time. As the door closed I knew I had lost her forever.

Lisa was diagnosed with breast cancer in 2016. She had a good oncology team who put her on the latest cancer meds and amazingly, she went in remission for years. Then suddenly at the end of August 2021 it spread to her liver. She fought it for a while, but by the first week of September, it had gone past the point of no return and they sent her home to die with me. The first thing Lisa and I ever did when we first met was hold hands. Now, the last thing I did with her was hold her hand.

For so many years no matter which way I turned you were there. To the left or to the right, front or back, your smile, your heart. You were there. I would always see you. Now, no matter which way I turn you are not there. You are gone, and I will never get to see you again.

Lisa's passing marks the end of my life up to this point. My life after this will be different. It will not be as full and amazing as it was with her in it. My life now is forced to begin again, separate from what came before. I have imagined many forms of my life over the years. I thought I was ready for anything. The one thing I never imagined was a life without Lisa. It was never something I ever thought would actually happen. With her I was always happy, without her I'll never be happy again.

Lisa was an incredible scholar, a much better writer than I've ever been. She was a meticulous researcher who checked sources in painfully excruciating detail. Her book *The Robot: The Life Story of a Technology*, though it was aimed at a general audience, still corrected decades of misinformation and commonly held myths about artificial life. She was such an expert on the history of robots she had been filmed for an episode of *Ancient Aliens* to talk about robots. The footage was never used. No matter how hard they tried, she refused to say that aliens had shown humans how to create artificial life. She had always been proud of that. She was not one easily pushed around. In addition to robots Lisa was a Shelley scholar.

---

[9] Judy Rittenhouse, who had known Lisa since high school, had been kind enough to come over to help me, and Terry and Lou had rushed over from Staten Island.
[10] Every book I've ever published is dedicated to Lisa.

Her 1997 "Frankenstein: In a Better Light" is still one of the most downloaded articles on the subject.[11]

She had led an amazing life. She fought for the rights of farm workers, visited the Holy Lands with a group of nuns, and was picked up at the Vatican by a smooth-talking Italian tour guide. She supported herself for a time as a nude artist's model. She hobnobbed with some of the world's leading scholars, historians, and scientists. She mentored many students who went on to important careers. She was loved by all of them. In her writing, she exhibited an ability to turn a phrase. When I began to clean out her office I came across the last article she was working on. It was unfinished and so will never be published. It concerned the ethics of Artificial Intelligence. The title was going to be, "No Way to Treat a Robot."

After a lifetime of being a non-believer, Lisa's death made me hope desperately that there was an afterlife: that she still existed on some plane, and that I might meet her again. My despair only deepened at the realisation that there was no such thing. I only had one real way to deal with pain. As with so many other bad things in my life, I went to my writing to get me in off the ledge, and to be honest, a little alcohol as well (okay, maybe more than a little). I had just finished the Columbus project, so I went back to Darwin. I went back to monsters: the playground of my childhood. The project that almost became my doctoral dissertation twenty years before but didn't, (because I didn't think they'd let me write about monsters), beckoned again. I wrote up an outline on the white board in my office and stared at it. I had written my way out of my time in the service. I had written my way away from Newark. I wrote my way out of the depression I felt over the death of my father, of being in Manhattan on 9/11, then anxiety about whether or not I'd have a job in academia, then the loss of my mother. Writing always helped me out of the cesspool that is human existence. Now I had a sneaking suspicion, however, that I'd never be able to write my way out of the abyss of losing Lisa. Her death did not make me think of God. Contrary to the old adage, there are plenty of atheists in fox holes.

Lisa Nocks was the best bet I ever made. It paid off for years with many dividends of joy that I will never forget. Now, the game is over, and I can never repeat it. With this loss I felt I had lost everything. It is a cliché, but she really was my everything. She was the one I enjoyed all of life with. Lisa was the only person to whom I told everything. We fought everything together. Cancer was the only problem we couldn't defend against no matter how hard we tried. We knew all of each other's monsters and kept them at bay. The monster of Newark, however, the one that failed to get into my room back in the Ironbound when I was a kid, had finally made it in. I swung at it over and over again with my baseball bat, I screamed and cursed at it, but I couldn't chase it away.

You and I have memories longer than the road that stretches out ahead.[12]

Lisa was the real place of my own. When I received her ashes from the crematorium, I couldn't bear to leave her in a plastic box, so I put her remains inside a ceramic robot we bought a few years before. She wanted to live long enough to witness the singularity. This was as close as I could get her. She found me once and saved me, and redeemed me. Now all the telescopes, astrolabes, armillary spheres, alchemical potions, fossils, and maps in the world will ever let me find her again.

[11] Lisa Nocks, "Frankenstein: In a Better Light," *Journal of Social and Evolutionary Systems* 20:2 (1997): 137-155.
[12] The Beatles, "Two of Us," *Let it Be* (1970).

Conclusion

I chose monsters and the history of science as a field of study because I wanted to do something fun. I never considered "making an impact." I've tried to make my life a place of my own. In my work, I chase people as an historian because I am chasing myself. If I can learn something about them, maybe I can learn something about me. That's why I have used the methodology of biography. To do a synthetic analysis of economic growth trends in Colonial America or Medieval England, for example, or trade concerns of post-Communist China, might lead to a better understanding of those places and times, but what does it tell me about myself? I've always been a selfish being, that's how I have approached the history of monsters, and of myself. I'm still not sure what I've learned.

As a kid I disliked the world around me. That's why I spent all those years trying to make my life a place separate from the world. That has always been the way with me: if the place you are in is not what you want it to be, go find a place to build what you want. Now I have finally achieved that goal. I thought maybe I had found my place and the library I always wanted. Lisa and I built it together, but we would not get to enjoy it together. It made me wonder what had it all been for? It felt like some grand cosmic joke on me. I couldn't even have the luxury of blaming God. How can you blame something that doesn't exist?

Nothing made me happier than writing about the past, it's true.
But nothing ever made me happier than you…

Conclusion

No Desire to Go Home

Home is not where you were born.
Home is where all your attempts to escape cease.
- Naguib Mahfouz

I woke up not knowing where I was. Something was pounding on the door. I thought it was a ghost, but it was only a monster. I study the history of monsters. It's what I do for a living. After years of doing this I realized I had been writing about myself as much as about anyone else. In doing conscious biographies of monster hunters, I was, in an odd sort of way, writing an unconscious autobiography as well. Autobiographies can be used by writers to do various things. They are often used by writers to "go home." I've always had a problematic relationship to the concept of 'home.' My parents had many flaws, quirks, idiosyncrasies, and failings, but they tried their best. They tried to give us a good home. Despite their best intentions it didn't quite work out for me. I'm not sure why we lived in that terrible apartment for so long. It was likely at Betty's insistence. Whatever the reason, as a kid I lived in that place the better part of a decade (then for a time after I returned from the service). Some kids never knew that type of stability, yet, somehow, I never really learned to appreciate it. I thought this book might, amongst other things, be a way to find a path home: to reconcile my past, to excise the monsters. That didn't really work out either. To be honest, however, I never really wanted to go back home. I always wanted to go forward, to see what was next.

Sometimes on Sunday afternoons in the mid-1980s my friend Al's dad, who had owned a pizzeria in the past, would make a dozen homemade pizzas. Al had this big extended Italian family who all lived in a giant house on a corner lot just off Kearny Avenue. Al's mother always treated me nicely. If I was lucky, I could somehow manage to conspire to be there for this Sunday ritual without it seeming too obvious. The pizzas tasted terrific, but I was secretly envious of Al and his family. All of them sitting around eating pizza, yelling, laughing and being happy. I was just watching, not being able to really participate. I've always felt like an alien presence, a clueless entity, wherever I was, even at home. I always had the sneaking suspicion that most people barely tolerated my presence, and that sooner or later they would find out who I really was and that would prompt them to end the relationship. It happened more times than I can count (Lisa was one of the few who never made me feel that way). What's worse is I could never figure out what was so wrong with me that people reacted like this. I always felt like people allowed me to be there until someone better came along. Like a mirage on a desert I could sometimes see or imagine 'home,' but could never really get there.

I felt comfortable in Providence and in Oxford. It made me think it would be nice to retire there, if I could ever afford it. Those were just dreams as well. Lisa always made me feel comfortable. She's the one person I've always been happy to see, who I felt was always happy to see me. She made me feel more at home than anyone.

When I was a kid all I could think about was getting out of where I was. I walked ten thousand miles around the world to get as far away from that place as I could only to wind up back where I started. I've always felt a powerful impetus to go forward not backward. Going backward held an unnamable dread for me. Lisa would get upset with me if we left the house to go somewhere and a few blocks away would notice I left something behind. She would say, "Let's go back and get it." My response would be, "no, I'm not going back. I'll get another one," or I'd say I'd put it off until next time, or, "I didn't really need it." "I'm not going back" does sound like an odd thing for an historian to say.

In 2003 when Lisa and I bought the house on Webster Place in Plainfield it was not just the first house I ever owned, it was the first I ever lived in. I could not wait to show M&D. I especially wanted Henry to see it. He was getting sicker and frailer, and I wasn't sure how much time he had. A few weeks after we moved in, we picked them up at the apartment and drove them to Plainfield. Upon arriving, Betty went right in with Lisa, while Henry and I stood on the porch. I asked him how he liked it and he said quietly, "very nice." I stepped towards the door, smiled, and motioned for him to follow. He just stood there and said he would be in in a moment. I went in. After a minute or two he followed me in. I could tell he had gotten a little teary eyed, but as usual did not want anyone to see so I didn't mention it. He had always wanted a house, to have his own home, his own place, but was never allowed to have one. Now his son finally had one. It meant a lot to him that we had our own house, and that he had helped us get it (he had given us $5,000—all he had in his account—to use as a down payment, then bought us a washer/dryer pair with his first ever credit card).

They say we want those things most that we can least have. I've always longed for a place I could relax in. I've rarely felt really *relaxed*. I've always felt anxious. I've always felt like I had to be ready to jump up and go into action any second; like I had to be ready to go twenty-four hours a day. I've always looked for somewhere to relax. To be able to spend some time without stress. Resting on a warm sunny day, maybe in the grass in a field. That new mown grass smell, the only sounds a bird or two in the sky: a few minutes without responsibilities calling me, dragging me away, demanding of me, insisting of me: without the anxiety. Lisa there with me. Holding my hand. To loaf under a tree looking up at the branches that appear like the roads on a map leading to Cathay or Babylon or Norumbega or some future adventure.

> I wish I had a river
> I could skate away on…[1]

After Henry died, I dreaded going to see my mother in Kearny. She was always happy to see me and Lisa when we went over. She insisted on cooking us dinner and seemed to enjoy it. We'd sit around the kitchen table and chat about the family and about the latest neighbourhood news (once the TV show, *The Sopranos* was shooting a scene on the avenue in front of St. Cecelia's church and they parked some of their trucks by the apartment causing traffic congestion. My mother leaned out the window and started yelling at the film crew to move their vehicles because they were wrecking the neighbourhood). Beyond that, however, there wasn't much for us to talk about or to say to each other. She wasn't looking for any kind of absolution, and I didn't expect her to explain my life to me. Lisa always thought it strange that I never wanted to stay with my mother very long.

Sometimes while I was there, I would feel suddenly very tired. Not just regular tired, but bone tired, life exhausted tired. I would think, "if I just laid down for a few minutes I'd be okay." Betty would certainly have allowed me to. I would then be struck with this strange and startling fear that if I did go lay down on the couch or, God forbid, go to my old room, and lay down, I'd never be able to get up again. I'd be surrounded by monsters. I would disintegrate into oblivion yet be stuck in that spot for all eternity. Stuck there with all the old ghosts and goblins and monsters. I would be perpetually ten years old and unable to get away. I've had nightmares like that. I'd find myself at the back door of the apartment. I go in and everything is gone. Then I see Sherman in the corner of the kitchen. He's emaciated and shivering just like the day we found him at the Bideawee Home. I pick him up and hold him. He looks into my eyes and asks, "Why did you abandon me, why did you leave me alone? Everyone's gone!" I then say, "It's okay, I'm getting us out of here." I turn to leave, and the door would be locked or completely gone, and I'd know I was stuck there forever. I'd wake up in a sweat and out of breath. I always know I'm at my lowest emotionally and most depressed when I have dreams about Sherman where he's in some kind of trouble. It was my responsibility to take care of him and Lisa, and I failed both.

My other bad dreams always involve me being somewhere like a shopping mall or a train station or airport, and I need to leave, but I can't find my way out, or I can't find Lisa. Many of my nightmares take place in the apartment in Kearny. Sometimes it's in another house that I don't think I was ever actually in, but it's the same house, and something bad is always happening. Maybe that's why I've studied maps and history: I always have a feeling I'm lost and I'm trying to find my way out, but I can't find it. I could click my heels all I wanted, but it wasn't going to take me home, because there was no home to go to.

I began this project thinking about monsters. While I was writing it, however, I heard from a lot of ghosts. They called, but not home. I guess you've had to have felt 'at home' in a place before you can be called back to it. I've never wanted to go back. Unlike Harry Potter, I never dreamt of being back home with my parents. I've always felt the need, the desperation, to go forward, and to leave all the debris and wreckage and the monsters behind. One last question. What happens when you've lived the adventures, and fought the monsters, and you realize you have no metaphors left?

Last night I dreamt of you again. The *Alvis Stalwart* waited at the curb, its white paint shining brightly in the sunshine. I could see you through the passenger side window. You smiled and waved. Sherman was there, his tongue wagging and his tail swiping back and forth in happy excitement. The black of the six wheels seemed sharp as obsidian. The yellow of the bed tarp was so intense you almost couldn't look at it. The green letters down the side of the truck said it all, EXPLORATION. I climbed up and slipped through the roof hatch and dropped down into the center mounted driver's seat. Sherman barked as if to say, "let's go!" I put one hand on Lisa's. We looked at each other and smiled. Life is always better with your pal by your side. With my other hand I pushed the starter button and the big engine roared to life: that throaty, guttural sound, then a contented hum. I eased it into drive and pushed the gas pedal, and we moved forward.

Heading out to somewhere, won't be back for a while.

CFZ Press is our flagship imprint, featuring a wide range of intelligently written and lavishly illustrated books on cryptozoology and the quirkier aspects of Natural History.

CFZ Classics is a new venture for us. There are many seminal works that are either unavailable today, or not available with the production values which we would like to see. So, following the old adage that if you want to get something done do it yourself, this is exactly what we have done.

Desiderius Erasmus Roterodamus (b. October 18th 1466, d. July 2nd 1536) said: "When I have a little money, I buy books; and if I have any left, I buy food and clothes," and we are much the same. Only, we are in the lucky position of being able to share our books with the wider world. CFZ Classics is a conduit through which we cannot just re-issue titles which we feel still have much to offer the cryptozoological and Fortean research communities of the 21st Century, but we are adding footnotes, supplementary essays, and other material where we deem it appropriate.

http://www.cfzpublishing.co.uk/

Fortean Words is a new venture for us. The F in CFZ stands for "Fortean", after the pioneering researcher into anomalous phenomena, Charles Fort. Our Fortean Words imprint covers a whole spectrum of arcane subjects from UFOs and the paranormal to folklore and urban legends. Our authors include such Fortean luminaries as Nick Redfern, Andy Roberts, and Paul Screeton. . New authors tackling new subjects will always be encouraged, and we hope that our books will continue to be as ground-breaking and popular as ever.

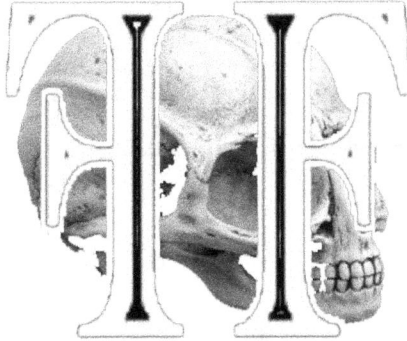

Just before Christmas 2011, we launched our third imprint, this time dedicated to - let's see if you guessed it from the title - fictional books with a Fortean or cryptozoological theme. We have published a few fictional books in the past, but now think that because of our rising reputation as publishers of quality Forteana, that a dedicated fiction imprint was the order of the day.

http://www.cfzpublishing.co.uk/

BACK COVER

Written as if recounting a sixty-one year long, and deeply personal dream, The Monster of Newark charts the life and career of historian of monsters, Brian Regal: author of Searching for Sasquatch, The Secret History of the Jersey Devil, and others. He has appeared on radio and television and dozens of podcasts discussing cryptids and pseudoscience. Placing his career as an historian within the context of his life from the streets of Newark, New Jersey, across America, through the English countryside, Germany, and even China and back, the narrative careens across the closing days of the US involvement in Vietnam, 1970s rock music, changing social norms, the Cold War, September 11th , the Age of Trump to the Corona Pandemic. All the time pursuing, despite suffering from Dyslexia, Lead poisoning, and being told he would never amount to anything, those elusive creatures known as cryptids. More accurately, pursuing those who pursue cryptids. This is the story, not of a monster hunter, but of a hunter of monster hunters. It is also a commentary on the field of cryptozoology and the place of monsters in our lives, and how one becomes an historian.

Dr. Brian Regal is Professor of the History of Science, Technology, and Medicine at Kean University where he teaches classes on science and medical history as well as pseudoscience, and alchemy.

He is the author of The Secret History of the Jersey Devil: How Quakers, Hucksters, and Benjamin Franklin created a monster (2018) written with co-author, and Kean University professor, Dr. Frank J. Esposito. He is also the author of Searching for Sasquatch: Crackpots, Eggheads, and Cryptozoology (2013). Earlier works include Henry Fairfield Osborn: Race and the Search for the Origins of Man (2002), and Pseudoscience: A Critical Encyclopedia (2009). He has appeared on the History Channel and Science Channel talking about monsters in the series True Monsters and Mythical Beasts, and 2021s HULU special Sasquatch. He was an invited panel speaker at Comic Con NYC, 2018 and 2021, and an NBC TV special on Harry Potter and alchemy.

He is also the author of numerous articles and Op Ed pieces. His latest book is on American discovery myths and is titled, The Battle Over America's Origin Story published by Palgrave-Macmillan in 2022.